QUE SERA, SERA

QUE SERA, SERA

Manchester United
Under Dave Sexton
and Ron Atkinson

Wayne Barton

Foreword by Ron Atkinson

First published by Pitch Publishing, 2020

Pitch Publishing
A2 Yeoman Gate
Yeoman Way
Worthing
Sussex
BN13 3QZ
www.pitchpublishing.co.uk
info@pitchpublishing.co.uk

ISBN 978 178531 626 5

Typesetting and origination by Pitch Publishing
Printed and bound in India by Replika Press Pvt. Ltd.

Contents

Dedicated to Dave Murphy.
This was your team.

Foreword

MANCHESTER UNITED always had the reputation of being the biggest club in the world. I had grown up as a young player seeing, and playing against, the Busby Babes. By the time I became manager of the club in 1981, that reputation was founded on historical success rather than their recent accomplishments. For the previous 13 years or so, results hadn't gone as well as hoped. Other clubs had surpassed them in the meantime, namely Liverpool.

Restoring that success, to me, meant re-establishing United as a top European club. United had this great tradition of playing in European competition, but since winning the European Cup it hadn't really happened that often. It was when I was managing Manchester United in ties abroad that I was given a greater appreciation of the size of the club and how they were loved worldwide. But we are talking about a special kind of reverence that might be difficult for today's younger supporters to fully appreciate; today, the club could probably survive on revenue from the megastore, and back in the 1980s the club shop was owned by Sir Matt Busby and only opened sporadically. When I took the job at Old Trafford, one of the first things I spoke to Martin Edwards about was my ambition to make United a major force on the Continent again.

I intended to do that playing good football. I never considered this to be the Manchester United way. I had my own ideas and belief about the way the game should be played, and I think my track record at clubs like Aston Villa and Sheffield Wednesday would vindicate that. Supporters of those clubs are always quick to tell me that my teams played the best football they saw in years. Even at Oxford, I remember that I was bemoaning the lack of a top-quality winger and I was chided by a reporter who reminded me that we were the top-scoring team in the country without one! So people talk about the Manchester United way, but nobody took me to one side and said 'this is the way you need to play' ... I always tried to have my teams playing the same way. Fast, progressive, aggressive football with flair. I would always like to have one or two players who could produce the unexpected.

That was a philosophy of football taught to me at Aston Villa by the great Jimmy Hogan. I hadn't realised the influence Jimmy's ideas had already had at United; in this book, Wayne Barton has finally brought that to light. As I've said, my role in this was coincidental, but I wholeheartedly believed in Jimmy's maxim. Different circumstances might come into play, depending on the game and the opposition, but one of his fundamental philosophies was: 'When we have the ball, wherever we are on the pitch, we're attacking. When they have the ball, anywhere on the field, we're defending.'

Jimmy emphasised the importance of taking care with the ball and accuracy of your passing. Those ideas have helped influence some of the more popular and prominent styles of football you see today. But Jimmy wasn't only about short passing, he wasn't against the odd long pass (as opposed to walloping the ball!). He could mix it up. A long pass could be considered just as important. He would stress that we had to look after the ball. The wing-half, he would say, is like a waiter in a restaurant serving the ball to the forwards. There was a commitment to hard work and entertainment.

That was what Manchester United fans wanted to see, and I suppose I was hired because I'd brought that to West Brom, along with European football.

At United I succeeded Dave Sexton. Allow me to go on record, as I have many times before, to state that Dave was the best coach I have ever seen. I've been on coaching courses around the world, I've observed the top international coaches at work in World Cups, and I've never seen anyone more inventive than Dave Sexton was. The sessions he put on were as good as any I've ever seen; I witnessed him actually on the courses, delivering better sessions than the ones the instructors were putting on.

Dave was the victim of many misconceptions. I've often seen his personality described as dour. I worked with him at Aston Villa, when he came to Villa Park as a youth coach when I was manager, and at the dinners at the end of the season he would get up and do a few renditions of one or two old London songs. I always found him great company.

Dave believed in good football as much as I did. The difference between us, as is astutely observed in this book, was that I believed in allowing and trusting players to play off the cuff, whereas Dave was a big believer in repetitive drills. At Villa, I had him working with every player at the club who was 21 or under, even if they were in the first team. One of those players was Dwight Yorke, a player who would go on to be renowned as one of the great natural instinctive forwards. And he was. He had a lot of natural flair. But so much of his movement, so much of the intelligence of his play, was a result of Dave's work with him. I can't say why it didn't work out for him at United. If I didn't have such respect for him, I would have wanted him at Old Trafford with me, working to bring through those young lads. Of course, he would probably have been offended by that; but when I went to Villa, I had no hesitation in getting in touch with Dave. I hope that readers of this book will have a greater appreciation for his footballing ideals.

My primary intention wasn't for my teams to turn up *just* to entertain. I didn't go in to training every morning and say that on Saturday we wanted everyone to go home pleased because they'd seen good football. I wanted to win. I played to win. I happened to think that the things I believed in would help us to win. On most occasions, it did. Yes, I thought winning football and entertaining football could go hand in hand, but given the choice, I'd always go for the victory.

It is tremendously difficult to pick out a single highlight from my tenure at Old Trafford, but it is no surprise given what I've said above, that all of the ones which spring to mind had entertaining aspects but also that certain amount of tension which comes from the high stakes of managing at the highest level.

That game against Barcelona at Old Trafford in March 1984 was incredible for the atmosphere above anything else. It was unbelievable. That was also the case in the 1985 FA Cup semi-final replay against Liverpool, which was a great night. Coming from behind to beat them at Maine Road was truly memorable.

The FA Cup was the highlight of every season. Again, this is something that perhaps has a different perspective in the modern age, but in my mind, it is the greatest domestic cup competition anywhere, and that was certainly how it was viewed in the 80s. It was watched all over the world. So coming up against Everton, who had just won the First Division and European Cup Winners' Cup, and defeating them, and then doing it in the circumstances we did, has to rank as number one.

When you look at the great club teams and I'm talking right the way through from the Honvéd team of the 50s to the modern era, most if not all of them play some variation or format of their game based on Jimmy Hogan's principles. Naturally, as so much of my footballing education came from Jimmy, so did mine. It's for others to comment on how well it went; I can only say I managed United according to the beliefs I had of how football should be played. Winning football games mattered the most; if we could entertain our fans along the way, then all the better.

Ron Atkinson, 2019

Acknowledgements

I AM immensely grateful for the assistance of a number of people; this book simply would not have existed without them. To Ron Atkinson and Martin Edwards, I am so thankful for your time and contributions. Thanks to Gary Bailey, Mick Duxbury, Norman Whiteside, Clayton Blackmore, Sammy McIlroy, Martin Buchan, Graeme Hogg, Alex Stepney, Paul Parker, Gordon Jago, Alan Brazil, Bryan Robson and Gordon Hill. Thanks also to Tommy Docherty. To Brian Greenhoff, still sorely missed.

As always, I owe a huge debt of gratitude to Eifion Evans and Dan Burdett. A big thank you to Paddy Barclay and Rob Smyth for their advice, guidance and eye for detail. To Barney Chilton and RedNews. Thanks to Stan Chow.

To Jane Camillin, Duncan Olner, Michelle Grainger and all at Pitch for their sterling work and dedication to this book.

A big thanks to my friends and family, including anyone I miss out from the following … ! Kim Burdett, Caroline Murphy, the Winstons, the Roberts', Mike Pieri, Stel Stylianou, Matt Galea, Oyvind Enger, Tyler Dunne, Ben McManus, Nipun Chopra. Charlie and the family. Special thanks to Dave Murphy. To mum, for your support. To Freddy and Noah. My wife, for always being my biggest supporter, the voice of reason, I couldn't do this without you.

Introduction

IN THE early summer of 1977, Manchester United Football Club were riding the crest of a wave. After watching their team defeat the First Division champions Liverpool in the FA Cup Final, United fans had optimistic thoughts about the year ahead, and after seeing the Anfield club win the European Cup days after losing at Wembley, there was some reason to believe that the sky was the limit as far as Tommy Docherty's young side were concerned.

That belief was not unfounded. The average age of Docherty's side was under 24; similar in age and composition to the United side who also defeated Liverpool in the 1996 FA Cup Final. All but three of that squad tasted European glory in 1999. That journey included step-by-step building on a solid platform and a trial-by-error approach to competing on the Continent. Their education came against European greats, and the exam was passed in thrilling fashion. Manchester United were allowed to fulfil their potential.

Following the 1977 FA Cup Final, however, it was a very different story.

Tommy Docherty was dismissed in early July following revelations that he had been having an affair with the wife of Laurie Brown, the club's physiotherapist. He had hoped that his confession to the board – belated though it was – might save his job. It didn't. It was consequently suggested that the affair was a convenient excuse for United to sack Docherty, as members of the board had allegedly grown frustrated with certain aspects of the manager's behaviour.

Certainly, there were a number of legendary figures associated with the club whose tenures had been ended by 'The Doc' who would not have been sad to see him go. George Best, Denis Law, Willie Morgan and Paddy Crerand had all departed Old Trafford but they still had friends at the club.

Yet, when taking everything into consideration, you cannot help but conclude that, for United, sacking Docherty was a reluctant decision. It seems to be proven by the facts; the suggestion that he had initially been reassured that his job was safe, the timing of it coming as it did in July and not sooner, and the simple fact that identifying a successor was not an obvious journey.

Also, it was fair to say that, although Docherty's rebuilding job had been brutal, most of the United team had a certain affection for him. That even extended to veteran goalkeeper Alex Stepney, who had only survived the axe himself by Sir Matt Busby's refusal to sanction the signing of Peter Shilton. 'My feelings towards Docherty had mellowed,' Stepney admitted when reminiscing over the days before the cup final. 'I knew all about his weaknesses. I had in my own mind the values that he represented. But I also knew that during the season, when all the activities connected with my testimonial were getting under way, he had promised that he would help and support me in every way he could. He did, too. On that I could not fault him. And so at this eleventh hour as we were listening to the final, heart-stirring briefing I felt a certain warmth towards him. He wasn't such a bad guy after all, I concluded.'

Stepney, though, admitted that he did feel some senior figures at United had sensed an opportunity when the news of the affair broke. 'In cases such as this, where private lives and morals are involved, people tend to sit in pious judgement on others,' he said. 'I knew that one group leading the attack upon The Doc would be the wives of the Manchester United directors. I felt sure that they would be trying to influence their husbands' thoughts. The Doc said that he thought he and Laurie could still work together. He did not know that there were other outside characters working against him as well as the directors' wives. For some weeks a group of Manchester business-men had been employed to keep an eye on him. A lot of resentment had grown up around Tommy Docherty. His treatment of Denis Law, Willie Morgan, Pat Crerand and others, his many outrageous statements, his larger-than-life image, did not go down well with those well-heeled hangers-on who are forever on the fringe of United affairs. There was a concerted effort being made to find evidence to bring him down, long before the surprising crunch arrived – and no one will ever know for sure who recruited these investigators. Personally I think the Mary Brown affair gave the board the most positive excuse for sacking him. The feeling among many of us was that they were just waiting for the chance.'

If there is any substance to the theory held by some that there was an internal or external campaign to oust Tommy Docherty from the manager's job at Manchester United, it is at least, as stated, unsupported by the club's succession plan. Some believe that there was a select group of individuals who were not only happy to see Docherty go, they were actively engineering a set-up where the Scot's position would be untenable.

The suggestion is given weight by the nature of the discussion where the outgoing boss was informed of his dismissal. It could have been enough to say his extra-marital affair with the wife of the physiotherapist had created an impossible situation, but that reason was then supplemented with others such as allegations of selling cup final tickets behind the club's back.

However, this decision was not taken until early July in 1977, some six weeks after Docherty had led United to the FA Cup. And, coming as it did just a day after chairman Louis Edwards had dismissed rumours Docherty would be fired as 'nonsense', it does appear to be the case that the sacking was done somewhat impulsively and without any foresight. This is borne out by the number of names linked to the job on the morning of Tuesday, 5 July. Jack Charlton, Johnny Giles and Jimmy Bloomfield – all unemployed – were linked as possible successors for Docherty. So, too, was Dave Sexton, who was also tipped to leave his post at QPR, although his destiny was surely for bigger and better things after the success of his work at Loftus Road. Sexton had been linked with a return to his old coaching job at Arsenal; he was out of contract at QPR and the incumbent Gunners boss Terry Neill wanted him on the staff.

On 11 July England manager Don Revie stunned the country by announcing he was resigning as coach of the national team. Most of the press anticipated the most logical move was to Old Trafford, but on 12 July Revie shocked football further still when he said he was going to the United Arab Emirates. It was suggested that Bobby Robson, Ipswich Town manager, and Brian Clough, boss at Nottingham Forest, would both be courted by the FA.

Clough, according to Paddy Crerand, had been quite open about wanting the United job when the pair worked together to provide punditry for ITV in their coverage of the 1974 World Cup. The United board, however, would surely have been reluctant to follow the controversy of Docherty with the unpredictable Clough. When asked if Clough had been considered as a potential successor to Frank O'Farrell in 1972, Martin Edwards said decisively, 'No.' It is unlikely that decision would have been influenced positively by Clough's career in the meantime, which included that ill-fated spell at Leeds. There was no doubting that he was a brilliant coach, but it was clear that the conditions had to be right, and it was also clear that appointing him did come with a risk. In 1977 it was in no way obvious that taking the risk could bring the benefit of European cups. The only thing that was obvious was that he would not be taking over at Manchester United.

It did, for a moment in time, appear that the same could be said of Sexton, too. Arsenal believed their former coach would be returning in his old capacity. On 12 July *The Express* reported that Sexton would be flying out to join them on their tour in Singapore. By that time, however, the QPR manager had been identified by United as the man they wanted.

'As soon as we realised it would be impossible to keep Tommy because of all the circumstances surrounding what had happened, then we had to find a successor,' says Martin Edwards. 'We had tried for Dave Sexton before, so we approached him again and this time he accepted the position. He'd done so well at QPR and in fact they were challenging for the title. We'd looked at him before when we hired Frank O'Farrell, but the timing wasn't right then. We kept an eye on him and Father (then-Chairman Louis Edwards) obviously thought he was the right man to succeed Tommy. He seemed a fairly obvious choice. I wasn't involved in the negotiations at that stage because I was still a junior director; I just remember that it was a decision taken by Matt and Father because of how well he'd done elsewhere.'

It was also influenced by another factor. Back in 1969, after his first retirement, Sir Matt Busby wrote a newspaper column identifying the necessary traits a Manchester United manager must have in order to succeed, or conditions they must meet; it was criteria such as an age of 45 or younger, a commitment to playing young players and entertaining football, and a conviction of opinion. But the controversial reign of Docherty had seemingly prompted another category – that of character and perhaps the necessity of a more reserved dignity. Sexton was quiet and reserved, especially at the side of Docherty. It seemed fairly obvious that it was a calculated decision. 'I think it was,' Edwards admits. 'Frank [O'Farrell] was quiet, Tommy was outspoken and brash, and after that I think they just wanted someone to come in and steady the ship. Dave's personality did have a bearing on why he was hired.'

News of United's interest broke. Sexton sent a telegram to Arsenal chairman Denis Hill-Wood saying he intended to speak to Busby and Louis Edwards. Hill-Wood told reporters: 'I'm very fond of Dave. But right now I'm mad at him, furious with him. I was hoping that telegram was a hoax. Unhappily it wasn't. I have the highest regard for Dave and it's a great pity he won't be joining us. I only hope he will be happy at United.'

Arsenal had won the league and FA Cup double in 1971, but it was Liverpool who had emerged as the country's 'eminent force' after the demise of United in the post-Busby era. Three league titles and a European Cup had established Bill Shankly's and, later, Bob Paisley's team as the one to beat. Clearly, their succession plan had been more effective than the one put in place at Old Trafford. And yet there was still a draw about United which made them the most captivating club in the country. Aside from a brief period in the club's relegation year where attendances dropped, United had been the most handsomely supported club in the country, even during their time in the Second Division.

So it is interesting to observe Dave Sexton's reaction to being offered the United job, after confessing to members of the press that it took him 'about thirty seconds' to accept the offer of a three-year deal: 'It's been a traumatic and agonising few days. I intended going to Arsenal to work with Terry Neill, but United was a once-in-a-lifetime thing. If I lose the job tomorrow, I'll still have been manager of the country's most famous football club for a day. I've sent telegrams to both Denis Hill-Wood and Terry, explaining my decision and hoping they will understand ... I've got to be honest and say the image of Manchester United overawed me to a certain extent, but this job must be the peak of ambition for any manager or coach. My ambition is the championship then the European Cup. Potentially there is no limit to what they can achieve. I want to see the team winning and playing attractively. Which comes first? It must be winning. All I know at the moment about the job I have taken on is that I certainly cannot improve the crowd figures.'

Louis Edwards told reporters: 'It was a unanimous board decision to appoint Dave. What influenced us was the fact that he is a gentleman with a wonderful record.'

That record had been the sensational work he had done at Queens Park Rangers. It must be said, to give credit where it is due, that Sexton did not build the team at Loftus Road. That work was done mostly by Gordon Jago, who signed star names like Stan Bowles, Dave Thomas and Don Givens and had Rangers competing at the top of the First Division before he resigned in September 1974 due to a fractured relationship with controversial chairman Jim Gregory. Sexton did inherit a very good QPR team and in the 1975/76 season they finished second, one place above the newly promoted Man Utd. Their season in 1976/77 hadn't been great; a 14th-place finish was not much to shout about, though good runs in the League Cup and UEFA Cup had excited fans.

Sexton was still seen as one of the most promising coaches in the country, and with those players he had a team playing very attractive football. Alex Stepney was encouraged that he was the right man to follow Docherty. 'I have enjoyed watching QPR over the last few years and it has been super to play against them,' the goalkeeper said, 'so obviously Dave Sexton is not going to try to stifle our game. I think he is a very distinguished sort of person. He has the right sort of attitude to be a manager of Manchester United.'

As the news rippled through the country, it was indeed his contrasting personality to Docherty which most people were mentioning about Dave Sexton. Frank Blunstone, the coach at United who had worked with Sexton at Chelsea, echoed Stepney's thoughts: 'Dave can be twice as hard as Tommy Docherty,' Blunstone said. 'When he shouts people jump because he rarely raises his voice. And he is the best coach in the country. Dave is flexible and open to changes in the game. If United's style does need modification a little, he'll modify it. He moves with the times, and ahead.'

However, there was some reservation from a surprising source. QPR striker Don Givens felt Sexton lacked the hard side to his character that some felt was required to succeed at the very top. 'Basically, he's too nice,' Givens said. 'I don't think Dave has it in him to be nasty even when he needs to be. We all liked him at QPR, he's a hell of a good fellow. But he always gave me the impression that he would rather do without certain aspects of a manager's job. He loved to work with the players and put all his ability into practice and I don't think he wanted the aggravation caused by things like having to leave players out of the team, which is an essential part of the job. The only criticism we could have of him was that perhaps he wasn't strict enough with certain players. It happened to Dave at Chelsea and there were signs that it might begin to happen at QPR.'

If there was one thing that could be universally agreed, people wanted Sexton to succeed, if only because of his niceness. Indeed, that would be a caveat added by every single one of his critics. On 15 July, journalist Paddy Barclay wrote in *The Guardian*: 'Everyone interested in the finer things in football will want to see Dave Sexton succeed with Manchester United. He is widely regarded as the best tactician in England, and he has an absolute commitment to the attacking outlook that made United so attractive under Tommy Docherty.'

There was every reason to believe that Sexton would be the man to add substance to United's cavalier style; an educated approach that would surely be necessary in order for their football to have the genuine substance it required to translate good cup performances into a league championship challenge.

Style

OVER THE years which have followed Dave Sexton's reign as manager of Manchester United, the quicker, more succinct assessments of his tenure include the descriptions of 'dull' or 'boring' when referring to the style of football. A closer inspection, however, suggests that the issue was more to do with a certain incompatibility, for a number of reasons, than it was a matter of philosophy.

It is fair to say that from the off there were certain elements of the philosophy that caused a conflict. Sexton believed in the virtue of the counter-attack as the most profitable form of attack, and, while some could say with a degree of certainty that 'counter-attacking' was a fair description of one of United's most potent, and most attractive, strengths, it was also accurate to say that under Tommy Docherty the prevailing emphasis had always been on United imposing their own style. Docherty was proactive and Sexton, whilst not necessarily reactive, was always guarded and mindful of the negative consequence of leaving his team open, and so his primary approach was to establish a solid defence from which his team could attack. Which, in fairness, makes a lot of sense.

'I believe the counter-attack to be the most effective way of penetrating the opposition's defence,' Sexton said in his book *Tackle Soccer*. He likened this to a golfer pulling back his arm to make the swing on the ball, or a boxer pulling back his arm to unleash more power in his punch, emphasising the power of kinetic energy: 'The action of recovering your original position is the source of energy

I'm talking about. You must make the effort to get into position and regain the ball before you can do damage to the opposition.'

Sexton's explanation of the boxer, however, demonstrates his cautious nature: 'The boxer who throws a punch but fails to get his gloves back to cover will get whacked.' Sexton quoted New Zealand rugby coach Freddie Allen, who said, 'A good attack is a thrust to which there is no parry,' and translated into football parlance as a 'thrust by a team which does not allow the opposition time to get back, cover or defend.'

It certainly seemed fair to describe Sexton as much more thoughtful and considered in his approach than his predecessor. The more obvious and pronounced example of the difference would best be personified by one player: Gordon Hill. The winger's job was to go at the opponent and, when they had the ball, his instruction was to 'tuck-in'; his former manager and team-mates were well aware that his defensive deficiencies meant he was not suited to a more pragmatic role and made allowances for that.

For Sexton, however, there were no concessions. It was about balance and responsibility, as far as the new man was concerned. 'An interesting problem arises when the opposition play a 4-4-2 formation with four players in midfield,' he explained. 'Don't sit back with four defenders marking two forwards while the opposition take control in midfield. Push a defender into midfield to even the contest. You still have the three defenders needed to mark two forwards, so that is in your favour. It's all a matter of what to do with your spare man at the back. He can move into midfield or he can push further forward if you discover the opposition are struggling at the back.

'When we think in terms of human nature and natural instincts, it is natural for a forward to want to run at the opposition. But it is an unnatural action to put the same amount of effort and enthusiasm into getting back, recovering. Midfield players are faced with the same problem. Here the coach holds the key. He must educate these responses until they become natural responses. Midfield players play a big part in good lines of defence. The left-side midfield player should help the left-back, the right-side midfield player should help the right-back and the central-midfield player should work with the central defenders ... your winger may rarely get a defensive touch. But just by being there, he makes the opposition think twice before giving the ball to that player: their pass has to be accurate and their winger has double the problems to overcome.'

It did seem as if there was some room for understanding the personal differences of each player. 'Keep discipline in perspective. Know your players as individuals,' Sexton said. 'This will make the application of discipline easier. Aim to be positive when correcting a player. Don't just lay into him. Treat your players as adults and they will respond as adults.'

The same principle could apply to knowing your team. And, despite having such a heavy emphasis on pragmatic responsibility (that would perhaps become *too* heavy), there were indications within Sexton's approach that adventure could be accommodated; although the addendum of the mathematical equation hinted at the inherent incompatibility with United's explorative style under Docherty. 'Football is not an academic exercise,' Sexton explained. 'There is a point to the game. That point is that when you have possession of the ball, aim to produce a move that ends either with a goal or with an attempt at scoring a goal. The gift of being able to score goals is not something coaching can manufacture. Certainly, good coaching can improve a striker's technique by giving him confidence and a good, basic education around his talent. But before you can do anything, the gift must be there from the beginning. No amount of teaching, practising or brainwashing can substitute for nature in this instance … Finishers are born, not made … but they can be helped, encouraged and improved. A simple way of ensuring that you get a finishing response is to demand a certain number of attempts at scoring in each half. It does not matter whether those attempts comprise shots or headers. Perhaps your players will fail to achieve your target on occasions. But as long as you maintain your standards, they will maintain theirs. Always remember you are working with human beings. Gentle reminders and good, positive and well-planned coaching stimulate – and excite – players.'

The way he explained his belief in the value of quality wingers almost seemed like it could be music to the ears of a player like Hill: 'The forwards are the spearhead – the cutting edge on the knife. Their game should comprise five essential qualities:

1 goal flair;
2 aerial strength;

3 directness;
4 control;
5 speed.

'Therefore, the coach who can field three forwards, each possessing all five qualities, has the ideal forward line ... There are many attacking advantages to be gained by playing as wide as possible. For example, if the ball is on the opposite wing, let's say the right wing, the left-winger can either come inside or stay out by the line. Let us assume he stays wide. Now the right-back begins to worry. He has to keep one eye on the left-winger and also watch what is happening on the other wing. There are few more exciting sights in football than a winger in full flight, ball at his feet and the full-back backing off, waiting for the opportunity to dive in and make a winning tackle. When taking on a full-back, the winger's angle of approach is extremely important. The best way is to attack the defender on his inside foot.

So how you divide up your midfield is what matters. A good midfield player in the wrong role can look a mediocre player – the coach must see and know his players. The Germans exercised their systematic brain to analyse the jobs that need to be done by a midfield unit. What they evolved is what we now use as our midfield blueprint:

1 The attacking midfield player who pushes up behind the forwards in support, looking for goals and backing up in all attacking situations.
2 The midfield general who positions himself in as many central areas as possible to take and give passes to all sides of the pitch. He is the link within the link.
3 The all-purpose midfield player who is good at winning the ball and who tends to get back into defensive positions more than the other two.

'Having set the pattern, it is extremely important to understand that all three midfield players should be looking to do their jobs plus a share of their colleague's responsibilities ... By dividing up your midfield, you ensure that all vital jobs are seen to. But you do not restrict your midfield players to rigid roles. Flexibility, once the number-one jobs are done, is a great strength in any team.'

Sexton had typically thoughtful and extensive views about goalkeeping; that the difference between a 'liner' and a goalkeeper more comfortable with coming out and collecting the ball could have a profound difference on the defensive line and also require different attributes from defenders. 'The ideal goalkeeper has a safe pair of hands, capable of holding the ball under pressure and when it comes at him from different angles,' the coach said. 'He must have good agility, sharp reflexes, quick anticipation, positional sense and also be a good kicker of the ball. Properly coached, the goalkeeper can become the most versatile footballer in the team. I emphasise the words "properly coached". The coach who spells out the importance of creative thinking throughout the team – beginning with the goalkeeper – will produce a positive response.'

Again, it did seem as if his approach veered more towards the cautious end of the spectrum, although his words suggested otherwise. The idea of a goalkeeper as a member of the outfield team and not the last line of defence was nothing new at Old Trafford. Harry Gregg famously hated 'liners' and one of Alex Stepney's most desired qualities was his distribution. Sexton had inherited Stepney, of course, but stress as he might about taking personal attributes into consideration, even a goalkeeper in Sexton's team would have to be prepared for all eventualities. Which, again, in theory, was no bad thing, but it was a contrast to the emphasis being on the damage United could do to the opposition.

Stepney, the veteran 35-year-old that he was, might have thought himself to be an old dog who could not be taught any new tricks. He was in for a shock in pre-season training. United travelled to Germany and Norway to play four games.

'My first introduction to Dave in his role as United manager came in our pre-season tour of Norway,' Stepney recalled. 'He took Paddy Roche and myself for specialised goalkeeper training. As we walked out to a pitch that was hard and bumpy and flecked with gravel, I thought about something Phil Parkes, the QPR goalkeeper, had told me. He had worked with Dave for a long time and had nothing but praise for his knowledge of training and preparation. Phil had also warned me that the demands of the early, specialised goalkeeper training had been killing. The warm-up routine on this warm Norwegian morning was fierce enough. Then he made Paddy take a turn in goal. He had two footballs on the go. One ball would be driven to the bottom right-hand corner and then, as soon as you were across for it, the other would be sent to the opposite side of goal, and you had to spring over to save that one. The balls were fired with rapid, relentless timing. I watched Paddy lurching from one side to the other. He is rather pale at the best of times; I could see what little colour there was beginning to drain from him. The sweat stood out on him. Suddenly he reeled away, slumped to the ground and threw up. Then it was my turn. I was determined not to give in. From side to side I went. The pain was searing through the muscles in my legs. My breath was tight and I could feel a band tightening around my head. But I would not give in. My legs were starting to seize up and I felt as though I was falling from one side of goal to the other like a helpless drunk. I could hear Dave beginning to make cracks about my fitness, or the lack of it. Suddenly my senses cleared as a hidden, reserve supply of adrenaline burst into my brain igniting my dormant temper. I kept up the training, moving from one side to the other; I did not even pause as I shouted to him: 'Don't take the piss out of me when I am working.' From that moment on we had an understanding. We had a relationship going. He knew I was tough, and I knew he was prepared to drive people until they cracked. The training was marvellous, and I returned for the start of Dave Sexton's first season as manager of Manchester United feeling like a new man.'

Stepney had actually spent some time with Sexton, coincidentally. 'I had long been an admirer of Dave Sexton,' he admitted in his 1978 autobiography. 'I once spent a week's holiday with him in Sardinia. We did not go together but found ourselves in the same hotel, and, even though we had both taken the break with the idea of forgetting about football for a while, we still got the ball out, both on the beach and in our conversations ... His arrival in Manchester was something of a challenge to the press. Those journalists who fed daily upon the deeds of Manchester United had only to finger the pen in their top pockets for Tommy Docherty to launch into a string of quotes that were often sensational, usually unconventional, and rarely failed to make the back pages. Dave is a different animal. He cares little for publicity or personal glory. He would probably admit that he is not a very good communicator, and those journalists who spent the first few days close to him, as close as they are ever likely to get, said that drawing words from him required the same precision and strength as chipping away at a rock. They quickly dubbed him "Whispering Dave". The players enjoyed the contrast after The Doc's abrasiveness. Dave was polite. He treated us like gentlemen and we were all aware of the magnitude of the job he had taken on.'

Sexton had that rarest of opportunities afforded to any football manager – the chance to take over a club in the ascendancy. The usual scenario is for a manager to be sacked when things have gone horribly wrong and so there would be issues to address for the new man. There are for any manager, good *or* bad. But the usual immediately critical concerns of turning around form or confidence were not problems for Dave Sexton at United. Instead, he was effectively tasked with the further education of this young group. In the early days, that meant getting to know them better, through their application to the new training schedule. Under Docherty, Blunstone and Tommy Cavanagh, training had been a relaxed affair. Now there were routines that were being practised until perfected. Sexton was closely observing how the players adapted.

'We rarely finished with five-a-side, it would usually be some routine where the clipboard came out,' Brian Greenhoff remembered. 'He would mark things down, scoring things and tell you what you'd done – I always felt under pressure, which for me isn't what training should be about ... Dave's monitoring may well have been intended to motivate but it certainly didn't do that for me.'

However, at that point nor had Sexton's different approach to Docherty pushed anyone's nose out of joint just yet. In late July *The Guardian* reported that Steve Coppell had signed a new contract, with Greenhoff and Lou Macari set to follow suit. It was clear that the new manager was more focussed on continuity than making big changes.

Pre-season went well; a defeat against Werder Bremen was followed by three huge scorelines against admittedly weak Norwegian opposition – 8-0 over Rosenberg, 4-0 over Hamarka-meratene and 9-2 against Strømsgodset.

During the last part of the tour, Sexton granted a feature interview to Bob Russell of *The Mirror* regarding the forthcoming Charity Shield against Liverpool. 'This is an important game for the boys, though it's not really my occasion because I had nothing to do with them qualifying for Wembley,' he said. 'But for me the really important one is still over a week away – the kick-off in the league at Birmingham ... Starting with the Charity Shield, we'll be going for the lot – league, European Cup Winners' Cup, League Cup and FA Cup again. I don't believe in listing priorities, because if you miss out on a particular one you can be left in limbo with nothing to go for. By going for everything, even if you finally finish with nothing, you maintain the momentum right through.' It was pointed out that the only previous manager whose first game had come at Wembley was Brian Clough at Leeds. 'I hope to last a little longer here,' Sexton grinned.

On the eve of his first official game in charge, the new United boss told reporters: 'If you can repeat a win over Liverpool you let the whole football world know you are a force to be reckoned with.' The Charity Shield, however, was a non-event; on an energy-sapping hot day where Kenny Dalglish made his debut for Liverpool, United were untroubled but were unable to make any attacking inroads of their own thanks in part to an early injury to Jimmy Greenhoff. He came off in the 20th minute to be replaced by utility man Dave McCreery. Though still fairly competitive as far as Charity Shields go, both teams went through the paces in the final moments, and Gordon Hill recalls signalling to the referee to blow for full time with three minutes still to play. The official obliged and the shield was shared after a goalless draw.

Jimmy Greenhoff was ruled out for weeks and so young striker Ashley Grimes was called into the squad; but Sexton decided that he would move Macari up front, with McCreery in midfield and Grimes as the substitute, for the opening game.

The Express's James Lawton ran a feature on both Manchester clubs on the first Saturday of the First Division season. The United side was headlined: 'Sexton: We have to win a certain way' and the new boss was asked how he would cope with the relentless attention of the media. 'I could always hide,' he joked. 'It's no secret that I love the coaching side of the game and of course it is hard to imagine a club with more outside pressures. And it is not just simply that of winning things. That is always around in football. But you have to win things in a certain way here. We are talking about sport, a thing that ebbs and flows. What you can do is work as well as you know how and you can give everything you have to keeping the club healthy. That way you can get to sleep at night.'

City manager Tony Book believed that he was in charge of the more prosperous club in the area. 'We are in a take-off situation,' he boasted. 'The other day we opened our 40th fan club – in York – and the crowds are going to threaten United's old supremacy. They are under pressure all right. I don't want to sound arrogant about this, but the truth is we have the scope to go further. The pressure on Dave Sexton is that United have done everything – their problem is one of keeping to a level.'

While City were drawing 0-0 at Maine Road against Leicester, United were putting another Midlands club to the sword; two goals from Lou Macari, first in the fifth minute and then again in the 22nd, put Dave Sexton in dreamland. Birmingham pulled a goal back early in the second half, but in the 75th minute Gordon Hill scored one of the most astonishing goals of an impressive catalogue. Arthur Albiston clipped a pass into the box, the ball dropped over Hill's left shoulder around 12 yards from goal and the winger connected with a first-time volley that flew into the far corner. Eight minutes later, Macari put a perfect footnote on the afternoon with another goal to complete his hat-trick and a 4-1 win. The only disappointment from the game was the withdrawal of Stuart Pearson, who came off with a trapped nerve in his neck.

Sexton was thrilled with his team's capability of scoring despite the main strikers not being there. 'It was smashing,' he said. 'Everything came off for us even though Jimmy Greenhoff was out and Stuart Pearson had to go off. I'm very pleased about the way things have gone, particularly as I've always found Birmingham a very difficult side to beat.'

Hat-trick hero Macari was keen to praise the new manager: 'It's so easy to work for Dave,' said the Scot. 'He has changed our style very little, just making sure that every member of the side plays to his strength. He's a quiet man, but after the first day's training with us it somehow seemed he knew so much about us that he had been with us five years.'

Pearson was cleared to play the next game – the first home game, against Coventry, four days later. In his programme notes, Sexton addressed the supporters formally for the first time, insisting he was the right man for the job. 'Manchester United are my kind of team,' he wrote. 'I suppose there is nothing particularly special about that because they appeal to people all over the country, indeed all over the world. They are the best supported club in the business and have been for some years. Their name is an international byword in football circles. So it is with particular pride that I have become manager at Old Trafford and an honour that I shall do my best to justify. I was on the point of joining Arsenal, after leaving Queens Park Rangers, and there is magic in working for the Gunners as well. But when the vacancy suddenly materialised at Old Trafford it was an opportunity that I felt I could not miss. It was a chance that fired my imagination and I was delighted to be appointed. I will not be making changes simply for the sake of change. I don't think I am one of those support ego people who must turn everything upside down just to let everyone know who is boss. I hope I won't be afraid to change things if I feel it is right and necessary because after all I have a job to do and I would be letting the club down if I shirked it. But United are a successful team with consistency in both cup and league for the past couple of years. They have achieved this by producing an extremely attractive type of football. I neither want to spoil the attractive nature of their game nor obviously do I want to do anything that will interrupt the run of success … United have evolved a pattern of play that has proved successful and entertaining. I don't want to alter it because it's good. I simply hope to add to it … I shall do my best to uphold the proud traditions of this famous club.'

It wasn't a classic introduction to life at Old Trafford. Hill scored an early penalty and David McCreery scored a late winner in a 2-1 victory; McCreery for Jimmy Greenhoff the only change from the FA Cup Final team as Sexton kept as close as he could to the winning formula Docherty had.

Already, though, the idea of United's capability to challenge moving forward was being called into question. Playing Pearson backfired and he was ruled out of the next game at home to Ipswich Town.

It wasn't so much that United weren't good enough. Their first team had proven that they were. But whenever that side are questioned on how they would have done, they are generally split into two camps; they can usually be determined by those who come under the description of Docherty loyalists, and those who don't; those who did would insist the first team was easily strong enough to challenge, and those who didn't would stress that more quality was needed in certain areas. One thing both sides agreed upon was that strength in depth was needed in the event of an injury crisis. It wasn't a crisis for Sexton – yet – but he was discovering quickly that the drop in quality from first team to reserve was significant.

For United, the first consequence of the change of manager was coming home to bite them, although it was too early to categorise it as an error (if calling it an error at all was fair). The decision taken to sack Docherty meant sacrificing the loss of momentum when considering the manager's plans. Docherty might, or should, have been able to attempt to sign two or three players to build on what he had achieved. It was difficult for Sexton to do that without the risk of upsetting one or two players in the first team, and so one would consider his approach was the most reasonable one.

Without their first-choice strikers, McCreery and rookie Chris McGrath were selected in midfield to play against Ipswich, with Macari remaining up front to be joined by Steve Coppell. Just before the hour mark, Sammy McIlroy had to come off with a knock, and Ashley Grimes, a player more defensive, was brought on. Ipswich held on for a 0-0 draw.

McIlroy was out, but Pearson was back for the League Cup visit to Arsenal. Proving the theory that United at their best were a match for anyone but anything less would make it difficult for them to compete with the top teams, the Gunners controlled the tie and were already safely 3-1 in front before a late consolation from Pearson helped the scoreline look more respectable at the end. That setback was followed by an impressive 1-0 win at Derby County which just about spelled the end for their manager, Colin Murphy.

The Rams had struggled since Dave Mackay left in November 1976 and there had been rumours that they were interested in appointing Tommy Docherty in the build-up to the 1977 FA Cup Final. That speculation had forced United's hand when it came to renegotiating a contract with Docherty, and a new deal had been agreed but was left unsigned, with The Doc set to formally agree to it once he returned for pre-season. Murphy was sacked two weeks after the defeat to United, and Derby were finally successful in hiring Docherty. Within days, he returned to his former club to attempt to bring Tommy Cavanagh and Frank Blunstone to the Baseball Ground.

By that time, however, Docherty was merely adding to Sexton's growing list of headaches. The win at Derby meant, after four games and heading into the first international break of the campaign, United were level at the top but third behind Manchester City and Liverpool on goal difference. It was a strong start and a solid foundation. The first game following international duty was at Maine Road.

Tony Book played up the intensity of the occasion by saying: 'There is nothing I detest more than losing to United.'

For Dave Sexton, this was a new experience. 'The only experience I have that can remotely compare with this sort of game is that I have twice been concerned in Arsenal-Spurs matches. Somehow, although the adrenalin runs on those occasions, I don't think it will be quite the same,' he said. 'The picture is clear. Everyone believes in the reputation that Manchester United have built as an attacking side and it is clear to me that we shall have to keep things that way. People look to us to entertain and I think we have the players that can do that and win. It won't be just another game, will it? The fact that a win could put either of us on the top makes it important enough without the rivalry. I don't really know what to expect, except I am looking forward to it. And I am expecting us to play well.'

But they didn't. Jimmy Greenhoff was joined on the sidelines by his brother Brian, and Sexton replaced the younger brother, with Jimmy Nicholl replacing him; a full-back who would have to moonlight as centre-half. It was only Nicholl who ironically would emerge with any credit, scoring a blockbuster 30-yard shot in the 87th minute. By that time, though, United were 3-0 down, with former Old Trafford forward Brian Kidd getting a couple of goals against a team who were as unfamiliar with each other in defence as they were in attack.

Brian Greenhoff was back for the next game, the first leg of the Cup Winners' Cup tie against St Etienne in France. There, United actually played well, scoring through a fine Gordon Hill goal (Hill also had two goals disallowed). The hosts equalised and the game ended 1-1.

The occasion was marred by controversy in the stands. There was a comedic undertone as both sets of supporters threw sticks of French bread at each other; but the bread was followed by bottles, and because the stadium had no segregation there were lots of fights between fans even before kick-off.

'A barrier collapsed and more than 100 St Etienne fans climbed the 10ft wire fence which surrounds the pitch to escape,' reported David Lacey of *The Guardian*. 'United supporters fought for several minutes and were then routed by French police who drove them to the terraces and in some cases out of the ground altogether.'

'About 100 Britons started a fight behind one of the goals,' read the report in *The Times*. 'Armed with bottles, sticks and knives, they went for the supporters of the French team. Panic-stricken supporters rushed down towards the wire netting around the pitch where they were piled up. People following jumped over the bodies to the safety of the pitch. The rest of the crowd shouted, "Les flics, les flics (Cops, Cops!)" because the riot police on hand were slow to intervene. It took three charges by truncheon-swinging police to clear the battlefield, expelling most of the Manchester supporters.'

United were immediately defensive about their role in the events; Sexton and club secretary Les Olive were singing from the same hymn sheet by claiming United fans had been provoked. In truth, the trouble had started much earlier: 'The night before the game, a small group of Manchester supporters, some with knives, broke shop windows, ransacked the hall of a hotel and looted a shop in the city,' *The Times* reported. 'Five were arrested and will appear in court.'

St Etienne chairman Roger Roche was furious. 'They were the worst hooligans I have ever seen,' he said. 'This ground had been without a blemish until these gangsters came here and started drinking.'

The initial leak from UEFA was that they were strongly considering expelling United from the competition, though Robby Herbin, the St Etienne manager, insisted he did not want his team to win 'in a boardroom'. The English team were supported by the minister for sport, Denis Howell, who was preparing a report which would lay blame at the poor organisation of the game by the host team. Before he had chance to submit it to UEFA, the governing body had acted on that threat to kick United out. A statement read: 'The commission were of the opinion that the violent behaviour of the Manchester United supporters seriously endangered public security and the physical wellbeing of the spectators.'

Howell responded immediately via the press to complain the decision had been taken far too hastily. 'My preliminary report from the Foreign Office suggests that the official Manchester United club did everything they were asked to do in the way they were asked to,' he said. 'I would have wished that UEFA had read this report before they took official action.'

United goalkeeper Alex Stepney made an extraordinary blast at the fans of the club, telling the BBC, 'It's too ridiculous for words. As far as I'm concerned as a player for United, United fans have nothing at all to do with me. We went over there and gave an advert for football, both teams. I mean, we're getting condemned for something we haven't done.'

On 21 September a United contingent including Sir Matt Busby appealed to a three-man UEFA committee for the club to be reinstated. They were buoyed by a statement from St Etienne who now said the ban was 'unjust' – UEFA relented and allowed United to play the second leg, on the condition that it would be played at least 200km from Old Trafford, and the club were also ordered to pay a fine.

Busby was pleased, declaring 'Justice has been done.' But the news was not greeted with encouragement or co-operation by the FA or the Football League. The most obvious choice for a venue that would meet the conditions was one of the big stadiums in London. Arsenal offered Highbury, but, bizarrely, Alan Hardaker intervened to veto the plan. 'United have a lot of fans in London and they are worse than anyone,' Hardaker said, a comment only likely to infuriate those with long memories at Old Trafford.

Plans to hold the game in Aberdeen were ruined as the Dons had a League Cup game against Rangers. An invitation to play at Glentoran's ground in Belfast was politely declined as United finally settled on Plymouth's Home Park, a compromise Hardaker agreed with.

United manager Dave Sexton was relieved his team could continue to play in the competition. 'It is a fantastic situation,' he said, surely meaning the literal rather than positive sense of the word. 'The club is absolutely correct in everything they do and the players could not do more. They have won the fair play award for two years on the trot.'

The form of the team continued to be bumpy amidst the controversy. Chelsea scored within 90 seconds of their visit to Old Trafford and United were unable to recover; their issues compounded when captain Martin Buchan was forced off the pitch with an injury.

'United played into our hands by knocking so many high balls into our defence,' said Chelsea captain Ray Wilkins. Sexton complained that the Blues were 'masters in the air and we couldn't break them down our way.'

That defeat was followed by a draw at Leeds. On the eve of the game at Elland Road, Tommy Docherty revealed he had approached United to take their staff. 'I spoke to Dave Sexton today and was given permission to speak to Tommy Cavanagh,' he said. 'I hope he decides to join us. I will be meeting him later tonight.'

Cavanagh and Docherty, the two Tommys, were a double act. Some of the players remarked on the difference in Cavanagh's demeanour now Sexton was at the club, as opposed to how he was under Docherty. Brian Greenhoff claimed Cavanagh had tried to stress that the players at United were more productive with a more relaxed approach rather than the methodical instruction laid out by Sexton. To some of the United players, and to Cavanagh, Sexton's well-intentioned style of coaching was redundant. They already felt equipped to do the things he was instructing them to perfectly. Cavanagh's knowledge of the players meant he tried where possible to encourage them to play in the way he knew came naturally, but he was unsuccessful in trying to convince Sexton this was the right way to go about things.

'Ultimately, he had no choice but to coach us using Dave's methods,' said Gordon Hill. 'It was get on the bandwagon or find yourself another club ... Cav would still encourage us where possible to express ourselves but training was a world apart from how it had been under the boss.'

It seems – to give Sexton some benefit of the doubt – that there had been a miscommunication. Both the squad and the manager had their tried and tested, and successful, manner of doing things. As the manager, Sexton felt it was natural that his method should prevail. That was why he was hired, after all, and it stands to reason that he should want to do this. He wasn't familiar with the players and their ability in the same way Cavanagh was.

Under the previous regime, there was a strong element of trust and faith in a sport comprised hugely of chance; the players were good enough to get it right on the Saturday. Sexton was different; he wanted *proof* that the players were good enough on the Monday-Friday. It meant relentlessly working on particular drills until they were successful. Corner-kick routines would be repeated time and time again to the frustration of players who would eventually take it upon themselves to agree to contrive to make the routine successful just so they could get off the training pitch. United's star men couldn't understand why Sexton was so intent on the repetition. Was this meant to improve them? Was this supposed to be constructive in bridging the gap of quality between United and Liverpool?

Sexton was almost obsessed with the idea of planning the game so well so that as little as possible could be left to chance. Hence the repetition of these routines; an outsider can most certainly see the value in working until perfect, because even in a game of chance where crosses can largely depend on the technique of an individual, the purpose is to improve that technique through that repetition so that the chances of a successful delivery are higher. Perhaps, then, some blame can go to the players who were uninterested and uninvested.

Whenever there is such a crossover where one manager replaces a successful one, as rare as it can be, the natural resistance to the new man's methods can sometimes translate into performances. Certainly, United's players would complain about what they felt was an over-complicated approach which had too much emphasis on protection and defence.

Yet even when that does translate into performances, as well it might as players struggle – but struggle honestly, with their own best intentions – to put into practice the training through the week into a game at the weekend, there come the odd occasions where the buttons of pride are pushed and they evoke a different reaction. If players are at all concerned about their capability to get a result, you might often find them naturally reverting to the methods which had served them so well. Buchan and Jimmy Greenhoff were back for the visit of Liverpool on 1 October. It was more like the old United as their second-half performance was thrilling, and rewarded with goals from Lou Macari and Sammy McIlroy.

If the players had seen, noticed and felt the change on the training pitch, then the idea of a 'new' and 'old' United was at least not evident from the stands yet. Supporters were patient and willing to give the new manager plenty of time and they were sympathetic with the injuries and the controversy which had faced him in the early weeks. The victory over Liverpool was a very welcome boost.

It was a shot in the arm for the players who had a renewed confidence ahead of their second leg against St Etienne. In footballing matters, United had been the superior side, and bizarrely it did seem as if their hopes of progression depended as much on what happened off the pitch at Home Park as what happened on it. Plymouth Argyle were playing in the Third Division and their average attendance effectively halved after their relegation earlier that year. Home Park saw an average of 6,752 at the gate, which was the lowest since the turn of the century. Yet despite the regulations which were intended to make it difficult for United supporters to get there, 31,634 were present at Plymouth to watch the game. (To put this in some sort of context, United's lowest crowd in their relegation season was 33,336 for the game against Burnley – this was a mightily impressive turnout.)

'Home Park was packed to the rafters,' Arthur Albiston told *The Mail*. 'I don't think their players were used to having fans so close to the pitch like we were in England. The United fans made it a little bit unsettling for them and that helped us.'

Stuart Pearson scored after 32 minutes and midway through the second half Steve Coppell secured the result.

It was the first time since the Charity Shield Dave Sexton had been able to name the same 11 that had won the FA Cup, though the luxury didn't last too long as Pearson had to come off. In better news, the fanatical support which had travelled to Devon largely behaved themselves. The authorities in England would have breathed a huge sigh of relief, and not just the footballing ones;

the British government were counting on United to play a friendly game in Tehran in late October as part of the British Trade Week export drive and so the game passing without incident would have been welcome indeed.

United lost against Middlesbrough at Ayresome Park three days after winning in Europe; the arduous journey that saw them travel the entire length of the country probably had something to do with their below-par performance. With a week's rest they were preparing to take on Newcastle at Old Trafford but were unwittingly hit by an illness epidemic when, the day before the game, the players had to have vaccination injections before their travels to the Middle East.

United were able to get through a tough game against Newcastle at home but were paying the price; Brian Greenhoff, already feeling the pain of a knee injury, became ill, as did his brother. Gordon Hill picked up a cold, as did Arthur Albiston. 'Tommy Cavanagh said it's like somebody had taken a syringe and taken everything out of us,' Hill said. 'We couldn't run.'

'The injections made the lads' arms swell up a little bit,' Sammy McIlroy remembered. 'That knocked a few of the lads for six.'

Not ideal preparation then for the Cup Winners' Cup game in Porto, which meant a flight to Portugal as well. With players desperately struggling with illness, the hosts took clinical advantage and registered an emphatic 4-0 victory. Despite the size of the scoreline, there was more than a smidge of sympathy for the beleaguered United side who weren't in any shape to give their best.

Martin Buchan did not give any excuses. 'There was only one team in it,' the skipper said. 'And only one team gave the impression that they were going to win.'

However, when Sexton saw his team defeated by the same scoreline at West Brom a few days later – their sixth loss in 11 games – there were more people beginning to agree with *Express* reporter Alan Thompson, who had written in the wake of that defeat in Europe: 'Now United must buy – and quickly.'

'They were shattered and dejected from a lesson in the arts and crafts handed to them by a Portuguese side not all that highly regarded in their own country,' Thompson said. 'So where do they go from here? They will live in hope that they will pull back the goals in the second leg. And Dave Sexton must buy if he wants to put United truly back on the map. Not just one player, but more … simply because they do not have sufficient playing strength to make a dent on the domestic scene, let alone compete against the sort of class we saw Porto produce.'

One name linked with United was Gordon McQueen of Leeds. The Scot had the height that United's defence had been lacking since the departure of McQueen's compatriot Jim Holton a year earlier. Sexton decided to wait until Brian Greenhoff was ready to return, but there was already enough evidence from the opening weeks and months of this season to prove that the suggestion of United being equipped to challenge for the biggest honours as they were was way off. The defeat at The Hawthorns had seen Nicholl at centre-half again and young Martyn Rogers given his one and only game.

Tommy Docherty made an enquiry for Stuart Pearson. *The Mirror* reported that he was not 'completely turned down' and there was talk of a £250,000 offer, though Docherty was told he would have to wait until United's injury crisis eased up. The openness to selling Pearson and the link to McQueen were the first indications that Sexton felt United would need to change their style. More signs were to follow very soon.

After the ill-advised trip to Tehran (United won 2-0 against an Iran 'B' side), United travelled to Villa Park and were 2-0 down at half-time. After failing to start the second half in the manner he would have liked, Dave Sexton made a symbolic move, bringing off Gordon Hill for Ashley Grimes. The away fans couldn't believe it. The substitution didn't pay off, although perhaps in Sexton's mind it did – United did not concede again, and were able to get a late consolation through Nicholl.

Sexton was finding Hill to be the biggest obstacle in terms of players who were resisting his style of coaching. After training, he asked Hill to join him in his office where the pair watched videos of the hardworking Hungarian wingers in their great 50s teams. Sexton was keen for Hill to contribute more defensively and felt that part of the reason they had been so porous of late was because they were so open further up the field. Hill had not shirked his duties as he understood them from the Docherty days, but that was not enough for the new manager, who wanted Hill to drop further back and help Arthur Albiston. It had only been in January of that year when Old Trafford was witness to one of the most peculiar sights in history – Martin Buchan running up to Hill and scuffing him around the ear after losing the ball and putting the team in trouble. If you think that supports Sexton's theory, it was actually quite the opposite; Buchan was scolding his team-mate for taking a liberty in an unfamiliar area. Hill's strength was not defending and his captain was making him aware of that and sending him back to where he was of use to the team. It is said that some members of the team may have been growing frustrated with Hill for not working harder defensively; if Sexton was reading it this way, then perhaps he was taking their complaints too seriously, for by all accounts it seems that for most of the players it was light-hearted. They were more than happy to accommodate Hill's talent. Sexton, however, was not willing to accommodate anyone who would not work to his plan, and Villa Park was the first public sign of things going wrong.

The United boss could not afford to take such a gamble when playing against Porto in the return leg. To his credit, he sent his team out to overturn an unassailable advantage, and when Steve Coppell scored an early goal Old Trafford responded loudly. What followed was frantic, breathless and relentless as United hunted in packs. The visitors dealt a body blow by hitting the home side on a counter-attack on the half-hour to equalise; it meant Sexton's team now needed to score six to go through. But they got two before half-time for a 3-1 lead and renewed hope. Coppell netted again in the 65th minute to set up a grandstand finish, but a Porto goal in the 85th minute finally ended the hopes of the hosts. A fifth United goal followed in injury time to round off a memorable night, even if it was in vain.

The next few weeks were also memorable for the wrong reasons. Four defeats in seven games followed the Porto game as injuries to Brian Greenhoff, Buchan and Albiston continued to undermine the defensive solidity (and the elder Greenhoff also missed games, putting the goalscoring responsibility on Hill and Pearson). Sexton did not do much to help matters, however. After the defeat against Arsenal on 5 November – the first game after the Porto elimination – the United boss decided to make a big change.

'On the following Thursday I received the summons to report to his office,' Alex Stepney said. 'He told me that he was leaving me out of the team for the next match. He said he did not think that the goals were my fault, or that I was playing badly. But there were so many goals going in that he thought I was in danger of becoming punch-drunk, like a boxer who had taken too much stick.'

The legendary stopper had shipped 18 goals in seven games. Sexton told Stepney he would be calling Paddy Roche into the team. Stepney had been in this position before. Previously, Roche had made mistakes and Stepney had soon been recalled by Docherty. 'I asked Dave what he would do about the goalkeeping situation if Paddy failed to change the team's luck and performed no better than I had,' Stepney recalled. 'He did not answer for a while, and I suggested that he would probably go out and buy a new goalkeeper altogether. I had Phil Parkes at the back of my mind. There had always been some speculation, and it seemed logical to me that Dave would go back to his old club for a goalkeeper who was on the fringe of the England team. Dave looked at me and said that if Paddy failed to do his job I would be given another chance. Although I had no reason to doubt Dave's word, I felt that probably I had finally come to the end of the road as United's goalkeeper.'

Stepney was already beginning to have concerns about the compatibility of Manchester United and the manager he had high expectations for. 'Something was wrong,' he said. 'The team was not fully responding to Dave. It seemed that he had not taken the dressing room by the scruff of the neck.'

Roche's introduction to the first team did not help matters, though, to be fair to the understudy, it was not conducive to good form that the defence in front of him kept changing. Buchan and Brian Greenhoff did come back for his first game but the captain was only back for three games before missing the next two. He was back again for the visit of Nottingham Forest but United's campaign sunk to a new low when they were absolutely destroyed 4-0. Brian Greenhoff said it was, 'the worst performance I ever had at Old Trafford. Martin and I had just come back from injury and I just could not put a foot right and we got run ragged.'

Forest were now top of the division. They had been with United in the Second Division and so their progress and the sheer magnitude of their victory put the decline of Sexton's side in a very harsh light. *Express* reporter Alan Thompson, who had urged United to buy after the defeat to Porto, gave a damning report on the afternoon: 'When fans leave Old Trafford in their thousands long before the end, the situation with Manchester United must be critical,' Thompson wrote. 'Twelve months ago, this same United side was being hailed leaders of the movement to bring back attacking skill and enthusiastic running. Where has it all gone? The finger of suspicion can't but be pointed towards manager Dave Sexton. The aggressive style that won them the cup only seven short months ago has disappeared. In its place is something which this Sherlock Holmes cannot detect. But whatever it is supposed to be, the number of empty seats 20 minutes from the end should be enough to convince Sexton that it is not within a million miles of being the "Manchester United brand". A commanding centre-half, a courageous centre-forward and a dominant goalkeeper – the backbone of any side – are initial requirements. Don't tell me they have not been available. In the past 18 months Nottingham Forest have signed Peter Withe, Kenny Burns, Peter Shilton, Archie Gemmill and David Needham. Brian Clough has transformed an average Second Division side into First Division leaders. Those players were available to any bidders ... and any one of them would be an asset to Manchester United. If lack of available talent cannot be accepted as an excuse, neither can poverty be accepted as a plea. It was not the fact that Manchester United lost 4-0 to Forest on Saturday which disturbed me – it was the manner of it. They were outclassed in all departments – and in the second half they dropped chins and accepted slaughter like chickens. Forest should have won by eight clear goals. Now there are two courses open to them. Either they will have to settle down to at least a five-year wait for young players of certain styles to emerge or they will have to spend heavily. About £1m should do it.'

Sexton was a patient man and he had a patient board, but the former option was not one that was available, considering the quality of the squad he had inherited. Some may have been willing to concede that United were not quite as ready to challenge Liverpool as some had heralded, but they were most certainly much better than their form over the first half of the season had suggested. Going into Christmas 14th place in the table was a dismal start, and Sexton felt that even despite the injuries he had a greater conviction over his belief in the weaknesses of the squad. He appeared to concur with Thompson's assessment; having already dropped Stepney, he also viewed the Forest defeat as more of an indication that Buchan and Greenhoff shouldn't be first choice as a pair, instead of it being a blip. Stuart Pearson did not seem best suited to Sexton's preferred style of delivery for centre-forwards, and Gordon Hill did not seem best suited to the manager's preferred attitude and work rate.

Over Christmas in 1977 there was plenty of speculation. Manchester City's Dennis Tueart reportedly turned down an advance from Sexton, while Aston Villa refused an offer of £200,000 for their striker John Deehan. Birmingham said no to an approach for Trevor Francis. There was a strong link to QPR's talented midfielder Gerry Francis, but the London club had put a stunning £500,000 price tag on his head.

Stung by the public criticism and the very real possibility that any number of them could be at risk, United's stars responded in style, trouncing Everton by a 6-2 scoreline at Goodison Park on Boxing Day, and then putting another three past Leicester the following day at Old Trafford. But the manager had already made up his mind, and the reality was that those two victories were the last hurrahs of the Docherty side in the guise that supporters were familiar with. They were projected for further success and, in the eyes of some, might have even taken the place of Forest or Villa on one of their European Cup-winning nights; yet, the team with a young average age and a bright future did not even make it to the end of the calendar year before it was torn apart.

On one hand you can't help but feel sympathy for Sexton when it comes to the criticism he received for 'tearing the team' apart. He had not had a proper opportunity to play the 11 who had won the FA Cup. That team had played together just twice and both times the manager had to make a change because of injury. And because of those injuries, which were mounting up, Sexton was already finding that Old Trafford was no place he could hide; no place where these mitigating circumstances would mask failure, even if most observers *did* feel sympathy. Importantly, the players could not complain now that Sexton was looking to make high-profile changes. Individually, they might, and indeed would, but it was plain to see the squad needed reinforcements. From championship hopefuls to being in a 'critical' condition; Manchester United were experiencing the familiar, unsettling feeling of a bumpy transition once more.

Personality Clash

DAVE SEXTON attempted to change the tide at the start of 1978. The hint of positivity that came from the back-to-back wins against Everton and Leicester City was completely wiped out by a 3-0 capitulation at Coventry on New Year's Eve and a dreadful 2-1 home defeat to Birmingham on 2 January.

Sexton was sufficiently convinced to spend £350,000 on Leeds United striker Joe Jordan. 'I am delighted that we have got such a talented player,' the Manchester United boss told journalists. 'His signing in the morning will be a great boost to us. Jordan is a top-rated player in every country in Europe. He will be a great signing for Manchester United.' But Jordan had scored just 47 goals in 223 appearances for Leeds. His record that season so far was three in 20 First Division games. It was clear he was being brought in for his aggressive style and imposing presence ahead of any genuine goal threat.

If this was an indication that Sexton wanted his United team to be tougher, then Brian Greenhoff took it a little too literally in the FA Cup third-round game against Carlisle United. Greenhoff admitted he should have already been sent off for a worse tackle than the one that eventually did see him dismissed. His team-mates held on for a 1-1 draw at Brunton Park, and the versatile defender could have no complaints for being dropped for the replay four days later, which United won 4-2.

But when Greenhoff was dropped for the next game against Ipswich Town (a 2-1 United win), he wasn't told, and confronted

Sexton afterwards, with the United boss telling his player that he wasn't told because he thought it would upset him. 'It didn't sit well with me, particularly as he was a slightly nervy character at the best of times and when he knew he'd done something wrong he didn't handle it very well,' Greenhoff said. 'The manager should have you on the back foot but it was the other way around.'

Sexton felt suitably concerned about the form of the player who had been the man of the match in the 1977 cup final to seek a replacement partner for Martin Buchan. That player would be Jordan's former clubmate, Gordon McQueen. 'Again, the signing of Gordon and the effect it had on my position in the team was something Dave decided not to talk to me about,' Greenhoff said.

McQueen had voiced his intention to leave Elland Road days after Jordan's move had been completed. 'I feel that my game will not improve further if I stay at Leeds,' he said. 'The departure of Joe Jordan to Manchester United brought the matter to mind, although he did not result in my decision to seek a transfer. I only hope that this matter will not drag on like it did for Jordan. I hope I can get away quickly. I am perfectly serious and if they want me to put it in writing I will do so. I'm not worried about the loss of money in making this request.'

Bob Armstrong of *The Guardian* tipped United to make a move, writing, 'McQueen is the sort of versatile attacking defender who would fit in admirably with the positive philosophy of Dave Sexton.'

But the move, much to the player's chagrin, *was* protracted. Indeed, for a while, it seemed as if the British record fee that Sexton was tipped to spend on his next signing would instead go on QPR midfielder Gerry Francis. On 16 January several journalists reported that United had agreed to buy Francis for £440,000. United fans had reportedly acted angrily, calling the office of *The Express* to suggest the club should sign Gordon McQueen on account of the need for a defender and also Francis's recent injury problems. It seemed as if Sexton had hesitated based on the backlash from fans as Rangers believed a deal had been done.

'The announcement regarding Gerry Francis is premature, as we are still in the process of negotiating with QPR,' Sexton insisted. 'It is my intention to present all the details when finalised to my directors at a board meeting on Thursday.'

Jim Gregory, the Rangers chairman, was insistent that the player was moving to Old Trafford. 'Gerry said goodbye to the rest of the team on Saturday,' he said, 'and we felt we acted in a proper manner by making the transfer public.'

QPR boss Frank Sibley concurred with his manager and complained about United's stance: 'I'm disappointed Dave Sexton has denied the deal has been completed. He rang both Gerry and me on Friday night and said everything was agreed.'

United fans, fuming at the idea of signing a player in the one area where the team was fairly strong, had not been placated by the fairly low-key arrivals of defender Kevin Moran and goalkeeper Gary Bailey. Bailey had been training with a club in Holland when he saw an advert in *Shoot!* magazine which said United were actively looking to give a young goalkeeper a trial. He asked his father Roy, a veteran of the English game, to arrange a trial on his behalf, and Bailey joined up with the United team in the December defeat at West Ham. He approached Martin Buchan in the hotel United were staying in and told him he was there for a trial. 'Yeah, you and the entire world,' Buchan quipped, and walked straight past him. 'Some introduction to the English sense of humour,' Bailey jokes now, although there was a distinct difference once more between that and Buchan's dry take.

Bailey was still some way away from being considered as being ready for the first team but was given a handful of reserve team games before the end of the season, as was Moran.

In the last week of January, Sexton had an experience with the past and future at Old Trafford. The first was a very joyous event; Tommy Docherty's Derby County were destroyed 4-0. Gordon Hill scored two goals in the first half but even so was described by John Course of *The Guardian* to have had a 'rotten' opening period. Hill then provided goals for Pearson and Buchan; it was the captain's first goal for six years, and one that might have felt sweet for the Scot, as he was tasked with confronting Docherty on behalf of his team-mates due to the former manager failing to keep true to a promise to pay the players an agreed bonus after the 1977 cup final.

If they wanted a bonus for retaining the trophy they would have to overcome West Brom, who had just hired Ron Atkinson; Joe

Jordan made his United debut, in place of Jimmy Greenhoff, who had scored the winner in the previous year's final. Albion scored in the 77th minute and United needed a last-minute equaliser from Steve Coppell to force a replay. At The Hawthorns, they needed another to force extra time – Hill getting this one, though Cyrille Regis finally gave Albion the result they deserved with a 94th minute winner. Atkinson was ecstatic. 'I said that this replay against United would be an Everest; it was!' he said. 'Now let us climb every mountain all the way to Wembley.'

One player who certainly was not ecstatic was Hill, whose primary concern was not actually the defeat. 'I'll always remember Joe Jordan depressing John Wiles's cheek at West Brom,' he said. 'I was absolutely disgusted with it. I was playing in the game and I couldn't believe what I looked at.'

Atkinson's side would stumble at the penultimate hurdle, losing to Ipswich in the semi-final at Wembley. For United and Dave Sexton, the defeat to Atkinson's new side meant the end of hopes of silverware just six months into a new era which had started with supporters dreaming of the biggest prizes in the game. Fans would have accepted that those prizes would not have been immediately forthcoming, but it was the regression in both results and style which meant they were concerned.

Two days after the FA Cup exit, *The Guardian* ran a feature interview with Steve Coppell where the midfielder tried to allay those worries. 'It sounds corny, I know, but injuries made us struggle. With Martin Buchan, Lou Macari, Stuart Pearson and Jimmy Greenhoff out at various times we were unable to consolidate the work which Dave Sexton was putting in,' Coppell said, before insisting that Joe Jordan would prove to be a valuable asset. 'He gives us the let-out of a high ball into the middle, which we never had before. It has been drilled into us that we must play football right into the penalty area and get to the line, keeping our crosses low. Now we have more options. We never had tactical talks with Tommy Docherty. We had a set way of playing and innovated around that. We never discussed other teams before we played them. The changes have not been too extensive, but what has been done has tended to involve the players more. It is appreciated, and results will soon begin to show it.'

However, supporters voted with their feet, and for the 8 February game with Bristol City the lowest crowd of the season came to Old Trafford – just 43,457, almost 14,000 fewer than the attendance for the game against Derby. Hill scored again, but City equalised in the first half. The game ended 1-1. *Guardian* reporter Paul Fitzpatrick said that more than one fan went past the press box and said, 'What the hell are you possibly going to say about that?' Well, Fitzpatrick described the game as '90 minutes of purgatory'.

The consequence of the result was greater than a dropped point. Martin Buchan suffered an injury and had to come off; Jimmy Greenhoff moved to right-back. 'We think that Martin may have flaked a bone in his right ankle,' Sexton said. 'It could mean that he'll be out for three weeks at least, and perhaps even longer.'

It prompted the manager to accelerate plans to sign Gordon McQueen; the day after the game, Sexton made an offer of £450,000 for the Leeds man, who said, 'If the deal with United should come off, I wouldn't say anybody had won. But I won't believe anything until it is official. Quite honestly, I didn't think they would go so high for me.'

The following day, the deal had been agreed and McQueen was presented to the press. He told reporters, 'Ninety-nine per cent of players want to play for Manchester United, and the rest are liars.'

The new player was not in the team to face Chelsea the day after signing, but Brian Greenhoff was back in the team to replace Buchan. He expected, as vice-captain, to be named skipper. No conversation had taken place to the contrary; but embarrassment was felt by Greenhoff when he picked up the match ball to lead his team out. 'Dave took the ball off me and said, "Stevie's the captain today!" and gave the ball to him,' Greenhoff said. 'He said it in front of everybody.'

United rescued a 2-2 draw at Stamford Bridge in the last minute when Hill scored a penalty, but Greenhoff was axed for the following game at Anfield, which marked McQueen's debut. Sexton's side lost 3-1 and were never in the game. It was a disappointing first game for the record signing. 'I don't blame the players, only myself,' a disappointed Dave Sexton said.

'The problem for me is that after leaving Leeds I started to try to play like a £500,000 defender,' McQueen said in 2018. 'That was the wrong way to go about it. I should have stuck to what I was good at. But you want to impress when people pay that amount of money for you. There was a lot of pressure initially at United, but I soon settled down. At the start I didn't like having that big fee hanging around my neck. But after a couple of games I was absolutely fine. Joining Manchester United never phased me. Old Trafford was an intimidating place for a lot of players, but it didn't bother me.'

McQueen was an ambitious and adventurous defender; perhaps not quite as proficient on the ball as Greenhoff, but taller and more robust so that he should ostensibly be better prepared for the physical tests a defender in the First Division could expect to face. McQueen was left out for the visit of his old club and Leeds's 1-0 win at Old Trafford on 1 March left his new side in 12th.

Middlesbrough's visit to Manchester three days later saw United (and Jordan, yet to score for his new team) draw another blank; Hill missed a late penalty and the game ended 0-0. *The Guardian* reported that supporters gave 'Sexton the bird' and angrily demanded that the manager made a change to bring Stuart Pearson on. 'But who could I have taken off?' Sexton responded, though it was suggested that it was obvious the supporters meant Jordan.

A 2-2 draw at Newcastle was United's eighth without a victory. Sexton recalled Alex Stepney but his side got the same result at home against Manchester City. Four days later they drew at home again against West Brom. For the third game in a row, United were denied by a late equaliser. 'It's just not going for us, is it?' Sexton said to reporters afterwards.

Stepney had been unfortunate as he made an outstanding save, only for Albion to score from the rebound. The only two players who emerged with credit according to the press were McQueen, who scored his first goal in the 30th minute, and Gordon Hill, whose form of late had almost single-handedly made Sexton thankful that he had draws instead of defeats to lament, having scored at Newcastle and then both goals in the derby. Hill scored again as United finally won in their following game at Leicester, but his goal in the next game was just a consolation following two Bob Latchford goals for Everton at Old Trafford. It was ten strikes in 12 games for the winger but when his team were getting a comprehensive beating at Arsenal on 1 April – Hill's

24th birthday – the player was given the public embarrassment of being substituted in the second half.

'Some people would give anything to get rid of a headache,' David Miller of *The Express* had written on the morning of the game. 'Dave Sexton has spent almost £1m acquiring one. Sexton takes his big-money Manchester United side to Highbury this afternoon, attempting to make his million make sense against Arsenal ... It is, perhaps, an exaggeration to say that the team Sexton inherited from Tommy Docherty was successful. Although it won the FA Cup, there were signs that the momentum of Doc's Double Wingers was slowing down ... there were increasing noises from inside Old Trafford that Sexton was thinking of a 4-3-3 formation, with one winger and more midfield control as in his successful QPR team. His problems will come not so much on the field, as from the players he has to leave out, confided one Old Trafford source as the cheques started to fly.'

It seemed that Sexton had identified Hill as a major cause of the recent form and not a silver lining in it. He decided he was going to drop the winger for the following game against QPR and would play him in the reserves.

'In the run-up to our game with QPR in April, Dave told me he intended to rest me and play me in the reserves at Preston,' Hill said. 'Later, I got a call saying he'd changed his mind and I was going to play. Even later, I had another call saying he'd changed his mind yet again and I wasn't. When Dave called once more, indicating another change of mind, I made the decision for him by saying it would probably be best if I played for the reserves at Preston. I was all over the place and informed Dave that I was concerned that if I had a bad game he'd be on my back again. So I went to Preston, but at half-time Jimmy Curran said to me that he'd had a call from the boss and they were bringing me off. He told me that the club had accepted a bid from Derby County.'

Tommy Docherty, who had been rebuffed in a February move for Jimmy Greenhoff, found his advance for Hill successful. Sexton accepted a bid of £250,000, which would be a United record for an outgoing transfer. Hill, feeling the discussions had been engineered in such a manner that it was obvious he was not wanted – and the evidence certainly supported it – accepted the move.

'I'm delighted for Derby County that we have signed Gordon but I feel sick for the United fans,' Docherty said on 14 April. 'I am flabbergasted that he even came on the market. It's a joke really, a catastrophe for United.'

Hill, naturally upset at being personified as a reason for United's poor form when his goals had helped the club mask how grave the issues really were, blasted: 'It seems United have changed their style and I don't think it's for the better. It seems they don't want entertaining football. It has left me baffled. You need 'O' levels or a university education to understand our tactics because they have become so complicated.' The player later expressed his frustration at the timing of his departure. 'From what I knew we were all capable of,' he said, 'I knew that the form we were in was not a true reflection of our quality.'

But Hill was gone and his comments were the first real public statements of discontent about how things were going since Dave Sexton came to Manchester (news of the transfer was also reportedly followed by supporters daubing 'Sexton Out, Hill In' on a wall near Old Trafford).

'Gordon Hill's outburst on leaving Manchester United that you need 'O' levels to understand Dave Sexton's tactics might be tinged with bitterness but could nonetheless be 98 per cent true,' wrote Alan Thompson of *The Express*. 'The coach is the curse of modern soccer. Not all of them. I can, if pressed, name perhaps a handful who have actually improved the game both to play and as a spectator-entertainment. But as a breed they do seem to me to have an extraordinary skill for making what is essentially a simple game, to be enjoyed, into a difficult one. That is not what the public would prefer to pay to see. Manchester United are finding that out – their gate last Saturday was down to 42,000, which is still magnificent by most standards, but is hardly a quorum for the Stratford End. In the last couple of years they have flopped from a high point of being one of the great crowd-pleasing entertaining sides ... to a position wager they steadily rock in mid-table upsetting nobody and winning nothing. How on earth United could justify selling their only match-winner on the ground that he does not work hard enough in defence is beyond my comprehension. But, then, I am not a coach. Dave Sexton, who took over a successful, winning, entertaining, spectacular outfit, has not so far rekindled a spark, let alone started a bush fire, with the club that, in Europe at any rate, is still regarded as the greatest British side.'

Dave Sexton exercised his right of reply. 'The fact is that Gordon is a very selfish player,' he said. 'The other lads here have had to do a lot of work to accommodate him. Talk of a vendetta is immature and not fair to the lads Gordon has played alongside for three years. He has scored his goals, of course, but the other lads have had to pay the price for them. Gordon talks about being asked to tackle back, for example, and says it is just against his nature. Well, I never wanted him to tackle back, just to do some retrieving, something called teamwork. Apparently he says also that he loves the Manchester United fans. Well, he didn't want to play for United last Friday when he came into my office. Before he stepped through the door he was in the team but then he said he wasn't in the right frame of mind. Doesn't he know that playing for this team is playing for those fans? This is a team game and whatever problems Gordon may have felt he had here are going to happen again wherever he goes – unless he changes. If he does change then he will get into the England team regularly. If he doesn't, he won't.'

Sexton may well have felt vindicated by the form of his team towards the end of the season. Hill's exit from the team and departure from the club coincided with four consecutive wins before the season concluded with a disappointing defeat at Wolves.

In the game against QPR where Hill was dropped, it appeared as if Sexton was stressed to impose his own style on an occasion where the spotlight would be on him as it came against his former side. 'We of Manchester United cannot afford to indulge in too much sentiment about our visitors because as I am only too well aware we have problems enough of our own to worry about,' the boss wrote in his programme notes. 'It distresses me that we have not been able to strike the winning sequence we all wanted, particularly at Old Trafford, and after strengthening the squad with two top-class Scottish internationals. Much has been made of our failure to win more than one game in our last dozen games, though I feel it is only reasonable to point out that there is another way of looking at the recent sequence. We have in fact lost only four of our last 12 league games.'

It was not a fortunate rephrasing. No one at Old Trafford would have been convinced by the reframing of that argument. Injuries to

Jimmy Greenhoff and Lou Macari did have an impact on selection, meaning that there was no genuinely coherent and consistent selection and strategy as Dave Sexton's first campaign in charge of the club came to a close. It was clear to see that Sexton wanted a greater emphasis on structure and sensible play as opposed to the gung-ho attitude of his predecessor, and he had added height and physicality where United had previously not had it. Jordan and McQueen did bring qualities United didn't previously have, though it was fair to question whether these were qualities the team needed.

United had kept just three clean sheets after McQueen's arrival, whilst Jordan scored just two goals. This is not necessarily a reflection of their quality or form and it may well have been that Sexton perceived the late flurry of victories *as* that vindication that a corner was being turned. The final home game against West Ham came on the back of two wins. Sexton was again keen to try to put a positive spin on the events of the season, and also to put a lid on the talk about Hill.

'It was the run of draws that cost us a place in Europe next season, which of course is a big disappointment to players and supporters alike,' he wrote in the programme for the game against the Hammers. 'But we have never been far away from qualifying and I find the fact that we have lost only five of our last 20 league and cup games quite a firm basis on which to build … I think we can look forward to the future with every confidence; I thank you for your support this season and hopefully we can all go forward together to an exciting year next season … Finally after the unpleasantness of last week I would like to wish Gordon Hill good luck with his new club and thank him for his efforts for Manchester United, not least his goals, some of which will remain among my most spectacular highlights of the season. A parting of the ways came in the best interests of all concerned in the end, but football is a big game and we wish Gordon well as we fight on to try and provide a few more highlights in our remaining games before the curtain finally falls on the season.'

Brian Greenhoff and David McCreery filled in Hill's vacant number-11 shirt; both hard-working utility players who would confess to having little of their former team-mate's wing-play ability. Yet even Brian Greenhoff had been told to play with more conservatism. 'It was essentially the same bunch of players that less than a year previously had finished sixth and triumphed at Wembley against the European Champions,' he said. 'My theory is that it was down to the training and the profound difference now was that players simply didn't enjoy it ... The things that came naturally, Dave Sexton seemed to make too much of an issue over. He didn't like me bursting forward too much, but that was my game. The very purpose of me playing at the back in the first place was so I could start attacks from deep.'

There was an emphatic change of approach that was given a personification in the sale of Hill; a moment that was just as symbolic in the changing style of United's football as Docherty's dismissal itself had been. Sexton was evidently hoping that the changes would be positive for the fortunes of the club in the long term as they had appeared to be in the short term after the sale of the star man and the top scorer.

United supporters were not convinced. The graffiti on the walls at Old Trafford was clearly more reactionary to the heartbreaking news that their hero had been sold than they were a genuine plea for the club to sack the manager. But it was clear that in making such a bold decision, Sexton had accelerated invitations of judgement. The mitigating circumstances which he had not been responsible for had just about helped him avoid shouldering the majority of the criticism for the club's significant underperformance since winning the FA Cup. He would not have the benefit of the doubt in his second year.

* * *

The 1978/79 season was Manchester United's centenary year. The drama of the last decade alone at Old Trafford would have been enough to fill the complete history books of most other football clubs in Britain, with a European Cup win, a relegation, a promotion, an FA Cup win, numerous semi-finals and five different managers.

It had seemed that under Tommy Docherty, the identity crisis of the club had also been resolved, but since his controversial exit and the contrasting approach of the more methodical Dave Sexton, there was once more a concern about the style of football being played at the club.

United supporters had turned out for the final home game of the season with a strong attendance of 54,089, but the two games before that had been 42,677 against QPR and just 41,625 for the game against Aston Villa on 29 March. Fans were voting about the style of football with their feet.

Perhaps they were fearful of their football becoming less about the beautiful game and more about the physicality. The successful Leeds team of that decade were infamously aggressive and Sexton had acquired two of the prize assets to play in his team in Manchester. If these were reservations on the terraces, then the same concerns were not necessarily felt in the boardroom.

'There was no reservation about the signings really because Leeds were so successful at the time and they were two of their great players,' Martin Edwards said of Joe Jordan and Gordon McQueen. 'A strong centre-forward was needed and Gordon McQueen was riding high at the time for club and country. He was scoring goals as well. We felt they were two players who would improve the squad. Even after all of Tommy's success and exciting football, there was still a general feeling that the team wasn't quite good enough to win the league. It was a good cup team but to take us to the next stage we needed to strengthen the side. Forget their style of play, Jordan and McQueen were just very good players in Division One who we felt might give us that extra quality to get over the line and win the league.'

Edwards felt that the 'physical' tag which was associated with the duo was somewhat unfair: 'Gordon wasn't particularly hard, I never thought of him as a crunching tackler, he was quite exciting for a defender. Jordan, of course, was hard and we hoped he would give a presence up front for us.'

That was a fair assessment and it was still equally fair at the time the players were signed to emphasise that Sexton was adding qualities to the squad that were not present before. Indeed, that much had been hoped for. It was when Gordon Hill was sold that Sexton had made a symbolic statement when it came to letting United supporters know how his team would play, and so the concerns that the exciting style of play was being phased out for a physical and slower approach were heightened.

'Obviously it was a big move,' Edwards admits. 'But we had gone for so many years without winning the league that if Dave felt another player would improve us on that side at the expense of Hill, you go along with it because you have to support the manager really. It was only over time, four years later or so, and you realise you're not getting any closer to winning the league, when you realise it's an error. But at the beginning, when he's making such choices, you have to support him.'

The difficult year had done little to damage United's profile as a football club. They had continued to be the most well-supported club in the country with an average attendance that was over 6,000 greater than Liverpool's, even accounting for those drops after the turn of the year.

Dave Sexton had walked into the top job at Old Trafford speaking so excitedly about the size of United that it put into perspective just how the club were seen in comparison to his former employers Arsenal, another of British football's greatest institutions. The schedule of the club continued unabated towards the end of Sexton's first season – first he took United down to Loftus Road to play a testimonial game for his former defender Dave Clement. Then United played two games in Norway, before heading to America to play Tampa Bay Rowdies and Tulsa Roughnecks (who were coached by United legend Bill Foulkes).

Flyers for the game against the Rowdies included the following billing for United: 'The team that won the 1977 Super Bowl of soccer. The team with more English world-class players than any other. The team with the largest international following. The most expensive team ever assembled. Manchester United, the #1 soccer club in the world.'

That logic made Tampa the best side on the planet, then, after they won 2-1 in sweltering and humid conditions which were made all the more unfamiliar for the United players with the sound of a commentator playing over the public address system asking the home fans if they wanted to see 'one more goal'. Against Tulsa, United won 2-1 thanks to two Brian Greenhoff goals.

It was finally time for Sexton to prepare for that centenary season and he felt confident that the hiccups of his first year were just that. 'I believe we have the basis for a more consistent and skilful effort this season,' he told David Meek. 'We have got the side more balanced and we can look forward with optimism. Towards the end of last season we were creating more chances and we seemed more able to keep the pressure applied right to the end of the game, instead of losing our grip in the way that lost us a lot of points at one stage. It often takes a little time for a new manager to get to know a team in depth, and the last year has been a finding-out period for me. There were disappointments and setbacks, but I think we learned from them, and in any case there were a lot of good things in my first season … Looking back over the season, there was a lot to be pleased about and give us encouragement for the future … I am also extremely satisfied about our two big signings from Leeds United. We shall really reap the benefit of Joe Jordan and Gordon McQueen this season as we build on the foundation created by their arrival when we eventually turned a run of draws into a winning sequence. It was the kind of improvement which I am hopeful will be continued this season and provide some kind of reward for the supporters of Manchester United who rallied behind us so encouragingly again.'

Sexton was outspoken on the controversy of the Hill sale which continued to divide opinion. 'Gordon is a very selfish player and to accommodate him other players have done extra work,' he said. 'They were, in fact, brilliant for him and he was ungrateful to say what he did. He scored goals but we had to pay a price for them. The teamwork and spirit will be better without him.'

The United boss was keen to stress that he felt Steve Coppell had been a particular beneficiary of Hill's departure in the final weeks of the campaign. 'It is as if Steve has had a harness taken off him,' he said. 'He is attacking again with all his old flair and success.'

In the short term, Hill's replacement on the left-hand side was identified as Sammy McIlroy, though it seemed as if Sexton was shifting to a 4-3-3 shape with McIlroy tucked inside, which gave the impression of new freedom for Coppell, who Sexton knew he could trust to work in a manner that nobody expected of Hill. For a while it seemed as if Sexton would instead replace McIlroy in the middle when United were linked with a renewed move for Gerry Francis. Doubts over his injury record meant the club were unwilling to part with a club-record fee (these fears were heightened by the fact that Gordon McQueen had suffered a knee injury) and Francis moved to Manchester City instead.

United did not make a senior signing but were forced to restructure. Chief scout Norman Scholes retired from full-time work but would be helping with administration duties following

Gordon Clayton's move to Derby. Joe Brown, the youth team manager, became chief scout, and Syd Owen took Joe's old job.

The club had a low-key pre-season schedule in Germany that was marred by some supporter trouble (Sexton was compelled to urge his supporters to 'behave') but the glamour fixture of their build-up was undoubtedly a match to mark the centenary against Real Madrid. On the eve of the game on 7 August, Tommy Docherty took a swipe at his successor. 'I've heard of a team taking four years to build, but not four weeks to destroy. That must be a record,' he quipped to the *Sunday Express*, before going on to say United must win the league or 'something's wrong somewhere'.

Sexton had already outlined his ambitions in the *Manchester United Football Book*. 'I set myself standards and if I don't reach them I'm prepared to depart,' he said. 'United have given me three years to do a job and with a club of their standing and quality of players it's long enough to win something. I left QPR only because I had been there for three seasons and though we had done reasonably well we did not actually have a trophy to show. Managers are fighting for their lives and their jobs all the time. It's just like the situation for players. If a goalscorer does not score goals, a schemer does not scheme, a defender does not defend, a goalkeeper does not keep out the goals, then the club gets someone else to do the job. It has to be like that for the manager as well. If he does not win something the club must get someone else who might. If Manchester United have no trophy to show after three years with me as their manager, I shall be quite happy to apply the philosophy that prompted me to leave Loftus Road. If a manager does not win a trophy, his influence lessens. By winning something he earns himself time. People like Sir Matt Busby, Bill Shankly and Bill Nicholson stayed with their clubs a long time because they kept winning honours and it was this that gave them their authority.'

Despite all efforts to put a brave face on things, the occasion of the Real Madrid game was a fairly forgettable, and regrettable, one. The game itself was encouraging. United won 4-0, with two goals each for McIlroy and Jimmy Greenhoff. David Lacey of *The Guardian* said, 'One of the most pleasing features was the strength of understanding which lay between Buchan and McQueen at centre-back.' But there was some controversy when it was revealed that a number of former players had not been invited, most notably some of the survivors of the Munich air crash, such as Bill Foulkes, Dennis Violett, Albert Scanlon, Johnny Berry and Kenny Morgans. Harry Gregg, who had been invited, pulled out of the event in disgust, forcing the club to make an official statement where they regretted they could 'only invite so many guests'.

When the club concluded their pre-season schedule in a game in Denmark three days later, Joe Jordan was dismissed, providing a realistic reminder of the present state of affairs at Old Trafford. Perhaps Sexton would have given second thoughts to the £60,000 bid he had accepted for Jimmy Greenhoff earlier that week; as it transpired, Greenhoff turned down the move to Chelsea, saying he would 'play it by ear' when it came to his future.

Sexton, as he had done consistently, tried to be positive about the pre-season. 'In each of our four pre-season games we've shown a nice gritty quality that was once missing,' he insisted. 'Add that to the skill that is always present in any United side and you've got to have a chance of winning something. My first year here has flashed by and I've no regrets about taking on United. It's my biggest challenge. Indeed, probably the biggest challenge in the game. Other teams can scramble for their results. United have to do it with open football and there's never been any question of me wanting to change that. Don't forget that if we'd shown the form throughout last season we hit in the last half, we could have been in Europe.'

The United boss was also minded to defend his signings, saying of Jordan: 'He hasn't scored many goals, but he's played so well that if he'd added goals to his game he'd be the greatest thing since sliced bread.' And of McQueen: 'We played more football at the back than Gordon was used to at first. Now he's really bedded in – and as a bonus he'll get us ten goals a season.'

In his programme notes ahead of the season opener at home to Birmingham, Sexton seemed peculiarly keen to reframe the events of the previous season as a basis on which expectations should be formed moving forward. Those reading his column ahead of the game would not have been filled with optimism. 'I expect to find the going harder than ever this season with the championship outsiders proving as difficult to beat as the fancied teams like Liverpool,' he admitted. 'For our part, we at Old Trafford are anxious to make our mark after a fairly modest season. To finish tenth in the championship is hardly failure, but at the same time we were not up with the title challengers for very long and we are all anxious to do better. We feel we have the resources and the players at the club now to make a determined bid for honours.'

United lined up with this 11 against Birmingham: Roche, B. Greenhoff, McQueen, Buchan, Albiston, Coppell, Macari, McCreery, McIlroy, Jordan, J. Greenhoff. There were already four changes from the FA Cup-winning side of a year before, with a fifth in the case of Brian Greenhoff's move to right-back to accommodate the new partnership in the middle. The attacking line-up was more about working than thrilling; compared to the exciting performance against the same opponents in the opening fixture a year ago, this was a United in Sexton's moulding, and they laboured to a 1-0 win earned with a Jordan goal 20 minutes from time.

A few days later United went to Elland Road to play Leeds United, who had just appointed Jock Stein as their new manager. Stein had famously turned down an opportunity to manage at Old Trafford back when Sir Matt Busby was searching for his own successor but was now out of work after an acrimonious exit from his post at Celtic. Unlike Sexton, Stein had inherited a bit of a jumble in Yorkshire and the visitors took advantage of that early uncertainty by winning 3-2. Stein lasted a month and a half before admitting he wanted to leave to manage Scotland.

Despite winning the opening two games, United were no more convincing. A humbling 3-0 defeat at Ipswich was followed by four consecutive 1-1 draws. They were eliminated from the League Cup at home to Third Division Watford in front of just 40,534 supporters. Attendances in the league hovered around and just over 45,000 as Sexton struggled to put together an 11 who felt comfortable together. On 21 October he selected Arthur Albiston at right-back against Bristol City, such was his dissatisfaction with Brian Greenhoff. But Bristol won 3-1 at Old Trafford in a stunning result which now exposed that it was more likely to be the manager's choices which were more instrumental in the increasing regression in the performances and results. Perhaps sensing this, when Gordon McQueen was out for the visit to Birmingham on 11 November, Sexton went with Greenhoff and Buchan at centre-half. The idea to impose some stability was quickly thrown out of the window as the hosts tore United to shreds, winning 5-1. Even Greenhoff conceded that the taller Stewart Houston should have been selected to combat the height of the unplayable Don Givens.

One *Daily Express* report had dubbed United's ground 'Cold Trafford'. It provoked the powers above Sexton to make statements of their own; it was revealed that shares in the club would be sold in order to generate transfer funds of around £2m for the manager to spend. 'I'm very concerned about recent events on the field,' chairman Louis Edwards said on the day he announced his retirement from business 'to concentrate as much as possible on club affairs'. 'I'd be a fool to say we have been playing well. In fact, our last performance was shocking. I haven't been satisfied with our performance in a few matches. We are trying to do everything possible to fill one or two gaps in the team. We are not afraid of buying and no one can accuse us of that. One or two players we have inquired about are not available, but we are watching and are on the look-out all the time. Anyone who is suitable at home or abroad will be considered. We are injecting a greater sense of urgency into the club's buying policy. Money is there immediately and if they want more there is £1m to come from the issue of rights shares.'

The day after those comments, a much-publicised court case was concluded when Tommy Docherty withdrew his accusation of defamation against Willie Morgan. Neither were at the club, but it was their relationship at Manchester United which continued to make the club headline news for all the wrong reasons. So it was hoped that, moving forward, the positivity generated by potential incoming transfers might get a good feeling back at Old Trafford in the short term. The names included Steve Daley of Wolves, Robbie James of Swansea and winger Dave Thomas of Everton. The World Cup that year had attracted the eyes of British clubs to Argentine talent – the host nation winning it as they did – and Spurs had already signed Ricky Villa and Ossie Ardiles. Experienced River Plate striker Leopoldo Luque was offered to United for £500,000. More was to follow. Amidst the speculation, Dave Sexton did make one move for definite that week when he made an offer to sign Coventry's Scottish goalkeeper Jim Blyth. Alex Stepney had seen the previous season out after being dropped, but Paddy Roche had been an ever present in the 1978/79 campaign until the Birmingham game, which seemed to be the final straw. Coventry knew it was a seller's market and slapped a £440,000 price tag on their man. United, who had only wanted to pay half that, had no option but to agree.

Blyth failed the medical then the deal broke down over the question of insurance, which refused to guarantee a policy on the player. 'I've never been so upset in my life,' the player said. Coventry manager Gordon Milne said he planned to reopen talks with Dave Sexton about a compromise where the fee might be broken into instalments as Blyth played a certain number of games.

On the same day, Paddy Roche complained to *The Guardian*, saying: 'I went straight to the boss but he explained that I was not being made a scapegoat for our performances. It was more a question of consideration for my feelings after what has happened this week. He did say he thought I had been looking a bit shaky in recent games, but we went through all the goals and he agreed that I couldn't be blamed for any of them. He assured me that I am still the first-team goalkeeper.'

However, having had that conversation, Sexton instead chose Gary Bailey for the visit of Ipswich Town. It was a dramatic change in fortunes for Bailey. 'In my mind, I was thinking I would be going in for a knee operation,' Bailey says. 'But on the Friday Dave came up to me and said I would be playing because the move for Jim had fallen through. It was probably a good thing because if I had known further in advance I would have panicked. I thought they would still sign Jim and if it was only one or two games I would have, I wanted to take the opportunity.'

The youngster kept a clean sheet in a 2-0 win. His performance in torrential rain was described by *The Express* as 'sensational'. Ipswich boss Bobby Robson said: 'I thought Brian Greenhoff was great. He showed the kind of spirit Manchester United need at the moment.'

The inconsistency of the team showed when United followed that win with a 3-0 defeat at Everton. Bailey learned just how quickly the press could turn; he also discovered that his manager was not wholly convinced. 'I played against Ipswich and I played really well and made all the right decisions, and the crowd seemed to take to me,' Bailey explains. 'The day after, at The Cliff, the press grabbed me and asked if I would take a picture with an umbrella. They captioned it "Singing In The Rain". Three days later we played Everton. We got hammered and I got smashed by Bob Latchford. The papers use the same picture with the caption "Drowning in the rain"! Ahead of the next match against Chelsea, Dave said to me, "Look son, if you don't play well I can't keep you in the team." He told me they were looking at the Argentinian goalkeeper but if I did well I might keep my place. I did.'

Sexton pushed ahead with plans to sign new players. On 21 November (as United lost at Goodison) an offer of £250,000 for Wrexham left-winger Mickey Thomas was rejected. The Welsh club wanted £300,000, and they got it three days later when the deal was swiftly completed. Sexton was delighted. 'He will give us a lot more balance on the left,' he said. 'He's an exceptional player.'

The hope was that Thomas would be a perfect foil to Coppell on the left, hard-working, efficient and consistent. He made his debut against Chelsea in a 1-0 win and was in the side to face Derby. The Rams were still coached by Docherty and had former United stars Gordon Hill, Gerry Daly and Jonathan Clark in their team. Daly scored in the third minute but a rejuvenated United responded to lead by half-time, and added another to secure a 3-1 victory in the second half. In truth, it was already a very different Gordon Hill; he had suffered a serious knee injury earlier in the season and had rushed back after being misdiagnosed, a decision that would have tragic consequences as far as his top-flight career in England was concerned. If the country never saw the best of Hill, the same could be said of Docherty, who appeared to have lost all of that showbiz after the controversial events of the last 18 months. United, in victory, had a temporary last laugh, but there were plenty of Reds supporters sympathetic to the plight of their former heroes.

A 2-0 win over Spurs was followed by more transfer speculation. It was reported that there were approved applications in the Foreign Office to allow Daniel Passarella and Ubaldo Fillol into the country 'to discuss football with Manchester United'. Derek Potter of *The Express* wrote: 'After the methodical 2-0 destruction of sweet-moving Spurs, United don't need to cry for Argentina anymore.

There's still cash-saving talent around Old Trafford as Andy Ritchie and Gary Bailey proved with astonishingly mature performances.'

John Couse of *The Guardian* reported that the Edwards family would be putting in £750,000, with other shareholders contributing to make United's transfer fund £1m. 'The object is said to be to buy players,' Couse wrote. 'The result is that the price of any player wanted by United is automatically doubled. So the more money you brag about, the less you get for it. The news has obviously reached Argentina. United have been after a couple of their World Cup stars, but manager Dave Sexton announced on Saturday that River Plate had priced Passarella so highly that even he was not interested; and the goalkeeper Fillol was not for sale at any price.' Couse went on to say Sexton would have 'preferred to spend a ridiculous £440,000 on a man playing for Coventry City reserves and was only saved from doing so by doctors and insurance brokers.'

On 21 December Docherty enquired about David McCreery. Sexton was clearly annoyed. 'I won't let McCreery go there,' he fumed. 'I have already sold Docherty two players. In any event, McCreery is not on the transfer list and we have a busy programme over Christmas followed by the FA Cup in the new year. He has not asked for a move and we could need any of our players for this programme.'

Any except Alex Stepney, who was given permission to join Dallas Tornado the following February. One United goalkeeping legend was departing, but Sexton brought in another when he added Harry Gregg to his coaching staff. He had been approached as a goalkeeping coach but Gregg insisted he would only return as a general coach. The hero of Munich returned to his former club though admitted to holding some concern. 'Dave Sexton appeared to be the ideal choice – quiet, dependable and, perhaps most importantly, uncontroversial; he offered stability where before there had been volatility,' Gregg said. 'Caution, though, has never been the United way. Of equal importance to delivering trophies is the flamboyance and excitement which characterised the greater sides which had gone before.'

Both Gregg and Stepney would have watched with despair and sympathy in equal measure as United succumbed to consecutive 3-0 defeats at Bolton on 22 December and then at home to Liverpool on

Boxing Day. The rookie Bailey was blameless. Debutant Thomas Connell was thrown in at the deep end to play left-back (McCreery's place apparently not so urgent that he would be called to play) in these two games, his only appearances for the club. Sexton had enjoyed some success with young striker Andy Ritchie but it was clear that United were paying the price for Docherty's concentration on the first team, which had resulted in a certain neglect of the youth set-up in the mid-70s. Under Sexton, that appeared to be changing. Later that month renowned scout Bob Bishop would brag to the press that he had found the 'best since Best' in a 13-year-old striker from Shankill who 'scores goals, makes goals and plays for the team'. 'He's a good boy ... not romantic. And he's got short hair,' Bishop said of the prodigious Norman Whiteside.

McCreery was called into the team to play against West Bromwich Albion on 30 December 1978. Even the festive period could not entice a crowd bigger than 45,091 to come to Old Trafford – a huge drop from the 54,910 against Liverpool. Those who did make the trip saw an incredible game of football. The only problem for United fans is that their team were once more on the wrong end of the result, scoring three times but capitulating in defence to concede five. Incredibly for a goalkeeper, Bailey was one of United's best players, but it was becoming increasingly clear that the partnership of McQueen and Buchan was not as resolute as Sexton would have hoped. United were chaotic and disorganised; their visitors, on the other hand, were slick, stylish and decisive, punishing Sexton's side time and again in the second half.

There was something fairly symbolic about the sight of Sexton and Ron Atkinson standing on the side of the Old Trafford pitch to be interviewed by Granada Television's Elton Welsby for their programme *The Kick Off Match*.

'Well I thought, you know, after the two defeats we'd had previously, I was very pleased, I thought everybody worked very hard and tried very hard, and we got three cracking goals,' Sexton said. 'Unfortunately this fella's team got a few more than us. But overall I was very, very pleased with the way we responded and the way we fought back. We might well have got the result from the game when it was 3-3 in the second half, just before they scored their fourth goal. I thought we looked as though we were going to score a fourth goal, but they got one on the breakaway and it brought them to life again, and you can't give a team as good as that that time.'

Atkinson was magnanimous and diplomatic in victory. 'I would say that was a great Saturday afternoon for everybody if you don't take the result into account,' he said. 'I mean, if you come out on a Saturday afternoon to enjoy football and think, "Cor I've had my money's worth there!" then nobody can have any complaints.'

The problem being that Manchester United supporters did take results into account. Neither results nor performances had been up to scratch, and while Dave Sexton had benefitted from the benefit of the doubt due to the injuries he had also made a number of major decisions to alter the identity and personality of the team. The object of that particular goal was to make Manchester United harder working and tougher to beat – an objective that was clearly not being met after three consecutive defeats where 11 goals were conceded. It was a landmark defeat; one Sexton could ill afford considering the political motives for selling Hill in the early part of the year.

In a weekend preview for *The Guardian* on 16 December 1978, Robert Armstrong had commented that there had been 'sufficient cause for serious doubts about Dave Sexton's future with Manchester United'.

The run of defeats and embarrassingly emphatic nature of them could only have weakened the manager's position. Martin Edwards insists, though, that this feeling wasn't shared by the board yet, which would go some way to explaining why they were still handing the boss big transfer funds. 'Things weren't right and there was some discontent among supporters because of the style of football,' Edwards admits. 'As a junior director it was very much a case of Matt and Father running the show and making the important decisions, while I and the other directors went along with them. But I cannot recall that there were any serious concerns about the job Dave was doing at the time. Not at board level.'

But when under 40,000 turned up to watch United win 3-0 against Chelsea in the third round of the FA Cup, it was beginning to feel as though the powers that be would be unable to avoid the question for much longer. It was a race against time for Dave Sexton – would he be able to prove that his approach would be successful before supporters voted against it being completely intolerable?

Five Minutes

MANCHESTER UNITED suffered – if that is the right term – their lowest attendance at Old Trafford for over five years when just 36,058 turned out to see them defeat QPR 2-0 on 28 February 1979.

Reporting for the *Manchester Evening News*, David Meek's piece on the game was headlined 'Golden days are finally over' and featured the line: 'Manchester United's magic bubble has burst and it's sad, but more constructively honest to concede that the halcyon days are finally over.'

The Guardian reported that Louis Edwards and Sexton were 'both of the opinion that the drop in attendance at Old Trafford is part of a national trend after the recent bad weather'. It may have been generous on Edwards's part and oblivious on Sexton's (and there were further social and economic reasons for drops across the sport in general), but by that point even the United manager could not have been ignorant to the harsh reality. There was an element of truth in how the harsh weather had hit British football; United played only two games in January 1979, and both of them were in the FA Cup.

Their win over Chelsea was followed by a draw at Craven Cottage, but only 41,200 turned out to see the replay on 12 February; supporters were not even encouraged by the fairly handsome 3-0 win at Maine Road two days before, or the opportunity to say farewell to Alex Stepney.

United won 1-0 against Fulham to set up a fifth-round game with Colchester United. A Jimmy Greenhoff goal decided the game, but Dave Sexton was more impressed with Gordon McQueen's defensive contribution. 'Gordon was getting up so high tonight that Brian Greenhoff asked him if he could see his car parked outside,' he quipped.

It was the elder Greenhoff brother who decided the next round, too, with an 86th-minute winner to spare the blushes against lower league opposition. On this occasion, Sexton expressed sympathy for his beaten opponents: 'I thought Colchester battled splendidly. They were a credit to the competition and I feel sorry for them that they cannot come to Old Trafford for a replay next Monday. They earned it.'

Far from being convinced about a cup run which now saw United in the sixth round, supporters had grown concerned and frustrated about the below-par showings against poorer opponents. When it was 0-0 at half-time against Aston Villa in the next home league game, another below-average crowd of 44,437 booed their own team off the pitch. Villa took the lead on the hour but Jimmy Greenhoff scored a penalty with 15 minutes left. United limped to another draw. The fans booed the players off just as they had at half-time; it seemed clear that this was aimed at the manager.

'The football spectator is a long-suffering creature,' wrote John Couse for *The Guardian*. 'From where I stand at Old Trafford, I have grown accustomed to missing part of the action because so many people have been herded into the paddock. That is not the case anymore. With 12,000 or so fewer spectators, there is an excellent view. The trouble now is there is not much to see.'

There was a remarkably candid response from one of United's stars when asked about the game afterwards. 'Diabolical,' Sammy McIlroy said, 'diabolical.'

Harry Gregg, who spoke of the 'unease in the crowd' he could sense in the Villa game, decided to take it upon himself to talk to Sexton ahead of the game against QPR four days later. 'It wasn't easy to speak my mind,' he said. 'I didn't want to appear out of place, but as far as I was concerned this was for Dave Sexton's benefit, not mine. I told Dave that in my experience there was no way the fans, or the board for that matter, were going to put up with the current situation indefinitely. I reminded him that United was expected to play with vitality, that failure was just as likely to lose him his job as poor results. Dave said he had been manager and coach at all his previous clubs, but at United the coach was Tommy Cavanagh. He walked over, shook my hand and thanked me for the advice. We led QPR 1-0 at half-time, yet the players were still booed off the pitch. At the end of 90 minutes United had doubled their tally, yet one woman hit Dave Sexton with her shoe as he walked back up the tunnel.'

If United supporters were beginning to vote with their feet – quite literally, in that instance – then the next game indicated they were willing to take the greatest of sacrifices. Over 3,000 tickets were returned unsold for the visit to Bristol City, a place where United had only travelled to twice in recent years. It was unheard of for fans not to travel to away games in their droves, and it was yet another truth Sexton could not shy away from. At least, in this instance, he could point to a recent run of good form, backed up by the 2-1 victory at Ashton Gate. The manager defended his team as a 'young team in transition', saying: 'We always play with a lot of spirit. We've got a good fighting squad. There's also a lot of skill there.'

That fighting spirit was called upon as Spurs and United battled to a replay in the sixth round of the cup, United coming out on top in the second game at Old Trafford. 'Manchester United have recaptured some of their pride but not the old daredevil panache,' David Miller wrote in *The Express*.

Against Coventry at Highfield Road, United were embarrassingly 2-0 down inside eight minutes. It was 4-1 in the 47th minute; Sexton's side regained some respectability with two consolation goals.

Out of nowhere, a thrilling victory against Leeds followed, with three goals in the first 20 minutes. That 4-1 win was followed by a draw which on paper seemed to point towards good strength of character as United recovered from two goals down to salvage a point at Middlesbrough ahead of the FA Cup semi-final against Liverpool. But the performance at Ayresome Park was shocking, with the hosts dominating a fixture they should have won by a number of goals. 'It wasn't the ideal way to prepare for the cup, but my concern was to get everyone fit, and that happened,' Sexton admitted afterwards.

In the Friday feature interviews for the press, however, the United manager was in somewhat defensive form. 'I believe passionately in the blokes we have at Old Trafford ... that they can do something important for the club,' he said. 'I believe they can get into Europe even without winning the FA Cup ... if we can sustain the sort of form we showed last Saturday, this squad is good enough to win a European trophy. I know there's been some criticism of me from time to time about the way United have been playing, but, believe me, whatever has been said publicly, it's never as bad as what I'm saying about myself if things don't go as well as I hope. I don't reckon the criticism when we played QPR at home was fair. At other times, maybe. People don't criticise for nothing. The win over Leeds was the first time we've blasted the opposition off the park. That's what the crowd expect. If we'd done that a few more times at home, there would be no criticism. Obviously, there has been a lot of talk about my handling of the team since I came to Old Trafford. However, it's not a question of getting the team to play the way I want, but how it's best for them. United played with two wingers under Tommy Docherty, but Steve Coppell tucked into midfield when needed because he had the strength to do it. He was a holding player, while Gordon Hill was more attacking. The only difference now is that it's the other way round, with Stevie having more freedom, and Mike Thomas picking up in midfield. The arrival of Mike made a lot of difference to us. Sammy McIlroy improved immediately because he had more freedom, and it's made things better for our left-back, first Stewart Houston and now Arthur Albiston, who's probably been our best player over recent games. The improvement of Gary Bailey under Harry Gregg's tutorship has also been important. If you're going to do something big, things have got to be right in goal, got to be reliable. I know my signing of Joe Jordan was controversial, but, believe me, there's much more to being a centre-forward than scoring goals. He has pace, fearlessness, mobility and the opposing defence are always looking for him. With United, he's had to fit into their style, which means he gets the ball to his feet more often, and he's revealed more control and dribbling ability than people supposed he had. I must admit that when I came to Old Trafford it was really daunting, knowing what I'd got to live up to. But that quickly faded when I found myself among such good people as Tommy Cavanagh and Jack Crompton, who were already part of the fabric. The knowledge at Old Trafford that it's not just enough to win but that you have to win well with style, put pressure on the players as well as me.'

FA Cup semi-finals carry a sense of occasion all of their own; add Liverpool as the opposition and choose Maine Road as the arena and you are including some extra ingredients on top. United were playing in their change strip of white with black stripes and Liverpool were in all yellow, lending a visually memorable aspect to the encounter. Kenny Dalglish scored a clever goal in the 17th minute when he outfoxed McIlroy and Buchan before slotting in. Less than two minutes later, United were level; a hooked cross by Jimmy Greenhoff was headed in by Jordan, the sort of direct move which did play to Jordan's strengths. Liverpool were then generously awarded a penalty but hit the post.

Ten minutes into the second half, United were ahead; an awkwardly bouncing ball was miscontrolled by Coppell into the path of Brian Greenhoff, who showed fine improvisation to loft the ball into the net. Liverpool equalised late on to take it to a replay, which would be played at the home of their rivals, Everton. 'I began to think that the disappointment might start to be getting through to the players,' Sexton said. 'We had to raise our game three times, first when they took the lead, then to go ahead and again after they had equalised. There's a great spirit in this team, and you always think you've got a chance.'

In the 78th minute of a very tense replay, Mickey Thomas showed fine composure to measure a cross for the head of Jimmy Greenhoff; the man who had scored the goal which decided the final two years before had knocked the same opponents out to take Dave Sexton's team to Wembley, where they would face Arsenal. Having ended Liverpool's treble hopes in 1977, now they served a terminal blow to their double chances. With the winner in both games, Jimmy Greenhoff cemented his place in Manchester United history. The sight of the elder Greenhoff heading in, and then celebrating in the timelessly cool white shirt with black stripes down the left breast, is forever recalled as an iconic image of the decade. In the pursuit of glory, Greenhoff's role as 'scouse spoiler' would never be forgotten.

Three days after the replay, United repeated their Middlesbrough trick when they came back from two goals down to get a draw at Norwich; but again, this was not indicative of a renewed spirit or a turnaround in fortunes for Sexton. The team's form for the last 13 games was horrendous, with just two wins; the first of those was a last-gasp victory over Norwich at Old Trafford in front of just 33,678 fans. The second came in the game before the cup final when United faced Wolves at home, and many players seemed to realise that they needed to put in a performance to get a place in the final team.

Thankfully for Gary Bailey, his own goal didn't affect his own position as there was no competition for him; unfortunately for Brian Greenhoff, trying to rush back from a calf injury he'd picked up in the semi-final was causing complications. He was injured early on against Wolves and suddenly the man of the match in the 1977 final was a significant doubt for the 1979 occasion. United won 3-2 against Wolves, but a better indication of their form overall came in the nine games before, when they had drawn five and lost three, never scoring more than one goal in a game and drawing a blank in four of them.

There was no dressing it up; United were every bit as abysmal as they had been in their relegation season in the spring weeks. They were clear second favourites going into the final. As the build-up to Wembley got under way, Sexton confirmed that both Greenhoff brothers were doubtful. He had also given Bailey an early nod to let him know he would have his place in the final; on 10 May the goalkeeper told reporters: 'Pat Jennings is the man to feel sorry for, not me. Everyone is expecting me to make mistakes at Wembley and if I do they will be written off as just a kid learning the job. But Pat is expected to be perfect and despite all his experience he is going to feel the tension. There is no point me getting scared, screwed up and tense about the final … I chucked the ball in the net [against Wolves] and that was probably the best thing that could have happened. I saw it as a bad game behind me.'

Sexton backed Bailey to recover just as he had from that difficult three-game period over Christmas. 'That spell didn't affect him or shake him and we stood by him,' he said. 'Gary showed his nerves were good in a job where you don't mature until your mid-20s. He's going to make mistakes, but he won't crack.'

The day before the game, the talk centred on whether or not United's semi-final winner would be available. 'I won't take a chance over Jimmy,' Sexton insisted. 'You need all hands on deck for a final. But if Jimmy says he can play, he can play. His word will guide me.' The United boss knew it would be an important event. 'Of course, I desperately want United to win tomorrow – for the players, for myself, for our supporters. But it is just as important that we should play in such a way that everyone, not just our own supporters, admires our own performance.'

The veteran forward said he would be sensible. 'If I don't think I can last the game, then I'll be ready to drop out in the morning,' Greenhoff said. 'I would not take a risk. It would be a terrible decision to have to take but at the moment I feel very confident.'

On the morning of the game, Liverpool boss Bob Paisley gave his verdict on United to the press: 'Tommy Docherty's legacy to the club was an outright commitment to open football and this has only been partially modified by Dave Sexton. Habits die hard. The result is inevitably a Jekyll-and-Hyde football team. This can be very exciting. But it can also be very disappointing.'

Sexton was never as open with the press as he was in the build-up to the final, speaking in particular with David Miller of *The Express*: 'Throughout my football life I've always had one ideal,' he explained. 'That is to have a team which plays 11-man soccer, in which every player is in tune with the other. It is when this happens that you get a great spectacle for the public, and it would be marvellous if that could happen when we meet Arsenal at Wembley tomorrow – a final for people to remember, whether we win or lose … I think there is a lot of misleading talk in football about man-management and motivation. In my opinion, the strongest impulse that can be tapped among players is that they all want to be thought of by their fellow professionals as good craftsmen. More than money, more than medals, we all want that photograph on the wall which recalls the moment of triumph. Some years ago when I was a player I sat down to make a note of the things I most wanted from football and this was how it came out: 1. I wanted to play well myself. 2. I wanted my team-mates to think I was a good player; that I contributed in helping them to do what they wanted. 3. I wanted the opposition to think I was a good player. 4. I wanted the opposition to think my team was a good team. 5. I wanted it to be a good game for spectators. 6. And then, I wanted to win. That's not to say I lacked the will to win. That is something I take for granted, as sure as night follows day. Of course, I desperately want United to win tomorrow – for the players, for myself, for our supporters. But it is just as important that we should play in such a way that everyone, not just our own supporters, admires our performance ... It's going to be a fascinating final. We're well aware of the problems Arsenal are going to pose for us, of the way they will attempt to neutralise our strength. We know because they've done it before, and our job is to break out of any grip they try to put on us. In that sense, the result is likely to be determined by the comparative tactical intelligence of the two sets of players. And, of course, we think we're going to win! The tactical areas fall quite conveniently into attack, midfield and defence. Arsenal rely heavily on their offside tactics, intending to kill off the willingness of the opposition's forwards to run, attempting to make us run out of ideas ... the key to our game will be to get forward quickly when we gain possession. This is our centenary year, and more than anything this gives us the incentive to achieve something unique. What makes me optimistic is that since the opening pre-season game against Cologne the team have shown tremendous determination. Whenever there's been a setback we've bounced straight back ... Although Manchester United have this great tradition for flair and attacking football, which is of course something I always want to see, the greatest improvement in the side this season has been in defence.'

Words were all well and good, but the fact of the matter was that the entertaining games United had been involved in that season had never seen them on the victorious side of the scoreline. If it was true that the board hadn't considered Sexton's position over the winter, then surely it was only the FA Cup run which had stopped his future being one of serious discussion in May 1979. This was a time when the FA Cup was so highly regarded that progress and success in it was a major factor when considering the value of the work done by a manager. Should Sexton emerge victorious from the game at Wembley, he would have a significant case to suggest on face value that he had returned United to where they were when he came in, even if all evidence continued to suggest the regression was continuing unabated.

If supporters could predict how the final would go from the performances of their centenary season, then it would likely be tight, with United coming out losers in a poor game. As for the Greenhoff brothers – both were passed fit, so Jimmy started and Brian was on the bench. Stuart Pearson, out of favour anyway, missed out with a knee injury. The composure Sexton was hoping for was absent as Arsenal scored from their first real foray forward; Buchan, for once, was caught out, as Bailey came out and left space for Brian Talbot to score in the 12th minute. These weren't great errors from either United player but showed some indication of the consequences of Sexton's changes, the minor details he was usually so clinical over which were his undoing – Bailey, the 20-year-old, with a moment's impulsiveness, and Buchan's decision to commit when that had not been his role in his previous defensive partnership. To all intents and purposes, alongside Greenhoff, Buchan had been the 'McQueen', the player who had the greater defensive mind to sweep up any problems. Now Buchan was tasked with the more tigerish aspect of active ball recovery more often. He was certainly capable of it, though given the choice you would want him in the other role. With these particular responsibilities, he had been caught out for the Dalglish goal in the semi-final and again here; caught out by good opponents who took advantage of poor organisation in defence, which might have been avoided had Buchan been given his normal duties.

United were okay in response; a well-worked move including a good run by Mickey Thomas presented a chance for Jimmy Greenhoff, who fired over. It was the sort of move you could tell had been rehearsed. McQueen thought he had scored an equaliser but knew in his heart it would be disallowed for handball. Minutes later, the game plan was completely out of the window when Liam Brady's marvellous dribble into the box gave him space to pick a cross for Frank Stapleton, who had positioned himself away from McQueen and behind Jimmy Nicholl. His header made it 2-0.

Despite their need being urgent, United were unable to make a dent in the Arsenal backline for the majority of the second half.

The Gunners threatened to make it even more embarrassing but Bailey pulled off a fine unorthodox save to deny Stapleton a second.

With four minutes left, and Sexton's team looking for a miracle, United got a free kick on the right. Coppell crossed it in, Jordan played it back across goal and McQueen fired it home. The method, the execution and the identity of the major players were all matters of vindication for the United manager. Arsenal were rattled and when Coppell found McIlroy with a clipped pass, the Belfast-born schemer took advantage of the rashness and desperation of the tackles from the Gunners defenders, evading two before stabbing the ball into the corner. It was a magnificent goal; the sort of genius, the sort of miracle United supporters had been praying for.

Arsenal's players were crestfallen. Tommy Cavanagh instructed Brian Greenhoff, who had been warming up, to get ready to come on. Dave Sexton said no. The United manager would wait for extra time. But extra time didn't come. The United players, hoping for the breather that the substitution would have afforded them, were forced straight back towards their own goal from kick-off. Jimmy Nicholl, exhausted at right-back and the player tipped to come off, was caught out on the right. A cross from the left sailed too high for Bailey, who made the fateful decision to try to catch it anyway. It meant he was unable to provide cover when Alan Sunderland got to the ball ahead of Arthur Albiston and pushed the ball into the goal. Emotions had been switched in the space of 60 seconds. Events were carved in history; it would forever be known as 'The five-minute final'. United were unable to recover. The cruelty of the consequences of the wrong decisions made on impulse inflicted excruciating pain on the supporters.

If they could depend on one predictable thing, it would be Sexton's sportsmanship in defeat; it wasn't exactly what anyone at United wanted to hear, but the dignity in defeat was a real touch of class. 'I'm proud we were part of something as dramatic as this. Yet it was very cruel for us – having to run uphill for almost the whole game, reaching the top, then falling off,' he said when talking to the press afterwards. 'I haven't had a chance to study any film, but I don't particularly blame our boys. They'd expended 88 minutes of draining energy, mental and physical. It wasn't that we relaxed, but just that Arsenal caught us on the counter-punch. The fact that we came back to make such an historic finish of this final typifies the quality and character that has developed in the United team. Arsenal's three goals were very similar – one of their players getting through almost to the line. That's ideal, the goalkeeper has to come to the near post, and from that moment you just sit and pray. They were three good crosses and three good goals, though the ball bobbled in Price's favour in the tackle just before he centred for the first goal. Of course, I'm unhappy that we gave three goals away when you consider the amount of play we had. It's our responsibility to prove that the way we play is superior, say, to the way Arsenal play. But I do believe the way Manchester United play makes it more difficult to win the league, because the public demand entertainment in conduction with success. But I agree with that. In defeat, Manchester United's honour and pride were still intact.'

McIlroy had tasted defeat with United at Wembley in 1976, but losing like this was an entirely new experience. 'We didn't deal with Liam Brady to bring him down because we were still on a high,' he said in Sean Egan's wonderful book *Doc's Devils*. 'I'm not knocking anyone when you say it should have been discipline. We were on a high from getting back from 2-0 to 2-2. We were still celebrating the goal and they just broke away again and got the winner.'

Was the goal any consolation for him? 'No, not really. Wembley is only a place for winners. You have lost the game and it's a horrible place to lose. Score a good goal at Wembley and not lift the cup – it doesn't make up for it.'

Brian Greenhoff was less forgiving, describing Sexton's U-turn in sending him on as 'the worst decision' the manager ever made. Greenhoff felt he wasn't alone when it came to feeling the change should have been made at 2-2 to force Arsenal to wallow a little longer, and give United's players a breather. The difficult relationship between player and manager would spectacularly implode over the following months. Incidentally, Greenhoff's room-mate was Steve Coppell, who recalled that Brian was sleepless with anxiety and called Laurie Brown to see if there was anything that could be done to help him get a good night's rest. 'His chances of playing went with that call,' Coppell said, 'though I still believe Brian could and should have played.'

When Joe Jordan was speaking in 2005 (as United and Arsenal were scheduled to face each other in the FA Cup Final again), he relived the experience with *The Independent*. 'There was nobody to blame but ourselves,' he admitted. 'We all wanted to do it so much for our manager Dave Sexton – he was a great coach, a great manager and a great man – and you don't get that combination so often – and it was hard, if not impossible, to look into his eye afterwards. We had been beaten once, then come alive and we had the game. Arsenal, after controlling affairs, were suddenly beaten. They just needed a little push and it was ours. But we did the most unforgivable thing professionals can do: we took our eyes off the ball for a few seconds, we thought about what we had done, not what we had to do.

'The consequence is that 26 years on I have still not seen a single frame of film from that game. I couldn't do it. It would be like watching an old nightmare come back to life, my worst memory in football. It would be just too painful.'

Liam Brady, man of the match for the opposition, agreed with the consensus that if the game had gone to extra time his team would have probably lost: 'We had the game and then we lost it, and if we had not conjured that goal in the last minute, I believe that United would probably have won in extra time. I just don't think we had too much left, and they had come from the dead.'

The season concluded with a draw at Old Trafford against Chelsea. Just 38,000 turned up. 'The last week has been a hectic whirl of activity and I was delighted that we were able to bring the season to such an exciting finish with a run through to the final of the FA Cup,' Sexton wrote in the programme. 'It provided a suitable climax for our centenary season and ensured that we had something at stake until almost the very last kick before the summer break ... What we have got to do now, of course, is to aim for more consistency in our game at Old Trafford. That must be our prime target next season. It's always disappointing if you don't please in front of your own fans and we did have a couple of frustrating spells at home this season. There were reasons. We brought one or two new players into the side and they had to settle in as well as regular men getting to know the newcomers. It worked out all right in the end – or we wouldn't have been playing at Wembley on Saturday!

We shall undoubtedly profit from experience next season, but that is looking to the future.'

But United finished ninth; their second consecutive mid-table finish. Their last six home games had all seen attendances below 50,000. Only eight home games in United's centenary year had drawn attendances over that figure. Supporters were not being entertained. In order to justify continued faith, Dave Sexton had to demonstrate that his caution was necessary in order for the club to be stable. If there was any weight to the theory that Tommy Docherty's methodology was too erratic to invest in the long term then it was never substantiated with anything tangible other than an opinion. One could understand the logic that a top club like United needed to have a more stable game plan, but it was proven that this particular strain of sensibility was conflicting with what the supporters wanted to see.

The ironic twist in the FA Cup Final hadn't even been the devastating sucker-punch; the short-term effects were bitter bruises and memories, but fans knew that the kitchen sink had only been thrown in the last few minutes because the game plan had failed. They had only seen their team entertain on occasions where the plan seemed to go out of the window. That possibility of free-spirited risk taking had reduced with the sale of Hill and the omission of Greenhoff and Pearson. There was little chance that Sexton would observe the final and decide that a more relaxed coaching approach would be the way to go now. He had already invested time and the club's money in trying to adapt to his style and, as most managers would, he would believe that *more* coaching and *more* players capable of adhering to his style was the way to success, rather than any flexibility or change in himself. Martin Edwards admits the style was 'too cautious' and 'a world away from the excitement' of Docherty's football. It would be fair to say that few United supporters would have grumbled if Dave Sexton had been fired in the summer of 1979. But the board took the decision to back him once more, investing in the theory that the cup form could translate into more consistent league form, and therefore giving Sexton the confidence to build in the manner he had been.

In His Own Mould

HAVING BEEN given a fair vote of confidence, and not the ostensible one often bestowed upon football managers just before they are ruthlessly sacked, Dave Sexton worked with the conviction that he must ensure his approach to managing Manchester United would be successful. He was helped by a change in the post-season schedule which put the emphasis on any friendlies being part of the preparation for the following season, instead of the money-spinning opportunities that often came up in late May.

Sexton did not use the extra time to perform major transfer surgery on his team. In the wake of the FA Cup Final, United were linked with a move for young Chelsea captain Ray Wilkins. It took almost three months of protracted negotiations to get the only transfer of the summer over the line. Wilkins finally arrived in mid-August for a club-record fee of £750,000. 'I have looked forward for a long time to get this chance,' Wilkins told the press. 'Now I hope everything goes smoothly and I'm a United player in time to play at Southampton on Saturday … United play the kind of football I like.'

Sexton spoke confidently of the change he hoped his new player would bring: 'I have known the lad since he was a 12-year-old schoolboy and I don't think anyone knows more about him than I do. He's a midfield general and I think things are made for him at Old Trafford.'

Sexton likened the negotiations to toothache, joking: 'I'll have to find something else to worry about now.' It was no laughing matter for Stuart Pearson or Brian Greenhoff, both of whom were sold in August. For Greenhoff, although he had felt his time may well be up, the nature of his departure was deeply upsetting. One of his sons was ill in hospital during pre-season and Greenhoff had tried to compromise with Sexton to miss an open training session on the eve of the season. Sexton was uncommunicative, forcing Greenhoff to toe the club line and miss picking his son up. The breakdown in relationship was made more evident when West Ham manager John Lyall called Greenhoff at his house to inform him the Hammers had bid for him, and it had been accepted. Greenhoff confronted Sexton at The Cliff and said he was going to London to speak to Lyall; Sexton apparently responded surprisingly, confessing that he had accepted the bid but bizarrely saying he didn't expect Brian to accept the move. Sexton then told his player that Leeds were interested, whilst Tommy Docherty (now at QPR after being sacked by Derby) made advances once he had been made aware of Greenhoff's availability.

Brian was mulling over his options but was reluctant to move to London. He was called in to Sexton's office after training a couple of days later, where he was told the manager did not want him to go. Greenhoff was furious and in haste accepted the offer from Leeds. The transfer fee was a club record for an outgoing player of almost £390,000 – reflective of the genuine quality the underrated star had. It was another symbolic departure after the sale of Hill and one probably more emotionally felt by fans; Greenhoff had been the shining light, the supporter's player of the year in the relegation season. They had wept with him as he sat in tears on the Wembley pitch after the 1976 FA Cup Final, cementing his place in their affection in the process. Greenhoff angrily told Martin Edwards on leaving: 'That man is not befitting of the title of manager of Manchester United.'

An indication of how loved Greenhoff was – and how unpopular his exit was – came from the ultimate source. 'I wasn't happy about him being allowed to leave United for Leeds,' Sir Matt Busby said, 'but the decisions was up to the manager. The manager must be allowed the freedom to do his job, back his judgment, stand on his own feet.'

Greenhoff didn't go to West Ham, but Pearson did, helping the Hammers in a glorious chapter of their history which included an

FA Cup Final win in 1980. Greenhoff regretted not joining him, but insisted he could not have stayed at Old Trafford. It wasn't just Docherty's players Sexton wanted to move out. Before the season kicked off, there was renewed speculation that he wanted to sign Dave Thomas, and that he was even willing to part with Mickey Thomas, the player he had brought in less than a year before. It transpired that the move didn't happen; on 18 August a report in *The Guardian* indicated Sexton had been keen to use Greenhoff as a makeweight for a move for Everton's Thomas. Dave Thomas was not quite Gordon Hill but closer to him than Mickey Thomas, and close enough to Sexton to have both known and appreciated his approach from their work together at QPR. Just observe the player's different reception to one notable technique of Sexton's: 'He used to collect cine films of old 60s football and he'd sit us all down and say "I'm going to show you a video on tackling or crossing, or scoring goals from outside the box" and Dave would spend hours at home in Brighton editing all this together himself. He was so far ahead of his time it was untrue.' The much-rumoured reunion never came to fruition.

The 1979/80 season got underway at The Dell. Southampton scored a penalty on the half-hour, but five minutes before half-time McQueen's header from a corner hit the post and went in via home defender Holmes. A promising first half was followed by a dreadful second, in which United failed to fashion a chance. The game finished 1-1. Sexton conceded that his side were 'poor and lost cohesion' in the second half, but did insist he was pleased with the contribution of Wilkins in the middle of the park.

Ahead of the opening home game against West Brom, Sexton was keen to stress to supporters via his programme notes that there would be reason for them to be excited through the season. 'There are several youngsters in the side who have not yet reached their full potential just yet, but the coming season sees them another year older and with the practical experience of playing in the First Division,' he said. 'We are aiming for greater consistency in our league performances and Ray is going to help us achieve it along with our other seasoned international stars and the young players who are maturing in splendid style.'

And United were good against Albion, certainly in contrast to their December showing against the same opponent. There seemed to be a maturity and control to their play, as well as an energy more associated with the Docherty reign. 'Manchester United turned the clock back to the old, bold days and walloped West Bromwich,' reported John Bean for *The Express*. 'For sheer energy, Dave Sexton's new men were the equals of the infectious United of old.' A goal early in each half earned a 2-0 win.

'We got it right tonight, Wilkins has given us a midfield platform and Mickey Thomas was superb,' Sexton grinned after the game.

Next up was a sterner test; an early rematch with their conquerers at Wembley. United travelled to Highbury with Ray Wilkins in high spirits. 'For me this is a chance to build on what we considered was a smashing win against West Brom on Wednesday,' said the new man. 'We made Albion, a very good side, look ordinary and I think I got the feel of the way United play in that game. I'm excited about coming to London to reproduce that form. Manager Dave Sexton is not asking me to play much differently than I did at Chelsea. I am doing the fetching and carrying and that helps to release Sammy McIlroy and Mickey Thomas for forward runs. But at least I'm in the situation now where I'm not having to shoulder all the responsibility. I feel more than ever it was the best move I could have made.'

Wilkins was impressive in a pragmatic goalless draw. Sexton told some journalists that he felt his side were good enough to challenge Liverpool for the First Division championship. It was some boast, that looked a little foolish after a defeat to Spurs at White Hart Lane in the first leg of a League Cup tie, but a home win over Middlesbrough in the league quickly got United back on track. What's more, it was the sort of performance that got people talking. 'They are as quick and inventive as they were perhaps a couple of seasons ago with the little men, Macari, Thomas and Coppell, almost impossible to mark at times,' wrote Leslie Duxbury for *The Guardian*. 'Jordan looked in great shape and Wilkins too seemed to have been caught in a collective euphoria which has kept them undefeated so far.'

After a 3-0 victory at Aston Villa, journalist Bob Houston wrote: 'Dave Sexton's featureless Manchester United may not be winning the country's admiration as of yore, but they're steadily amassing points.'

A win over Derby County the following week put United top of the First Division. There still seemed to be an issue getting a complete 11, but for the first time Dave Sexton appeared to know the majority of his strongest team, with a solid defence and midfield to build upon. 'It would be wrong to suppose Manchester United are top of the table solely because of Ray Wilkins,' David Miller of *The Express* wrote after the 1-0 victory over the Rams. 'But it is no coincidence. What Wilkins has given to United – and gives to England – is not particularly dramatic or instantly obvious to the man on the terrace. But it is what is missing in so many teams – balance and rhythm.'

United tasted their first league defeat of the season at Wolves, and then were given a 4-1 pasting at Norwich to send them out of the League Cup (the Reds had recovered to eliminate Spurs as part of their impressive run of form). Recovery was emphatic; a 4-0 victory over Stoke City was enough to prompt one *Express* sportswriter to say Sexton had 'now completed the rebuilding of the side he inherited from Tommy Docherty'.

This was no backhanded compliment. It was a statement which said it was now Sexton's Manchester United as opposed to Sexton's caretaking of Docherty's United. It is important to point out a couple of things about the era; coverage of football on television, while still somewhat in its infancy with regards saturation, was still far more prominent than it had been just five years before. There was more to pick from when it came to assessing the pragmatic qualities of a Sexton team against a Docherty team. Additionally, a couple of points about the Docherty reign itself need to be spotlighted in order to project a fairer context. The first was that the Scot himself had spent the first 18 months of his reign feeling that a protective style of play was necessary (Docherty was inheriting a side which had just shipped five to Crystal Palace, but the point remains valid). During this period, as Docherty fought for control, it is no surprise that he made most of his enemies at Old Trafford. He did eventually turn his side into the cavalier, expressive machine it became, and perhaps it is fair to say that he placed so much emphasis on attacking and the ability of his own team in the last two to three years that not even Sir Matt Busby or Alex Ferguson could claim to have been so 'gung-ho'. And, indeed, now that quality was preserved and crystallised, with no way of knowing how it would transpire, Docherty's brand of football could forever be canonised, free of the concerns of its sustainability at the time. It had been suggested that in order for that side to take the next step in its progression and maturity, they would need to become tougher and more organised. To that end, hiring Dave Sexton made perfect sense. The transition hadn't been as smooth as many would have liked, and there had been some major casualties along the way, but there now appeared to be some proof that his methods could be successful.

Ray Wilkins had played a massive part in the early-season transformation. His intelligent screening in front of the defence, as well as his peerless use of the ball, made him the perfect player to sit in front of Buchan and McQueen. It was no coincidence that United racked up six clean sheets from their first nine league games. Their tally of 16 goals was comparable with the best teams in the division (only Forest and Norwich had scored more).

However, the jury was still out when trying to predict whether this was a permanent shift or a temporary run of form. Sexton was clearly still trying to sort out his front line; Lou Macari had been moved back up top as a consequence of Wilkins's arrival, and, while Joe Jordan was sidelined with injury, the United boss felt that he needed a more substantial presence up front. When Wolves made a move to sign Dave Thomas, United made a late bid of £400,000, which was accepted by Everton; perhaps influenced by earlier delays which made it look as if Sexton wasn't all that keen to get him, Thomas plumped for a move to Molineux. The first bump in form came in October; a defeat at West Brom was followed by a draw at Bristol City. Sexton described the latter as a 'good fighting point' and said, 'We've got to get a win – home or away – when we're on top, but the way we play, with so much running, is bound to take its toll eventually in a game.'

A 1-0 win over Ipswich was followed by a 0-0 draw at Everton, where Sexton was forced to play Coppell alongside Macari. 'We are very lightweight up front and have to work everything to a T,' Sexton said after the result at Goodison Park. If this seemed like a candid admission that United's place at the top (which had been maintained despite the patchy form) was fortuitous, then the boss was in slightly more positive spirits after a 1-0 win over Southampton on Bonfire

Night. 'When we get the goals to match our football somebody is going to catch it,' he promised.

It didn't seem as though those goals would come from Andy Ritchie. The promising young striker was deemed surplus to requirements as early as November, when Sexton accepted a £350,000 offer from Aston Villa. The move would have made Ritchie the most expensive teenager in British football history, but the youngster rejected the offer. Sexton, who had previously said the size of the fee was the only reason they accepted, declared: 'The fact that Andy has turned down Villa makes it certain he wants to stay here and we will not be considering any other offers. We are happy to see him here fighting for a first-team place. I felt it was only fair to tell him about the offer from Villa and let him make up his own mind. I must say I am pleased he has chosen to stay.'

Not for the first time, Sexton had sowed the seeds of discontent in the mind of a player by accepting a bid; his subsequent insistence that he was happy for Ritchie to stay sounded hollow.

The victory over Southampton was followed by a 2-0 defeat in the Manchester derby and then a 1-1 draw with Crystal Palace at home, in which Joe Jordan scored an injury-time equaliser on his return. That result saw United displaced from top position on goal difference by Liverpool; Sexton was confident that the record of four goals in seven games was about to dramatically increase. 'I've no doubt the goals will come,' he said as his team prepared to face Norwich. 'Some team is going to catch a cold against us. My confidence is partly due to Joe Jordan being back, but we have been consistently getting into scoring situations.'

The Canaries caught a cold alright; United smashed five past their visitors, with Jordan getting two, and Kevin Moran – playing just his fifth game, standing in for the injured McQueen – also grabbing a goal. 'Joe is so unselfish that he would be a great asset even if he never scored another goal in his life,' Sexton purred. He was in equally buoyant mood ahead of the following game against Spurs. United's title hopes were being talked up, and he initially said, 'Sorry, I just don't want to talk about it!' before relenting to say, 'Well, yes, it's going quite well, Gary Bailey has come on a lot in goal, Ray Wilkins has given us balance and rhythm in midfield, and we keep knocking away up front, where we were without Joe

Jordan and Jimmy Greenhoff for a while.' Asked if United would 'go for it' at Spurs, Sexton was bullish. 'Attack? Of course we'll attack, we want to win to stay at the top,' he smiled.

At White Hart Lane, Spurs were the more entertaining side, whereas United had to show a different side to their game in order to get a result. Gary Bailey had already been forced into a magnificent save before Glenn Hoddle scored a fine goal. It took an hour for United to fashion a genuine chance, and thankfully, when Sammy McIlroy was able to, Lou Macari was on hand to convert and equalise. With three minutes remaining, Jordan did some good work down the left-hand channel and played a clever ball into the middle. Mickey Thomas was unable to connect, but the goalkeeper came out of his goal to try to deny the Welshman, and was powerless to stop Steve Coppell converting into the empty net.

David Miller of *The Express* said it was Sexton's Scufflers compared to the Busby Babes. Sexton cared little. 'There must be a reason why we're there at the top,' he said. 'Today the team showed real resolve. At half-time we simply discussed the fact that we had to pressurise them. Their midfield had been running through us. The real reason for our victory was that Joe Jordan and Lou Macari kept battling away up front.'

That week, United were linked with legendary Brazilian defender Carlos Alberto, and veteran Czech winger Marián Masný. The boss dismissed the speculation, saying he 'had no intention of buying for the sake of it'.

Three big games awaited United over Christmas – Forest at Old Trafford, Liverpool at Anfield on Boxing Day, and then Arsenal at home to close out 1979. Sexton described them as 'games of the century'. As Forest arrived in Manchester, people were keen to remind Sexton of the 4-0 humbling almost exactly two years ago. 'Forest caught us on the hop that day and my ambition since then has always been for us to get our own back,' he said. 'I want to redress the balance. We've been playing tremendously consistently, toeing the line every week. We have set a high standard and now the challenge is to maintain our momentum.' There was some sweet revenge; by 3:30pm it was 3-0 to United, with two Jordan goals and a strike from McQueen. It remained three, but it was by no means an anticlimax.

The same could not be said of a 2-0 defeat at Liverpool. Sexton was upbeat, insisting: 'This result decided nothing.'

Mickey Thomas, though, realised it was a blow. 'It's hard to back against Liverpool and they must be a good bet to win it again,' the midfielder said, 'but we'll keep trying.'

The mood in the camp was good; United retaliated in some style, putting Arsenal to the sword with a comprehensive 3-0 win. They were two points behind Liverpool but six points ahead of Southampton and Arsenal below them (it was still two points for a win at this stage). United lacked the cutting edge of Liverpool up front and were not quite as miserly in defence, but their resilient defensive structure, which made them hard to break down, did now appear to be the difference that made them contenders.

A shock third-round exit to Spurs in the FA Cup meant United had only the league to play for from January. Nikola Jovanovic, the Yugoslav defender, was signed from Red Star Belgrade for a fee of £300,000. He was the first player to be signed by the club in the 80s, and also the first official foreign player to play for the club (Italian-born Carlo Sartori was recognised as a home-grown player as he moved to Salford as a child and came through the club's famed youth system). A move for Watford's Luther Blissett was also touted, though never amounted to more than speculation.

United started the decade in somewhat patchy form. They drew at Middlesbrough where Dave Sexton unfortunately spoke to reporters about a 'very exciting game'; he was not aware that two supporters had been killed.

Paddy Barclay wrote in his *Guardian* report: 'As Manchester United supporters waited in their segregated pen for police to signal the beginning of the journey home, the rest of Middlesbrough's biggest crowd of the season streamed away contentedly absorbed in discussion of a thrilling match. 'You couldn't have better entertainment than that at any price,' was one man's view on the wooden stairs leading down from the main stand, and nobody argued. The same happy thoughts no doubt engaged the minds of Norman Roxby, aged 51, and his wife Irene, 52, as they walked out of the ground and passed the 10ft double doors behind which, by now, the United supporters were heaving. As the couple passed, the bulging doors burst down, bringing with them the fatal brickwork of a pillar and a wall. Witnesses suggest that a group of Middlesbrough supporters outside had taunted their United counterparts into attempting to break out and engage in a fight. Earlier, it had been thought that impatience at the sight of gates closed without apparent reason was their motive. In the past, of course, it has been argued that crowded pens in themselves induce conflict. The fact remains that if those people had behaved as, for example, a flock of sheep would have been expected to do in the same situation, Mr and Mrs Roxby might be alive today.'

Sexton's team were involved in a bizarre game at the Baseball Ground where they fell behind in the 33rd minute and equalised five minutes later; 1-1 remained the scoreline until injury time, when Steve Coppell grabbed a dramatic winner and then Barry Powell, who had earlier given the Rams the lead, put the ball into his own net to give the visitors a 3-1 win. If that result was flattering, at least Sexton wasn't hiding from the truth when his side lost 1-0 at home to Wolves on 11 February, describing his team as 'a bit below par'. Another late Coppell goal earned a draw at Stoke.

But even when United did get a win – and a big one at that – some remained unsure of their capability to go all the way. 'To win unconvincingly is one thing. To win 4-0 is usually another. But there was little excitement in Manchester United's victory over Bristol City on Saturday,' Paddy Barclay wrote for *The Guardian* on 25 February, before he went on to say the most excitement came from the terraces late on as news of Ipswich's equaliser against Liverpool came in.

'We are so bloody close,' Sexton insisted. 'Only two points behind Liverpool, and I can sense the fans willing us to win the title. I can understand how they are feeling. They are tremendous supporters and it us up to us to repay them by providing exactly the kind of football we played today.'

Ironically enough, the win came in front of the lowest crowd of the season – 43,329 turned up, only the second time a crowd under 50,000 had been registered at Old Trafford that campaign. The other had been that 5-0 win over Norwich, after similarly patchy form.

Two days after beating Bristol, United were rocked by the death of their chairman, Louis Edwards. Edwards had been under considerable strain after the Granada Television series *World in Action* ran a show alleging that the club had been involved in a number of highly irregular and downright illegal transactions to secure business contracts and also as inducements to convince young players to sign for them. Edwards strongly denied any wrongdoing but felt the stress, as you would imagine anyone would in those circumstances. He suffered a heart attack on 25 February and died; his son Martin believed it was a direct consequence of the stress.

It was suggested that Sir Matt Busby was keen to step into the breach and become the chairman of the club. In October 1979, at the club's annual general meeting, it had been revealed that the Red Devils souvenir shop was owned by Sir Matt, with all the proceeds going to the former manager. Louis Edwards had been pushed on the matter as it was mentioned that the proceeds were not on the club's accounts. He was uncomfortable answering, but Busby himself answered, saying: 'With the chairman's permission I shall answer that. About 10 or 12 years ago I had ideas of starting a souvenir shop, separate from the club. The shop is mine and that is why it is not in the accounts. The club have simply been good enough to give me facilities on the ground.'

Though it would take some weeks to officially resolve (the announcement was made on 23 March), Martin Edwards stood his own ground to insist to the other directors that he would be more suitable for the role of chairman than Busby.

'I wasn't really daunted,' he insists. 'I had been running the family business and had experience of dealing with more staff and greater financial turnover. Moving to United wasn't frightening, it was something I wanted to do. I had been a director for ten years at that point. The other directors suggested that Matt should become chairman and I should wait my time, but I didn't feel that was the right decision because I felt Matt was getting on, he hadn't been very well. They reconsidered and made me chairman and Matt president.'

One theme of the post-Busby era had been the suggestion of interference; under Wilf McGuinness, senior players would often go to Busby if they disagreed with a decision. When Frank O'Farrell was in charge, Busby did in fact approach him to advise him against dropping Bobby Charlton. Tommy Docherty was mostly able to get

on with things and make some critical calls, such as letting Denis
Law and George Best go, but still felt as if Busby had vetoed signings
such as Peter Shilton. Then there was the difference of opinion
when it came to assessing just how involved Busby had been in the
dismissal of Docherty. By now, though, Busby seemed to accept
that when it came to influencing matters on the pitch, he was a
glorious part of the club's past. 'I'm not sure Matt interfered with
the way Dave ran the club,' Edwards says. 'I've read that managers
didn't always get the players they wanted, but I'm not sure that Dave
would ever have felt that. I think more was made of Matt's influence
than actually occurred.'

In Smith and Crick's *Betrayal of a Legend*, they described the
set-up left to Edwards to run: 'The United manager he had inherited
in 1980, Dave Sexton, was, superficially at least, also a rather grey
figure. Sexton seems in many ways an unlikely person ever to be
a football manager. In his spare time he reads philosophy books,
studies the lives of thinkers like Wittgenstein and Mill and reads the
poems of Robert Frost. His approach to football is highly scientific.
One of his first acts at Old Trafford had been to buy a video camera
and projection screen so that United players could watch and analyse
their previous games. Training was largely coaching and tactics,
whereas in the Tommy Docherty days it has been mostly games of
five-a-side football.'

Grey seemed an apt description. March was miserable. On
the first day of the month United went to Portman Road to face
Ipswich. Gary Bailey was in incredible form. He saved two penalties
– one of those had to be retaken, and he'd saved the first one too.
The only problem was that United lost 6-0 in their heaviest defeat
for almost 30 years. They were 4-0 down by the 53rd minute and
Sexton was so fearful of how bad it would get that he was forced to
bring on Jovanovic to play in a three-man central defence to try to
stem the flow.

Against Everton in the next game, United were held to a goalless
draw. Sexton was forced to bring Jimmy Greenhoff off the bench to
try to find a winner; just two months earlier, it had been suggested
that the player's career might be over because of a pelvic injury.

At struggling Brighton, Sexton's side were once more unable to
score – and waited almost an hour to have their only shot on target,

which was a McQueen header from a set-piece. The United boss admitted he needed to 'build up morale' after the Ipswich defeat, but supporters were fuming at the approach in this game, which seemed set up to take a point. One fan got into the press room after the game and insisted that reporters printed that the game had been 'real rubbish'. They obliged.

United were now four points behind Liverpool; form improved with wins against Manchester City and Crystal Palace, but the league leaders matched that form, and when Forest defeated Sexton's team at the City Ground, it appeared as if Liverpool's trip to Old Trafford could all but seal the title. They had a six-point lead with seven games left; their goal difference was a point in itself, being 23 superior to United. It was an occasion worthy of a gamble, which came in the shape of Jimmy Greenhoff, who would play from the start. 'This realistically is our last chance,' Sexton admitted. 'The only way Liverpool are going to drop points is by putting pressure on them – which is exactly what we intend to do. For that reason, it's nice to have Greenhoff's touch and influence there again.'

Just 14 minutes in and it seemed as if the league title race was over; McQueen rushed out of position and mistimed a tackle on Dalglish, who coolly dodged his compatriot and finished past Bailey. Five minutes later, United managed to restore parity, though the style and execution of the goal in comparison to their opponents said much about the respective quality in the teams. Coppell's cross was fine, and Thomas showed good perseverance to force the ball in after a scrappy first touch, but it was a scramble rather than a refined move.

There was a strange incident when Alan Hansen flicked the ball up over the United defence and raced on to it himself; the home side had advanced in a pack to try to catch their opponents offside, and only ended up making a disastrous mistake as Hansen had the entire freedom of the United half. He advanced on Bailey, and was accompanied by Dalglish; Hansen squared the ball, and somehow Dalglish fired wide, though he had also advanced into a slightly offside position. Remarkably, Liverpool had made an even bigger mess than the catastrophic defending which had allowed them in.

In the second half United got their act together. Mickey Thomas was denied a second by a goal-line clearance from Phil Thompson.

The resistance of the visitors was broken shortly after; Jordan headed a corner towards goal, and Greenhoff – showing the sort of opportunism that he had in the FA Cup Final – flicked the ball into the net. The veteran striker, who before the game had hoped for a 'Roy of the Rovers' moment, had seen his wish granted. Old Trafford rejoiced in putting their old classic chant 'Greenhoff!' back into the rotation of their terrace jukebox. From then, United were in the ascendancy, and Ray Wilkins was unfortunate when his magnificent shot cannoned off the crossbar. Their 2-1 win was narrow, but richly deserved.

Bob Paisley was fuming with his team afterwards. 'There's no way we should not win against a team like that,' he said. 'I don't want to take anything away from United, they're not a bad side, but we completely dominated the game in the first 20 minutes. Then a few heads stopped working.'

There were now slim hopes of a championship miracle. United were at least the closest competitors to Liverpool; this was the closest they had come in 12 years to challenging for the title. They would have to be perfect from now until the end of the season, and accept that even if they were it might not be enough.

Lucky Seven

ASKING FOR Manchester United to win seven games in a row doesn't seem like the impossible task. But, to put it into context, it was asking them to produce their best run of the season, and also asking them to massively up their own game; only twice since Christmas had Dave Sexton's teams won consecutive games, which seems astonishing when you think about it.

They did follow the Liverpool game with a win at Burnden Park and then Andy Ritchie scored a hat-trick (the second of his fledgling career) to put Tottenham to the sword on 12 April. It was the team's best run of the year so far and they went into a crunch game at Carrow Road in high spirits.

'We need full points to remain as challengers for the title,' Dave Sexton said. 'It is a tall order. But we've won five out of our last six games and there is no reason why we can't do it.'

Ray Wilkins expected a tough game. 'We've got to win tomorrow,' he admitted. 'When points become so valuable, teams do become scared and are afraid to open up. We went through a patch like that. But I believe we are out of it and I think the Norwich fans will see a Manchester United team looking to win.'

Joe Jordan struck in the 57th minute to settle nerves; he then added a second within two minutes to secure a crucial victory. The home defenders had concentrated so much on the predatory threat of Andy Ritchie that Jordan was able to catch them off guard. 'Andy scored a hat-trick against Spurs last week, but I felt he contributed just as much today,' said Jordan. 'He's a young player and will get better. At 27, I don't consider myself past it either and there is no reason why the partnership shouldn't flourish.'

Sexton played down talk of building momentum after learning that Liverpool had drawn with Arsenal, saying: 'It will still take a Jack Nicklaus charge for us to win the title.'

Another Jordan double earned a victory over Aston Villa on Wednesday, 23 April. United were in touching distance. Life at Old Trafford for Dave Sexton never got sweeter than it must have been on Saturday, 26 April 1980. The day started with the announcement that he and Tommy Cavanagh had been offered new three-year deals. Martin Edwards said: 'We are delighted with the progress under Dave Sexton and Tommy Cavanagh and we want them to continue the good work.'

Sexton said, 'I am already looking forward to next season.' There was, however, the small matter of the current season to put to bed. Sexton, who had said he would quit if he went three years without winning a trophy, was tantalisingly close to landing the big one that evening. He was keen to talk up the ability of his squad in his final programme notes for the season. 'I said at the beginning of the season that I felt we had a squad good enough to challenge for the championship. I'm delighted to say that the lads have more than justified my faith and confidence,' he said. 'We have, in fact, a great bunch of fellows at Old Trafford. I think they are the most unselfish team I have ever managed and that goes for both on and off the field. They play for one another and you find a similar spirit in the dressing room and away from the actual football. They are prepared to help each other. No one hogs the limelight and there is an absence of cliques and particular circles that can destroy the spirit of a club if you are unfortunate enough to have those kind of players on your staff.'

Another brace, this time from Sammy McIlroy, was enough to overcome Coventry in a tight game at Old Trafford.

News came through that Liverpool had drawn again, this time at Selhurst Park against Crystal Palace. The teams were level, though Bob Paisley's men had a game in hand which would be played on the Wednesday.

All eyes were on that game at Anfield, with United supporters praying fifth-placed Aston Villa would do them a favour. After a tense first half, Liverpool had a rampant second period, winning by four goals to one. The title race wasn't technically over so far as mathematics were concerned, but there was no chance of United winning the league; Liverpool had a two-point lead with a goal difference of 52, compared to United's 30. Both teams lost their final games of the campaign in one of those odd twists of fate you often find in football. United's defeat came at Elland Road; lining up for the hosts was Brian Greenhoff, who admitted that he did not feel any sympathy for Sexton.

* * *

It was still fairly difficult to accurately assess the true quality of the Manchester United squad in the summer of 1980. They had shown such dramatic improvement to finish second after two mid-table finishes following an equally dramatic fall from grace when such big things were expected. Had they overachieved again? Had Dave Sexton finally found a formula that was conducive to success? He was at least entitled to think so. Most of the summer was spent on an ultimately doomed chase for Arsenal midfielder Liam Brady. United appeared to pay the consequence for allowing the negotiations to drag on, but Brady's wage demands were similar to Jordan's – these prohibitive figures for United were on offer from Italian clubs.

On 2 July Martin Edwards said: 'Things are at a preliminary stage, although everything is going along nicely,' and updated reporters on 18 July with the following: 'No fee has been agreed as yet with Arsenal. I understand Brady can sign for us and if the two clubs cannot agree on a fee it will go to a tribunal. But I don't think we will match their asking price. He seems keen to sign for us and that is the main thing.'

On 19 July Sexton told *The Guardian* that he expected a call 'any time over the weekend' as Brady asked for more time to consider the move; on the 28th, United were still linked with a record £1.25m move. It was a sickener for all concerned when Juventus were able to take advantage of the delay and convince Brady to move to Italy; due to his contract situation, the Old Lady were able to get him at a snip and paid just £500,000.

Having missed out on his primary target, and keen on a centre-forward but not sure who, Sexton resolved to work with the squad he had in the hope that another year's familiarity would be of benefit when it came to performances. Sammy McIlroy was certain that a full pre-season for Ray Wilkins would be great for everyone. 'His use of the ball is so good, and he sprays it around just like Giles,' he said. 'Next season I feel you will really see something special from him. He is a great passer of the ball, and he sees situations that are "on" all the time. Wilkins is going to be a great midfield general. Despite his lack of pre-season experience, he has fed himself into the system tremendously well at Old Trafford, and next season he is going to be even better.'

Sexton, meanwhile, talked up the impact Andy Ritchie could make: 'He's stronger physically now and that much better a player. He will always score goals. The reason he hasn't had more chances in the team is the same reason David Fairclough hasn't at Liverpool. We've been doing very well and so I have stuck with my successful players.'

For some, though, the idea of getting that close to Liverpool only to fail continued to hurt through the summer. 'Manchester United's failure to win the championship after chasing Liverpool for much of the season was a sickener. But at least we ended as runners-up – a place in Europe for the first time in three seasons,' Gordon McQueen wrote in his column for *Shoot!* magazine, before praising the team who did win the league. 'They turned in so many classic performances, it's amazing in a way United managed to keep pace with them. We've a tremendous squad now. There aren't many teams around who could afford to lose players through injury with the experience of Jimmy Greenhoff, Lou Macari, Ray Wilkins and myself and still keep in the championship race. That's a sure sign we have a squad good enough to win honours next season. Another very important factor in our favour is the tremendous team spirit at the club. The lads are a first-class bunch.'

Martin Edwards's concern about Sir Matt Busby's health appeared to be justified when the former manager suffered a stroke in July 1980, putting the disappointment of missing out on signing a player into perspective.

As United prepared to take on Middlesbrough on the opening day of the 1980/81 season, Dave Sexton extolled the virtues of continuity. 'We made a dramatic improvement in our league performance last season to finish runners-up to Liverpool after finishing in much more modest positions the previous two seasons,' he said in his programme column. 'So I think the results suggest we are heading in the right direction and naturally we are keen to continue the progress. Last season's achievement is no guarantee of course, because we all start again with a clean sheet and the consistency we struck does not come easily. We did well last year because everyone played to their full potential in an unselfish way. This is not a quality like skill that once acquired is there for all time; it's a factor that has to be summoned up for every match and does not allow the slightest easing up in effort and concentration. So it won't be easy to strike the same consistently high standard, but at least we have proved what can be achieved if the players are prepared to work for one another and play to their maximum ability. It's also reasonable to expect several of the players to raise their standard because we have a number of youngsters who are still learning and adding know-how to their ability and physical effort ... I shall be looking for that shade more confidence in our play that can make all the difference.'

. His words were prophetic. Middlesbrough were comfortably dismissed 3-0 but United's form following that was nothing short of horrific; they scored just one goal in five games as they were eliminated from the League Cup and stumbled in the league. A 5-0 win over Leicester gave false hope as that win was followed by five consecutive draws (a run that saw United eliminated from the UEFA Cup by Widzew Łódź on away goals).

Sexton felt it was necessary to act swiftly in the transfer market, and used Manchester United's trip to Nottingham Forest to negotiate a deal for home striker Garry Birtles. Forest were open to it; in another event of foreshadowing, Birtles was guilty of a number of missed chances for his side as United escaped with a 2-1 win.

The deal wasn't concluded in any swift manner and appeared to depend on United finding a home for Andy Ritchie. Brighton eventually made an offer for Ritchie, and United signed Birtles for a record fee of £1.25m. Birtles had started the season in good form, aside from that game against United, with nine goals in 14 games; yet United fans were still upset to see Ritchie go. If you were to be extremely critical in your evaluation – though this is with the benefit of hindsight – you might say that swapping Ritchie for Birtles was not the sort of upgrade that made a statement. It is worth remembering, though, that Birtles's success had come in a league-winning and double European Cup-winning team. There was a certain pedigree Sexton was investing in. The rejig to the forward line continued. In October Sexton accepted a bid from Blackpool for Jimmy Greenhoff; he refused to go there, but when a Crewe Alexandra offer was also accepted in December, he accepted his time was up.

Nottingham Forest's success had been another factor – if relatively minor – in accelerating a more critical judgement on Sexton's own work. Competing with Liverpool was one thing; the Anfield club were well placed to seize advantage of United's decline post-Busby and they most certainly did that. But Forest had been in the Second Division with United and since then had enjoyed a ridiculously rapid rise to the summit of the game. On a straightforward comparison, United had the resources to be in that position; as the newspapers had suggested after Forest's 4-0 win at Old Trafford, there was no excuse for Sexton's team, as it now was, to have missed out on the sort of players that had tormented them so.

The rot well and truly set in after that win at the City Ground. United won just three from their next 16 games. A 3-1 defeat at West Brom on 27 December left United in seventh place, which was probably a fairly generous representation of the way they had played so far. After 25 games, they had drawn 15. They had won six – as many as Leicester in the relegation zone, and only one more than bottom-placed Crystal Palace. They had lost only four and boasted the equal-best defensive record in the division. A year before, United had been the beneficiary of the narrow margins of such form, so much so that references to the club now being in the image of their manager were a positive thing. Now, though, it was difficult to tell whether they were unfortunate to have so many draws; though, considering their approach to games and the angry responses from supporters, one must conclude that United had got their just desserts for a lack of ambition.

In fairness to Sexton, he had tried to address that with the signing of Birtles. Perhaps it was something of an admission that the Jordan signing hadn't been as effective as he'd hoped, as Birtles was definitely more in the Pearson mould. 'He's a goer, he's a trier,' Sexton had said of his record signing ahead of his debut.

Seven games in to his United career and Birtles hadn't scored; even on that rare occasion when goals came easy, in a 4-1 win at Brighton, he couldn't get his name on the scoresheet. Sexton repeated his earlier comments, and revealed what he believed the reason for the poor form was: 'He won't give in, he's so much of a trier. He's the sort of player you have to look after. We've got a clear week ahead of us and it could give Garry the time he needs … If our scorers had been in form we would have been so far in front by now that we would be out of sight of the rest of the pack. Let's hope the spree we went on here is a sign of better things to come.'

But even United's own supporters appeared to give up hope. A crowd of over 57,000 attended the goalless Boxing Day clash with champions Liverpool, but that was very much a spike owing to the occasion. The fans had not been convinced by the second-place finish as a sign of genuine progress and back-to-back goalless draws at Old Trafford against Coventry and Wolves in front of low crowds prompted Martin Edwards to make a bold statement. 'Money is a big problem in the game today,' he told reporters, 'and while it might be blamed on the recession, that may be only part of the story. A lot of responsibility lies with the managers and coaches to make the game attractive enough to pull in the missing fans.'

A 1-1 draw against Southampton at home at the end of November (a result rescued by a late Jordan equaliser) saw tempers fraying. 'Sammy McIlroy snapped and niggled like a poor man's Peter Storey and Tommy Cavanagh left Manchester United's dugout to berate the occupants of Southampton's; Dave Sexton later bristled at a journalist: it all showed frustration born of impotence, and another unsatisfactory experience at Old Trafford,' reported Paddy Barclay.

Sexton came out fighting and rejected criticism of a lack of adventure, instead blaming the 'boring tactics' of all three opposing managers.

But United legend Paddy Crerand was not so sure. Normally so defensive of the club, Crerand blasted to reporters: 'Teams that came here to defend got five past them.'

Three games against Brighton opened 1981. Andy Ritchie returned to haunt United, scoring twice in those games, but Sexton's team emerged victorious, winning the FA Cup third-round tie after a replay (where Birtles scored his first goal for the club) and at Old Trafford in the league. But those wins were followed by defeats at Forest and Sunderland – the latter could have been even more embarrassing, but Bailey saved a penalty in the first half, before conceding one in the second in a 2-0 defeat.

They bounced back to defeat struggling Birmingham 2-0 at Old Trafford. Sexton responded strongly after that game, telling journalists: 'It is still within our capabilities to climb high enough to get into the UEFA Cup. We have had a couple of disappointing results, but there are still 30 points to play for.'

It said everything about the size of United as a football club that the relatively poor attendance of 39,081 was put into perspective against the rest of the football world by Charles Burgess of *The Guardian*. 'The strong allegiance of the fans, who watched most of Saturday's match in subdued mood, could mean that Sexton keeps his job, whereas if he had been at another club, and the gates had dropped dramatically, the directors would have taken action immediately,' Burgess wrote. As Edwards had already said, and would later repeat, however, even attendance that looked positively healthy for anyone else would not suffice for United.

That win, however, was far from being a springboard for Manchester United to turn their season around. It was a rare positive result in a run of poor ones that, unbeknown to the manager, was sealing his fate. The pivotal period came in early February. A 1-0 defeat at Leicester seemed crucial. Supporters were now more direct, and there was a vocal section demanding the manager be sacked. Their performance at Filbert Street was described as 'continuingly [sic] out-of-sorts' and a 'hollow display' by *The Guardian*'s Ian Ridley, who reasoned that if not for Bailey United would have been several goals down by half-time.

Sexton once again rejected the suggestion that his side had not been adventurous. 'If we set out to be defensive we would use that tactic away from home,' he said. 'We played our part in a magnificent attacking game.'

On 9 February 1981 the chairmen of the clubs in the First Division met to discuss conduct with the approach to hiring and firing managers. In *Betrayal of a Legend*, Crick and Smith reason that the meeting saved Sexton temporarily: 'What probably gave Dave Sexton a reprieve was a gentlemen's agreement among league chairmen reached on 9 February 1981, right in the middle of United's worst spell. Many clubs had suffered severe disruption from managerial changes in the middle of a season, with knock-on effects on a string of clubs. It was agreed that in future chairmen would not poach each other's club managers during the season. Martin Edwards had probably already decided to get rid of Sexton, but had he sacked him then it would have been impossible to find a replacement without breaking the no-poaching agreement almost straight away, or going outside the league.'

In an interview for this book, Edwards rejected that theory, saying: 'I don't think it had any bearing on Dave's future. I don't think the decision had been taken then.' However, it may have planted the seed, as it was clear that if the decision came afterwards, it happened within a month. 'The football we played in that final season made it obvious fairly early on to me that we would have to make a change when we got to the end,' Edwards says. 'We weren't getting any closer to winning the league. The seven wins made it all look rather unfortunate but the decision to sack Dave was made earlier than that, and we thought it was right to wait for the end of the season to make the change.'

United had another scoreless draw at home against Spurs before travelling to Maine Road for the derby. There, Dave Sexton found an ally in City boss John Bond. Bond felt his opposite number should be cut some slack because of the number of injuries he'd dealt with. 'If that can't be understood then there will not be any tolerance at all,' Bond said. 'Dave Sexton has got my 100 per cent support and respect. He has done a good job for football and sometimes these things go unnoticed. When I was manager of Norwich last year, we got stuffed 5-0 at Old Trafford and if I had not been the opposition manager, I would have enjoyed it.'

City won 1-0 in a poor game. Afterwards, Sexton told one journalist, 'I wish we could begin all over again,' and it wasn't clear whether he meant the game or the season. Bond was fair to give

Sexton some leeway. Injuries had affected the seasons of Buchan, McQueen and Wilkins, who played just 26, 11 and 13 league games respectively. This triumvirate were so crucial in providing the solid foundation for United's consistent if unspectacular form which had earned them second place the previous season. Nikola Jovanovic, the expensive recruit intended to stand in for Buchan or McQueen, had a significant back problem which limited him to 19 appearances. Without that foundation, the other United stars were even more reserved and protective than usual; even Mickey Thomas, hardly as carefree as Gordon Hill but still productive, missed around a third of the campaign. The weight of creative expectation fell on the shoulders of Sammy McIlroy and Steve Coppell; as United's only real expressive talents who were fit on a regular basis (though McIlroy himself missed 10 league games), opponents found them easier to shut down. The City defeat was the first in a run of three consecutive 1-0 defeats and the third in a run of five games without a single goal being scored.

Those defeats came in widely different but equally agonising forms – first, an injury-time goal by Brian Flynn gave Leeds a dramatic late victory at Old Trafford, and then Kevin Keegan scored in the third minute to give Southampton the lead at The Dell. Sexton appeared as defeated as he ever had been. 'I've been a manager for 13 or 14 years, and for 13 or 14 years I've lived with the possibility of losing my job,' he said. 'The thought is always there – you've got to live with it. I've got to persevere with what I think is right for the inspiration to come.'

But United looked out of ideas and Birtles and Jordan looked completely ill-suited as a front pair. Jordan, having had the most impressive season at the club so far, was attracting admirers from foreign clubs; in the coming weeks, Sexton would be found pleading with the forward to stay. Supporters in the modern era may well find the situation completely relatable – the club and manager becoming vocal in their hopes to convince a player who was symbolic to the supporters as a negative change in the style of play. That is not to do Joe Jordan a disservice; he had a cult following of his own and most certainly made an impression in his time at Old Trafford. It was fair to say that when Dave Sexton's style of football was successful, Joe Jordan was a crucial player in the team.

Defeat at The Dell appears as if it was the final straw as far as Sexton's future was concerned. So we return to the theme of the qualities required to make a successful Manchester United manager. Or the criteria demanded by the history of the club, which usually falls into three categories as far as the supporters are concerned: playing well, winning trophies and playing young players developed by the club.

It can't be denied that for the majority of supporters, the Dave Sexton period at Manchester United featured a brand of football that was difficult for them to appreciate. As the 1980/81 campaign, and Sexton's tenure at the club, came to an end, this would be a topic impossible to ignore. It is important in the pursuit of balance and context to present a fair appraisal of the work that Dave Sexton did. There were some positives, positives which would have some benefit for the long-term future of the club.

Sexton had combined his work at Old Trafford with his role as under-21 manager for England. He had proven to be capable in the development of young players at Old Trafford, though it would take a little longer for that to bear fruit.

It was important to the new chairman, who had grown up watching the Busby Babes, that the club continued to bring through their own talent. 'It's all part of the overall tradition and it does go back to Matt and the MUJACS,' Edwards says. 'When he became manager and brought Jimmy Murphy in, they decided they wanted to bring up kids in a certain way and play a certain style of football. The likes of Eddie Colman, David Pegg and Duncan Edwards were all brought through a very successful system by Jimmy, and when he would go and tell Matt that they were ready, they almost fit in to the first team seamlessly. It's no different to how Alex set it up in the 1990s. It's maybe more difficult now because there are more and more foreign players and the youth teams aren't seen as being as important as they once were. Chelsea are the best example – they win the Youth Cup regularly, but how many of them actually come through to play first-team football? Supporters always appreciated a player coming through, they got behind him perhaps even more than someone who was bought in. United like that because it is embedded with the club's spirit. I think those homegrown players give you more. You see it in the modern age – players who have come in from overseas, sometimes when it gets tough they move on or ask for transfers. You'd never have got that from Giggs or Scholes. Is that romantic or overplayed? Perhaps sometimes, but you can't deny there is a synergy there.'

Sexton had played his part in that. Ritchie had been sold, and was perhaps more of a Docherty find than a Sexton one, but it was the latter who gave him his big break. Scott McGarvey was starting to feature around the first team. Gary Bailey had been brought through the right way, though did come to the club a little later. There were some very exciting young players in the youth system, such as the previously mentioned Norman Whiteside. The big success story of that season, though, had been Mike Duxbury.

'Unsurprisingly – and this is often the case when it comes to describing the manager who gave a footballer their big chance – Duxbury is generous in his appraisal of Sexton. What comes across in the defender's recollection is a greater affection for the methods that had been criticised by others.

'I never thought he ever promoted defensive football as such,' Duxbury insists. 'I think he looked into the game a lot more than Ron Atkinson. He thought about the game a little bit more. That's what came across to me. We used to study, maybe if we were in in the afternoon, he kept the young lads back and showed you a video of Beckenbauer coming out with the ball from the back. So, as I say, he probably thought more about the game. They always said he was a student of the game, that sort of thing. But for me personally, I never thought he promoted defensive football ever. The first thing he said to me was, "When Stevie, he gets the ball, go past him." So how that's defensive, I honestly don't know. And that's the way that we played at that time. Yes, we had certain things to do, defensive-wise, with organising at free kicks, which you would imagine every team does ... but apart from that, it wasn't, "When this happens, do this, do that," it wasn't robotic. We were still free to play.'

Frank Blunstone concurred: 'I played under Dave as a coach. He was always an attacking coach,' he said. 'As a matter of fact, he was the first person to get full-backs to attack, 'cos at one time they never went above the halfway line.'

Duxbury concedes that it wasn't as cavalier as Docherty's style of football, but remains defensive of it. 'Well, they went down and then played their way back the way they did and then they continued in that style when they got back in the First Division,' he says. 'So yeah, it was always going to be difficult to follow in that cavalier style. A lot of the fans from that era will say it was some of the best football they'd seen. And so from that you can see that it would have been a change ... It's hard to say, from my personal point of view, it never came across to me that we were defensive, but I could see how people would think that and maybe, at that particular time, United didn't play the best of football in between Docherty and Atkinson. So yeah, you could label it that way. I'd never any problems in training. For me, as you can imagine that at that young age, 19 or 20, all you're wanting to do is get into the first team. So that's your target. It doesn't matter what you're doing, you do it and you know, you do it just for the love of the game, and then you hope to be selected. You can see from the older end, and maybe if I was in that position, it would've knocked me a little bit, if it was a little bit more negative and there was a different approach to it. But for me going the other way, it didn't matter. All I wanted to do was play in the first team.'

Another theory is that Sexton's approach wasn't as emphatically based in pragmatism as it was in improvement. Under Docherty, under Busby, so much value had been placed in the trust in players to express themselves. If there had been any football education at Old Trafford it had come from Jimmy Murphy, whose approach to teaching was in instilling the benefit of repetition and teamwork. Sexton was different; he came into a dressing room of talented players and effectively challenged them to improve. Some players responded to that, others found it an insult to their ego.

'I suppose it's a fair point to ask how much any of the players had been genuinely coached, even with Sir Matt,' Duxbury reasons. 'I didn't ever play under him, but from all accounts it was always a case of "just go out and play", and that seemed to be the same under Tommy Docherty too. Just a faith in good players to show what they can do. So, probably that side of it under Dave Sexton, a more detailed and thorough analysis, was a little bit alien in a way.'

Duxbury, a hard-working and dedicated professional, appreciated that approach, and as such it is no surprise that his own relationship with Sexton, who he also worked with as a young under-21 international, was fine. 'He was great,' he says. 'There was no problem whatsoever. It was the same at England as well. We were free-flowing there, there was no massive tactical plan or anything like that ... within reason, you know, obviously you have to do certain things, but the message was again, as country as it was for the club, just go play.'

And Martin Edwards revealed that even though there was a dominant element in the support that wanted the manager to go, Sexton still had his fans. 'There were some letters of support for Dave,' Edwards says. 'In the context of how many letters we got complaining, or how big our support was, it wasn't a huge number, but there were some because he was a genuine football man and a lovely guy.'

Duxbury's breakthrough was just about the only positive in the winter months; but United appeared to finally spring into life with a 3-3 draw at champions-elect Aston Villa, having been 2-0 down at half-time. McIlroy's late penalty rescued a point, and afterwards Sexton beamed: 'I'm more than happy – I'm delirious.'

Ahead of the next game with Forest, he was hopeful his side were on the verge of better things. 'Though recent weeks have proven rather a lean spell for us, don't run away with the idea that we have shrunk in our estimation of ourselves,' he wrote in the match programme. 'We have had some problems getting back into gear following serious dislocation with injuries to experienced players and it has perhaps taken longer than our supporters, indeed all of us, would like, but have no fears, our luck will turn. The signs are there and I have every confidence in our ability to get results in keeping with an overall improvement in our play. A little while ago we were not troubling the opposing goalkeepers, and this worried me; but of late we have been getting in our strikes at goal and it is only a matter of time before we break through this scoring barrier.'

They needed an own goal to get a draw against Forest, but, when his team beat Ipswich 2-1 the following weekend, the boss said, 'It was a great win. I think we might have turned the corner.'

It was reported that Joe Jordan was demanding £1,000 a week to sign a new contract. David Miller of *The Express* said it was 'so grotesque an absurdity I trust United will swiftly invite him to go and join the dole queue, or Stockport.' (In the book *Betrayal of a*

Legend the authors claim that Jordan's demands were actually in the region of £2,000 per week.)

Jordan proved his worth with goals that earned victories at Everton and Highfield Road. Gordon McQueen scored the only goal at Anfield on 14 April, while Jordan was on the scoresheet again as United got a sixth win in a row against West Brom. It was a fantastic end to the season, though all but one of those wins had been by a single goal.

United closed out their league campaign against Norwich. It was clear from Dave Sexton's programme notes that he felt personally disappointed by the criticism he had faced from the press. 'We complete our league programme by welcoming Norwich City to Old Trafford this afternoon, and do so with more than a twinge of regret. We could have done with a few more games, for our star is rising, and if the season had gone on for another fortnight I feel sure we would have qualified for a place in the UEFA Cup,' he said. 'Unfortunately our run has come a little late to put us high enough to make sure of Europe and it leaves us sad about the wobble that saw us slip back after our FA Cup defeat in January. It was particularly disappointing because, considering the high incidence of injuries to experienced players, we had done brilliantly to stay in the top flight during the run-up towards Christmas. Then after being narrowly pipped at Nottingham Forest in the cup we began to lose ground … What was surprising perhaps was the length of time it took us to get back into our stride. I think, looking back, that it may be fair to say that if we had not taken such a knocking from all sides after the cup setback then we might have picked up quicker … and therefore had enough fixtures left to stake a place in European football. Sometimes the so-called guardians of public interest do more harm than good. They hurt the people they claim to be protecting by knocking the wind out of their sails. They assume the guise of looking after the supporters' interests and in that role give you deep wounds. So in the long run they hurt the people they are supposed to be helping. What kind of friends to the public are they? Fortunately our supporters were good and showed great patience when it was needed … But I don't want to leave the season on a sour note because the team are playing magnificently now. We have everything to look forward to next season, and hopefully we shall have benefitted from a rather bitter experience by learning from it. I would like to thank you all for your great loyalty. Once again you have made us the best supported club in the country and we shall strive to deserve that distinction by our efforts in the future.'

United won 1-0 – Jordan with a goal in the 57th minute in front of a crowd of 40,165. It was a game as laborious as those which had caused such a drop in attendance. Paddy Barclay's review of the match included this damning line: 'Sexton's last instructions of the season had been that United should go out in style. This was a bit like asking an SAS unit to perform Swan Lake.'

Criticism over poor play or poor crowds were now included in the bigger picture; Martin Edwards was questioned about the future after the game, and his response provoked inevitable speculation. 'I have made up my own mind, but there are six directors and it is one man, one vote,' he said ominously. 'Obviously, the way we have finished has helped the manager's position, but as yet no decision has been taken.' *The Express* perceived that to be an indication that the end was near, with their headline on the match reading 'Sexton on knife edge'.

Edwards's decision was indeed to sack Sexton. 'One, I didn't feel that under Dave we would win the league, and two, it was obvious that there was some discontent amongst the supporters. It was starting to affect the attendances. There was general unrest,' he explains. 'Those last wins didn't take away from the overall mood at the club. The sad thing was that I liked Dave as a man; I thought he was a good character. Over history, it's funny, but some managers have understood the United tradition and way, and they've embraced it. Some haven't, and they haven't been able to deliver the style or the success in the same way. It's funny because even successful and experienced managers like Louis van Gaal and Jose Mourinho didn't really grasp what the style of the club was about. I put Dave in that category. I think Ron and Tommy *did* get what United were about.'

The chairman did speak to the directors. 'Of the six directors, Sir Matt Busby is known to have opposed the sacking,' Crick and Smith wrote in *Betrayal of a Legend*. 'Perhaps it was because Sexton had been his recommendation. Busby felt that, because of the bad injuries the previous season and the winning run towards the end, Sexton deserved another year.'

On 30 April the decision was made public; Dave Sexton was sacked as manager of Manchester United. 'There has been unrest among supporters and, in spite of recent results, we felt that commercially we could have a bad time with season ticket sales if we didn't make a change now,' Martin Edwards told *The Guardian*. 'The easiest thing would have been to give him a vote of confidence and let him carry on, but we have got to think of the long-term interests of the club and we needed a change. Seven wins at the end of the season made us give it a little more thought and if we had lost them it would have been easy.'

In his summary of Sexton's tenure, Paddy Barclay appeared to strike the right tone (after rightly singling out the Birtles transfer as, so far, hugely unsuccessful considering the striker hadn't scored a league goal in his 25 appearances): 'In general, Sexton's record in the transfer market has been just about satisfactory. He brought McQueen and Joe Jordan from Leeds, Mike Thomas from Wrexham and Ray Wilkins from Chelsea. None could be described as a failure, but they have been blended into a practical combination rather than an entertaining team, and entertainment remains a prime requirement for the Old Trafford supporters.'

Practical, satisfactory; the sort of dependable buzzwords that could have probably been used as predictions for the work Sexton would do at Old Trafford back when he was hired in 1977. But he was also immensely likeable, despite his growing reservations about the press, and in David Miller of *The Express* he most certainly had a friend. 'Mob rule has moved off the terraces at Old Trafford and into the board room,' Miller wrote on 1 May. 'The sacking of Dave Sexton is the most blatant capitulation to public opinion. It can bring only odium upon the board. Better Manchester United were back in the Second Division out of harm's way. It will serve them right if they win nothing for the next five years, because they have surrendered, off the field, all that they once stood for under chairman Harold Hardman in the early post-war years. Manchester United used to be a proud English institution. Now they have revealed themselves as being just another scuffling, avaricious average club.'

The outgoing manager had his friends within Old Trafford, too. Duxbury, for starters. He felt that despite the problems, and despite the issues Sexton had clearly had with some players at the club earlier in his tenure, there was no question of the players at Old Trafford not playing for him, even if he accepts some of the longer-serving players might not have completely enjoyed the manager's style. 'Fans might have had a lot to say with it, that the style of play wasn't United, etc.,' Duxbury says. 'It wasn't as if we were struggling. Certainly that last season when we won those last seven games. Previously, it could have been a problem. But, for me, the timing wasn't brilliant. The directors, they obviously thought we're going to have to look at bringing in somebody else and then to win those last games, it couldn't have been easy, then, for them to say we're looking to change the manager. It's probably the same with any manager ... You've got people who are going to like you and play for you, and then you've got those who ... it's a horrible thing to say, if you're not playing for the manager, you're playing for the club, the fans ... It's absolutely scandalous really ... You know, I can understand the mentality, but I still find it hard to accept. As a youngster, maybe I was naive, maybe when I was older I might've been in that way ... but as a youngster, that certainly never entered my head.'

In 1979, having been given the confidence from the board and chairman to continue, Sexton had felt confident in doubling down when it came to imposing his style on the club. As a likeable coach, one can't help but wonder if he had shown some willingness to compromise, if he had considered the backlash from the supporters and the criticism of former players, and accepted that the growing feeling of uncertainty was at least partly due to his reluctance for players to express themselves rather than go through the drills, perhaps there could have been a future for him. If, for example, he had decided that such a compromise would be the best way to build on the second-place finish. Instead – and it should be said, sensibly so, as with most decisions Sexton made – the coach opted for consistency.

Duxbury feels it's just one of those things. 'Who knows, who knows?' he says. 'Would Dave have come around? Would he have thought I need to maybe loosen up a bit? Some people are like that, initially they want to put their stamp on things and maybe, and hopefully be big enough, then think well maybe I need to change, or would he have been adamant to carry on for that next season, whatever. Nobody really knows. Nobody really knows. But it would have been an interesting one, certainly.'

Harry Gregg, part of the coaching staff who had tried to talk to Sexton in his early days back at the club, felt the way it ended was inevitable. In one training session Gregg recalled filling in at right-back in a practice game; even he, as a retired former goalkeeper, grew infuriated by the instruction that every ball must be played along the defence instead of looking for openings at every chance. 'He was a likeable enough man, but I don't think he was the right man for the club,' Gregg said. 'He loved United, of that there's no doubt, I never felt he truly understood its ways ... To outsiders Manchester United's last season under Dave Sexton was not altogether unsuccessful ... But then, United are not like other clubs. In the end even seven straight wins wasn't enough to save him from the chop. The record books might suggest an impressive run of form, but a more telling statistic is that nearly 12,000 fewer fans watched Joe Jordan's winner in the 1-0 defeat of Norwich City than the brace he scored in the corresponding fixture the previous season.'

Paddy Barclay went as far as to suggest that the timing of the sacking might have been a shock. 'Immediately after Saturday's victory over Norwich in the final fixture, it was assumed that Edwards would have to give Sexton perhaps another year in which, building on such encouraging results, he might introduce the missing ingredient that the Old Trafford supporters had come to expect after the great era of Matt Busby and the lively one of Docherty,' Barclay wrote.

Edwards, perhaps reasonably, could deduce that such an ingredient might be a player like Gordon Hill, for example. But Sexton had already had one of those and got rid of him. He had also already shown a reluctance to move away from his preferred style. The chairman knew he would be investing in something that would not happen. It was time to make the change. Perhaps the time was right for Sexton, too, who had said at the outset he would leave after three years if he hadn't won anything; the pull of Old Trafford had proved too strong, but in that fourth year there had been tangible and definite regression within his era. The change, therefore, was almost inevitable.

Total Football

THE MOST popular theory regarding the immediate post-Tommy Docherty era at Old Trafford is that Dave Sexton was a fantastic coach, but was ill-suited to being a football manager – particularly at the highest level, because the sport at that elite standard was too cut-throat, too cynical; it chewed up nice guys and spat them out. This is a nice summary, though the purpose of books like this is to scratch beyond that summary and look into the many complex reasons why the period of 1977–1981 was so disappointing for Manchester United. It should have been the perfect marriage – a team with a nice composition and a young age, with a manager who was widely regarded as having the premier coaching mind in the country. But it wasn't.

The truth is that further exploration only muddles matters further, because the more you look at the facts the more it appears to defy conventional logic. The biggest criticism of Dave Sexton's Manchester United was that they did not possess the flamboyant qualities one would normally associate with the club.

It should not have been such an incompatible relationship. Dave Sexton had been credited with bringing 'Total Football' to QPR, and if you are a time-served United supporter who lived through his time at Old Trafford and are impulsively inclined to scoff at that description of his brand of football then you may be surprised.

If it is accepted that Sir Matt Busby was the mastermind who implemented what this idea of 'the United way' was supposed to represent, then it was Jimmy Murphy and his coaching of the 'Babes' which was the greatest visual representation of that. Murphy worked tirelessly on the training ground extolling the virtues of hard work, repetition and simple, effective use of the football. He had been this way as a player but it was in observing the teachings of the great coach Jimmy Hogan that influenced Murphy's way. Jimmy Hogan is the oft-forgotten man when it comes to describing the origins of 'Total Football'; the great Rinus Michels learned what he knew from Hogan.

It is apt, considering the nationality of United's greatest managers, that Hogan himself was influenced by a Scot. When he was at Fulham in 1907 he was coached by Jock Hamilton; Hamilton had the distinction of being the first professional coach to work in Brazil. Jimmy had always had a personal drive for self-improvement but British football was stuck in its ways, with training sessions based on running and strength; Hamilton promoted the use of the ball in training and also felt that superior skill could best sheer physical power. It seems elementary now but it was revolutionary in the domestic game at the time. Hogan, a deep thinker, took these ideals on board and tried to implement them where possible in his own game.

Three years later, Hogan was at Bolton Wanderers, and the club went on a summer tour to the Netherlands in 1910. The standard of the opposition was significantly weaker than in the UK. In one notable game, Bolton destroyed Dordrecht 10-0. The locals were keen to improve and Hogan saw an opportunity; over the preceding years following his relationship with Hamilton, Hogan, at the tender age of 28, had tried to encourage a passing game wherever he went. He once said: 'I don't care whether a pass is long or short, forwards or backward. I just care if it is right. It has to be right for the team.'

The resistance he found in England was not there abroad. It was ironic in a sense that the aggressive British style which had forced such a heavy beating had inspired the Dutch to listen keenly to Hogan, who took the opportunity to see if his own approach might bring some success, splitting his career as an occasional player for Bolton (he played 54 times in five years) and a part-time amateur coach in the Netherlands and Austria between 1910 and

1913. From there, he established such a promising reputation that when he retired from playing at the age of 31 (having been bitten by the coaching bug), he was recommended to become manager of MTK, a team in Hungary who had recently had another British player, former Scotland international John Tait Robertson, as their boss. He stayed in Hungary for seven years, transforming MTK's fortunes as they won consecutive league titles.

The First World War occurred during this period. Hogan tried to return home to his family but was unable. When he finally could, after the Armistice, he went to the FA and asked for the £200 compensation payment that was due to footballers who were caught up in the hostilities. He was refused and he was effectively accused of being a traitor. Left with no option but to return to Europe if he wanted to continue working as a football coach, Hogan went to Switzerland and then later Germany. A brief spell with Austria Vienna at the start of the 30s helped rekindle his good friendship with Hugo Meisl, the manager of the Austrian national team, who hired Hogan to work alongside him.

Whilst on a day off in France at the end of his international career as a player for the Welsh team, Jimmy Murphy learned that the Austrian international team was training nearby. They were led by Hogan, who Murphy was familiar with from Hogan's days as a Fulham player. Murphy was astounded to see Hogan conducting training with the ball. 'We never saw [the ball] from Saturday to the next,' Jimmy would later remark, referring to the training sessions at West Brom. Murphy would later say that this was the first time he'd ever seen an actual football coach at work and he was keen to learn more, so he hung around and introduced himself to Hogan; from this moment, a friendship was formed. For a brief moment in his long career, Murphy was the disciple, keen to engage and absorb as much knowledge as he could.

To Murphy, Hogan was brave and revolutionary. He played with attacking centre-halves and strongly believed in innovation. In one of their many conversations, Hogan said he believed that Continental soccer was on the verge of a huge shift which would see many European countries surpass their British counterparts as they embraced these new ideas. At the time, Murphy was disbelieving, but by the late 1940s it was clear from the emergence of the Hungarians that Hogan was absolutely correct. It is worth pointing out that this was still some time before the 1953 'game of the century' which made the philosophy one that was widely accepted as a successful one. After the match, Sándor Barcs, president of the Hungarian Football Federation, told journalists: 'Jimmy Hogan taught us everything we know about football.'

Gusztáv Sebes, the Hungarian footballer and coach, said of Hogan, 'We played football as Jimmy Hogan taught us. When our football history is told, his name should be written in gold letters.'

It made Murphy even more of a convert to Hogan's ways and it was without apology that he adopted the same approach when he arrived at Old Trafford. 'Mastery of the ball and of the simple way of doing things were the basis of football,' Murphy later said. 'I used a lot of Jimmy Hogan's ideas when I joined Matt Busby at Manchester United. He was a very influential coach.'

Sir Matt Busby, too, was a fan, who said: 'Ball practice, that's what the youngsters need, not just boring themselves loping round the track. I saw the Hungarians – a great side because they made the ball their slave. Teams have got to play to win, not just to avoid being beaten. I'd rather see a player lose the ball because he's trying to do something with it, instead of having it taken from him because he's doing nothing.'

It is interesting to note how Busby referenced the Hungarian triumph at Wembley; Murphy's own influence from Jimmy Hogan pre-dated his working relationship with Busby by some eight years, and it is unclear whether or not Busby's comment is indicative of his own beliefs or if, instead, he had become so enamoured by the quality of his young players he had simply felt it was the fruit of his own work.

Perhaps it is important to make some distinctions now as things become clearer. There are a number of managers in Manchester United's history who subscribed to these ideas. If we include Murphy because of his prominence and importance in the development of Busby's young players, then there is him, Tommy Docherty, Dave Sexton, Ron Atkinson and Louis van Gaal who were all effectively students of this style of football. If a couple of names on that list stand out as odd against the others then that too should become clearer soon.

First of all, Murphy, Docherty and Atkinson all had one thing in common: first-hand experience of Jimmy Hogan and his ideology. Michels interpreted Hogan's methods and developed a style of play that was so successful it was only natural that his peers were inspired. Sexton and van Gaal could be counted among those who were influenced by Michels. So perhaps that is one factor. It shouldn't be, because, as is clear, Michels's brand of football was not negative or dull in the same way as plenty perceived the eras of Sexton and van Gaal.

Perhaps one fundamental flaw in their approach was their style of teaching. Both managers had achieved magnificent success with that approach prior to their appointment at Old Trafford and so one can immediately appreciate that they would feel vindicated enough, even if by virtue of their appointment in the first place, to replicate their approach at United. Both managers inherited squads of different characters, and though van Gaal did take over a David Moyes team that was low on confidence, to all intents and purposes that was a squad (with two new players) who had been schooled by one manager and the club appeared to be in tune and harmony; so, in some aspects, not too dissimilar to the one Sexton walked into.

What happened with each of these managers (and others) does at least seem to feel consistent with the general rule in the history of Manchester United; one feels this could be true of footballers in general – though the likes of Sexton and van Gaal clearly serve as examples that it isn't always – but, historically, players at Old Trafford have mostly been receptive to the conveying of a message from a mogul who inspired by his words. There seems to be a clear divide between the managers who enjoyed the theoretical side as opposed to those who primarily considered expression and the abilities of the players on the books; the coaches who wanted the players to fit the system, and the coaches who made the system fit the players.

The change was more gradual with Sexton than van Gaal, perhaps owing to the respect the former had for the success of the previous regime. It is certainly a complex situation; Steve Coppell's take on it is that the players deserved to take a greater share of the responsibility, but that over time Sexton became too obsessed with trying to educate the players on what they already knew. 'Given that we had the same players we had before he joined, it can only be that it was the players themselves who failed to fulfil their potential,' Coppell said of the first year. 'Dave Sexton was very introspective and at the same time kind and generous. He made exactly the right note when he arrived by making the point that he was taking over a talented, successful side and saw no point in changing the status quo. He was as good as his word, standing back to let Tommy Cavanagh take those pre-season sessions and carry on with the sort of fitness training we had done in previous seasons.'

But that changed, and despite the best of intentions, and some slight indications of the positive effects of Sexton's ideals, his inability to simply trust the players with the basics created some difficult relationships. 'I suppose I have to come to the conclusion that, despite my deep respect for him and my initial excitement at his arrival, Dave Sexton was not the right manager for Manchester United,' Coppell said. 'He introduced a lot of training routines designed to practise various elements of the game; he was a great technician and he wanted the players to do certain things a certain way. He even had a huge library of videos that he would use to illustrate his point and which would show the great players heading, shooting, tackling, trusting and so on. His training routines would incorporate practice in these basic skills and concentrate on trying to improve technique, but how can you teach Martin Buchan to tackle, Gordon McQueen to head the ball or Jimmy Greenhoff to score goals? We could see what he was trying to achieve and would try and improve for him, but you could see how much better his coaching works with the younger players.'

Or, with players used to his style – perhaps in that regard, United might have been better off investing just a little more patience to see long-term benefits. Perhaps there is some truth to the idea that Sexton was ahead of his time. If any visionary worth his salt is forced to endure patronising and condescending put-downs from his misunderstanding contemporaries, then it has to be said Sexton was tremendously well-respected and held in the highest of regard by all of his peers.

The same could not always be said for how his style came across on the pitch; Ron Atkinson had nicknamed Ray Wilkins 'The Crab' due to the generally accepted perception that Wilkins was a midfielder who was more skilled in the recirculation of possession than he was at risk-taking, lung-busting bursts from the centre of the pitch. This style of footballer was admired to the extreme on the Continent, and it would take another couple of decades at least for British football to appreciate such a style with envy and not dismiss it with derision. It is important to include the context of the time; this was not necessarily 'backward thinking', considering the dominance of English teams in European competition at the time. And, even when attitudes did change, and a modern 21st century equivalent of Wilkins came along in the form of Michael Carrick, he was still largely unappreciated until the latter stage of his career.

Joe Jordan was unfortunate in some regards, as was Dave Sexton; Jordan's qualities were somewhat complementary to the likes of Jimmy Greenhoff and Stuart Pearson and he certainly brought something to the table that the pair didn't have. However, having been brought in for fairly big money, he was expected to replace one of two players who had scored in the FA Cup Final the previous year. What's more, those bruising characteristics he boasted became symbolic of an uncultured style of play, which was a million miles away from Sexton's intention, and consequently both he and Jordan suffered the damage caused by the reputation.

'I felt the criticism of the players Dave brought in was a little harsh,' Mike Duxbury says. 'The type of football with Ron was very open, free-flowing and Gordon McQueen was part of that. Joe went on to bigger and better things, went on to a big club over in Milan. There was a different style of football with the Italians at that time. Mickey Thomas was a contrast to Gordon Hill so I could see why people would see that as a more defensive move. Mickey was very hard-working. It's hard to say, from my personal point of view, it never came across to me that we were defensive, but I could see how people would think that and maybe at that particular time United didn't play the best of football in between Docherty and Atkinson. So yeah, you could label it that way.'

Different environments, track records and levels of expectation all play a part in how receptive certain elements of a football club can be to change. Dave Sexton went to QPR with such a fine reputation that the Loftus Road club felt lucky to have someone of that calibre. Therefore the players were mostly inclined to fully engage with his methods so that they could improve. With all due respect to QPR, their history of having an established style of play that was recognised and renowned internationally was not quite as pronounced as the one Dave Sexton found at Old Trafford.

In some ways, Tommy Docherty's era ought to have alleviated some of that pressure because his team's style was different to that of Sir Matt Busby's, showing that there was more than one way to succeed at the club. Maybe one reason Sexton didn't is because Docherty's team could feel a sense of genuine legitimacy after a decade of pressure at Old Trafford; this was the team who had thrilled fans again, won a trophy again and so had the confidence that they were representing United in the right way. The players did not feel as if major changes were necessary. Most of them went on record as saying that additions would have helped, some said that additions were crucial, but few, if any, ever went on record saying the United players themselves needed to improve. Perhaps there is an implied professional pursuit of improvement and the maturity of decision-making that comes with age, but then again maybe it is in this, in the individual make-up of the personality of any footballer, where Sexton found his primary and ultimately most challenging obstacle. While some players appreciated a coach who concentrated so heavily on the fundamentals and the basics, others felt insulted; you would understand, then, a natural resistance to those sorts of drills, and it was hardly a resistance some kept private, as was obvious very early on when players questioned the repetition and then just conspired to contrive the success of a routine to get back into the changing room.

Perhaps this is running the risk of turning into something of a manual on coaching philosophies, but it is really a matter of the human and psychological reactions to change. When focussing on a more theoretical style of play that finds great merit in repetition of drills, you will naturally find resistance from players of greater creative ability, where the value is more in encouraging them to express themselves as individuals. Making them watch videos of other players, many of whom would arguably be less talented than the player watching, sent a conflicting message.

It would effectively be the *same* message, because what Sexton in particular was striving for was a technical proficiency and efficiency as a basis for the flamboyant side to be built upon; instead, this was interpreted by some as a sacrifice of that flamboyance in order to achieve the efficiency.

Yet, Sexton clearly understood what was expected of him – he had admitted as such with his earlier references to 'open football'. There were miscommunications – and when that happens with egos, which it should be said are required to achieve big things at big clubs, something generally has to give.

Some players respond and others don't. The trick is balance. But Sexton didn't go for balance, nor did David Moyes when he tried the same approach, nor did van Gaal, nor did Jose Mourinho (albeit his was a different style of football altogether); all of those managers instead felt strongly that the key to success was in the perfect and complete adherence to their ways, and if not, then players were quickly culled – you can think of Hill, Ferdinand, Rafael, Mkhitaryan.

Hill's exit from Old Trafford came in Sexton's first season and remained the most controversial and symbolic move that the manager made. The criticism Hill had of the manager's tactics and approach to his development was as clear as Sexton's general misunderstanding of the player's strengths and, also, possibly, his relationship with his team-mates who were willing to put up with it.

Conveniently for this book, Sexton did once discuss the role of left-wingers specifically when describing his interpretation of Michels's style at Ajax: 'With their pressing and rotation, the Dutch created space where there wasn't any before. Everyone else still played in a rigid way, in straight lines and fixed positions,' he said. 'The Dutch approach was quite different. Michels never talked to me about it in theoretical terms, but he didn't have to because if you were in football, you understood immediately what it meant. Instead of straight lines, his concept was people changing positions. By itself, that freed up huge amounts of space and gave defenders a problem: if the Dutch left-winger moves infield, what should the right-back do? Go with him, or stay put? If he goes, it leaves a hole where immediately the Dutch left-back will pop up. But if he doesn't go, the winger gets the ball to his feet in midfield and turns and runs at you to the centre.'

Hill did understand this under Docherty, but his instruction was much more direct and straightforward: 'Tuck in when you don't have the ball.'

'Merlin' is fond of the saying, 'Football is a simple game complicated by coaches'; he has been a coach of young players for almost two decades and it may be ironic to some that he heavily promotes becoming proficient at the basics through repetition. This, however, is with children; and Hill believed he was a competent enough footballer to not have the whys of a situation exhaustively drummed into him. A player like Steve Coppell, or Ray Wilkins, on the other hand, could be completely receptive to that approach. What made Manchester United so great was that they had both and loved both for the qualities they brought. Sexton would have preferred two Coppells. United fans would have been happy with two Coppells; they might even have been happy with Mickey Thomas, if Hill hadn't been sacrificed in order to have him. Thomas was hard-working and disciplined; he was the things Sexton wanted that Hill couldn't provide. And Thomas is well-loved by United fans in his own way. But he wasn't as relentlessly consistent as Coppell on the other side, and he also had anxieties about representing such a big club.

A team of Steve Coppells would be no bad thing, but United supporters were used to a blend of styles, with the spectacular to complement the hard work and reliability. It was ultimately Dave Sexton's responsibility to find a balance because, as he found out the hard way, the fans would make their opinions known. He was fortunate, in a sense, that the club tolerated this for as long as they did, though when the supporters made their statements in the ultimate way by not even turning up, the consequence of that failure to compromise and find a balance was the loss of his job.

As a footnote, it is somewhat crucial to observe the recollections of Sammy McIlroy, who usually served as Hill's replacement on the left in the months before Thomas arrived. It would make more sense for Sexton to make McIlroy sit through the same videos Hill had to watch. McIlroy, however, tells this writer that he never had to.

* * *

Jimmy Hogan was present at Wembley to see Hungary beat England 6-3. He was employed at Aston Villa as youth-team coach at the time and had taken some of his team to Wembley, telling them they would witness something special. He was at Villa Park until November 1959, when he retired aged 77. One of his last protégés was a wing-half by the name of Ron Atkinson.

'I can remember virtually all of the sessions we did with Jimmy Hogan,' Atkinson said in 2013. 'A lot of coaches I got involved with later on, I couldn't even remember one thing from them. It was enjoyable, but, not only that, you could tell it worked. It was working with the ball, keeping the ball, passing the ball, little passing drills.'

Speaking to BBC Sport on the anniversary of the England-Hungary game, Atkinson also said: 'When Jimmy came to Villa, he was revolutionary. He would have you in the old car park at the back of Villa Park and he would be saying, "I want you to play the ball with the inside of your right foot, outside of your right foot, inside again, and now turn, come back on your left foot inside and outside." He would get you doing step-overs, little turns and twists on the ball and everything you did was to make you comfortable on the ball.'

Atkinson explained how Hogan was ahead of his time, but felt that his inability to progress as a manager in the way he ought to have was due to the lack of knowledge from his contemporaries and fellow coaches who were too deeply rooted in the more traditional, historical British style. He described Hogan as his 'biggest influence'.

'It was the way he put it over,' Atkinson says. 'In those days when I was a kid at the Villa we had about 15 teams or something like that. You would get in Jimmy's team and Jimmy was completely unique. I spent a bit of time as a kid at Wolves at the time when they were one of the best teams in the country. Wolves were very much based on statistics and fitness; on the other hand, when I went training with Jimmy Hogan, it was an eye-opener because everything was done with the ball. Even running was done with the ball. Even a running exercise had to be finished with a pass or something like that. At the time in British football that was not known. You would play in that team in the Birmingham League as kids. It was a hard old league against seasoned pros. He would get the team in a group huddle. His standard thing was, "Wherever you are on the field if we have got the ball we are attacking, and if they've got the ball, wherever it is, we are defending." He would tell the wing-halves that they had to be like waiters in a restaurant serving the wingers and serving the front players. He had a lovely way of delivering it. I could never remember him swearing. The irony of it all was you would get in the reserves after that and the trainer in the reserve team would say, "Forget what tip-tap has told you, give it some altitude!" All of the young lads used to love playing for Jimmy.'

It feels like a simplistic way of putting the same ideas across, but consider this recollection from Tommy Docherty, as told to BBC Sport: 'He [Hogan] used to say football was like a Viennese waltz, a rhapsody ... one-two-three, one-two-three, pass-move-pass, pass-move-pass. We were sat there, glued to our seats, because we were so keen to learn. His arrival at Celtic Park was the best thing that ever happened to me.'

Digestible for footballers of any background to understand, it is no coincidence that Docherty and Atkinson had such similar outlooks, or that supporters have a particular fondness for those teams and the way they played (we defend together and we attack together could be a nice rephrasing of that Atkinson recollection, and was also a phrase uttered by Jimmy Murphy). Sexton theoretically held the same ideals. His interpretation was different; as mentioned more than once, his obsession with drills and routines over-complicated the approach, and led to supporters becoming bored with seeing the same things every week.

'Maybe [the players couldn't understand Sexton],' Atkinson says. 'What I always wanted was high-intensity training. I would have rather trained hard for an hour and a quarter than slogged it out for two hours. I would never hear a bad word said about Dave. I was always very impressed with him. People have their own way of working. Cloughie, for example, you would look at his teams and think they were the most coached teams you've ever seen. And yet you would talk to people and they would say he was never there! I heard similar things about the great Liverpool teams. I liked enthusiasm and high intensity.'

Manchester United's relationship with 'Total Football' is, then, more closely linked than is widely credited. That is surely because there are additional elements, or different interpretations of what constitutes an effective or efficient execution of it.

Eric Cantona, later to be a United legend and as of May 1981 a worshipper of Michels and Johan Cruyff, once described his perfect goal as each member of the team touching the ball once and the last scoring. In 2015, under Louis van Gaal, United scored a goal at Southampton after 45 passes (a feat that not even Pep Guardiola's Manchester City managed to surpass as of the summer of 2019, though it must be said Spurs hold the Premier League record at 48 passes set in August 2014); it was celebrated for what it was but the general perception of United's style of play under van Gaal was as unfavourable as it was under Sexton. Therefore, the goal was representative of something else completely. For some, the idea of some of the best players in the world in one team monopolising possession is the pinnacle of football; it is even often elevated to the subjective position as the height of Total Football, and consequently the most aesthetically pleasing style in the world. It cannot be surpassed. Those who subscribe to this are referred to as purists, as if to confirm the interpretation of the style *as* that pinnacle. There is a certain elitist snobbery around this as it is implied that preference for another style or interpretation of that same style is to be uneducated.

Pep Guardiola, a fantastic coach in his own right, has also been largely fortunate in some respects. The squad he inherited at Barcelona had already won a European Cup in 2006, had Xavi and Andres Iniesta coming to the peak of their powers and Lionel Messi breaking through. Barcelona had been enjoying the benefits of the Michels ideology since the arrival of Johan Cruyff and, in the time between Cruyff's departure in 1996 and Guardiola's arrival as coach in 2008, the Spanish club had hired Louis van Gaal on two occasions as well as Frank Rijkaard. All four managers showed different interpretations of Michels's style and Guardiola's was to monopolise the ball. This was done to great success but there were many who wondered how the coach might fare at a club without three of the greatest players ever.

At Bayern Munich, it is fair to say that while the period was successful, Guardiola's style of coaching did not have the same sort of influence. In fact, one might even argue there was a regression in the quality of their football, as the side he inherited had absolutely obliterated the Barcelona team he had left behind in the year he took a sabbatical, and were European champions to boot when he arrived in Germany.

At Manchester City, the Spaniard has been able to cherry-pick fantastic players and then replace them with better, more expensive players, sometimes after only one season, if their form has been poor. Some say this is a triumph of coaching insomuch that it is reflected as a relentless pursuit of perfection.

That is one way of looking at it; another is that a triumph of coaching is taking your principles wherever you go and improving the group of players who you work with, however long it takes, or however quickly it comes together, within the usual boundaries of what is considered normal at a football club (the odd transfer instead of wholesale). This seems, at least on the face of it, more in line with the ideals of Hogan or Michels. You might even include Sexton and van Gaal in that category too (although van Gaal's tenure at Manchester United is a different story altogether).

The prevailing point in how all this relates to Manchester United, Tommy Docherty, Dave Sexton and Ron Atkinson (and forgive me for straying somewhat from the point to return here) is that the teachings of Hogan were best received at Old Trafford – be it by the players, the supporters, the board, the cultural heritage – by putting the emphasis on efficiency and economy. Economy of possession meant trying to score a goal as quickly as possible; it meant speed of movement, physical pace, and quick, inventive thinking. For Docherty and Atkinson, as with Busby before them, this meant trusting the intuition and creative thinking of the players, whereas for Sexton it meant perfecting different routines.

In so many ways, then, Ron Atkinson seemed so right for the job of Manchester United that he was almost the perfect – the only, even – choice. But he wasn't even the first.

Old Hollywood

CONTRARY TO the popular story of Lawrie McMenemy turning down Martin Edwards's advance for him to leave Southampton and become manager of Manchester United, it transpires that the man who had inspired the Saints to FA Cup success over the Old Trafford club in 1976 did, in fact, initially agree to succeed Dave Sexton.

'It was a blow,' Edwards admits. 'He had been managing a very successful Southampton side and I felt he would have a lot to give us. I approached him and he said yes, he was very keen. Then some time later he said he had changed his mind on the basis that his wife didn't want to move, and he didn't want to move his kids who were being educated in Southampton. It was a blow because I was relying on him when I had made the decision that Dave was going. It had all been agreed, but then I dismissed Dave and Lawrie changed his mind at the last minute.'

The story played out in the press in traditional fashion. Sexton was sacked on 30 April, so one might deduce that between that date and 25 April – United's last league game – Edwards had reached an informal agreement with the Southampton manager. On 2 May McMenemy was named the favourite for the job. Southampton would demand £150,000 compensation according to reports. It was not straightforward, however. McMenemy deliberated and wanted more time before making a final decision.

John Bond, the Manchester City manager, had told reporters United should pay want-away striker Joe Jordan the money he was

127

demanding. City apologised but then Bond told a sports forum on Monday, 4 May that United should stand by Sexton. It prompted a spiky response from the United chairman: 'Now John Bond is openly criticising our board for sacking Dave Sexton. I am sick and tired of his comments on our internal affairs. For a man who walked out of a ten-year contract with Norwich, I would have thought he would have less to say. He is hardly in a position to moralise.'

The days went on and United flew out to play a post-season friendly against the Israeli national team under the tutelage of Jack Crompton and Tommy Cavanagh. The days turned into weeks with no news of an appointment. On 17 May it was reported in *The Express* that McMenemy was facing a 'tug-of-war between his family and his ambition to manage Manchester United'. That tug-of-war was won by his family. On 19 May it was reported that he had turned down the opportunity to succeed Dave Sexton.

'Naturally we are disappointed,' Edwards told the press. 'We set our hearts on bringing McMenemy to United and now we will have to advertise the job. We would have liked a new manager in time for our pre-season tour to the Far East on 1 June, but it is not the end of the world. We felt that McMenemy fitted all our requirements, and we would like someone similar to fill the post.'

McMenemy's refusal poses one of the great 'what ifs' in United's history, considering how close they came to appointing him. In 2002 he told the *North East Chronicle*: 'Yes, with hindsight, I should have taken the Man U job.'

In his 2016 autobiography McMenemy finally went into detail to reveal the chain of events which led to his decision. 'The one approach and offer that made the headlines was the one I received from Manchester United in 1981,' he said. 'Martin Edwards made contact by phone on behalf of the club and offered me the job. The Southampton directors were determined to keep me. They threw the fact at me that I was under contract and then those "benign" olde-worlde gentlemen directors reiterated that I had to continue as manager of Southampton FC. They expected me to honour my contract. No messing. In 30 years they had to deal with two managers, Ted Bates and myself. They were not easily swayed by insubordination. They looked after you so you must look after them. That was their creed. They saw all the talk about Old Trafford as an aggravation they did not need and would not tolerate. I did not have to be educated on how big a club United were, massive compared to any I had been involved with. Sheffield Wednesday was big when I joined them in the 60s but United was an institution. That meant the manager would have so many things other than pure football matters to contend with. I thought I could have handled that despite it being the hardest aspect of the job, the one managers found most difficult to cope with. For me it would also have meant uprooting the family, but that comes with the job. We were used to so many moves in a relatively short space of time from Gateshead to Sheffield to Doncaster, Grimsby and Southampton. At that stage our elder son Chris would have been 19 and while the others were not babies it would have meant a huge amount of organisation for Anne, Sean and Alison. The security of my family and their rights as youngsters in the middle of their education – the potential trauma involved in changing school – was an important factor in my decision. I never talked money with Martin. I assumed money would not be a problem. It would have been the best of everything. That is the way the club is and continues to be. It was a family thing. I did not want to put the children through what would be a dramatic change at the very time they needed stability and both Anne and myself as a presence in their lives. I was proved right when I later foolishly left Southampton for Sunderland, a move that had a serious effect on my family. I agree that managing United could have been the highlight, the pinnacle, the peak of a career if you had been successful – and you would have to have been that. I could have taken the family to Manchester overnight and stayed in the best hotel suites or a rented house. That was not the problem. It was the effect on your family life of moving on after being in one place for eight years. We had formed friendships as a family and living on the south coast is a bit different. It was not fear of the job; I wasn't chickening out. I understand the question remains: can a football person turn down Manchester United? You would have to say only one in a hundred would. But I didn't need United to satisfy my ambitions. As I saw it I could continue successfully at Southampton. We were a top-six club dabbling in Europe and I felt we were good enough to hit the heights. Ted Bates, wily fox that he was, put it in perspective for me. He asked if I could achieve with United that which I couldn't at

Southampton. He said I would get greater satisfaction from winning the league with Southampton than I would with United. While people may laugh at the assertion now, it should be remembered we did finish second in the league while I was at Southampton ... As a professional do I regret it? Well, I wonder how far I could have taken them.'

The news that United would advertise was a blow for Harry Gregg; the legendary goalkeeper had been encouraged by some of his colleagues to put his name in for the job. He was hurt that he wasn't automatically considered, but made a formal application nonetheless, only to have his pride hurt again when that wasn't seriously considered.

The Guardian reported that Edwards had told a journalist: 'Brian Clough would never be considered because he would want to run the whole show.' Sportswriter Peter Thomas of *The Express* discussed the likely candidates. Bobby Robson was likely to stay at Ipswich. Howard Kendall of Everton? Too late, and frankly it would have been too soon to take him to Old Trafford. Ron Atkinson had '*the flash touch*, as does Watford boy wonder Graham Taylor, but that was not quite the thing for United, I should say'. Ken Knighton of Sunderland had 'too much boardroom trouble to endear him to United's directors, and anyhow he is a Clough disciple, as was Alan Durban of Stoke. Malcolm Allison was dismissed, Terry Neill of Arsenal would 'provide headlines but boring teams', Keith Burkinshaw of Spurs would 'produce a lavish, Fancy Dan team and little public contact', while Ron Saunders was 'a man of his word, and right now it seems his word is Villa'.

John Bond 'had taken Manchester by storm' but 'wouldn't be the John Bond I respect if he upped and offed across the city' (nor was Edwards a fan, it seemed), Bob Paisley was 'a fixture at Anfield', his predecessor Bill Shankly was 'too old'; Thomas felt it might be Billy McNeil of Celtic, for whom there 'is certainly one thing in his favour more inclined to belief than to football' or Jock Stein who, Thomas felt, 'must really now be heartily sick of managing Scotland'.

With no truly obvious name, Thomas closed with another suggestion: 'Could it be that United, once the European trendsetters, might even plunge into the market and bring in a Continental boss?'

Edwards was determined to stick with a British coach. 'My next choice was Bobby Robson,' he says. 'I rang him and spoke to him. He was very courteous but he felt he was going somewhere with Ipswich Town, and he had a very good relationship with the two chairmen there, the Cobbolds. He'd built a team there and he felt it would be wrong to leave at that time. I had to respect and appreciate that … I looked around and thought, "Blimey, there's not much choice!" I approached Ron Saunders who was at Aston Villa. He built the side who had won the European Cup. He declined my offer.'

On 25 May, Robson's decision was made public. *Express* reporter Steve Curry suggested United turn back the clock and give Tommy Docherty a call: 'He was United's most successful manager since Busby, with the right charisma for the post, and the backing of the best supported club in the country. Are the United board now big enough to swallow their pride and bring back the man who would almost certainly be welcomed by the fans as some kind of Messiah?'

Two days later it was reported that the United directors now had a shortlist of Saunders, Atkinson and McNeil. Having been turned down by three men, Edwards was reluctant to approach his next choice – if Saunders's rejection was made public, that would have been embarrassing enough. But fate intervened.

'The first time the position at Old Trafford had been mentioned to me in any kind of context was in May 1981 at a pre-FA Cup Final sports forum organised by the *Daily Express* in London,' Ron Atkinson said in his book *United to Win*. 'On the panel were the two Wembley managers, John Bond of Manchester City and Keith Burkinshaw of Tottenham Hotspur, who are united in their scathing condemnation of the sacking of Dave Sexton at Old Trafford. Both insisted that any other manager who was offered the job should turn it down out of hand. Finally the question was put to me. While I expressed sincere sympathies for the sacked Sexton, I can remember vividly adding, "The manager of Manchester United has, without question, the top job in British soccer. Any member of my profession offered the position should not have the slightest hesitation in taking it."

'When I spoke those words, Manchester United and Ron Atkinson seemed a million miles apart, and yet within a couple of months my name began to crop up more and more in connection with the job, one of those occasions being during our trip to Florida. We were staying in Fort Lauderdale and we had just watched Tampa Bay Rowdies in action. Back at the hotel we're all sitting around having a relaxing drink when Frank Worthington arrived from England and told me that Lawrie McMenemy had turned down the opportunity to leave Southampton to take over as manager of United. With a wink, Frank added, "I'm told they are coming after you now." We had a few laughs and more drinks, but I have to admit that Frank's remarks started me thinking. Within a couple of days I received a telephone call from an English sports journalist who has become a close pal over the years and whose sources of information were invariably impeccable. He told me in no uncertain terms that Manchester United wanted me as their new manager and strongly suggested that I apply for the position immediately. He added, "If you are asked, will you be interested?" I replied, "You'd better believe it!"'

The news filtered through to the United chairman. 'I got a call from a journalist who informed me Ron Atkinson might be interested in the job,' Edwards says. 'He had taken West Brom to third in the league and had been in charge for their great 5-3 win at Old Trafford. There was no doubt about it, Ron would have been my next choice, but the fact that I was tipped off that he was keen definitely sealed it. The expression was that he would walk to Old Trafford for the job. I met him and he was dead keen … I met with Bert Millichip at the services at Stoke and agreed a package with him. He realised it would be difficult to keep Ron so I agreed a termination fee of £60,000.'

That meeting occurred on 1 June; on the 2nd *The Express* said Atkinson was due to sign as United manager by lunchtime that day. Edwards and Atkinson met and a rapport was established. 'I was extremely impressed by Martin Edwards,' Atkinson said. 'He is personable and businesslike. I knew in an instant he was the kind of man I would enjoy working alongside. Also possesses an impish sense of humour, which is essential for a complete understanding of how I work. Mind you, it is just as well he can take a joke, because when the negotiations came around to the kind of club car I was to be furnished with, we had a bit of a joust. Said Martin, "Right, Ron, now what kind of car were you thinking of driving?" I replied,

"Well Mr Chairman, at West Bromwich I had a Mercedes 450 SL and I was very impressed with the comfort and reliability." Martin thought for a moment and said, "Dave Sexton had a Rover." I countered instantly, "Mr Chairman, I have a dog called Charlie but I thought we were talking about motor cars not dogs." We both laughed heartily, and I can tell you that was merely the first of many humorous conversations between us.'

The time passed without news of an appointment and it seemed as if Edwards might be left with egg on his face again. This time it was Millichip who was unsure; on the 6th, several outlets reported that Atkinson could be forced to resign as manager of West Brom as they and United couldn't agree a compensation package. Millichip acquiesced, though, and Edwards had his man.

'I signed a three-year agreement with Manchester United,' Atkinson remembered. 'At the press conference officially announcing my appointment, on 9 June 1981, I said, "When I was offered this job I was both thrilled and flattered, but I could not help feeling that Manchester United and Ron Atkinson were made for each other. It doesn't bother me that I was not the first choice. I prefer to think that I was offered the job in front of the best manager in the country – Brian Clough. I will not be just United's manager, I will be an ardent fan. If the team bores me it will be boring supporters who hero-worship the players, I will not allow these people to be betrayed." At the time it was my opinion that West Brom would have been much better served in placing their confidence in Mick Brown and the reserve-team coach, Brian Whitehouse ... Mick and Brian had played a fundamental part in creating a successful set-up at The Hawthorns ... I wanted them with me at Old Trafford, but I didn't want them to join me to the detriment of their own careers. Both indicated immediately that they would like to make the move, then I advised them strongly to wait for a short while to see if West Brom offered to let them take charge at The Hawthorns. Just a couple of days later they contacted me at Old Trafford and said they both wished to take up my offer ... West Brom's loss was certainly Manchester United's gain. I had acquired the vital backbone of my staff. Brown and Whitehouse were major signings for the club and every bit as important as the expensive purchases of Bryan Robson and Frank Stapleton that would be made in the coming weeks.'

On 9 June Atkinson was unveiled to the world as Manchester United manager at a press conference. He was immediately taken to task about the style of football he intended to play at Old Trafford. 'Players don't like to be restricted,' he said. 'They like to go forward, and they will get plenty of encouragement from me. We will attempt to play positive football, although I am not saying that out of the hat we will produce another George Best. I have never gone out and closed a game down, although obviously sides have to defend sometimes. I believe in positive football – the type of football that not only the crowd and directors like to see, but also the players like to play … Dave Sexton did well for United, but the situation arose and he was relieved of his job. My style must be a little more conducive to success but that is no criticism of him. I don't want to talk about the past, I'm more interested in the future … I believe I'm the best man for this job … I can't understand anyone turning this job down.'

Martin Edwards, sitting alongside him, stated: 'The more time I spend with Ron Atkinson the more I am convinced we've got the best man of the four we've considered.'

Atkinson decreed his first job would be convincing Joe Jordan to stay. 'I will move heaven and earth to keep him at Old Trafford,' he said. 'My priority is to win, but I want United to play positively and attractively – and I certainly don't envisage sweeping the current players out.'

There *would* be changes. Brown and Whitehouse came in. Tommy Cavanagh and Laurie Brown were let go. Harry Gregg knew that his time was up due to a spectacular disagreement he'd had with Atkinson when he was Shrewsbury manager but went through the procedure of meeting with the new man anyway, where it was agreed a parting of the ways would be best. When Edwards mentioned Ron Atkinson might be coming in, Gregg says he told him: 'United was the Hollywood of football and it didn't need a John Wayne.'

It did need some of the stardust back, though. According to Atkinson, the football club had been trading off their past glories for a little too long and needed to accept the current state of affairs. 'From the moment I stepped through the door at Old Trafford, I was under no illusions about the size of the task which confronted me,' he said. 'Although both the club and its fans claimed they were the greatest in the world, the argument did not hold water in terms of recent achievements. The brutal truth is that Manchester United and its supporters were living in a fool's paradise and had been doing so for some considerable time ... Manchester United was simply not good enough even to contemplate tilts at the major prizes in the game ... Certainly I was not at all optimistic of immediate success in the forthcoming 1981/82 season. Yet from a personal point of view it was a good time for me to take over. The size of the crowds at Old Trafford, by their own huge standards, had begun to plummet and the supporters were not enamoured by the quality of the football they had been watching. I could only improve things. It was time for some positive action and that had to mean I must break with my own tradition in management of allowing the existing staff an opportunity to prove their worth to me. Reports and informed rumours had already reached my ears, which suggested that, under the management of my predecessor, Dave Sexton, not all of the staff had been pulling in the same direction. While I had enough experience to know that if there is not complete harmony in the coaching staff there is little or no chance of harmony or success on the field of play, what had occurred during Sexton's reign at the club was no business of mine. Nevertheless, I was already convinced that new spaces of my own choosing were urgently required and consequently some people had to go. Harry Gregg, the Manchester United goalkeeper at the time of the tragic Munich crash in 1958, had been employed by the club to help out with the coaching, with particular responsibility for working with the goalkeepers. I had come across Harry a few times in my early days as a manager. He had been in charge at Shrewsbury and later Swansea, and, quite frankly, his methods had never impressed me. Some of his thoughts on the way the game should be played could never have been reconciled with my own. Harry had to go and it should not have been a surprise to him when he was informed that he was now surplus to requirements. Gregg became bitter after his departure and had quite a go at me in the newspapers. Also to go in what was growing into a major purge were physiotherapist Laurie Brown and the reserve-team trainer, Jack Crompton, plus youth-team coach Syd Owen. All of these people could consider themselves to be unfortunate. Sadly for them I had become more convinced than ever that if I was to do the job required at Old Trafford I would first have to implement a clean sweep of the place. This was a big job, perhaps the biggest and toughest in the game. It was vital I had my own men around me to give me a sporting chance of success. I needed men I knew within myself I could trust 100 per cent every minute of every day. I had to have men I could work with, men whose talents I knew and respected.'

Owen might have considered himself particularly unfortunate. He had done some fine work bringing through young players. The wait for an FA Youth Cup win had been even longer than the wait for a First Division title, but a semi-final finish in the competition with a team which included Graeme Hogg, Clayton Blackmore, Norman Whiteside and Mark Hughes suggested that the prospect of bringing quality footballers through wasn't exactly dire.

You could say Atkinson was ruthless with his dismissal of Owen but his intention was clear: 'Despite the fact that United is regarded as one of the wealthiest clubs in England, I have always taken a particular interest in producing first-team players from the ranks,' Atkinson insisted at the time. 'The man I wanted for the important role of bringing them on was Eric Harrison, who had recently left Everton following the departure of Gordon Lee as manager at Goodison Park. I invited Eric to join the team and he accepted immediately.'

In 2019 Atkinson spoke about Harrison in an interview for this book: 'I knew Eric and liked his views on the game,' he says. 'We played together when we were in the RAF and we always kept in touch. He had been first-team coach at Everton but he was getting so intense that they wouldn't have him on a bench on Saturdays. When I went in at United, I asked him if he would fancy coming down and helping us with the youth players. I don't know why I thought that was a good idea; it might well have been that I wasn't looking for a first-team coach because I had Mick Brown, and the youth-team coach position was available. There is a school of thought in football that says your best coach should be your youth-team coach. He was so insightful; for example, knowing that at Old Trafford your defenders would have to be good on the ball because they would often have it. He would work so hard on their ability to pass the ball.'

Harrison was the obvious choice. He might not have been Atkinson's first pick, however. That honour might – in a different world – have gone to, of all people, Dave Sexton. Sexton was hired as Coventry City manager before Atkinson was even linked with the United job seriously, and so the idea was never seriously suggested. Nor would it have been anyway, as Atkinson would not have insulted Sexton in such a way, but the respect he had for him was clear. 'He was a brilliant coach, the best I have ever worked with, and had he not been my predecessor at United, I would have tried to take him with me to Old Trafford,' Atkinson later said. When Ron was named manager of Aston Villa, he did indeed appoint Dave as a coach.

Next to follow Eric Harrison was a physiotherapist. Atkinson appointed Jimmy Hedridge, of whom he said, 'His record of restoring full fitness to injured players in record time was well known in the game.' Within a month, however, Hedridge suffered a huge heart attack at The Cliff and tragically died. He was just 42.

'Eric Harrison mentioned to me that the Everton physiotherapist, Jimmy McGregor, might be interested in leaving Goodison Park,' Atkinson said. 'He spoke highly of the man, as did many other people I consulted, and events have proved that we were undoubtedly fortunate to persuade McGregor to join our team. In my opinion he is the finest football physiotherapist in England. His medical knowledge is profound and he is an expert at speedy diagnosis of an injury, which is absolutely vital in the treatment of professional athletes. Once I had got my coaching and medical team sorted out, the time was right to begin major surgery on the Manchester United team.'

Two days after being appointed manager, the fixture list for the 1981/82 season was announced. The first game for United was a trip to Coventry City and a reunion with their recently sacked manager. Their new one had other things on his mind, namely the players he wanted to bring in. Atkinson wanted to make a statement signing. 'My philosophy regarding the kind of players we needed was crystal clear from the start,' he said. 'If the best became available, it was my duty to both myself and the club to be in there bidding. On the day of my official appointment as manager I disclosed that my immediate target would be Glenn Hoddle of Spurs ... Hoddle is a player who appears to be involved in contract talks with Tottenham at the end of every season. There was strong interest from abroad in signing him up ... His football talents were well known to me. He is a player of rare skill and vision and a delight to spectators. In the end Hoddle decided to sign another agreement with Spurs, although I gained the distinct impression that Manchester United would be the only other English club he would consider playing for should he decide to quit his old club.'

He couldn't convince Hoddle to come, nor Joe Jordan to stay. Jordan had received an offer from Milan and informed Atkinson he would be taking it. 'The big Scottish international was a popular figure, especially with supporters,' Atkinson said. 'But his contract at United was at an end and within a week he was off to seek fame and fortune in Italy. He had enjoyed perhaps his best two seasons as a player and failed to agree terms on a new contract at United, but I wasn't too upset about his departure. He was already on the wrong side of 30, which can be vitally important as far as a footballer is concerned, especially a player like Jordan who thrived on physical contact. His exit also forced us to look hard at possible replacements.'

There was so much activity in those early weeks that Atkinson might have been forgiven for not knowing if he was coming or going. The Jordan headache was compounded by disciplinary issues on the trip to Malaysia that was occurring just as Atkinson had been appointed. Sammy McIlroy and Jimmy Nicholl took the decision not to join up with the club after playing for Northern Ireland. They would face fines, and possible further consequences. McIlroy showed contrition: 'I know that, as a contracted player, I have done wrong and must accept the consequences,' he said. 'But I simply put my family first.' McIlroy was concerned that his wife was struggling looking after three young children as their son was ill.

Mickey Thomas also refused to fly. He confessed that the struggle of living with the pressure of performing at Old Trafford was too much. 'Just before Ron Atkinson took over, I said to Martin Edwards I wanted a transfer because I couldn't handle the pressure,' he admitted.

Nicholl and Thomas would become possible makeweights for Atkinson as he sought to make big changes. He had not yet seen his squad close up, but newspaper reports linked United with a move for Everton's John Gidman, leading reporters to put two and two together and suggest that young right-back Mick Duxbury might be surplus to requirements.

Duxbury would not have the easiest of relationships with the new man but his initial thoughts were not apprehensive, even though he had perhaps wanted to work with McMenemy or Robson. 'I'd always liked them, as what I'd seen from Lawrie McMenemy at Southampton, he did a great job with the people that he brought in, the way they played, and Bobby Robson also at Ipswich,' Duxbury says. 'I mean, you would have thought they'd have been great signings for United, anybody would have taken them. But they turned United down. I certainly thought they would have been great assets at the time. I didn't know much of Ron. That he'd done a good job at West Brom. The team that were there, the players that were there. Things got off to a decent start, really, when he arrived.'

Around a week after the appointment of the new manager, United were linked with a sensational transfer which was dubbed 'the biggest player swap in British soccer history'. 'The proposal would send striker Garry Birtles back to Forest, along with keeper Gary Bailey, in exchange for their opposite numbers, Trevor Francis and Peter Shilton,' read one report.

There was some truth to it. In his 1981 book Atkinson explained: 'I admitted in the *Daily Express* on 29 July 1981: "I have a dream team in my head. I don't know if I will be able to get it together completely but I intend to have a damned good try. If I can get all of them … then only one or two players from the existing team will remain. To my mind this job is bigger and tougher than managing England." Consider the quality of some of the players I thought about bringing into Old Trafford. Trevor Francis was on my list at one time, and I went as far as meeting Brian Clough to discuss the possibility of signing Trevor from Nottingham Forest. Clough was demanding a fee in excess of £1m, so I gave the matter a great deal of thought. I had no intention of repenting at leisure after spending fortunes in haste. I finally decided not to go through with the transfer. Although I had always admired Francis, who, in my opinion, is one of the great players of the recent era, there had to be real doubts about his fitness and durability. His signing would have been just too much of a risk. I knew, however, that Trevor had set his heart on playing for Manchester United. When I backed out of the deal he was upset and disappointed. It was after I spent an evening with him and his wife Helen on a social basis that Trevor finally tackled me on why I had decided not to buy him. We were sitting in the lounge of my house at the time and I didn't see any point in wrapping up my words. We were friends and he was a professional. I told him straight out that the reason he would not be playing for United was that I considered him to be injury prone. He was deeply hurt. I know I was not top of Trevor's popularity poll for some time.'

Birtles had a short-term reprieve, and Bailey had a second chance – Clough did not want to discuss selling Shilton, and the United boss was impressed with what he had seen from the young goalkeeper to keep faith in him. Atkinson continued, though, to be frustrated in his initial search for reinforcements. 'Mark Lawrenson was another player I went after within weeks of my appointment at Manchester United,' he said. 'I was very annoyed when we lost him to Liverpool through no fault of our own. At the same time as we had expressed an interest in Lawrenson I was informed that Middlesbrough's David Armstrong was also available for transfer, and I was given the go-ahead to make strong attempts to sign both of these players. Simultaneously we were involved in a pre-season tour that was being played in Aberdeen. I had made an offer of £500,000 for Armstrong but was told that Southampton would be willing to pay £600,000 to beat us for his signature. The size of the fee daunted me a little, and when I finally received the first hint that Bryan Robson might be available for purchase from West Brom I decided to stop bidding for Armstrong, preferring to reserve cash for a major attempt to land Robson. At this point we had been in negotiation for some time with Brighton on a suitable transfer arrangement for Lawrenson ... We knew that Lawrenson was meeting Liverpool officials at Heathrow Airport but were assured by both the player and Brighton that nothing would be finally decided until he had talks with United as well. It was at 5pm the same evening that Mike Bailey, the Brighton manager at that time, telephoned me to make further enquiries about the availability of Nicholl and Grimes. I gave him permission to speak to both of the players, but in return I wanted Brighton's consent to interview Lawrenson. I was absolutely staggered to be told by Bailey that the player had already signed for Liverpool.'

There was some brighter news when United were successful in their bid for John Gidman, who became Atkinson's first signing on 22 July. 'It is the first one in the bag,' the delighted United boss said. 'I consider he is a United type of player. His strength is going forward and he can do that as well as anyone in the country. I see a great future for him here and I feel he can win back a place in the England team.'

Prospects of signing Robson did not appear bright when new West Brom manager Ronnie Allen declared on 6 August: 'My attitude is that Robson leaves here over my dead body.'

That might have been the case as far as Arsenal were concerned too, when it came to the future of their striker Frank Stapleton; but Stapleton was out of contract and able to move, with the fee being set by a tribunal. Arsenal wanted almost £2m; the tribunal set the fee at £900,000. The Ireland striker could provide the height United would be missing after the departure of Jordan. It was a positive move but the arrival, coming as it did so late in the summer (20 August, though the First Division season got underway on the 29th), left the United boss concerned about the lack of incomings.

'I knew the signing of Stapleton could only be the start of expensive transfer activity,' said Atkinson. 'In fact, I told Mick Brown and Brian Whitehouse in one discussion that unless we signed new players quickly we would do well to end the season in the top half of the league. Any thoughts of being equipped to make any kind of challenge for the championship with our current team was a joke. There is a tremendous amount of grandeur and opulence at Old Trafford. The club reeks of tradition. There are bars, restaurants, private suites and enough room on the terraces to pack in an attendance of 60,000 people. But at no time have I been overawed by the place ... I had immediately approached the board of directors to outline my plans for revamping the team. If I shocked them in any way, and I certainly suspected this might be the case, they certainly didn't allow it to show. Perhaps I was telling them what they already knew. I asked them to see their way to releasing almost immediately a tremendous amount of money for the players

I wanted to buy. But I did add that such instantaneous action could mean that they would not have to buy again for a couple of years. As it turned out, I was as good as my word in that vitally important meeting with my new employers.'

In an interview for this book in 2019, Atkinson elaborated slightly on why he wasn't frightened by the size of the club: 'I think it was a bit of an advantage that I had left a better team. I wasn't overawed by the stage. I didn't feel any pressure to behave a certain way, or to conduct myself in a certain way. West Brom were a big club and I was used to that.'

United were threadbare up front. Garry Birtles had not shown good form under Sexton, and Atkinson did not feel Birtles and Stapleton were a good fit. He wanted someone in the Jimmy Greenhoff mould.

'Frank Worthington is another player I seriously considered taking to Old Trafford, if only on a short-term basis,' Atkinson explained in 1981. 'Frank was already over 30 but I felt strongly that Old Trafford would provide the ideal stage for a crowd pleaser with delightful ball control. There was no doubt in my mind that Worthington should have played for one of the big clubs at some stage in his career. Frank might have stayed with us for only a couple of seasons, but he was a player of play and imagination. The United fans would have risen to acclaim his artistry. For some reason, though, he decided to join Leeds United from Birmingham. Perhaps he couldn't believe that a club like United would be interested in taking him on in the twilight years of his career. The fact is that had he hung on for another week or two he would have been a United player. I'm sure he regrets his impetuosity now. So Francis, Lawrenson and Worthington were not destined to become part of my new-look Manchester United, but I had signed the striker I needed in Stapleton.'

So just Stapleton and Gidman arrived in the pre-season; Atkinson may have insisted it was a 'joke' that he would have been expected to challenge for the league title with the squad he had, but on the eve of the season he spoke to his friend and future ghostwriter Joe Melling of *The Express* to declare he had big hopes.

'My great ambition is to win the First Division title for Manchester United in my first season as their manager,' he said.

'Let's face it, this great club has not exactly covered itself in glory on the field of play over the past 13 years. One FA Cup win in that time is not good enough for a club revered and worshipped throughout the world.' Atkinson said he told Martin Edwards: 'I have not come here to be patient. I've come here to win the league at the first attempt.'

It took the manager and the squad a little time to get to know each other and get over those first impressions that had been formed prior to them working together. Gary Bailey, to name just one, caused Atkinson to reconsider just how urgently he might need a goalkeeper. Another who had cause for concern was Mike Duxbury. The youngster was tipped as someone who could be used to entice another club into selling one of their stars. The arrival of John Gidman would surely limit his chances of football so soon after breaking into the first team, but Atkinson would keep him on, and the player himself responded to the challenge.

'He'd a good reputation and had done well with West Brom, with Bryan Robson and Laurie Cunningham,' Duxbury said of Atkinson in his autobiography. 'I felt it was a good appointment and just as Dave Sexton represented a huge personality shift from his predecessor, it was exactly the same with Ron. He came with a reputation of being flashy and instead of trying to move away from it or dispel it, he seemed only to live up to it and try and grow into it even more. He couldn't have been any more different to Dave! I wasn't exactly fearful for my future, but as someone with just one season in senior football under my belt you naturally have a concern about where you will figure in the new manager's plans. Dave himself had been no stranger to making huge and unexpected changes, so you have to prepare yourself for anything ... I could not argue to be an established member of the team just yet, in any case. I knew that from day one I'd be battling to prove myself; within reason, my form in 1980/81 would count for little as we returned for pre-season training.'

Duxbury confessed 'it didn't feel brilliant' but also conceded that all of the players were in the same boat when it came to trying to impress the new manager. The defender had only played a few games for the senior team so Atkinson could be forgiven for not knowing much, other than Jimmy Nicholl was on his way out and needed to be replaced. As for Gary Bailey, he had played a blinder but still conceded five in Atkinson's December 1978 visit to Old Trafford, and then there had been the error in the cup final which was high-profile. Ron was open-minded enough to give him a chance to erase that impression.

'I liked Ron from day one. He was good to be around,' admits Bailey. 'It was almost the reverse as it was under Dave; Mick Brown was good to be around too, but Ron might have benefitted from having an assistant who concentrated more on tactics alongside Mick ... I always thought that if Dave had a good number two it would have helped. Cav wasn't really a number two, he was more of a helper. Don Howe, for example, was a great number two. Maybe we would have benefitted from having someone who was lively and bouncy to counter tactical stuff with Dave. Cav believed more in Tommy Doc's approach than Dave's, and Dave might have been better off with his own staff. They didn't seem a natural fit together. That's not to say that Cav didn't do a good job, he just didn't do the job that Dave needed him to do. It's a fair argument to say Dave was maybe suited better to being a number two than manager. But he had done well at Chelsea and QPR. It's easy to say that after the fact, though, and getting us to second was still a good achievement. It was my impression that Dave thought we could improve as a group to challenge for the title. I felt we needed one or two signings because the other teams around us were improving.'

Perhaps most confusing of all was the pre-season speculation that Steve Coppell might be surplus to requirements – Coppell possibly a victim of the complex explanation of the perception of Sexton's Manchester United. It didn't help matters that the winger picked up an ankle ligament injury in pre-season; his determination to play through it and keep his place in the first team was to have a significant long-term impact on his career. Arsenal were interested, as was Sexton at Coventry, but it was West Ham who made a serious move when they offered £1m. Atkinson left it up to Coppell.

'When Ron first joined United I don't think he rated me,' the midfielder said. 'He had come from West Brom, where Derek Statham was playing at full-back. I never really felt like I played that well against Derek – he was difficult to play against and initially I think Ron would have been happy for me to move on. He said I could go if I wanted to, but I said I wanted to fight for my place and I think he respected that. We got to know each other better and I began to play some of my best stuff for him.' But Coppell's injury issues meant he started the season out of form and he was even dropped midway through the campaign.

Ray Wilkins might have had fairer warning that the new manager had reservations. 'I am going to take a long, hard look at him in the coming weeks,' Atkinson told the press. 'I am going to ask him why he is not the same player as he was when he burst on to the scene at Chelsea as a youngster.'

In 2019 Atkinson discussed the composition of the squad he had inherited, and the vulnerabilities he had targeted when he was at The Hawthorns. 'When I arrived, some of the senior members of the squad were not quite past the post, but going past the post. They were picking up a number of injuries,' he says. 'When we played United we used to think they had got a lot of weaknesses. I thought you could get about them in midfield. We had good pace up front at West Brom and we knew that United defenders did not like to be disturbed by players who ran the channels. We knew Martin Buchan didn't like to leave the middle, he liked to hang on to the last position; that's not decrying him because he had been a great defender ... if anything, we would always say if in doubt let big Gordon McQueen have the ball. In my second home game against Ipswich, Gordon started running with the ball. I think Dave had encouraged him to do that because I don't remember him doing it at Leeds. But he never looked comfortable ... I remember looking at the Ipswich lads and I'm sure they were laughing! Some time later we were playing Birmingham and I think their players had been told the same, to let him have the ball. He started running with it inside our half. They backed off; he got to the halfway line and turned left. He got to the touchline and I was thinking at that point, "Robbo, tackle him for crying out loud!" He ran down to near the corner flag, turned inside and the Birmingham players were still backing off him. When he finally got inside the box someone went to tackle him. I dreaded what came next because I saw Gordon move, and knew what he was going to try because he tried it all the time in training. A nutmeg. It didn't work. The defender won the ball and cleared it to the striker, Wayne Clarke, who ran through and hit the crossbar. I'm sure Gordon was being guided by the lines on the pitch! I knew they were doing what I had done when at West Brom. But, yeah, when I came in, it was clear a few of the key players were coming to the end and the squad needed refreshing.'

The initial impact Atkinson had on the United squad made it clear that things would be much more different than how it was under Dave Sexton. Sexton's style was so particular that any change would be pronounced. It would take some getting used to.

'People have been critical of Dave Sexton's personality but he was, to me, at least someone I could talk to. Ron was brash, larger than life – or at least wanted dearly to put that impression across – and sometimes in training it appeared as if he'd set up the session purely to satisfy his own ego,' Mike Duxbury remembers. 'He'd join in – which was fine, managers did that – but there were certain drills with crossing, finishing, and he'd be in those too. Who was the one who was supposed to be benefitting? The full-backs putting in the crosses, the forwards trying to finish them, or the manager who was just having fun? As a youngster who didn't have that kind of personality, I just observed it and felt he wasn't the kind of person I could approach seriously with concerns. That's not to say that I felt Ron didn't take the opportunity seriously, I'm sure he did, and his preparation for matches was good enough to show you that. There were just instances like the one above, or even unplanned pre-season training. We went to Heaton Park, which was a regular occurrence with United but was always well planned out. However, on this particular day, we went to do some running and when we arrived there was a woman with a pram – he was just telling us to run around the woman! Thoughts then occurred, what happened if she wasn't there, or even if she moved as we were running? There was no respect for how she'd feel with 30 blokes bombing towards her, and I don't think she'd be on the pitch on the Saturday either!'

As United prepared to face Dave Sexton's Coventry City in the first game of the season, it wasn't only the faces in the dugouts that had changed. The Football League had decided to award three points instead of two for a win in order to try to encourage more attacking football, particularly from teams who would be satisfied with a point in away games. This did not affect how United would approach the games, however. 'We always went for the win. We tended to just play every game the same,' remembers Mike Duxbury.

Atkinson's first team sheet included both of his new men and he was fortunate in that, Coppell's secret ankle issue aside, he had a fully fit squad to choose from. But it was Sexton who gained some revenge; his side stormed into an early lead, before Lou Macari levelled before the break. A goal just after half-time for the hosts gave all three points to the Sky Blues.

Atkinson's first home game at Old Trafford was against Nottingham Forest, the European Cup winners of 1979 and 1980. Brian Clough's team were in a period of regression domestically, having finished seventh in 1981. United fans had looked on jealously during their period of success, wondering if things had worked out differently might it have been them. If that was the level of hope and expectation that Dave Sexton had walked into, then it was hastily revised for Ron Atkinson. Most knew in their hearts that United no longer had a team that could be expected to challenge for the league, and some of the players who were in their prime in 1977 were now coming up to the period where they would be veterans who would need to be replaced. Macari, goalscorer on the opening day, was now 32. So was club captain Martin Buchan. Atkinson would have to deal with this transition and knew that most understood this was a period of transition rather than a team on the precipice of glory. Most of all, supporters wanted to be entertained again. And that was the hymn sheet Atkinson was singing from in his first programme notes.

'Welcome to Old Trafford for our first home game of the season, though perhaps the greetings should be the other way round. For I am really the new boy at Manchester United, while many of you are supporters of many years standing who have followed the club through the good years and perhaps the not-so-good,' he said. 'All I can say is that I don't think it will take long to get to know each other because we have a common purpose, which of course is to put Manchester United at the top. I think we have a few other things in common as well. Although I am the manager I am a fan of football at heart as well, and the last thing I want from my game is to be bored. So along with my staff (who share my beliefs) and the players, we will be doing our best to entertain you with attacking football. This doesn't mean, however, that in some games we may not be obliged to defend for 90 minutes. Football is about competition and we won't be able to dominate all the time. Mind you, we shall have a darned good go, and I think we have pulled off a transfer capture in Frank Stapleton which will enable us to back up those words with action.'

Atkinson described Stapleton as the 'best centre-forward in England, perhaps Europe', and continued: 'I haven't finished yet in the transfer market, though don't get the idea that I am a restless character who can't leave well enough alone. For instance, after one very traumatic period with West Bromwich when four or five players left and we spent heavily on replacements, it was two years before I bought another senior man. So Mick Brown and I do know how to get down to hard work and develop a team, once we are sure we have got the right make-up. So far I think we have made an excellent start and have improved the squad by 20 per cent. So we are starting with confidence and I hope you are able to share in the sense of excitement that grips me as I look ahead to the challenge of the new season.'

United were unchanged from their opening-day defeat, but a goalless draw against Forest did nothing to inspire fans. It got even worse four days later when Bobby Robson's Ipswich Town came to Old Trafford and won 2-1. Worryingly, in those first two home games the attendance already dropped by almost 6,000 from 51,496 to 45,555.

Frank Stapleton – who scored his first goal in the defeat against Ipswich – rescued a creditable point against champions Aston Villa at Villa Park, and the following week Garry Birtles finally scored his first league goal for United at the 13th time of asking to earn a win over Swansea City.

That game also saw the debut of Remi Moses, the hard-working midfielder who had played for Atkinson at West Brom. United had been trying to persuade Albion to sell them Bryan Robson when the unexpected opportunity to sign Moses occurred.

'I was staying at Haydock Park and I was negotiating to sign Frank Stapleton,' Atkinson recalls. 'I was trying to lock him away as I knew Liverpool wanted him. I knocked on the door and there was Remi. "What are you doing here?" I asked. "I've come to sign for you!" he replied. I said it was a good idea but I was a bit tied up so I gave him my room key. It must have been 2am when I got around to seeing him; he was sitting on my bed and I told him I was knackered but I would sort it out.'

As he was out of contract, the tribunal set the fee at £500,000. It was proving more difficult to procure Robson from a chairman reluctant to allow his best player to join the same club his manager had just defected to. Bert Millichip would no doubt have remembered Ron Atkinson saying he would not have sold Robson under any circumstances; in fact, Atkinson claimed that Dave Sexton had made an enquiry in November of 1980.

'I knew United had tapped Robbo, but I told him in no uncertain terms that the only way he would go to United is if I went,' Ron says. 'The day after I got the job, Robbo was on England duty, and called me from Hungary. "Boss, remember what you said!" He or a third party was ringing me every day. I had almost given up on it because I am a big believer in things happening quickly if they are to happen at all, but we were playing Swansea and Bill Shankly was at Old Trafford, having a cup of tea with me in my office. I asked him what he would pay for Robson and he said, "Whatever it fucking takes!" I felt a new motivation to get him.'

Martin Edwards admits that he was not aware of any prior bid for the midfielder. 'I don't ever remember Dave wanting to sign him, but I can remember when Ron approached me to tell me he wanted Bryan,' he says. 'He said he would give us fantastic service, years and years in midfield and then for the last five years of his career he would be a centre-half. He also spoke glowingly of how well Remi Moses would improve us. It was difficult to prise them away, especially after we'd just taken their manager.'

Talks for Robson would drag on. But five games, four goals and just one win was enough to provoke David Miller of *The Express* to write a scathing article entitled 'Why they all hate the new United style.'

'Like an ageing actress whose looks have gone, Manchester United are desperate for curtain calls but are succeeding only in appearing slightly ridiculous,' Miller wrote on 22 September 1981. 'Garry Birtles's first league goal for a year … did little to dispel the feeling that United may get worse before they get better. Instead of the popularity and success they crave, all they are achieving so far under sheriff Martin Edwards and hired hand Ron Atkinson is to become the most unpopular club in the country. It is a sad comedown for the great club built by Sir Matt Busby and Harold Hardman, but in the list for lost prestige they are forfeiting the friendship and affection of all but their own supporters. For almost the first time since the war, United directors have not been invited to lunch before next Saturday's match at Highbury, simply because Arsenal's directors consider United are no longer behaving like colleagues and gentlemen ... Were United to be relegated, their cries of anguish would be drowned in the laughter in the rest of the First Division. The sacking of Dave Sexton, leaving aside its highly questionable justification, was handled with the finesse of a smash and grab raid ... While we look forward with expectation to Swansea's future, those who conspired inside and outside Old Trafford to bring down Sexton should question the validity of their work.'

Miller might have wished he had held on a little while before tearing into United just as they appeared to be turning a corner. A 2-0 win at Middlesbrough with goals from Birtles and Stapleton was followed by a decent draw at Arsenal. Stapleton then scored the winner in a 1-0 victory over Leeds to make it three wins out of four and four consecutive clean sheets.

The following week saw United finally put an end to the Robson saga by paying the £1.5m West Brom were demanding. President Sir Matt Busby, in the rarest error of judgement, resigned from the board in protest at the size of the fee. But Atkinson was convinced he had to have the midfielder. 'United were in desperate need of a player around whom we could build a solid team,' he said. 'I don't believe there is another manager in England who watches more games, studies more videos or discusses more football than me. If there had been a player within the four corners of the British Isles or within the boundaries of Europe who fitted the bill more than Robson, I confess I didn't know of his existence; it had to be Robson.'

The signing was announced on 2 October 1981. At a press conference, Atkinson was challenged on the size of the fee, to which he replied: 'He is the most complete midfield player in the game. He can defend, he can create and he can inspire all around him. He is a great tackler, he is good in the air, he has a superb range of passing, shots, and scores goals. He's like Duncan Edwards and

Dave Mackay – a scruff-of-the-neck player. He can take over any game even when it is going against his own team. He is the kind of player who makes a good team great. He will increase considerably United's chances of winning the major prizes from day one.'

Atkinson's conviction only grew as Robson justified his worth. 'Robson's value has more than doubled,' Ron later said. 'The player has fulfilled so many of our ambitions for him. He is the captain of Manchester United and the captain of his country. He and Moses have proved to be wonderful value for money, although I must confess now that I was almost at my limit with the size of the fee. At the time I don't believe I could have gone to the chairman and directors of United and attempted to justify going any higher, even though I knew that Robson was absolutely vital to our future success.'

There was a certain amount of pressure alleviated from Atkinson's shoulders, having made Robson his number-one target. Whilst it didn't provoke him into any bold declarations or predictions, it did help him redefine his perspective to confirm that he now felt more generous in his appraisal of the players he had inherited.

'The excitement of signing Robson was enhanced by the fact there were several players at Old Trafford who had forced me to change my opinions on their quality and ability within my first couple of months of the club,' Atkinson explained. 'At the beginning I had had grave reservations about first-choice goalkeeper Gary Bailey. Big and blonde with the kind of physique which catches the eye, Gary is guaranteed to stand out in a crowd. I had noticed him all right when he played for United against West Brom, but he had grabbed my attention for the wrong reasons. He always seemed to concede goals that a top-class goalkeeper would have prevented. Within a month of working with the lad, I knew I had been wrong about him. I had obviously been unlucky enough to have previously caught him on the kind of bad days that happen to every goalkeeper. His attitude and capacity for improvement were first class. In fact, I was so impressed by the lad that I turned down the opportunity of signing the great Peter Shilton ... Arthur Albiston is another United player who took me by surprise. I had previously considered him to be little more than a steady full-back. It is often said that no manager can gauge the true value of a player until he has actually worked with him, and although I am not sure if that is always the case, it was most certainly correct where Albiston was concerned. Within days of my arrival he had proceeded to stagger me with his outstanding natural ability ... It was in those early days that Dave Sexton, who had joined Coventry as manager following his departure from United, tried to persuade me to sell both Moran and young Mike Duxbury. Fortunately for me, I decided I wanted to take a longer look at both players before making any decision on their future. It didn't take me long to realise that both were super players with a spectacular career at Old Trafford ahead of them.'

One player whose future had been less certain was Gordon McQueen. Having played only 11 times in the league in the final season under Sexton, the Scot was under pressure to remain fit to keep his place under the new regime. 'I told him straight out that if he wanted to stay at Old Trafford he would have to show me his fitness merited a new contract,' Atkinson said. 'His response was excellent. He worked tremendously hard and played in a fair quota of games ... Gordon is an incredible character who readily admits that he has no idea why he does certain things on a football field. Many is the time he has set out on one of his wayward runs from the back and confused himself, let alone his team-mates.'

He had settled alongside Buchan to form a good partnership that was somewhat reminiscent of the one Buchan had with Brian Greenhoff, in that the captain had made McQueen aware that he was the organiser of the backline. This did free McQueen up to make some of his more adventurous runs with the ball, and, although he was never quite as efficient with his distribution as Greenhoff had been, United fans did grow to have a strong affection for him. Unfortunately, just as things were getting into a groove, McQueen was injured in the win over Leeds. His place was initially taken by Kevin Moran.

Robson was unveiled in front of supporters ahead of the home game against Wolves on 3 October. The record signing wasn't enough to boost the attendance back over 50,000. Robson wouldn't play on the day and everyone knew he was a player who would play through the middle, but two players who felt immediate concern about their future were Coppell and Sammy McIlroy, who were playing on the right- and left-hand side respectively. McIlroy wasn't a natural left-sider like Gordon Hill, but had played there sometimes prior to Hill's arrival, and was at least more of a natural schemer than Mickey Thomas, who had been sold to Everton. Coppell, feeling the pressure to keep performing, was making his 200th consecutive appearance for the club.

It was McIlroy who gave the biggest reminder of his capability, scoring a fine hat-trick in a thrilling 5-0 win. According to Mike Duxbury, McIlroy still had plenty to give. 'There were still one or two players who maybe could have gone a little bit longer,' he says. 'I don't know. I can remember when Bryan signed on the pitch, Sammy Mac scored a hat-trick and he was one who was on his way out. So, you know, things were changing in that way. So I think Sammy was one of those, a great servant for United. Bryan had a terrific work ethic. Everything he did, his leadership and all those types of things that are well known, he was terrific.'

Coppell was dropped from the following game; Robson stepped in, wearing the number seven shirt he would become so famous for, though Coppell did maintain his appearance record by coming off the bench in a goalless Manchester derby at Maine Road.

Elimination from the League Cup was disappointing, but United's league form held out. Late wins over Middlesbrough, and, even better, at Anfield, continued the good momentum but United supporters were not yet fully convinced. Not since the first game of the season had they got a crowd over 50,000, and it would take some time for that to happen (though their average of 42,744 for the season was still a league best). United continued to win and a 2-0 win against Brighton, with Birtles and Stapleton getting the goals (Birtles had scored in four consecutive games!), put Atkinson's team top of the First Division.

The players had lived up to the manager's public intentions, despite his initial private reservations. 'In view of the fact that we had new players, a new pattern and consequently a new blend, I must confess I was surprised when we went to the top of the First Division by Christmas 1981,' Atkinson said (although for reasons of critical accuracy it must be pointed out that Swansea City were top at Christmas). 'We even held the position into the new year, but I would have been still more amazed had we managed to stay at the summit ... If I had been asked at the start of the season, before a ball had been kicked, what was the best I could hope for, I would willingly have settled for third position. It was of great importance for the club to establish itself again as one of the leading teams, and our finishing position ensured European qualification for the following season; a club of United's stature should never be out of the European mainstream, although sadly this has not always been the case. Overall, a splendid feeling of satisfaction prevailed at Old Trafford. We realise that there was a great deal of ground to be made up on Liverpool, but real progress had definitely been achieved. The way we saw it was that Liverpool had six or seven years' start on us and we had to cram three or four years' progress into just one year if there was to be any chance of quickly closing the gap. We believed it was of paramount importance that we at least suggested we were capable of making a serious and sustained effort to challenge their imperious reign as masters of soccer in England.'

One player in particular who had turned around some scepticism was Steve Coppell. Coppell had been asked to play on the left wing at Anfield, to do a man-marking job on Phil Neal; Atkinson gave credit to Coppell for influencing the performance.

Poor weather conditions in England meant that United didn't play a game between 5 December 1981 and 2 January 1982. Their run of good form had been hit somewhat by defeats either side of that Brighton win, in which United shipped three goals in both games against Spurs and Southampton.

On 28 December David Miller of *The Express* was not yet ready to revise his earlier pessimistic predictions. 'Having seen United lose twice away from home, I reckon Atkinson may have to pawn the odd gold bracelet or two to buy another defender,' he wrote.

It was certainly fair to say it was a mixed bag. Results were positive, but supporters were wary and apprehensive. Their midfield reinvention was taking some time to bear fruit, with Bryan Robson confessing that he initially struggled. 'Once I had become a £1.5m player, lining up with the biggest club in the country, it was an entirely different scenario,' he said in his autobiography *Robbo*. 'Suddenly, expectations soared and everything I did – every tackle, pass, run, shot or header – came under scrutiny. When we lost some of our momentum and results went against us, I definitely suffered ... After starting quite well for my new club, I was underperforming. The pressure of the feet and all the attention undoubtedly took its toll. Some players are adamant a big fee doesn't affect them, but that's not what I found. I don't mind admitting it affected my game. The more I thought about it, the worse the situation became. After games I was worrying myself sick because I knew I could play better than I had. I would think to myself, "I cost all that money, I should be doing a lot more than that, I should be changing the game." As a result, I probably tried too hard to justify the fee and started doing things I wouldn't normally have done. It took over my football brain and scrambled my thinking. I strayed away from my tried and trusted way of playing and started trying to do other people's jobs. I got myself into the wrong areas and did the wrong things. I couldn't get it out of my mind that Ron had spent a hell of a lot of money on me and other players, so surely we should have been up there at the top. The weight of expectation was so much heavier at United because of the club's illustrious past. There was simply no escaping that heritage.'

The enforced winter break came at the right time, then. Robson could take stock of those first few weeks and realise that his team-mates were good enough to be there or thereabouts even accounting for his struggle to acclimatise. They could be trusted to do what came naturally to them, just as Robson was brought in to do the things that he did naturally.

United's FA Cup journey was over at the first hurdle, with a defeat at Watford in the third round. It ostensibly gave them a free run to concentrate on the league, but the truth is that it didn't work out in that way. United jostled for top spot with Southampton and Swansea, but Ipswich and Liverpool were lurking ominously in fifth and sixth place with numerous games in hand on the teams above them.

Atkinson was surpassing the expectations of himself and everyone else in his first year in charge, but he was still trying to deal with the composition of his squad. The signing of Moses and Robson was always going to see one extra midfielder leave, and when he was relegated to the reserves at the end of January Sammy McIlroy took it badly. He was transferred to Stoke City in haste and later regretted moving so quickly.

Atkinson was still sorting out his best team and shape. After a draw against Everton in early January, Paddy Barclay summarised United's issues: 'They missed too many chances, lacked a controlling influence in midfield and in defence found great difficulty in coping with the impressive Sharpe,' Barclay wrote in *The Guardian*.

Bryan Robson and Ray Wilkins were still getting used to each other at club level, and there were definite issues in the team's penetration up front, with Barclay noting that Steve Coppell had been 'brought back a little earlier than they would have liked' after a knee injury he'd picked up playing for England against Hungary.

In the February international break, England had used Ray Wilkins as a sweeper in a 4-0 win over Northern Ireland and national team boss Ron Greenwood suggested clubs should use the system. Atkinson had his own say: 'It can be a successful system – if you have the players to operate it. Whatever the label, crowds still basically want to see goals – mainly in opponents' nets.'

This was right around the time when United hit a bump in the road; the drop in form that most teams suffer. A run of four games in five without a goal started with defeat to Sexton's Coventry at Old Trafford. Rather fittingly, that game was played in front of the lowest attendance of the season; journalist Robert Armstrong said the majority of the 34,499 who were at the ground were 'howling in frustration by the end'.

By the time Liverpool visited Old Trafford on 7 April they were top, five points ahead of Atkinson's fifth-placed team.

'I maintained right from the start of the season that any team with championship ambitions will have to beat Liverpool,' the United boss said in his programme notes. 'I remember at Christmas when Manchester City beat Liverpool 3-0 and there were a few diehard United punters who didn't like the idea of our local rivals notching such a good result ... I'm only too grateful that we also took three points off them with a 2-1 win at Anfield in October. Perhaps that was also in the period when Liverpool were in something of a transitional stage with their team and they were still experimenting to find the right blend and balance from their squad. They will undoubtedly be here this evening full of the idea of revenge, and they may well have looked at our recent home record and come to the conclusion that they in turn have caught us at just the right time. I'm hoping, though, that we might have a surprise in store for them. Certainly four games at Old Trafford without a win must be regarded as a setback. But we have not been far short of winning those games; no one has come to Old Trafford and dominated us and in terms of dictating the play we have done well.'

Liverpool won a close game by a single goal. It put paid to any unrealistic hopes United fans might have had of their team staging a late push for the title, but they did at least see them hit strong form. From their last ten games, Atkinson's side won seven and drew two to finish in third, some seven points above Tottenham (but nine points behind champions Liverpool).

Spurs had been defeated 2-0 at Old Trafford on 17 April. 'They're the sort of side I'd like us to become,' Atkinson admitted after the game. 'We're not far short of their stage of development – and don't forget, they took three or four years to reach it.'

There had been definitive improvement and a step forward. United were more ambitious in their approach but their reshaping, and the lopsided team following the departure of McIlroy, as well as the pressure on Stapleton to carry the can up front despite the improvement of Birtles (who would be sold back to Forest in the off-season), meant goals were hard to come by. Just 59 had been scored in 42 games, though United did at least boast the best defensive record in the league, a residuary benefit of the Sexton era.

Atkinson had focussed mostly on replacing Joe Jordan and bringing Bryan Robson in to build around. Robson had grown into his role with ease and looked a safe bet; the fanfare associated with the record fee he arrived for had died down somewhat as he became the model of consistency. At the end of Ron Atkinson's first season, Robson wasn't even the centre of attention; that distinction went to 17-year-old Norman Whiteside, who had just broken into the first team and was about to drastically change United's woes up front.

Que Sera, Sera

AS THE curtain came down on Ron Atkinson's first year in charge of Manchester United, he could look back on a year which saw his side guaranteed third place whatever the result against Stoke City.

'We bring down the curtain on our season this afternoon on a note of satisfaction,' the manager wrote in his notes for the programme. 'I hope that doesn't sound TOO self-satisfied and I know that there must be a lot of you out there who would have liked us to be a little hotter on the heels of Liverpool. I certainly would, but to look at the situation realistically the important thing for Manchester United is that we have made progress in the last 12 months. The club is stronger than this time last year. Our squad at first-team level has a higher playing level, something which also goes further in depth now, thanks to the arrival of quality players … It would have been nice to have won the championship in my first season as manager at Old Trafford, and that was certainly the ambition, but looking at it now, it wouldn't really have been logical to come so far so quickly and I think we should simply take a lot of quiet satisfaction from the progress made so far. It's progress on a number of fronts as well. Brian Whitehouse has done a lot of good, solid work with the reserve team, while Eric Harrison brought us a touch of cup fever with the success of his boys in the FA Youth Cup.'

That success was getting to the final against Watford. United lost after a dramatic 7-6 aggregate result which went to extra time in the second leg. There were high hopes, though, for the likes of

Graeme Hogg, Billy Garton, Mark Dempsey, Norman Whiteside, Mark Hughes and Nicky Wood.

This was not just good timing. At the annual meeting at Old Trafford in early December 1981, Atkinson stated his intention for the future. 'Unless it is absolutely essential I aim to concentrate on a youth policy,' the manager said, though perhaps that was out of necessity rather than choice considering the club reported a loss of £277,582 for the financial year ending 31 May. 'When I came here the side were not really good enough, in my eyes, and I went for quality players at a time when they were available. I probably did two years' buying in three months and we are now seeing the results. The players I brought are young enough to serve the club for some years.'

Whiteside in particular caught the eye due to his physical stature and aggression, which made Harrison recommend him to Atkinson for fast-track development. Whiteside became the youngest player since Duncan Edwards to play for the first team when he came on as a substitute in the win at Brighton in April, two weeks shy of his 17th birthday. Eight days after his birthday, he became the youngest scorer in the history of Manchester United when he scored against Stoke in a 2-0 win which closed the season.

'By April 1982 I was seriously considering introducing Whiteside to the senior set-up,' Atkinson recalled. 'I made him substitute for the first team against Brighton on 24 April and in that game he came on for Mike Duxbury. A little later I called all of my coaching staff together to discuss whether Whiteside was ready for a full game. Most of them were not sure it was a good idea. They believed it was too early for him to be thrown into a full 90 minutes of rough-and-tumble First Division action. But I had a gut feeling about the boy: I was sure the time was right. I had watched him closely at both youth- and reserve-team level. Even at the age of 16 he always appeared to me to be a man among boys.'

The Belfast-born forward continued to break records that summer. He broke Pelé's record of being the youngest player to play at a World Cup; by the end of the tournament, he had played more times for his country than at club level, helping Northern Ireland get to the second group stage on a run which saw them defeat hosts Spain in a famous victory. He returned to Manchester tipped to be the first-choice strike partner for Frank Stapleton.

That might not have been the case. Atkinson had made a bold and controversial move in the post-season of 1982. 'I spent the entire summer giving careful consideration to ways and means of improving the side still further,' the manager said. 'I came to the decision that if I could sign Kevin Keegan from Southampton I would not only be bringing another great player into Old Trafford but also showing Liverpool and the rest of football that we really did mean business. Keegan's contract at Southampton had expired and he was searching for fresh inspiration. I held talks with him but was quickly to discover that his personal terms plus fees involved would cost United a minimum of £500,000. I considered the implications of the deal. As big a name as Keegan undoubtedly was, he could not, at Manchester United, bring many more people through the turnstiles. The support at Old Trafford was already handsome enough. Keegan would have virtually had to guarantee that he would win a major trophy for the club; no player in the world can make such assurances. I knew in my heart that, much as I would have liked him in my Manchester United team, there was no way I could justify going to my board of directors with the proposition in view of the necessary financial outlay ... Certainly I would dearly have loved to pair Keegan with Frank Stapleton at Old Trafford. The two of them would have produced a host of goals and excitement. Sadly, even for a club of United's magnitude, the idea was just not economically viable.'

In late July it was reported that United were set to take advantage of the financial difficulties at Wolves by signing their forward Andy Gray for a bargain fee of £300,000. 'Gray is just one of several players I am looking at to strengthen our squad,' Atkinson said coyly, though the move broke down due to an inability to make contact with Brian Clough, the Nottingham Forest boss, who was on holiday and in no mood to expedite the signing of Garry Birtles just to benefit United. *Economically viable* was the perfect description of the major signing United did make that summer; schemer Arnold Muhren's contract had expired at Ipswich Town and it was said he too was looking for a new challenge following the news that Bobby Robson was going to take the England job. Muhren later went on record as admitting that he felt the opportunity to join United would be his last chance to move to such a big club.

'As soon as United showed interest in me I was determined to go,' Muhren told the fanzine *Red News*. 'When a big club with such a tradition and charisma is willing to sign you, well, that's a once-in-a-lifetime opportunity, so no reason to hesitate. I was going to a big club and was looking forward to getting acquainted, but it wasn't all new to me of course as I had been to Old Trafford before during my spell with Ipswich Town and the ground and its supporters were awesome, very impressive! So I was so happy and proud to be part of it.'

He was 31, so most certainly not a long-term solution to United's left-sided issue, but Atkinson's need was urgent and Muhren was a perfect fit. 'Arnold Muhren is a Dutch master and when his contract expired with Ipswich I didn't hesitate for a second in setting out to bring him to Old Trafford,' Atkinson admitted. 'I had been constantly on the look-out for a left-sided player to improve the overall balance of the side and Muhren fitted the bill beautifully. He never has and never will be the most physical of players, but to me he has brought art and beauty into the game. I can sit and watch him all day when he gets that left foot working as though it were a magic wand. He produces wonderful passes and has such exquisite control of the ball.'

The same could be said of Ray Wilkins; Atkinson had developed a greater appreciation for the midfielder in their year together, and even felt suitably convinced of his seniority to name him captain in the absence of Martin Buchan. At the age of 33, and due to some injury problems, Buchan was now in the final stages of transitioning to the reserve team, where his considerable experience and consummate professionalism would prove valuable for young players coming through.

'It was a great experience, with great experience you were playing alongside. Martin Buchan was coming towards the end when I was coming through, and I played with Gordon McQueen and Kevin Moran in defence as well,' Graeme Hogg remembers. 'Remi Moses was in and out of the team. The senior pros brought the young lads through really well, there was always only encouragement, no slacking off.'

Wilkins had blossomed with the responsibility. His form improved, though it has to be said it is clear that Atkinson felt he deserved some of the credit for it. 'My opinion of him was that he was failing to employ his considerable abilities as a creative player because of an infuriating habit of continually playing the ball across the field,' Ron said. 'I deliberately attempted to rile him by nicknaming him "the crab". It might seem a little cruel now, but I believe there was much more affection and concern for the welfare of the player in my little jibe than in Tommy Docherty's barbed comment that the only time Wilkins went forward during a game was to toss a coin at the kick-off. It is certainly true that Wilkins had to be constantly reminded to be much more positive with his passing, but United's purchase of Frank Stapleton seemed to help him cure himself of the "sideways bug" ... He grew to have a tremendous rapport with the Old Trafford crowd, who quickly sensed and appreciated his vast improvement. Previously the United public had not been so kind. There was one occasion when a cricket match had been played on the United pitch; the 22-yard strip of carpeting put down to form a wicket had left a clear imprint in the centre circle and one terrace wag shouted, "Blimey, they've even marked out a pitch for Wilkins to play now!"'

One can't help but think that with Wilkins in good form, and the classy Muhren now in the fold, United had a team that could play the Continental style of football Dave Sexton had craved. But the side that lined up to face Birmingham City at Old Trafford on the opening day of the season had a distinctly 'Ron Atkinson' feel to it: Bailey in goal; Duxbury, Moran, McQueen and Albiston in defence; Coppell (wearing number 11 on the right of midfield), Robson (in his number seven shirt), Wilkins and Muhren in midfield; Whiteside and Stapleton up front. Paddy Barclay felt United were 'in a more promising position at any time since Sir Matt Busby brought the European Cup to Old Trafford in 1968', saying Atkinson's squad 'looks capable not only of making a challenge for the championship, but, more important, playing a stylish and imaginative game worthy of setting before Britain's largest football audience.'

Just two players remained from the team which had won the FA Cup five years previously, and one of those, Steve Coppell, was going to face a professional tragedy in the coming months. You would not have thought it going by his form; he scored against Birmingham in a 3-0 win and again in a convincing win by the same scoreline at Nottingham Forest four days later. On 11 September, Coppell got one and Whiteside got two in a thumping win over Ipswich.

'We started the season convincingly enough,' said Ron Atkinson. 'Overall I was reasonably happy because the new signings had settled in admirably and a midfield blend was beginning to look better and better. Then a goalless draw with Liverpool, at Anfield, confirmed our right to lead the table. I had been expecting that result to inspire us further, but the reverse proved to be true.'

From then on, in fact, United's away form in the league was pretty dreadful. There were nine defeats and just two wins from their remaining 15 games on the road after the draw at Anfield on 16 October 1982. In addition, Valencia eliminated United in the first round of the UEFA Cup. The club were fined £1,350 due to supporter trouble in Spain, though there was no further action taken.

This was the second of what would be five seasons at Manchester United under Ron Atkinson and he had said from day one that his intention was to win the league. Third place in 1982 had been a fine start, taking everything into consideration, and in the pursuit of an explanation for why the team failed to win the league, well, it seems fair enough to reason that Atkinson was dealing with a team in transition and, after selling Sammy McIlroy, had to try to compensate for a glaring deficiency on the left side of attack.

With a year under his belt, and a lot of money given to him to bring in Stapleton, Robson, Moses and Muhren, the manager was under a little more pressure to provide an explanation for stuttering form. There were a few reasons. Norman Whiteside and Frank Stapleton were given the responsibility of leading the line for an entire season, which was a lot of expectation on the shoulders of a 17-year-old, no matter how high his potential. The veteran Lou Macari and the rookie Scott McGarvey made only a handful of appearances each to alleviate some of that pressure. McGarvey and Whiteside served as examples that Atkinson would give an opportunity to young players, and it was only fair that such patience and understanding was afforded to the manager as it was to the players who were adjusting to the rigours of playing for the most famous club in the country.

In a goalless draw against Arsenal in September, Atkinson played a 4-3-3 system as Coppell and Muhren were injured. Young Peter Bodak, the former Coventry winger, had signed for United on a free transfer in the summer but was not considered ready to step up despite scoring in his first two reserve games. Bodak was allowed to join Manchester City in November. Instead, the pressure remained on Whiteside, who 'was again United's greatest threat, at least until his lack of experience induced desperation in the second half' against Arsenal according to Paddy Barclay.

Barclay was more enthusiastic about United's performance in the Manchester derby a month later, saying supporters were 'richly entertained'. 'A wall of noise, formidable even by the standards to which they have been accustomed, greeted Manchester United and their response was a performance that in other circumstances would have brought colossal victory,' wrote Barclay. 'Their denial was due to goalkeeping of breathtaking quality by Corrigan.'

In fact, City looked like they would snatch a smash-and-grab win; they were improbably 2-0 up in the 48th minute before a Stapleton double rescued a point.

Despite concerns to the contrary, United hadn't necessarily suffered from a lack of goals – their only blanks so far coming against Arsenal and Liverpool. The genuine concern was what if Stapleton was injured, or who was there to pick up the slack to take the pressure off Whiteside to provide a moment of magic. The answer for many was in the feet of another young forward who had been recently signed and put into the reserve side – Peter Beardsley. The 21-year-old had been signed from Vancouver Whitecaps and had made an instant impression, scoring a hat-trick in a reserve game against Stoke City.

This story, and Beardsley's career in general, make the story of his Old Trafford spell all the more confusing. It is listed as an aberration on behalf of Atkinson, but some context has to be applied. In isolation, Beardsley scoring a hat-trick for the second string suggests he was much too good for that level, and history has proven that to be true. But he was competing for a forward place, even at that level, with Scott McGarvey and Mark Hughes. McGarvey was prolific and Hughes was sensational; both of them were getting their own share of goals, and when Liverpool's reserve side were beaten 6-1 in early November, it was McGarvey and Hughes rather than Beardsley who were the standout performers.

In midfield, Beardsley was hardly likely to displace Coppell (though a little bit of patience might have helped all parties in this regard), there was no way he would have got in front of Robson or Wilkins, or even Moses, while he would have been understudy too for Muhren. Even in the reserves there was Clayton Blackmore, Alan Davies and Paul McGrath who would all have a decent shout of getting selected if a spot became available in the first team.

'I often played against Peter Beardsley in training, he was a nice lad but in terms of being able to predict what he would go on to do in the game, he seemed a million miles away from that level. He caused me no issue,' remembers Graeme Hogg. 'It's a similar story with David Platt, who couldn't even get in our Youth Cup team in 1983. He left and went to Crewe and everything worked out for him but it was hard to believe from either of them at the time.' Beardsley made one League Cup appearance before being allowed to return to Vancouver.

In October the club held their annual meeting, where Martin Edwards stood before shareholders to announce what *The Guardian* described as 'the biggest loss in the history of British football'. Edwards tried to explain that the £2.3m deficit was now more like £1m after player sales and a new sponsorship deal with Sharp Electronics were taken into account. Ron Atkinson was also present and insisted that the team he had inherited had required 'major surgery' when he took over. One supporter stood up and replied, 'The next time we need major surgery, could we have it on the National Health?!'

The jab was thrown in good humour, though, as most accepted United were on a positive trajectory. At the end of that month, sportswriter Robert Armstrong reasoned that Atkinson's tenure required the First Division, 'or at least the FA Cup', to show for it in the summer of 1983 or it would be another year of failure. 'For a club that has to look back 15 years to its last league title, United's sense of their own worth at times seems absurd, rather like England's claim to be a leading soccer nation,' Armstrong blasted.

United went down 3-1 in a controversial game at Upton Park on 30 October. Just after half-time, Ashley Grimes – in for the injured

Wilkins – was punished for handball when the ball struck his elbow in the box. The Hammers scored the penalty; three minutes later, referee Dennis Hodges refused to award the visitors a spot kick in a similar position and Grimes was incensed. He remonstrated physically, and though the United camp vehemently denied intent, his hand struck the head of the referee; Hodges wasted no time in ordering Grimes from the field.

'As the referee spun round, Ashley's hands made contact with Mr Hedges's head,' Bryan Robson insisted after. 'The referee said, "You hit me – I'm sending you off."'

Atkinson admitted he hadn't seen the incident Grimes was complaining about but defended his player. 'It wasn't as bad as it looked and he definitely didn't mean to do anything violent,' he said. 'He will be disciplined by the club for being sent off but I hope he doesn't get into any worse trouble.'

Grimes was charged with misconduct; in late November he was hit with the biggest fine the Football Association had ever imposed on a player, £750, and banned for two further matches.

The United boss was more concerned with what he described as defending like 'kamikaze pilots' at the Boleyn; one player safe from criticism was Martin Buchan, making one of his final appearances for the club. Buchan was called upon again for the trip to Watford in early December. The Hornets were surprising everyone under Graham Taylor and had already enjoyed a high-profile victory over United in the FA Cup in January of that year. 'It's a bit of a surprise when you first play against them,' Bryan Robson confessed. 'First Division teams are used to opponents who play the ball through the middle and suddenly it's being knocked in high behind you. It's not so much the high ball that is the problem, more the quality of the knockdowns and the way they use them.'

United won 1-0, a goal from Norman Whiteside on the hour earning a very good result, though the visitors were somewhat fortunate that Gary Bailey wasn't sent off for handball outside the area. Atkinson felt Gordon McQueen's height played a big factor in dealing with Watford's aerial threat. 'No matter what anybody says, he's a bit of a lighthouse. He can see everything when it's upstairs,' Atkinson said. 'You have to have somebody at the back who can head the ball well and today McQueen did that when we needed him most.'

Vicarage Road was the venue for Buchan's 456th and final appearance for Manchester United. The clean sheet and victory, coming in a game where United's defensive mettle was under intense scrutiny, was a fitting testament to the legendary centre-half's career. Buchan saw out the rest of the season at Old Trafford in the reserve side.

He had been replaced by Ray Wilkins as captain of the first team, but by December 1982 Wilkins too had felt the disappointment of losing the armband. This was not due to a loss of form, or Atkinson returning to his earlier critical opinion of the midfielder.

'I confess I have nothing but admiration for the dignity and professionalism of a player who has fought his way back so magnificently,' Atkinson said of Wilkins. 'He was the Manchester United and England captain until sustaining a bad facial injury at Bournemouth when playing for United in a Milk Cup tie late in 1982. In his enforced absence from the teams he lost both jobs to Bryan Robson and was unable to recover them. He even lost his place in the United team when he had been restored to full fitness. Wilkins undoubtedly suffered severe mental torment because of this; it was a traumatic time in his career. Hs belief and attitude were a marvellous example to any youngster. He buckled down to the task of proving that he was the best man for the job in our team. He succeeded as well, through sheer courage and conviction. So rare is the personality of a man like Wilkins that through all the bad times he still continued to be one of the main off-the-field leaders. I used to tell Robson always to look at and listen to Wilkins, and he has subsequently learnt much about the art of captaincy from him. The two lads had played for England at youth and senior level and there was a strong mutual admiration. Ray is now the player his abilities demand he should be. He has marvellous control of the ball, great vision, undeniable authority and plays positive passes whenever possible.'

Wilkins's return to the first team was not fantastic. Consecutive goalless draws at Swansea and at home to Sunderland had come either side of Christmas, and Wilkins was back in a heavily rotated team that went to Highfield Road the day after the Sunderland game. It was a game packed with ironies; United, who had recently drawn a crowd of just over 33,000 for the game against Notts

County in mid-December, were up against a team who, under Dave Sexton, had their highest gate of the season. Much of that owed to the identity of the opposition but the home fans were rewarded by what *The Guardian* described thus: 'Dave Sexton's stylish side brought wit and imagination to a performance which had one wondering which manager had spent a few million pounds in the drive for success.'

Sexton would have felt sympathetic in that Gary Bailey and Ray Wilkins – two players he had given Old Trafford careers to – were culpable for first-half goals which put his team in the ascendancy. A 3-0 victory for Coventry was achieved in the second half and United were now eight points behind Liverpool.

The match was an exposing of United's squad strength. Whiteside and Muhren had been rested and McGarvey and Grimes were just not ready to step in and replace players of that calibre.

Also sorely missed was Steve Coppell, who would return imminently but not for long. He was back in the team for the win over Aston Villa on New Year's Day, and, what's more, scored what many decree to be the finest goal of his career. His left-footed long-range drive in the 64th minute secured all three points for Atkinson's side. Stapleton got two in a 3-1 win, but Paddy Barclay said: 'Ron Atkinson's side could well have recorded something closer to the rugby score they had threatened in the previous home match against Sunderland.'

With Coppell and Muhren on song, United were fantastic to watch. Remi Moses, alongside Robson, was also the recipient of praise from Barclay. 'United's midfield displayed a width and balance that makes it difficult to envisage where Wilkins could be fitted in,' he wrote. 'Certainly Atkinson will not wish to lose Moses's ball-winning qualities and he would be making a mistake if he deemed Muhren a luxury because the Dutchman's subtlety is beginning to rub off on the team.'

Villa were European Champions and had just come back from winning the Intercontinental Cup; they were a sizeable scalp, and proof that United, with a full complement, were a match for anyone. Barclay was in attendance to watch United take on West Ham in the FA Cup. Coppell scored an outstanding goal again and Barclay wrote that the winger 'still nagged by soreness in his left knee, can seldom have played better'. Muhren and Moses were also lauded, though Barclay did surmise that United could do with more experience up front. 'Whiteside is an admirable young player but he is beginning to look more and more like a 17-year-old as his touch deserts him and should be replaced for a while by Macari,' he wrote.

In mid-January, Brazilian club Flamengo offered to assist on that front when they offered United the opportunity to sign their 29-year-old striker Nunes for £375,000. Nunes was very proficient in the domestic game but did not make the impact many thought he should for the national team, though this was deemed to be because he was more of an English-style attacker. Ron Atkinson did consider making an offer, but ultimately decided it would be too much of a risk. Despite the problems of inconsistency and occasional profligacy, he was building a team that was playing some fantastic football.

Whiteside gave a good response to any critics by scoring in United's 2-1 win over Birmingham on 15 January. Peter Ball, reporting for *The Observer*, went on record to give Atkinson's team just about the highest praise anyone could muster: 'Recently, and somewhat surprisingly, a colleague compared this United team not unfavourably with the Munich side. Even if one accepted the individual comparisons, all that exercise proved is that a great team is more than the sum of its parts. A more pertinent comparison with the present Liverpool side suggests the same conclusion, for it is possible to make out a strong case on paper for United being stronger in all departments except at the front. United's defence, though, stands comparison with Liverpool. In goal Bailey has the safer hands and better judgement and his agility, certainly the equal of Grobbelaar's, showing through with two stunning saves.'

Even Paddy Barclay, despite retaining belief that it would be wise for Whiteside to be rested, did praise the Ulsterman for turning from 'an ugly duckling' into a 'swan, flying free in the penalty area, past Young and then Gray, whose mistimed attempt at a tackle brought United their breakthrough from the penalty spot' against Nottingham Forest. Coppell scored from the spot in the 64th minute to dampen the growing anxiety and United began to play some good football; Muhren scored six minutes later to secure a good win.

That Old Trafford victory was earned in front of just 38,615 supporters; the coming weeks would see even lower attendances, with a game on 22 March against West Ham attracting just 30,227 to the 'Theatre of Dreams'. This was comfortably lower than even the worst days under Dave Sexton, so what were the reasons for this decline? They had, after all, been compared favourably with the best teams in the country, and even the best team in their own history, in recent weeks. If such comments were over the top, then the pre-season assessments that the club were in the best place they had been since the summer of 1977 did at least seem fair. Surely the biggest reason, though, was the staggering, skyrocket price increases for match tickets which coincided with the recession in 1980 and the start of 1981. Season tickets in 1977 were priced between £26 and £32; for the 1982/83 season, the price range was £64 to £76. There had been incremental price rises through the years but it was unprecedented for them to have more than doubled in such a short space of time. United had started extending their Main Stand in the summer of 1980 but the truth was that all of football was affected by these financial changes and the ticket prices at Old Trafford were not even the highest in the country.

The only time there was a rise which was comparable was from 1987 to 1992, when season ticket prices went from £96–114 to £280. Then, supporters had the comfort of watching the best team in the country. In truth, though United's attendances were lower than they had been, this was more of a social and economic issue that afflicted football as a sport; within the context of football, their gates were still the strongest.

The recession and price rises must have affected attendances in the Sexton era too, though there were in-season declines which meant it was difficult to attribute the drop to much else than the poor style. At least, that was the primary reason. United then had sacrificed their style for functionality; one sure sign of a very good team is their ability to play in more than one fashion, and having been applauded for their expansive and creative play, Ron Atkinson's side showed they were still capable of looking after themselves if it came to a physical battle, which is precisely what they were faced with at Kenilworth Road in the fourth round of the FA Cup.

After a war of attrition in the first half, United started the second period well, with Moses scoring within a minute of the restart. A Kevin Moran goal in injury time secured progression. 'For all their dominance, United's football was far from exhilarating, especially in the first half, when Moses and Robson led the kind of dour midfield dogfight that drove fans away in their thousands in the 70s,' sportswriter Robert Armstrong reported. 'Ironically, the grim professionalism that marks United nowadays strongly resembles the functional style that earned Dave Sexton's team the league runners-up position in 1980.'

United, though, were merely able to show this side of their game, rather than it being the prevailing quality. Atkinson was not disappointed; he described Remi Moses as 'as good a player as we've ever had' after a fantastic showing. It was indeed a testament to how far they'd come that they were able to mix it up and come through games like those against Luton and Watford; a reminder of how far they had yet to go came at Ipswich Town. John Wark's performance put Robson in the shade for once; he scored a spectacular overhead kick just before half-time, but Ipswich should have been handsomely ahead at the interval and would have been if not for the brilliance of Gary Bailey in goal.

'We just didn't turn up,' Atkinson said of the first-half performance. 'At half-time we had a few words with people who were not playing as well as they could and, after that, full marks.'

A goal from Stapleton less than 60 seconds after the restart restored parity but a competitive second half ended with neither team managing to grab a second. United paid the price for their inability to find any sort of consistency on the road, as Liverpool won again to solidify their place at the top of the table. They had a 12-point advantage now, and United were in second; an equally telling statistic was in the 'goals scored' column, with Liverpool having scored a remarkable 63 after 22 games, and United the lowest scorers in the top six with just 36, despite their imaginative play.

Clearly a league title challenge was out of the question. But while nobody would hide from the fact that Atkinson was being asked to win the league, it remained important for United to have a clear sense of identity. The 25th anniversary of the Munich air disaster was the first major milestone in an end-of-season run that would have a few more.

'It's right, there should be precious memories about Munich for our fans,' Ron Atkinson told Steve Curry of *The Express* after United had drawn 1-1 at Ipswich. 'It's part of what makes Manchester United great, and what makes mine the best job in football.'

Curry confessed it was difficult to compare the teams of today and yesteryear, whilst acknowledging the unique pressure the Manchester United players must be under: 'Living with legend, matching a memory that has gathered mystique is a burden Manchester United must always carry. But the boys who watch them still share the same common commitment to the cause.'

There was some poetic symmetry in how events unfolded. The Babes' last game on British soil before Munich was at Highbury. It just so happened that this would be the next game for United in February 1983, in the first leg of the Milk Cup semi-final. They hadn't won at Arsenal for 15 years, when Sir Matt Busby was manager, before they'd even won the European Cup, and Atkinson's side had only won five games from 17 away fixtures in all competitions in the 1982/83 season so far.

Norman Whiteside was suffering from some difficulties, too; the rare flashes of brilliance were starting to feel like the exception, with the struggle the norm. The player conceded in his biography that the poor run of form had a 'psychological effect'. He was not helped by the words of his colleague Frank Stapleton, who insisted Atkinson was not a man with a long-term plan, and intimated that if Whiteside didn't pull himself out of it, he was likely to be replaced rather than coached to improvement. To his credit, Whiteside saw the threat and rose to the challenge.

It wasn't so much that a statement performance was needed by player or club, but it arrived nonetheless to effectively announce Ron Atkinson's United some 20 months after the manager had taken charge.

'We went to Highbury and produced one of the most devastating displays of power football I have ever witnessed,' Atkinson recalled. 'With ten minutes remaining of that away leg, we were four goals in the clear through Whiteside, Stapleton and Coppell [who took two] but in no way resting on our laurels. If ever I needed a positive demonstration that the players were determined not to be moved from their Wembley objective, it was most certainly provided in the Highbury dressing rooms after that game. Arsenal managed to flatter themselves by pulling back two goals late in the game from Tony Woodcock and Peter Nicholas, but not a single word of criticism was required from me. I thought the atmosphere would have been one of great elation at such a marvellous performance; instead the room was filled with sweat-stained footballers criticising and quarrelling with each other about the goals that had got away. The angry scene filled me with faith and hope for the future. Teams which win the major prizes must display a hard professional attitude, with each other.'

United aggressively pushed high up the field from the early stages. Whiteside, having gone close early on (with a shot that was saved, but not rewarded with a corner), struck in the 18th minute after a fine pass from Remi Moses. Stapleton then struck before the break as Whiteside turned provider. Steve Coppell, a semi-final hero of years gone by, got a brace in the second period to leave the hosts shell-shocked. Mike Duxbury could have made it five when he went on a remarkable dribble, beating three players and exchanging passes with the relentlessly creative Whiteside, only to see his effort tipped around the post.

The Gunners recovered with those two late goals but United's biggest headache, though they weren't to know it at the time, was the start of a running issue between the home players and Moses. After Peter Nicholas appeared to swing an elbow at Moses, the United midfielder responded by seemingly pushing his head in a 'butt' fashion. Moses then had to be held by the referee following a goalmouth scramble, where the United man had tried a shot but had been aggressively (but, apparently, not too aggressively) knocked off the ball by Kenny Sansom. Perhaps feeling as if he was being targeted, Moses exacted some personal revenge by injuring David O'Leary in a tackle. The former West Brom man might have won the battle and the war in the short term; he was never one to pick a fight, but come the end of the season it might well have been one he regretted getting involved in.

Cup fever continued to affect United as they travelled to Derby in the FA Cup in a repeat of the 1976 semi-final; remarkably, only Steve Coppell remained in the United team from that game. He was interviewed by *The Guardian* ahead of the match and quizzed on aspects of the evolution of the game in the intervening years. He spoke about how his own position had changed: 'An out-and-out winger can be the icing on the cake for a team if the other ten are prepared to support him. Forest did it successfully with John Robertson for a time, but even that had to change. Maybe United could do it – if they can get the right man. But my game is horses for courses. There are certain games when you know you are going to get joy from a full-back; other games, you're not.'

Another way the game was moving forward was the increasing number of games being shown on television. At a time when club owners were already concerned about huge drops in attendance, they were against more exposure on television as they reasoned that would only have a further negative impact. Coppell agreed with them. 'I'd like less football on television,' he said. 'Highlights of one game on each channel would be enough. But I'd keep the Saturday morning previews because they give people an appetite for the live game.'

It was that appetite in the short term that Atkinson was banking on from his players, though he listed three other attributes beginning with the letter 'a' as he spoke to reporters the day before the trip to the Baseball Ground.

'My players had better realise they have got to get their heads out of the clouds at Derby,' he said. 'Yes, we touched brilliance at Arsenal. Now we must reassess the situation and get our application, approach and attitude right all over again for Derby ... Our fans who went to Highbury will be there again tomorrow. They are the best in the land. Their job is to get behind us, realise this is a different situation. With their backing there is no reason why we can't compete in two Wembley finals this season. It can be done.'

Football has a wonderful way of providing all manner of victories that can send supporters delirious; the emphatic statement, a spectacular winning goal or a late, late show. At Derby, United fans were treated to the latter, and it was Whiteside who struck in the 84th minute to show he was as multitalented as his team-mates. The 1-0 win left Atkinson just as pleased as he had been a few days earlier. 'We've got the bit between our teeth at the moment,' he grinned. 'For a long time we played quite well but now we've got the belief that we're as good as most if not better than most. Now we've got a lot of natural competitiveness in the side. We can play but we're also prepared to sweat a bit.'

After seeing his team drawn against Everton in the next round of the FA Cup, the United boss was confident that his prediction would come true. 'It's looking good. The important thing is that we will be playing at Old Trafford after having to travel to Derby and Luton in the last two rounds.'

The big games kept coming. United were preparing to take on Arsenal in the second leg of the Milk Cup semi-final, and Ron had said that his team would be 'going all out to kill them off in the first 20 minutes'; all the goalscoring action took place in the *last* 20 minutes, whilst both sets of players took the killing part a little too literally with another scrap that Paddy Barclay described as 'intensely, often excessively, physical'. It started in the 11th minute when Robson was injured in a tackle and had to come off. There was an able replacement in Ray Wilkins, but Robson would be out for a month with ankle ligament damage. Moses was once more the target of Arsenal players' ire, with Talbot and Nicholas roughing him up. United responded in the most positive manner, scoring through Coppell to finally settle the tie in the 73rd minute. Arsenal equalised, but an injury-time winner from Moran added a little spectacular gloss to proceedings.

It was injury time again for Moran three days later against Liverpool, but this time in the more traditional manner one would associate with the Irishman; less than half an hour had been played against the league leaders when the defender had to come off with a cut shin which required nine stitches. He had earlier suffered a gash on his head.

Atkinson had described the encounter as another cup game. 'If we win, we will be in clinging distance,' he said. 'You can call this match the First Division's cup final.'

United scored in the 35th minute through Muhren, but the visitors levelled before half-time through Dalglish. The game finished level. There was no replay as there are in cup competitions and so Liverpool were able to bask in the glory of a 14-point gap at the top of the table.

Robson's absence hadn't affected United too much against Liverpool as the home players were pumped up for the occasion; it was a different case at Stoke the following week when Atkinson's men fell 1-0. A derby at Maine Road was enough to lift the spirits once more and United overcame an early deficit to win 2-1 thanks to a Frank Stapleton double. They needed Stapleton again a week later when they took on Everton at home in the cup. In injury time, as Atkinson threw everything in search of a winning goal, he made a bold move. United won a corner and the manager signalled to Mike Duxbury to come off. Lou Macari, his replacement, chested down a ball from Wilkins. The ball fell perfectly for Stapleton, who showed fine invention to volley the ball across goal into the top corner. Old Trafford erupted with a noise that can only be generated by the intensity of a knockout competition and the fine balance between victory and defeat.

'The substitution was a desperate gamble,' Atkinson admitted. 'We had a corner so I thought I'd throw Macari on. Duxbury was the nearest player to the touchline so I took him off. Lou's stamina is a bit suspect, so we only put him on for the last minute and a half. He's in the dressing room now, physically exhausted, shattered.'

Duxbury didn't see the funny side: 'I asked Ron right away, "Why did you take me off?" – he said it was because I was the nearest player ... which would have been okay if I hadn't literally just walked past three players to come off. I was at right-back and we were attacking the Stretford End – I couldn't have been further away! I would have taken any excuse but to just blatantly lie was ridiculous.'

It may have come as a particular blow for Duxbury, who was enjoying his best run of form at the club. Having overcome the initial blow of John Gidman's arrival, Duxbury had stood up to the competition and deserved his place in the team. He did acknowledge that he could have little complaint on this occasion as Atkinson's gamble had been a winning one. It seems likely that Atkinson said the first thing that came into his head rather than being deceptive, though this incident, coupled with Stapleton's warnings to Whiteside earlier in the campaign, as well as some events which were to follow before the end of the season, did appear to point towards the short-term nature of the manager's thinking.

It was a flat performance which followed against Brighton a week later. Robson was not yet back, Moses was suspended after an accumulation of yellow cards, while Moran and McQueen were also on the sidelines. With so many players missing it was no wonder Atkinson moaned 'we were like strangers' after the game. The 1-1 draw was unimpressive to the United fans who, according to *The Guardian*'s Charles Burgess, booed Ray Wilkins for a pensive display in the centre of the park. United were scheduled to play Liverpool in the Milk Cup Final the following week, with a game against West Ham in the midweek build-up before it. Atkinson described that as Wilkins's 'chance to redeem himself', though as he confirmed Robson would not be back in time for the game at Wembley, he knew that he would have little choice but to play the cultured midfielder.

It wasn't Robson or Wilkins who was the main talk as United took on the Hammers; it wasn't even a player who played at all, but instead, Laurie Cunningham, the Real Madrid winger who Atkinson had worked with at West Brom. Cunningham had suffered knee cartilage issues for almost two years and Atkinson signed him on loan with an option of a permanent agreement. 'First I want to see how he goes,' Ron said. He would need a few weeks of training before he would be ready to take part in a game in England.

United won 2-1 against West Ham but the victory gave nothing away in terms of who had played their way into Atkinson's Wembley team. Moses was back from suspension against the Hammers and would play against Liverpool. Whiteside would come back in for Scott McGarvey (McGarvey scored against West Ham, so might have felt his own nose pushed out of joint a little), while Paul McGrath might have found his axing a little unfortunate too. Duxbury had played alongside him at centre-half, but moved to right-back to play at Wembley, and Moran and McQueen were back from injury for the final.

'No one should doubt that, in Liverpool and Manchester United, the old League Cup has as its finalists the finest the domestic game has to offer,' reported Steve Curry.

Liverpool were strolling towards the title and United were banking on some complacency coming into their game; the league leaders had drawn their previous two games and had recently been eliminated from the European Cup by Widzew Łódź (who, you may recall, had eliminated United from the UEFA Cup in 1980).

For their part, United were not quite riding the same wave of momentum as they had been when they faced their biggest rivals on this stage in the 1977 FA Cup Final. They were, however, probably feeling in better shape than they had been in 1979. And this was undoubtedly their pinnacle so far under Ron Atkinson. It was Atkinson's own pinnacle so far too, and inevitably he was profiled by the press ahead of the occasion.

'Friends say that when coaching at United's training ground, The Cliff, he lives out his playing fantasies with his team of superstars,' Charles Burgess wrote in *The Guardian*. 'He can be heard giving a commentary to himself as he takes part in the daily five-a-sides ... "and it's Atkinson with a quick one-two with Stapleton ... He's past the goalkeeper and gooaaalll! The World Cup is in the bag ..." – just like every kid on every piece of wasteland in the country. Tactically Atkinson is astute, but players say that his main ability is to make some of his confidence rub off on them. They are allowed to play their own game. Typical are the performances he has wrung from Remi Moses, who along with his midfield partner Bryan Robson, followed Atkinson from West Bromwich Albion... Atkinson receives press at The Cliff just after he has changed from his tracksuit, showered, carefully coiffured his hair á la Bobby Charlton, and donned a red towelling bathrobe with the United crest on the breast. He orders tea all round and forgoes sugar for saccharine.'

The characterisation of Ron Atkinson as some sort of real life version of Brian Glover's Mr Sugden from the movie adaptation of *Kes* seems a little unfair, not to mention unkind. It certainly is fair to acknowledge Atkinson's personality as being part of the reason why he was hired, but Martin Edwards immediately understood that to be one facet of the man he was hiring. 'Ron was a football man, enthusiastic, and, yes, a larger-than-life character. But underneath that image, which I don't think did him justice, he was a very serious football man,' Edwards says. 'He liked attacking football and loved wingers. He was popular with the players. My impression of him was good right from the off.'

Atkinson himself knew that there was extra scrutiny on the personality of the man in the dugout at Old Trafford, in a way that wasn't the case at any other clubs. He interpreted that in a way that was similar to Docherty; by acting as the face to live up to the position of figurehead. If it was done to cultivate that attention and indulge in it, then there was an effective tool in there too. 'Whatever the situation was, you adapted to it,' Atkinson says. 'I didn't want to see players coming to training as if they were entering a prisoner of war camp. I wanted people to want to be there.'

And, for the most part, the players did want to be there, and they did respond. Sure, there were individual queries, mostly kept private, such as Duxbury's curiosity about just why Atkinson felt the need to be the man of the match in training – but even Duxbury conceded that there were benefits to the manager's approach. 'He wasn't as serious as other managers but he was probably not as flashy as he came across,' he admitted. 'To be fair, we played the best football under Ron definitely. So within reason, him going into greater detail didn't need to happen that often. He trusted us and we were capable.'

Going into the 1983 Milk Cup Final, Atkinson was confident his team were more than capable. 'We were ready and waiting for Liverpool that day and I suspected they could sense our intense determination,' he said. 'I looked carefully at all of my players. They were totally relaxed and ready for their big moment.'

As the teams took to the field, BBC commentator John Motson remarked upon the various newsworthy items to take from the game; that it was likely to be Bob Paisley's last Wembley game as a manager, as Atkinson was making his own first appearance; that Duxbury, Whiteside and Moses would be making their own Wembley bows; that goalkeepers Bailey and Grobbelaar were actually facing each other in a game in South Africa when United and Liverpool met in the 1977 FA Cup Final.

Their rise to fame had not been anywhere near as rapid as Whiteside's, and the 17-year-old made another historic contribution in the 12th minute. Closely marked by Liverpool legend Alan Hansen, Whiteside expertly controlled a long pass from McQueen with the sort of authority you would expect from a player ten years older. He turned Hansen inside out before slotting in coolly from the edge of the area. Just a year earlier he hadn't even played for the Manchester United first team. In fact, in March 1982 he wasn't even playing for the reserve side; his most senior appearance had been scoring two in the fourth-round replay of an FA Youth Cup tie against QPR.

Sadly, United's path to glorious destiny was not quite in sync. Bailey evoked memories of 1979 when he missed a cross but Liverpool were unable to convert the chance. They were, however, able to make their greater experience count. United seemed to be holding on until Kevin Moran was forced to come off in the 69th minute. Shortly after that, Gordon McQueen hurt his hamstring. Unable to make another change, McQueen was pushed up front and Atkinson was forced to play Duxbury and striker Frank Stapleton in defence. The reshaping hurt United badly; within six minutes Liverpool equalised, and threatened to win the game as Atkinson's men struggled to cope. They took it to extra time, but Ronnie Whelan scored a fine effort and United were unable to muster up the energy to fight back. Bizarrely, McQueen might have helped United's attacking cause; on one break, he appeared to be clear but Grobbelaar came out and brought him down. It seemed a certain red card but referee George Courtney decided to show only a yellow.

McQueen afterwards sportingly insisted he was glad that the Liverpool goalkeeper had not been sent off. Atkinson was equally magnanimous, citing Liverpool's winning experience as crucial and saying, 'If you want to get beat by anybody, he's the man' in reference to Paisley.

In his 1984 book *United to Win*, Atkinson recalled the events of the game: 'Looking back, I believe we were simply destined not to win. Norman Whiteside has provided the kind of story required with a superb goal after just 12 minutes. As could be expected, Liverpool stepped up the pace and the pressure but failed to cause us concern. We concentrated on forcing them to play the ball out to the wings and it was working perfectly. They were not making goalscoring chances and were becoming more frustrated by the minute. The gamer moved into the last 20 minutes when tragedy struck a double blow. Suddenly we had two players vital to our defences struggling badly through injury. Kevin Moran was forced to hobble off with damage to a leg and Gordon McQueen pulled a hamstring ... It was then that Liverpool hit us with an equaliser ... Yet, disorganised as we were with players cruelly put into team positions to which they were not accustomed, even the mighty Liverpool could not break through again before the end of normal time. Some of our men were exhausted by then. They had run themselves into the ground in the bid to shore up our defences, following the injuries to Moran and McQueen. Our only hope was somehow to survive the 30 minutes and bank on winning a replay. But it was just not to be.

'I don't think I have ever been the kind of manager to hide behind excuses, but I was bitterly disappointed at the reasons for our defeat. Fate had been against us and there was absolutely nothing we could have done about it ... My players were shattered by the experience. As Liverpool paraded the Milk Cup, our dressing room back in the bowels of the stadium was eerily silent. The players slumped down in disbelief at their outrageous bad fortune. They were exhausted both mentally and physically. I went to each in turn and urged that heads were raised and minds filled with the belief that we would be back in the FA Cup Final. That was our mission and all of us knew we would not fail.'

If Atkinson was genuinely inclined to believe in divine intervention then he might have felt reassured in the hours after defeat. There was a moment of historical familiarity. In April 1974, as he nursed the psychological bruises of seeing Manchester United relegated, Tommy Docherty was reassured by Sir Matt Busby about his future at the club. Now, Atkinson might have resembled Docherty in many ways, but neither would have been particularly fond of the comparison at the time, even if United supporters were glad of it.

Docherty was now thousands of miles away coaching with South Melbourne in Australia but was often quoted by the press and usually in times of trouble for United. He was also still immensely quotable Down Under, and no less controversial. He had courted controversy by saying there were 'only a handful of good coaches' in Australia and that those coaches were, 'for the most part, equipped with enthusiasm and not knowledge'. Former Melbourne coach John Margaritis blasted his successor Docherty, saying his claim was 'complete bullshit' and then launching an astonishing broadside at the colourful character: 'Certainly we could benefit from having a few of the world's best coaches here but I'm talking about the world's best, not about Docherty. He's playing 4-4-2 but he's rubbishing

4-4-2. Does he think Australian coaches are stupid? Does he think we're from the jungle?'

Docherty was not alone in being a manager who was cast into the footballing wilderness after being at United (when taking the size of profile and attention into account). It was a steep drop from a cliff edge. He was the first, perhaps, to find his credentials so brutally disregarded. Perhaps there was a sense of bitterness in Margaritis's forthright view, perhaps Docherty's reputation as a king of punchlines had not only preceded him but overshadowed his ability as a coach. It is almost certain that the magic he had, had dulled somewhat, and it is a matter of fact that from the moment he left Old Trafford, he was never as successful as May 1977. It has taken great efforts from several individuals – this writer included – to try to present a fairer reflection of Docherty's contribution, and dare we say *brilliance*, as Manchester United manager. At times that has meant attempting to penetrate the legacy of the ebullient personality Docherty himself still projected and cultivated even years after his retirement, in order to try to present that fantastic managerial nous. In many ways that journey is much the same as the one taken in this book; taking the opportunity to dig beneath the surface of a renowned motivator and character of the game, to demonstrate just how closely linked their philosophies were to the true identity of the club. After all, Tommy Docherty had been made for Manchester United.

It is safe to say that the Scot's career trajectory had gone the same way as the fortunes of the team he left behind, and he appeared scarred by the experience; when asked to speak about events at Old Trafford in the late 70s and early 80s, he was not particularly complimentary about Sexton, or Atkinson for that matter. One can understand why Atkinson, in return, might have felt that Docherty was embittered; the incumbent United manager would have been bracing himself for more critical words in the morning's press. Had he been trading on reputation, he might well have expected some interference from people inside the club, too; insinuations about Busby's involvement with first-team affairs had dogged each of Atkinson's predecessors aside from Sexton.

In some respects, Atkinson almost invited it, as he made the decision to travel back with the directors rather than the team. 'I've often been asked what it is like to work in the shadow of the great man,' he said in 1984. 'It might have been different for managers like Wilf McGuinness and Frank O'Farrell, when Sir Matt had just released the reins of management, but I have never experienced the slightest problem. Sir Matt is still very much involved at Old Trafford as president of the club, and rightly so in my opinion. I have always found him to be a very approachable and understanding man who is easy to talk to. Whenever I have sought his advice, he has always been willing to give it. Perhaps it was different for some of my predecessors, because when Sir Matt decided to give up control of the team to become general manager in 1969, many of the star players, who had been a part of the first English team to win the European Cup a year earlier, were still at the club. They had spent their halcyon days under Sir Matt, and for this reason I would suspect the new managers found it difficult. I will always be grateful to Sir Matt for the gentle way in which he raised my spirits following the disappointments of defeat in the Milk Cup Final against Liverpool in 1983. I spent most of the return journey from London to Manchester alongside him and he told me, "Don't worry, you will be back again very soon because you are on the right lines. You are getting things right at the club." His words provided me with a great boost. He was right again, of course, because within a matter of weeks we were back at Wembley again in the FA Cup Final.'

In a 2019 interview for this book, Atkinson described Busby as 'a god' and explained that he felt settled after their conversation. 'We always went past Oxford on the way back and there was a pub we would pass, and occasionally stop at, that we called the Sir Matt,' he remembered. 'On this trip I asked the driver to stop so we could pop in with Sir Matt himself!'

Moran was absent for the next game against Coventry, and Gary Bailey also missed the game. Atkinson was able to call on Jeff Wealands, the Birmingham keeper who had been brought in on a short-term loan. The slight Wealands kept a clean sheet in a 3-0 victory; an injury to Whiteside caused him to be replaced at half-time. That surely went some way to explaining Atkinson's incredibly understated assessment of Ray Wilkins's magnificent performance in the middle of the park: 'Ray played quite well.' Having 'seen off'

Bob Paisley in the last game, this was also the last time Dave Sexton would manage a game at club level at Old Trafford, as he would be dismissed by Coventry that summer.

Gary Bailey thought he was ready to return for the next game against Sunderland at Roker Park. Atkinson indulged in some of his unique brand of psychology. 'He said I should sit out the next game because my replacement was doing well enough. He did that more than once,' Bailey says. 'It was his way of winding me up, I suppose, and it worked for me because I would always be more motivated when I got back in the team. It was part of his psychology but I don't know how other players would respond to the same approach.'

Wealands kept a clean sheet in a goalless draw; perhaps Atkinson wanted to ensure that Bailey's concentration was as tight as possible after the dropped ball at Wembley. That last-minute winner over Everton had earned United another semi-final against Arsenal, this time in the FA Cup, and with that game fast approaching, the manager was trying every trick to get his players on top of their game. Bailey, and Bryan Robson, were back for the last game before the semi-final. Southampton took a 1-1 draw from Old Trafford. Robson scored just before the break for the hosts.

As some injury concerns were allayed – Whiteside was back, too – others were deepened. Steve Coppell had picked up an injury at Roker Park in a challenge with Iain Munroe that he initially tried to play down by playing on. 'It was a perfectly fair challenge, but I landed awkwardly and knew immediately I was in serious trouble,' Coppell said. 'To make matters worse, Lou Macari had gone off with an injury after only ten minutes and I more or less had to stay on or we would have been down to ten men. I stood out on the wing doing little more than making up the numbers for the last half an hour before hobbling off to the dressing room on the final whistle. The semi-finals of the FA Cup were coming up in a few weeks and I felt choked in the certain knowledge that I would miss it. I could not even face going into the players' lounge for a drink after that Sunderland game and all I wanted was to escape to the peace of the team coach. I was beginning to fear the worst.'

Fearing the worst but hoping for the best. As late as Monday, 9 May, Jim McGregor was working with Coppell on potential fitness for the end of the season. It was thought that Coppell might work better running than jogging; after two laps, the exercise was abandoned and the player's ambitions were reshaped into hopefully being fit for the following season.

Atkinson's hopes of replacing Coppell with Cunningham were a non-starter. The loanee was getting closer to fitness but the United boss was not willing to risk him in the semi-final. (A wise move, considering the bitterness of the last two encounters with Arsenal.) It meant a place in the team for Ashley Grimes and an unlikely reprieve late in the day for a player whose career was surely destined to be away from Old Trafford. As it was, he made his 100th appearance for the club against the Gunners at Villa Park.

Ten minutes before half-time, Bailey had a moment to forget. He attempted to smother an effort that went loose; from the rebound, the goalkeeper anticipated a shot, but Vladmir Petrovic tried to cross it. Bailey could not instinctively grab the ball cleanly and Stewart Robson challenged him for the ball before forward Tony Woodcock forced it over the line. United were trailing to an Arsenal team that were good, but not great; indeed, the spite in this recent rivalry appeared to have been provoked by the embarrassment felt by the Gunners when they were 4-0 down at home. The motivation to get revenge had served Arsenal well so far, but United responded well; in much the same manner, in fact, as Liverpool had in the Milk Cup Final. 'Our opposition that day was Arsenal who, to be perfectly frank, were steamed up at the way we had summarily dismissed them at the same stage of the Milk Cup,' Atkinson recalled. 'But my Manchester United team was again inspired by the occasion and brimming with confidence. We went about our business in positive fashion and took control of the game.'

It took just four minutes of the restart for United to draw level. Grimes played a ball into Robson on the edge of the area; the skipper turned and smashed home the equaliser. Norman Whiteside, who had spent the best part of 20 minutes trying to create a goal for his colleagues, took matters into his own hands, chasing down a hopeful clip into the area by Albiston, controlling the ball and smashing it on the half-volley into the far corner.

With five minutes left, Kevin Moran had to come off; he had earlier hurt his head, but bravely went into another challenge from an attacking set-piece. Blood was pouring from the wound on his head and the game was stopped while he was stretchered off. He was lucid enough to dangle an arm from the stretcher, putting a thumbs up to supporters who responded with a roar. Atkinson, beaming at a return to Wembley, quipped, 'We're going to give him a new contract next season. Part-time.'

Brighton – doomed to almost certain relegation, but still with four points won against United in the league – defeated Sheffield Wednesday at Highbury in the other semi-final to set up the final in May. As for United, they were in third place, with three games in hand over Liverpool but a 21-point deficit, which was more impossible than Brighton's chances of safety, to make up in eight games. Still, a runners-up place should have been comfortably achievable. Especially as United defeated second-placed Watford 2-0, a game which featured Laurie Cunningham's home debut and a fantastic goal from the on-loan winger; Atkinson was hopeful that the right-wing problems which had threatened to upset his preparation were over.

United took their eye off the ball, losing four of their last nine league games and winning just three – it was enough to finish third in the Fiirs Division. The biggest problem came at Highbury in a game that was most certainly not meaningless to Arsenal, even though the attendance of 23,602 was the lowest ever recorded for the fixture. United's players were looking forward to a short break in Majorca, and were flying out from Gatwick the day after the game. They would be nursing a few sore heads on the journey. The 3-0 defeat was not too much of a concern – United's ego was barely dented enough for Arsenal to claim even a moral sense of revenge – but when tempers inevitably flared once again, it was the visitors left counting the consequences.

Atkinson was left furious with Arsenal manager Terry Neill and his coach Don Howe, confronting Howe on numerous occasions as he felt the home players were repeatedly trying to wind Remi Moses up. In the dying stages of the game, they succeeded. After another altercation between the pair – not the first in this game, let alone their shared and storied recent past – Moses took exception to a challenge from Peter Nicholas and once more went at him with his head lowered. Referee Eric Read deemed it to be a butt and sent Moses off. The midfielder's prior suspension for accumulated bookings meant he would now pay the harshest consequence – a suspension from the FA Cup Final. Atkinson was livid.

'He [Howe] had been screaming for the referee to send off one of our players right from the start, when Norman Whiteside was involved in a foul,' Atkinson said after the game. 'He was at it all afternoon and he started again when Moses and Nicholas clashed. I did not believe Remi had actually butted Nicholas, I thought that the linesman had a better view of the incident than the referee.'

But the referee consulted with the linesman before he sent Moses off. Atkinson was incensed even more, and confronted the assistant before he too was sent from the sideline. 'I sent off Moses for violent conduct after a linesman had drawn my attention to an incident,' Read said. 'I sent off the manager for something he said but I cannot say much more.'

In 1984, with some time and clarity to reflect, Atkinson remained sure that the sending-off of his player was unnecessary to say the very least. 'I had a perfectly clear view of the entire incident and to this day I remain absolutely convinced that Moses, if not the cruel victim of outrageous gamesmanship, was unlucky that the referee was unsighted at that crucial moment,' he said. 'The punishment for the dismissal of Moses was automatic and crystal-clear: the player would be suspended from playing in the FA Cup Final. It was a tragic and unnecessary blow for a young man who had fought and overcome so many problems in his earlier life.'

United's players let their hair down at Gatwick. 'For no particular reason, [we] got absolutely plastered,' Steve Coppell, who was with the team despite the fact he wasn't going to Spain, remembered. 'The manager came down to complain about the noise at around 3:30am, but after he had gone back to bed our behaviour grew progressively worse. I vaguely remember trying to toss Ray Wilkins's shoes on to a huge model aeroplane that was suspended from the ceiling in the foyer before finally crawling into bed at around 6am.'

On the morning of 9 May, as Coppell accepted that he would not be able to play in the final, Atkinson resorted to fairly desperate measures to find a replacement. Ray Wilkins had picked up a knock against Swansea on 7 May, as did Cunningham. Wilkins was replaced by reserve winger Alan Davies at half-time. Paul

McGrath played from that side against Luton Town later that day, and, remarkably, scored two goals in a 3-0 win. 'At the time Ruud Gullit was starting to make a name for himself at Feyenoord and I thought that if Paul didn't make it as a centre-half, he might do a job where Gullit was playing, on the right-hand side of midfield,' Atkinson recalled. 'He scored twice against Luton just before the 1983 FA Cup Final but otherwise played so badly I had to put him back to centre-half.'

At the very least, United made it through to the final without any further injury concerns. Atkinson wrapped Kevin Moran, Gordon McQueen, Bryan Robson and Gary Bailey in cotton wool by taking them out of the last league game. They might have been heading into the final as favourites, but McQueen, who had been an unlucky loser at Wembley too many times to mention, was taking nothing for granted. The big Scot had found himself an unlikely favourite of Atkinson's; another case of the manager becoming fonder of the players as he spent time with them. 'I have been given more guidance by Ron than any other manager,' the former Leeds defender said. 'I might not always admit I agree with him, but nine times out of ten I have to say he's right. It's helpful that he used to be a centre-half. He understands the job. And in big matches that can be exhausting, physically and mentally. I never used to enjoy a game unless I was galloping on long runs. The boss stopped that. I used to keep going until I ran out of gas. It is not one of my strengths – but the roar of the crowd at Old Trafford used to go to my head like strong red wine.'

In cup-final week, Atkinson attempted to reframe the argument, painting the picture of Brighton as a team who were relaxed because they had nothing to lose, while insisting United's recent defeat at the capital stadium would ensure they would be completely focussed on the task at hand. 'Brighton might seem blasé now, but they don't know how they will react on the day,' he said. 'My players know because they have been there before only a short time ago for the Milk Cup Final. We'll go out and play it our way and we haven't talked about Brighton yet, but my players are the hungriest fighters ever to get to Wembley. We want that cup and we want it badly.'

One player who apparently didn't was Laurie Cunningham. He had been kept out of action since the Swansea game, with

Wembley in mind, but in the last knockings said he couldn't make it. 'Laurie was a great player,' Atkinson told me in 2019. 'He was misunderstood; people often thought he had a chip on his shoulder but he was a smashing lad. It was a weird one. He had an injury at Madrid that didn't get properly looked after. He did okay and got a wonder goal against Watford. He was down to play in the cup final. I always used to say about Laurie that he could run on snow and not make an imprint. It was worth paying for a ticket just to watch him run. He was magnificent. He had 20 flat-out sprints on the morning before the final and he looked good, but when I asked him if he would be okay for the game he said. "No gaffer ... I think I'll let the lads down." I tried to reassure him that he was playing on a big open pitch against a lad who wasn't the greatest in the world. I said, "Laurie, you'll murder him!" but he replied, "Yeah but if it goes, I'll let the boys down won't I?" So he cried off. One of the things I would say to the players all the time if they were umming and aahing about an injury, was, "If it was the cup final would you play?" The majority would admit they would. And Laurie didn't. He went back to Real Madrid.'

For Coppell, the problem was far more severe than missing the cup final. The day after informing Jim McGregor that he knew he couldn't play [9 May] he was given a grim either/or scenario by his specialist, Jonathan Noble – he could have the entire cartilage in his knee removed and possibly play for another year, or retire before running the risk of becoming disabled later in life. The former Tranmere man took some time to deliberate.

All in all, United's three right-wing options towards the end of the 1982/83 campaign were doomed to tragedy of differing definitions.[1] Of what little short-term joy there was, projected against the long-term perspective, Alan Davies was the unexpected beneficiary. United's staff wasted no time in talking him up. Atkinson described the Welshman as 'the nearest to Steve Coppell's style of player we have on our books', while coach Brian Whitehouse was even more effusive in his praise: 'He is probably one of the

---

1 Steve Coppell was eventually forced to retire due to his injury problems. On 15 July 1989, Laurie Cunningham, 33, was killed in a car crash in Madrid, Spain, after a year with Rayo Vallecano. On 4 February 1992, Alan Davies committed suicide at the age of 30, approximately seven years after leaving United.

most skilful players on the ball in the whole club,' Whitehouse said. 'What he has lacked at times is a bit of confidence. He has always had the potential.'

Davies's journey had been remarkable. One of Dave Sexton's last acts as boss was to sanction the release of the Welshman. That had been put on hold when Atkinson was hired; the new manager decided to retain the winger.

If Atkinson had been more diligent with regards his earlier thoughts about fate and destiny in cup finals, he might well have taken greater care in ensuring the morale of the good ship United was intact, especially considering the problems in the weeks building up to the game. There was a selection of United players who literally had insult added to injury on the morning of the game. 'The day was ruined when we were told that those not playing could not travel with the team to Wembley,' Steve Coppell said. 'We were to travel in taxis that would follow behind. Remi Moses was so upset that he even threatened going home.' The players reluctantly followed; Coppell was able to watch the match from the BBC gantry.

If United were deemed as the flashy, more expensive side, then Brighton tried to match them in terms of their own arrival. The team flew to Wembley by helicopter, passing the United coach. 'We were on the team coach watching the television and actually saw the helicopter flying in above us,' Atkinson recalled. 'I remember someone saying, "Wouldn't it be a laugh now if it fell out of the sky? What would we do for the afternoon?"'

That gallows humour seems particularly insensitive when written and read in a modern context, and even in a historical context considering United's own past, but it is worth remembering that considering the things that might be said in a football dressing room, that probably barely scratched the surface in terms of being close to the knuckle.

Following Coppell's injury, and with Buchan and Macari not part of the squad, United had no active players left from the team who had succumbed to Second Division Southampton in the 1976 final, but those who did play by and large deny accusations of complacency. They were a young team, and Southampton had plenty of experience. In 1983 there was no real hiding place and no such excuse. In the first ten minutes Robson and Muhren looked as if they would have a party. The United captain loved playing alongside the Dutch schemer. 'Arnold was particularly good for my game,' he said. 'He wasn't an orthodox winger who went past defenders. He was such a terrific passer and crosser of the ball that he could operate more as a "sit-in" player and still be devastating. With Ray also sitting deep, it meant I was free to make more forward runs.'

In fact, it was so easy that they were caught completely cold by a hopeful cross into the box that Moran was unable to intercept; Smith scored in the 13th minute to give the unfancied south-coast side the lead. In 1976 United had been hit with a fairly late sucker punch and couldn't reinvigorate themselves. Now, there was plenty of time to recover from the setback and reassert their authority. They were already in the ascendancy before the break and did not need a rocket from Ron to push them on in the second half. An equaliser came in the 55th minute; Duxbury and Davies, performing admirably under the spotlight, combined to find Whiteside, whose flick was smashed into the net by Stapleton.

Then 20 minutes later, Muhren showed some of that awareness Robson had spoken so fondly of, finding Wilkins with a searching pass towards the right. Wilkins took a moment to consider his options and measured a quite beautiful effort with his left foot, which curled into the far corner.

'If Arnold Muhren had not been on the ball I probably would not have made the run and saved my energy,' Wilkins recalled. 'But he had such a wonderful left foot that he picked me out from about 50 yards. The full-back [Graham Pearce] should really have shown me down the outside because I wasn't blessed with a lot of pace. But I managed to come inside him on my left foot and thought, "I'm absolutely shattered anyway so I'm going to have a blast". Thankfully it went into the top corner.'

United inexplicably went from clinical to casual and complacent, allowing Brighton back on to them. The ultimate price was paid when defender Gary Stevens was allowed time and space to control a pass from a corner and fire past Bailey. That 87th-minute equaliser took the game into extra time and seemed to give the momentum to the underdogs once more. It would take some effort to beat that for drama, but Brighton managed it; in the dying seconds of extra time, forward Michael Robinson outfoxed both McQueen and Moran and found Smith in an ideal position. No bobble, primed for goal.

'This was his chance of a lifetime,' Atkinson remembered. 'I stepped up from the bench and walked slowly, head bowed towards the touchline. I was hit by a terrific wave of nausea. I was desolate. I believed an entire season if not entire career had gone to waste ... It seemed an eternity and yet I still hadn't been battered by the roars of approval from the Brighton fans signalling that Smith had scored and Manchester United had lost the FA Cup ... I looked up. The ball was back in play. I had died a thousand deaths but Brighton hadn't scored ... It had been the greatest escape I had ever experienced.'

Smith took a touch and Bailey took a chance. In the same goal that Alex Stepney made the save against Eusébio in the 1968 European Cup Final, Bailey made his own mark on history.

'I get asked about the '83 cup final and the '79 cup final more often than anything else,' Bailey says. 'In technical terms neither were big moments, but in soccer terms they were huge. In '79 it was a good cross and I just couldn't get there. These things happen but of course when it happens in the last minute of a cup final it looks really bad. Especially in the circumstances of that particular game. In '83 there was nothing technically outstanding, it was just a case of coming out with my eyes open and getting to the loose ball. In terms of the best save I ever made, it doesn't even come close. I made better saves against West Brom in the game we lost 5-3, and against Juventus in Turin. The reality is people remember the saves which keep you in cup finals. It's definitely a harsher world for a goalkeeper. It's probably the worst position of any sport in the world.'

Not for Bailey in May 1983 it wasn't. Yes, like Stepney's, it did not require an exertion of miraculous proportions to prevent the shot going in. It did require reliability and concentration, and, *in soccer terms*, was just as important as something more spectacular. The game ended 2-2. Before the game that would have undoubtedly felt underwhelming for United; now, they had a palpable sense of relief. Atkinson might well have felt it was written in the stars after the late let-off, particularly when he realised the replay would take place on Sir Matt Busby's birthday. He was still wearing his game face when he spoke to the press afterwards.

'I thought we'd gone then,' Atkinson admitted to *The Guardian*, referring to Smith's chance. 'We'll have a few drinks tonight and recharge our batteries before we come back to Wembley again. We like this place, you know.'

The United manager kept the same team for the replay. Brighton boss Jimmy Melia succumbed to the temptation to play his captain, Steve Foster, who had been in a race against time to win a fitness battle to play in the first game. It was a decision that would not work in Melia's favour; Foster's recall meant Gary Stevens, who had played so well in the first game, was moved to right-back. United were devastatingly clinical this time, scoring in the 25th minute through Bryan Robson. Whiteside killed the game off five minutes later, and just before half-time Robson added a third to ensure the second period would be a procession.

In some respects, it was just as difficult for the United players to motivate themselves for that second half. 'We had to guard against the kind of complacency that we'd showed temporarily in the first Arsenal semi-final, but at half-time I couldn't help but feel there was a lack of impetus left in the occasion,' Mike Duxbury recalled. 'There's a little bit of uncertainty; you know the game isn't won after 45 minutes but with it not being quite as competitive in the second half, the final whistle wasn't quite as euphoric as it might have been if the game had been a little tighter.'

Midway through the second half, Robson was hauled back by Stevens in the box; a penalty was awarded. The skipper sportingly turned down the chance to score a hat-trick and allowed Arnold Muhren – who had never taken a penalty before for the club, but volunteered in the absence of regular taker Steve Coppell – the chance to score in an FA Cup Final. Muhren dispatched it with the coolness of a veteran to make it 4-0.

Through his act, Robson had bestowed a career-high moment for the Dutchman. 'For me every game was a big party but my absolute best moment was winning the FA Cup in 1983 against Brighton, and scoring,' Muhren told fanzine *Red News*. 'It was wonderful, the absolute highlight of my career as I was the first Dutchman to play at Wembley, and if you score as well what more can you dream of? Every year on cup-final day you get remembered by this when they stroll through the history of the cup. Unforgettable!'

Wilkins described Robson's gesture as 'the mark of the man' (although he was quite forgetful when it came to recalling what Robson actually said, considering Muhren hadn't previously taken a kick!). 'Robbo won a penalty in the second half and with us 3-0 up and in control everyone thought he would take it to complete his hat-trick,' he said. 'But he handed the ball to Arnold Muhren saying, "You've taken them all season so you take it". Arnie scored it but Robbo's gesture really stood out for me.'

The United supporters were in joyous mood and chanted the name of Sir Matt Busby, who took off his hat and waved it in the air to acknowledge and return the love. Whiteside almost made it five but his effort was tipped on to the crossbar.

'Manchester United presented Sir Matt Busby with a spectacular 74th birthday present last night – the FA Cup,' reported Steve Curry. 'He had difficulty fighting back the tears as the massed choirs of Manchester sent his name echoing round the home of soccer. For it was the style and the tradition laid down by the founder of the famous Red Devils that carried United to the biggest cup-final victory margin since Bury defeated Derby 6-0 80 years ago. The standards Busby set as manager were magnificently recreated in a new chapter of the club's success story by the man now in charge of the country's most famous club, Ron Atkinson.'

Atkinson was proud, but remained focussed on the future too: 'I have always said that the first trophy would be the hardest to win. Now the most difficult will be the second one.'

AC Milan were linked with a move for Bryan Robson in a transfer that might cost £3m. Prior to the final, Atkinson had said: 'I would not swap Robson for any other player in the world. I paid a hell of a lot of money for him, but he was worth every penny. I have never regretted that deal for a single moment.' Sportswriter Hugh McIlvanney said, 'Everyone in Britain should be grateful to Ron Atkinson' for rejecting the offer from the Italians, describing Robson as 'quite simply the best footballer currently available to England'.

But the United skipper was far from the only one to receive praise: 'Duxbury and Albiston were fluently impressive from full-back, Wilkins was forcefully influential in midfield, Stapleton led the forwards with mobility, cunning and a noble willingness and young Whiteside again performed like the prodigy he is,' McIlvanney wrote.

With a locker room full of talent, McIlvanney reckoned United should have lofty ambitions for the following campaign: 'The manager acknowledges that a league championship is the first essential, but he must also aim for stirring deeds in the European Cup Winners' Cup. Should he meet Alex Ferguson's Aberdeen along the way, there won't be too many tickets left lying on the sideboard in either city ... United will, it is pleasing to assume, invade Europe with adventurous football, since they are not noticeably equipped to play any other kind.'

Challenges

IF THE triumphant League Cup semi-final performance at Arsenal had been a watershed moment in terms of identity, style and performance, and if Ron Atkinson felt that fate had played a part in his first trip to Wembley, the conversation he had with Sir Matt Busby, and then winning the FA Cup on Busby's birthday, then the manager might well have been entitled to sit back and wonder how winning the grandest domestic trophy in the world might affect his standing in both present and historical terms.

The jury might still have been out on whether or not Atkinson's side were as fluid or entertaining as Tommy Docherty's team, but one thing was almost certain – 'Big Ron' would not be sacked that summer, and so he would have time to build his team and help them realise their potential, and hopefully not have it consigned to mystery in the same way Docherty did. Atkinson had matched Dave Sexton's effort of reaching the FA Cup final in his second season and had surpassed him by winning it. Everything was in his hands to become the most successful manager the club had employed since Sir Matt Busby retired.

Let us provide some context to the challenge facing Atkinson at the time, considering how people have perceived the bare facts and how that judgement has affected how people define or refer to his reign. It is perceived as an era of underachievement; of glorious failure, almost. Historically, the two most successful clubs in England aside from United are Liverpool and Arsenal. Atkinson was under pressure to win something from the off and the six years between FA Cups was deemed a long time. In fairness, it was. But take a second to compare that to the trophy droughts of Arsenal and Liverpool at the turn of the century; Arsenal went nine years between winning FA Cups in 2005 and 2014, while Liverpool went six years between 2006's FA Cup Final win and their 2012 success over Cardiff City On penalties in the League Cup, before then waiting another seven years before their Champions League win over Tottenham Hotspur. In terms of league titles, Liverpool haven't won one since 1990, and Arsenal haven't since 2004.

The way the Premier League has changed since more teams were allowed into the Champions League in 1997 has affected the strength of the competition as a whole, for a while making a quadropoly until the emergence of Tottenham Hotspur, and the takeover of Manchester City (the earlier takeover of Chelsea in 2003 affecting their own position). For a period between 2007 and 2012 English football was the strongest it has been in the 21st century, and some might say that at the time of writing and print there is possibly another such cycle beginning to take shape, but in the late 70s and early 80s it had arguably been even stronger. Ron Atkinson's team were not just competing with the greatest Liverpool generation of all time, but also teams like Nottingham Forest and Aston Villa who had been European Champions, and an Everton team ascending to greatness. There were no extra European Cup places (aside from a place for the winners, if they hadn't won their domestic league) so it was fiercer competition still. There were only so many cups to go around; it is worth remembering that, at the time, it was considered a sour note that Bob Paisley had never won an FA Cup, while Brian Clough also suffered a similar fate. It was a trophy coveted dearly; at this time of emerging national television attention, the FA Cup was the one day of the year when the schedule was dedicated to football.

'It was something I'd watched myself over and over again, sat on the settee at home and enjoying all the build-up,' Mike Duxbury recalled. 'It took some getting used to on the other side, though. We had the ITV crew with us as the BBC cameras were with Brighton and Jim Rosenthal was hosting their coverage. Me and Ray Wilkins were sat having our breakfast when the cameras came up and I was thinking, "Oh God" ... Jim said to us: "So this is just a normal breakfast for you boys?" Yeah Jim, we always have the cameras following us around!'

This is not to say that the pressure was not great on Atkinson to win a league title. It didn't make it all okay that he won the FA Cup. As Hugh McIlvanney had written, there was indeed a renewed level of expectation. But having found himself on the generous side of Busby, the incumbent United manager was now to have it re-emphasised how he, as each of his predecessors had, was walking in the shadow of greatness of the legendary manager. Atkinson had been reassured when it came to the job in general, and things were beginning to fall into place when it came to the style of play.

United were about much more than that, though. There were various facets to the job where you would be held accountable to the supporters. The three main categories were playing attractive attacking football, winning things and bringing through young players. So far, so good on the first two, but what about the latter category? This is an area which Atkinson is criticised for, sometimes directly but sometimes indirectly when it comes to acknowledging the work Sir Alex Ferguson did when he came in. As the story goes, the set-up was in such disarray that he ripped it up and started all over again. Certainly there can be no denying the magnificent work Ferguson did in that regard, but was it all that bad under Atkinson?

Did United not reach an FA Youth Cup Final in 1982? And would they not do so again in 1986? Had Atkinson not given Norman Whiteside a chance at just 16? Furthermore, he did that on his own judgement, having been advised by Eric Harrison and Mick Brown that they felt he was not ready. There was Mick Duxbury, who had stood up to the challenge of a player Atkinson brought in, John Gidman, to play the best football of his young career and make that right-back spot his own. If it is true to say that, under Ferguson, that conveyer belt of talent was more prolific, it is still true to say that under Atkinson United were still the standard bearers in English football when it came to developing young players and giving them a chance in the first team. Four players in the 1983 cup final were homegrown. If three of those (Duxbury, Davies and Whiteside) could be attributed to Sexton's work, then once again credit has to be given to Atkinson for continuing to give players the chance.

'The youth system that was in place at the time wasn't one that people talked about a lot but it was still prolific,' Graeme Hogg recalls. 'It was turning over three or four players who were getting chances in the first team every year and from that you'd get at least two who would play on a regular basis, and it saved the club a fair bit of money. It was still important for United to have a good youth system, especially with the money in the game back then.'

The prevailing criticism, or dominant undertone, to any reference to Atkinson's time at United is that he didn't take it seriously enough. That suggestion is rubbished by Hogg. 'Ron would come to all the youth games, the home games anyway,' he says. 'Mick Brown would be there too. It wasn't that different to how it was under Ferguson later on.'

It is often forgotten that Atkinson was the man who identified Eric Harrison and brought him to the club. That legendary school of hard knocks which educated the 'class of 92' was already operating ten years earlier. 'Eric Harrison did a fantastic job for years,' says Hogg. 'He wouldn't stand for any nonsense. He was old school. He would always say to give him a player who had less ability but was a grafter, someone who would work his socks off for the cause. He'd prefer that over someone who had all the talent in the world but only played when they felt like it. You had to be at it and you had to be consistent with it. You had to play consistently well or your position was on the line. That was in the A team, and in the reserves you were playing for your place every week.'

In the interest of balance, Mick Duxbury does have a different version of events when it comes to Atkinson's dedication to areas beyond the first team, while still accepting it was part of the club's philosophy. 'On the surface, maybe Ron didn't take as much notice as Dave,' he says. 'Dave took more notice of the young players; for example, he would take training sessions in the afternoon. What he was doing behind the scenes, I don't know, scouting-wise and all that type of thing, but it was certainly the case that he had that interest there. Ron, maybe not so much, but was he just happy to leave it to Eric Harrison? Someone like Eric who was trustworthy in what he would report. It might have been done differently but I never thought that there was less attention paid to bringing through kids.'

There is a story that does go some way to showing the trust Atkinson had in Harrison, and also the faith he had in the coach to instil the style of play he wanted in the kids. 'We had a good young defender, Simon Ratcliffe, who went down to Lilleshall,' Atkinson says. 'Charles Hughes, the director of coaching at the FA, insisted that Simon should play long balls. He came back up to us and Eric couldn't believe it. He was fuming and quickly told him he needed to play it to feet, not lump it up the pitch. Simon said that's what Charles had told him to do. So Eric and I called up Charles and told him in no uncertain terms that if that's what they were teaching down at Lilleshall, we wouldn't be sending them any more United players.'

In fairness again to Atkinson, Duxbury was a senior player by the time Sexton left, so may not have fully known just where the manager was at all times. But there is an element of substance to the criticism or suggestion that Atkinson was not quite as concentrated on that aspect as his predecessor or successor. Let us suggest that the 1982 team was mostly the product of Sexton's work; you have Graeme Hogg, Billy Garton, Clayton Blackmore, Norman Whiteside and Mark Hughes, who went on to make notable contributions of varying degrees in the Manchester United first team. There was also Phil Hughes, Andy Hill, Shaun Williams, Lawrence Pearson and Mark Dempsey, who went on to have good Football League careers. From the 1986 Youth Cup Final team, Gary Walsh, Tony Gill and Lee Martin all had good careers at United as squad players (Gill's was unfortunately cut short by injury) but the other players generally had lower-level careers in comparison to the 1982 side. The composition of the squad in the latter years of Atkinson's reign does suggest a heavier concentration in short-term solutions over long-term investment. We'll get to that in due course. There is a strong enough point to suggest that Atkinson deserves a little more credit than he gets for the youth structure at United, even if much, if not most, of the criticism is also valid.

In the summer of 1983, the Manchester United manager knew the challenge in front of him was to win the league title. He was able to plan for that with much greater personal stability. Martin Edwards offered Atkinson a new contract, which was gladly accepted.

'I had almost completed two years of the three-year contract with United which I had signed when I joined the club in the summer of 1981,' Atkinson recalled in his book *United to Win*. 'Chairman Martin Edwards offered me a further two years on the agreement and I immediately accepted: My job there had only just begun.'

To the press, Atkinson declared that the job of Manchester United was the biggest in the game, and also 'the biggest honour'. Quite a change of heart from the man who had described Old Trafford as a 'fool's paradise' when he took the job. Two years of dealing with the day-to-day life at the club had been enough to cause Atkinson to reconsider.

'I came to appreciate just how big United was, which is difficult to do when you haven't been there,' he admitted to me in 2019. 'You know the history, you know the story of the Babes. I was at Wembley in 1968. Maybe some of the glitter had gone since then, maybe people looked at them in the same way they would look at Tottenham these days. They wouldn't overawe you but you appreciated they were a big club. Liverpool and Arsenal had a special feeling. But once you are there and you get steeped in it and begin to realise how big they are ... We were also on the move a little bit. We were starting to get there. Ironically enough, after getting to two cup finals we were beaten in both domestic cups by lower division teams. After that we went on an unbeaten run for something like 15 games and we beat Barcelona. It's a bloody good job Barcelona didn't have to play Bournemouth!'

As Atkinson sought to build on his success of 1983, he made clear his intention to improve the squad. That would include the integration into the first team of some of the players from the 1982 Youth Cup finalists; Clayton Blackmore and Mark Dempsey would get little tastes of senior action, while Graeme Hogg and Mark Hughes would get a little more.

Hughes's own emergence had surprised the boss, who didn't think he would make a player and described him as 'sullen, morose' and that he was 'driven up the wall' by Hughes's sheer inertia. In the last minute of a Youth Cup game against Sunderland, Hughes beat a number of players and created a goal for Whiteside. Atkinson turned to Sir Matt Busby, who had vouched for Hughes's quality, and said, 'I think my judgement might have been a bit premature.'

The United boss still wanted more experience in his front line. He had been a long-term admirer of Alan Brazil, but Ipswich Town had rejected his advances. When Spurs moved to sign him in March of that year, Atkinson was caught on the hop, concerned as he was with the attempt to bring in Laurie Cunningham. Now Brazil was off the market, Ron switched his attentions to Celtic striker Charlie Nicholas.

'Any opportunity to strengthen the playing squad could not be missed and that is why, within days of the FA Cup win, I was hot on the trail of a player called Charlie Nicholas, a Scot who had just completed a season of prolific goalscoring with Celtic,' Atkinson recalled. 'Nicholas was with the Scotland team preparing to meet England in the Home International at Wembley. I drove south from Manchester to see him, along with my chairman Martin Edwards. We had what I considered to be a good meeting with the player over lunch. Later I discussed with Mr Edwards the lunchtime conversation and asked his views on what he thought the outcome would be. The chairman replied that he believed Nicholas was itching to join our club; the impression I, too, had formed.'

Nicholas has scored 48 goals in all competitions. The 21-year-old wasn't only wanted by United; Spurs and Inter Milan made concrete enquiries. Liverpool's overtures were arguably stronger than United's as compatriots Graeme Souness and Kenny Dalglish attempted to convince the striker to move to Anfield. According to Nicholas, his intention had been to move to Manchester, but he had changed his mind after the meeting.

'Atkinson talked more about himself than he did about Manchester United and me,' he told *The Sun*. 'I could not believe it. Then I realised that was his way. Atkinson came on far too strong and by the time the meeting was halfway through I knew my dreams of playing for United had ended. Ron and I would not have got on.'

Atkinson had a subsequent meeting with Nicholas's agent and came away with the impression he wanted to move elsewhere. He did not learn about the player's concerns until reading about it in the press. 'If my behaviour had been as he described, I was not aware of it,' the United boss insisted. 'I asked Mr Edwards if that was the way I had come across in the meeting. He was perhaps more indignant about the article than I was and it showed me that Nicholas's words in no way reflected the facts of the matter.'

An enquiry for Liam Brady, now at Sampdoria as he was midway through his tour of Serie A clubs, was quickly refused, and Atkinson was reluctant to bring in a player just for the sake of it. One opportunity was taken – Arthur Graham, the 32-year-old left-winger, was allowed to leave Leeds for just £45,000.

'My whole objective, despite winning the FA Cup, was to assemble a team to finish ahead of Liverpool in the league championship race,' Atkinson said. 'But there is never any point in signing players who are no better than the ones you already have on the staff. That's why, in the close season of 1983/84, no further signings were made. The player of the type and quality I demanded was just not available for purchase. I still believed I had the playing personnel at my disposal to give Liverpool a run for their money.'

Yet it might not have turned out that way. Atkinson had not fully dismissed the idea of cashing in while Bryan Robson's value was at its height, and even accepted an offer from AC Milan for Norman Whiteside. Whiteside was on holiday in Orlando, Florida, and on his first afternoon there Atkinson called his hotel room to let him know. The Northern Irishman was told that he had to decide immediately as there was a flight to New York at 10am the next morning (from where he would fly to Milan). Atkinson informed Whiteside that he would stand to get £100,000 as he hadn't requested a transfer, and more than ten times the salary he was getting in Manchester (£3,000 a week as opposed to £250 a week). The forward wanted more time to think and turned the move down.

Hogg's words have some resonance when it comes to how Atkinson saw the youth system – a cash cow as much as a developmental facility. His initial judgement on Whiteside had been proven right but was the offer from Milan truly one that he couldn't refuse? It would match the fee paid for Robson in 1981, and would have made the player the most expensive teenager in the world. Ultimately Whiteside turned the move down, saying he didn't want to make such a decision when he had literally just been on such a long flight to the USA.

That decision was most certainly to United's benefit. Even giving Atkinson the benefit of the doubt when it comes to how he saw the youth system, one quality he had underestimated was in fact the primary quality Harrison was instilling into the young players. There was a resilience about them in a way that hadn't been present for over a generation. One could argue that Harrison had a fire that was only comparable with Jimmy Murphy in the pre-Munich days. Murphy had softened after the disaster and became more of a father figure to the players he was responsible for bringing through. Harrison was as relentless as Murphy had been in those early years and the tenacity could be seen in the way Whiteside, and, ironically enough considering Atkinson claimed to have missed it at the time, Hughes, played.

Through the ideals of Jimmy Hogan and the personality of Jimmy Murphy, personified as they were in this context by Atkinson and Harrison, United were developing a culture and personality that was as close to its pre-Munich identity as it had been at any time since, even if that was by accident or coincidence. It certainly did not seem to be by design, at least if you were to ask Atkinson if his intention was to go back to the roots of what had made United great. It was his own philosophy as well as United's, so it was not contrived. And even that was a celebration of all that was glorious of the club's tradition. Had they not always embraced and encouraged individuality? United's kids, at their best, had always resisted the labels put upon them by the press in order to make names for themselves.

When Dortmund were beaten 3-2 in October 1957 by a Manchester United team with seven 'Babes' in it, Busby's side were declared the best in the world. In the post-Munich era, Jimmy Murphy somehow put together a youth team that would help United finally win a European Cup in 1968 and cement their own legacy. George Best became the best player in the world, playing a style unlike any other footballer before him. Brian Greenhoff was dubbed, at one point, the next Bobby Charlton due to his dedicated approach. He overcame that and became a top defender who was loved by all United fans. Sammy McIlroy was the first 'next George Best' but made a name for himself as a club legend. Norman Whiteside was the latest 'next George Best' and in the space of just one year of senior football had made his own indelible mark in history in his own name, playing in a World Cup and scoring in both domestic cup finals.

According to some players who came through the system at United, their education was different to the way Liverpool brought through players. The famous 'Boot Room' approach appeared to go down to the reserves and youth team, where the style was so embedded that United players would find it eerily familiar.

'We used to laugh and joke about that a little bit, that they were even alike physically to the Liverpool first-team players,' Mike Duxbury recalls. 'But can you replicate it? I don't think it's done nowadays, but certainly then, when the kids were brought through at United, they weren't replicating anybody. So I suppose it was a bit of a strange one that it never came across at United. You were just there for your ability, and of course everybody's going to be different. You might have a certain style of play, but everybody's different in that.'

There was also a different sort of preparation; United were trading from their historical reputation at all levels, and as the most successful youth team of all time with their storied history, they were still seen as the standard bearers and the team to beat at any level. United were the scalp. It made for a valuable experience for the players coming through. 'You hope it prepares you,' Duxbury says. 'It was always a message that was put across. It was something you grew up with that you became accustomed to, you certainly tried to handle it as well as you could, and it did, it stood you in good stead for if, and when, you did make the first team.'

That education is a crucial part in the personality and make-up in any Manchester United player, because it prepares a player for what to expect on that level when it comes to playing in the first team. This results in a work ethic which is synonymous with any great United team, so much so that it is usually this quality which is often first referred to. It is a quality that most certainly can be found in players outside of Old Trafford – United had Robson and Moses to lead by example – but there can surely be nothing as valuable in this regard as the three or four years a player might have playing for various different teams at United beyond that senior one, experiencing it on a game-by-game basis.

When signing players, especially ones intended to go straight into the first team, failures most often fell into one of two categories: either the player could not handle the pressure, or they felt that they did not have to work so hard at Old Trafford. Still, United could have a greater sense of expectation when they made a signing from a fellow English club, because having played against the Red Devils that player would have a genuine understanding of how much more committed opponents would be to get a result against United. The most famous reference to this was Sir Alex Ferguson's blast at Leeds United players in 1996, when he accused them of 'cheating' their manager Howard Wilkinson. In that era, the comment was more or less disregarded as 'mind games', and while there may well have been some of that Machiavellian spirit present in Ferguson's approach, his point was sincere.

This was not news for any United player who had lived with this for more than a generation. It is interesting, though, to observe just how the players refuse to use that as an excuse for any accusation of underachievement. It won't even be entertained. Anything else is fair game for discussion – were the players not good enough, were Liverpool simply better, was it the tactics, was it the lifestyle, was it the manager, was it the pitches? Anything will be discussed on merit, but not the commitment of the opposition. That is simply part and parcel of what you agree to expect when you represent Manchester United.

If a player is able to rise to that challenge, there is every expectation that they will be loved by United supporters. There is also that added quality which comes into the reckoning, that, at this point in the summer of 1983, was not even on Atkinson's radar – if we are to theorise that what he had seen in Whiteside was an individual trait rather than one which was representative of Harrison's school. That level of commitment which threatened to blow away any opponent if they were not adequately prepared. It had the potential to thrill supporters as much as a great goal or a fantastic piece of skill. It was this quality which had been present in the United team of 1977 and had been sorely missed since. Could it be back? It made for a fascinating subplot to the topic of trophies and expectation, as it was character and not quality which was often on the manager's mind throughout the 1983/84 campaign.

* * *

Manchester United won the FA Cup in 1983. Yet there was just something about the 1983/84 season that felt a little different. A little special. Okay, United didn't win anything, and as a matter of fact they also suffered one of their greatest modern embarrassments. But it was in 1984 when United arguably came as close as they realistically had done to winning the league since 1967, despite how appearances seemed in 1980. This was a season where Ron Atkinson could have genuinely felt as if his team deserved to be mentioned among the great European sides.

From the 1983 FA Cup Final team, only Bryan Robson, Arnold Muhren and Frank Stapleton had been brought to United by Atkinson, and yet the team had a far more cavalier, expressive and entertaining feel to it than at any time under Dave Sexton.

In goal Gary Bailey had proven himself to be a goalkeeper of great composure and agility. It was unfortunate in a sense that his errors had generally come on big occasions, but it showed a remarkable strength of character that he was often able to clinically objectify those moments as aberrations so that his confidence and concentration was on point for the next moment. Perhaps Bailey did not have the presence of a Peter Shilton but he had no less confidence and that went a long way to assisting his reliability.

There was a reliability in consistent form along the backline, too, and nowhere more than in the full-backs Mick Duxbury and Arthur Albiston. Duxbury's athleticism, endurance and professionalism had earned him the right-back spot ahead of John Gidman, a fan favourite because of his marauding forward runs. Albiston was rarely ruffled and rarely beaten on the other side. There was bravery in spades in United's defence, with Kevin Moran and Gordon McQueen having established themselves as the first choice. In the summer of 1983, Martin Buchan joined Oldham Athletic on a free transfer. Atkinson's back-ups for the defensive pair were Graeme Hogg and Paul McGrath, as the manager finally began to settle on McGrath as a centre-half. Having joked about Moran's tendency to get injuries, Atkinson would have been pleased to see the Irishman register 52 appearances in the forthcoming campaign, as dependable as he would ever be.

If United lacked anything it was pace down the wings, but Atkinson would compensate for this with formation changes; there was plenty of hustle and creativity in the likes of Remi Moses, Arnold Muhren and Ray Wilkins, while Arthur Graham would prove to be one of the more astute Big Ron gambles. Bryan Robson had even been seen as a gamble by some when he first arrived at Old Trafford, but he had now well and truly grown into the role of Manchester United captain. Acknowledged by most as the best British player, it was now time to see how Robson would fare against Continental opposition.

It was a good challenge for Norman Whiteside too, who would still have to carry some of the goalscoring burden on his 18-year-old shoulders alongside the more experienced Frank Stapleton. Having scored 19 goals in the previous campaign, Stapleton would match that tally again as he enjoyed his most prolific period at Old Trafford.

Without further signings, the young players like Graeme Hogg, Clayton Blackmore and Mark Hughes would all provide good supplementation for the first-team squad, as would Alan Davies, who had taken advantage of a series of unfortunate incidents with other players to play in the games against Brighton.

There was some slim hope that Steve Coppell would overcome his knee problem, but that chance was ruled out in September. It had been a mentally draining month for Coppell who had to deal with journalists telephoning him early in the month to say they planned to write feature pieces that he was finished as a player. The winger was not yet ready to face that and instead waited for an appointment with his specialist at the end of the month. On Thursday, 20 September Coppell's neighbour Bob Carolgees asked him to appear on his television show *Hold Tight with Spit The Dog* to talk about returning to the team after such a long spell out. By now, though, Coppell was beginning to listen to his body. The day after, Coppell's specialist returned from holiday to see him and booked him in for an operation on the 30th. As Coppell came around after the surgery, he was told that the medical advice was that he should retire. Perhaps that news prompted Atkinson's change in system throughout the season, where he would play a narrow diamond with Robson at the head of it.

Following the FA Cup Final, United had flown out to Swaziland to participate in a pair of friendlies against Tottenham and another game where a United and Tottenham combined XI took on a domestic team. The trip was lucrative and largely uneventful, save for a trip that a few of the players took to neighbouring South Africa; Kevin Moran had left his passport on the coach and faced problems with gun-bearing guards at the border until the issue was rectified. Moran's passport was returned to him by club officials but the guards remained initially unconvinced as the defender now had shorter hair!

It was an eventful trip. Ahead of the second of those games, Paul McGrath confessed to getting drunk beforehand – so drunk, in fact, that it affected his recollection of events – as he retold the story in his autobiography, he recalled John Gidman and Arthur Albiston abstaining despite, as McGrath thought, not playing later in the day. Both did. McGrath said his performance was 'abysmal' and that the manager was 'apoplectic' with rage afterwards, chiding his player for an extreme lack of professionalism and labelling him a 'bloody disgrace'.

Ron Atkinson often bemoaned his team's pre-season results but had another more individual complaint after a 1-0 friendly defeat at Ajax in which Gordon McQueen was sent off near the end. McQueen had reacted angrily to the embarrassment of being nutmegged by Jan Mølby and took the future Liverpool midfielder out. 'Never mind two matches – he should be banned for two years,' Atkinson said. 'It was stupid and entirely unprofessional. There's every chance he will be disciplined by me as well. But it was typical of our performance. Ajax should have scored ten.'

The most impressive pre-season result was a victory over Liverpool – a testimonial for an Irish FA official in Belfast. That served as a curtain-raiser for the curtain-raiser, if you will, as the teams prepared to face each other in the Charity Shield later that month.

Before that game – in one of those 'You wouldn't see that today' moments – Bob Paisley and Sir Matt Busby, guests of the FA, were carted around the side of the pitch on the back of a truck that also carried all the domestic trophies that had been won between the teams the previous season. The pair were warmly received by all supporters; it was perhaps an apex of good feelings between these two clubs, as relations would descend into unbelievably vitriolic proportions over the near future.

United won 2-0 thanks to a Bryan Robson brace. The first was a cleverly worked move through the middle with Wilkins and Stapleton combining to set Robson free; the midfielder skipped around Grobbelaar, who had come to the edge of his area, and finished in style. His second, on the hour, was less slick; a corner came in from the left, and Robson took advantage of the scramble to force the ball over the line.

Graham started on the right but switched to the left after the second goal as Atkinson trialled John Gidman in front of Duxbury for the latter stages of the game, in order to try to get some natural balance in the shape of the team. It was Robson, though, and Wilkins (who played 'beautifully' according to the manager) who impressed on a hot Wembley day.

United's win was comfortable and some perceived that as an indication that they were ready to take on Liverpool for the title. 'Losing has perhaps done Liverpool more good than winning and perhaps done the rest of us in the First Division more harm,' Ron Atkinson warned. 'Their pride will be hurt, they will be stung and they are still a team to watch.'

It was a show of respect but it would not do much to dampen expectations. It had now been 16 years without a league title for United; they hadn't put up a proper challenge for the championship in the previous campaign, but as well as winning the FA Cup they had gone unbeaten at Old Trafford for an entire season for the first time since winning the league in 1967.

It may have been different in years to come, but, according to some, the burden of that wait was not yet weighing heavy on shoulders. 'It wasn't too big. It was just a fact that it was 16 years,' insists Mick Duxbury. 'It wasn't hanging over your neck or anything like that. You're just there to win every game to get top of the league. But no, it wasn't a massive millstone. It never felt like that.'

When it came to addressing his own fans ahead of the First Division season opener at Old Trafford against QPR, Atkinson was not shying away from what most people expected to be the target for that campaign.

'The trophy cupboard has not exactly been packed in recent years, and yet our fans have continued to make us the best supported team in the country,' he said. 'That's a heavy responsibility when things are not going well, but I can tell you that it makes success much more meaningful when you can bring back a trophy for such great supporters. So thank you for your backing which helped us to success last season and which we look for again this year in an effort to go what we would all consider one better ... and win the league championship. That will be our aim and I believe we have the staff and players capable of achieving it provided we all apply ourselves with the same dedication and enthusiasm.'

It was the same team and same shape that started against the London side. United started in stunning style, scoring twice by the 17th minute, and going on to win 3-1. 'Stapleton's subtlety, the single-minded drive of Robson and Duxbury, the supreme passing of Wilkins and, perhaps above all, the reassuring perfection of Muhren's every touch suggested something close to a truly great team,' wrote Paddy Barclay for *The Guardian*.

Two days later, on the August Bank Holiday Monday, United took on Nottingham Forest at home. They scored early on through Kevin Moran but then got very sloppy in their play. In the second half, goals from Viv Anderson and Peter Davenport (both future United players) gave Forest the win. Atkinson was as furious as Barclay had been generous, blasting his players as 'complacent, overindulgent and unprofessional'.

Of all the players who might have warranted such a description, Mick Duxbury would likely be the last, but he was the only player to be dropped for the next game at Stoke City, where the hosts went to cunning lengths to try to level the playing field, as reported by Charles Burgess of *The Guardian*: 'A French brass band entertained the crowd at the Victoria Ground before the match. "They'll ruin the midfield," someone complained, to which the Stoke manager Richie Barker replied: "That won't worry us."'

United won 1-0 in a difficult encounter, but Atkinson was unapologetic. 'We had to do what we did against Watford last season,' he said. 'Sometimes people think it's a crime that Manchester United have to roll their sleeves up and get stuck in.'

Hostilities were resumed on a pitch more conducive to good football down at Highbury; United won 3-2, with pantomime villain Remi Moses making an appearance from the bench after missing the first few games. A routine win against Luton at home might have invited complacency back in as United were fortunate to escape with a draw in their first European game of the season. Dukla Prague had taken the lead in the Cup Winners' Cup first-round, first-leg tie at Old Trafford and threatened to become the first-ever foreign team to win at the 'Theatre of Dreams' until Ray Wilkins scored a penalty in the last minute.

United were not at the races in the next league game. Southampton were two goals up by the 17th minute and won the game 3-0. Atkinson was fuming afterwards, pointing the finger of blame squarely at McQueen: 'The first goal was a comedy of errors ... Their keeper punts the ball up the field towards 6ft 3in defenders and we still don't win the header ... Our back four, which has been pretty rock solid for the last two years, all of a sudden looks very, very brittle. We've got a good young centre-half, Paul McGrath, coming up. If that's the way we're going to defend then there's a fair chance he'll get his opportunity.'

Atkinson, who declared he wanted to see his team play 'the sort of football that punishes opponents' also said he would 'put in kids in place of the international stars if their application isn't 100 per cent all the time. I consider it to be an honour to be manager of Manchester United. I think players should have that same pride. All right, when you're three down and the sun's shining it's bloody hard sometimes. But if you're getting well paid for it you've got to sweat blood and tears sometimes. All we're sweating at the moment are tears.'

The inconsistent start brought its doubters. David Lacey of *The Guardian* said of Atkinson's side: 'His team have yet to acquire the definitive style on the field that their manager displays off it. Since Sir Matt Busby retired as manager only one of his successors, Tommy Docherty, has given United a strong identity.'

McQueen was given a reprieve and Duxbury was back in the side after an injury to Gidman took him out of contention. (Gidman would subsequently win his place back, but then fracture his kneecap in a win over Wolves.) There would be no danger of complacency against Liverpool and United secured a crucial win at Old Trafford with a Frank Stapleton goal. It was another Stapleton strike which secured qualification on away goals, as unconvincing as it was, against Dukla in the second leg. And United did nothing to quell those accusations of inconsistency when they were three goals up at Carrow Road with 25 minutes remaining, only to throw the lead away and leave with a point.

An Arthur Graham opening goal and starring performance – which Atkinson described as a 'bit of a revelation' (which would have been particularly timely considering Coppell's recent retirement) – against West Brom helped secure a 3-0 win at Old Trafford, and United went on a run of form of seven consecutive victories, which included another round negotiated in Europe against Spartak Varna. Atkinson's contemporaneous comments on the team's form had included some criticism, but when recounting that period in his 1984 book *United to Win*, he was much more generous: 'When the 1983/84 season got under way, the team performed with imagination and flair. We hit the top in the early stages and I was quickly convinced that only one team had a realistic chance of toppling Liverpool, and that was United.'

There was, perhaps, the slightest of revisions when it came to this target. Atkinson remained unconvinced about the firepower of his team and made a signing in November 1983. Garth Crooks, the diminutive Spurs striker, had lost his place in their first team, and the United manager felt he might bring a quality not present in his squad.

'I enquired about Crooks as I thought it was worth bringing him in on a loan to see if he still had that zip that set him apart,' Atkinson said in an interview for this book. 'I always have this theory that if you work with a player you don't make a mistake. You can make a mistake if you haven't, but once you've had a look at them, you can assess the level they can play at. Garth got us a goal at Ipswich, but he wouldn't have been good enough, he'd lost the thing which set him apart.'

Crooks played seven times and scored twice; hardly the spectacular gamble and failure that people sometimes suggest. Atkinson hadn't made the move out of frugality – in October the club had announced a record profit of £636,339 at the AGM, where the manager had said: 'I think that the youth policy at any club is of vital importance. We have to make sure we have young talent coming through and I intend to keep it that way here.'

United's coffers were boosted by a reported £500,000 insurance payout they received after Steve Coppell's injury. In November it was reported that they were interested in using that money to finance the move of Ajax winger Jesper Olsen. 'Olsen is a United fan and there is a chance that his desire to play for us may outweigh all financial considerations,' Atkinson told reporters. 'Ajax have made him a fabulous offer. Spurs have also offered him a lucrative contract. And he has been offered a king's ransom to play in Italy. I hope to persuade him that his career will benefit by coming to United.'

Olsen, a left-winger, would theoretically have to compete with Graham and Muhren for that position. But both of those players were veterans, and both of them were injured for the 3 December game against Everton at Old Trafford, forcing Atkinson's first genuine tactical rethink of the season. Considering it a temporary move, Remi Moses was asked to work the right-hand side, while Whiteside was played on the left. Muhren in particular was missed as United slumped to their third home defeat of the campaign.

'The accuracy and intelligence of the Dutchman's passing keeps their game neat and on Saturday, for all Robson's running and Wilkins's leadership, too many of their moves became ragged,' said journalist Paddy Barclay.

Despite already suffering four defeats, United were still only four points from Liverpool, who were leading the league. The defence, which had been so strong, had been fairly porous, shipping 17 goals in 16 games.

Graham was back for the trip to Portman Road one week later and scored early on before Crooks made his most significant contribution with the goal that secured all three points. 'Our whole theme on the way down was nothing but winning,' Atkinson said. 'We tried to play as if we were at home because we feared Liverpool might open up a gap at the top.'

The performance was described as 'stylish' by journalist Robert Armstrong. You might think, then, that United were starting to benefit from larger crowds, and if so, you might well be astonished to learn that for the following home game against Tottenham, only 33,616 turned up to Old Trafford. That was over 20,000 fewer supporters than were at the Liverpool game in September, still well below the average so far that campaign of around 41,000, and lower even for the game against Spurs in the 1974 relegation season, which was deemed a low point in the club's post-war history.

Well, there were some explanations; fair, mitigating circumstances. Firstly, the game was on a Friday night. Why? Because BBC were showing the game live on television. It was the first league game at Old Trafford to be shown live on television and came at a time when many were still undecided about whether or not the saturation was a good thing. Granada Television had taken the decision to reduce their football coverage in the pre-season, meaning Denis Law, their celebrity analyst, was out of work; their *Kick Off* show was axed, with soccer previews added to the end of *Granada Reports* news programmes on Friday nights. A Granada spokesman said at the time: 'People are saturated and bored. The audience for *Kick Off* fell ten per cent towards the end of last season compared to what it was two years ago.'

Ron Atkinson decided to look at things from a positive perspective as he addressed the matter in his programme notes. 'All eyes are on us tonight as we beam out our first live league television match from Old Trafford,' he said. 'We have got to make sure that we grab the opportunity that presents itself to us through switching the match to Friday for television. A win for us tonight would see us go top, and for a change apply a bit of pressure on Liverpool when they play Notts County tomorrow.'

The decision to reduce coverage was clearly to do with quantity instead of quality; certainly nobody could have complained about the magnificent game of football United and Spurs put on in an encounter the hosts won by four goals to two. Paddy Barclay, writing for *The Guardian*, insisted the spectacle could 'only have made good television'.

'Such entertainment merited a full house, but the combination of live television and cold, damp weather hit the attendance hard,' Barclay said. 'Among the spectators were such diverse celebrities as Bobby Robson and Eddie Shah but only 33,616 paid for admission, and since this was 14,273 fewer than watched the corresponding fixture last season United will be making a heavy claim on the league compensation fund.'

United had veered from the sublime to the ridiculous more than once so far this season and did so again after this impressive victory. First of all there was the matter of an embarrassing defeat to Third Division Oxford United in the League Cup after a second replay at the Manor Ground. There were then three First Division games to close out 1983, on 26 December, 27 December and 31 December (with a trip to Anfield to welcome in 1984 on 2 January!); a fixture schedule that would send modern managers apoplectic with rage.

The first of those was a draw at Coventry, before United contrived to throw away a 3-1 lead against Notts County, with nine minutes left, to only get a point. Complacency through being too good was not often a problem United had been afflicted by in recent years. Having spent so long building up that side of his team's personality, the United manager now found himself with a new dilemma of having to help his team focus as much as they seemed to do in the bigger games. 'If we don't win the title we will need our backsides kicking after a performance like this,' Atkinson fumed afterwards. 'We had a good chance of going closer at the top and we blew it. No way should we have allowed County back into the game.'

Much worse, and much better, was to come in 1984.

Money, Money, Money

CONSIDERING THE uncertainty and change in British football, as well as the inconsistency and relative underachievement of Manchester United, it must have raised one or two eyebrows when media tycoon Robert Maxwell attempted to buy the Old Trafford club in January 1984.

The purpose of this book is to chronicle the footballing journey the club took from July 1977 to November 1986, without concentrating so heavily on the politics and finances unless appropriate. Those matters are on record at length in the seminal *Betrayal of a Legend* and also Martin Edwards's own autobiography. Still, the takeover was big news, and the relevance cannot be totally ignored.

United were far from the cash cow they are today. In 1982 their shirts carried the logo of a sponsor for the first time ever when they struck a deal with Sharp Electronics. Their record profits announced in 1983 were still under half a million pounds and the value of the rumoured takeover was £10m. One can credit Maxwell for his foresight when it came to the financial boom football would enjoy, but at the time the concerns about attendances being so negatively impacted by television screenings of games were genuine enough for the matter to still be debated by clubs. Indeed, only weeks before these reports emerged, United were set to make a claim to the compensatory fund after the televised home game against Spurs.

When Bryan Robson arrived as United's record signing in October 1981, he was believed to be on a reported wage of £1,000 – roughly half of what Joe Jordan and Liam Brady had apparently been requesting that summer. In terms of bonuses, there was a tiered system based on a threshold of accumulated league points, which seemed a little confusing – for example, at one stage in the 1980s the first 35 points would earn the players £100 each, while for every point above the 55-point barrier, players received £400. The structure was not widely known, but those who did know of it were critical as they felt it incentivised players in the wrong way and sent out the wrong message. On some occasions United would end poor seasons with strong runs of form and some suspected that this was not completely unrelated to the tiered structure. Maybe the first thing to point out in that scenario is that it is supposed to be the entire reason *for* incentivising, so it should not be perceived in the manner it often is, and a second thing might be to acknowledge the fact that most at Old Trafford felt the terrible pitches throughout the British winters were very prohibitive when it came to the style Manchester United wanted to play.

The sums of money were not huge, though footballers were still well paid (the average annual salary in the UK in 1982 was around £7,000). Martin Edwards was a modern, forward-thinking chairman, but also protective of his club. He had lobbied for fewer clubs in the First Division, and for clubs to retain all of their home gate receipts. He felt there was a more prudent deal that could be struck with television companies and was part of the number of chairmen at the 'bigger clubs' who had threatened to form a 'super league' if the Football League was not more receptive to the requests of the clubs.

When Tottenham Hotspur were floated on the Stock Exchange in 1983, Edwards watched with interest. Before he could make that move, he was contacted by Robert Maxwell in late January 1984, who asked if they could meet to discuss Maxwell's interest in buying United. Both agreed to keep it quiet, but the following day, much to Edwards's annoyance, the story made the papers and continued to dominate until the pair agreed they would meet when Edwards travelled south for United's game at Luton in early February.

The first two games in 1984 summed up United's campaign so far. Garth Crooks, who was brought in as a player who might relieve some of the goalscoring pressure from young Norman Whiteside, instead set up the youngster to score a dramatic late equaliser at Anfield in a game that ended 1-1. Crooks had come on for the injured McQueen, but even his contribution could not earn him a stay of execution; the forward was sent back to Spurs.

It was suggested that Ron Atkinson may move for Juventus's Polish versatile midfielder-cum-forward Zbigniew Boniek, and that he might even be willing to use his star player Bryan Robson as a makeweight. Normally one to indulge in a little speculation, the United boss shut this one down immediately: 'I have heard all about the stories but it is sheer speculation,' he said. 'We have definitely made no approach and we are not going to.'

He would have been hoping that his team were in a similar no-nonsense mood as they prepared to face Third Division Bournemouth in the third round of the FA Cup down at Dean Court. McQueen was out, and Kevin Moran had also picked up a knock, meaning Atkinson had to field an unfamiliar centre-half pairing of Mick Duxbury and Graeme Hogg, the young Scot who was making his first-team debut. Remi Moses was deputing at right-back, a welcome opportunity for the tenacious midfielder.

But United were not at the races and, after a hard-fought first half, the Cherries took the lead on the hour. The holders were stunned and were hit with another blow less than 100 seconds later when Ian Thompson gave the hosts a two-goal lead. United didn't recover and did not look likely to.

'There wasn't the best feeling that came from that game,' Mick Duxbury recalls. 'We lost 2-0 on the day, which was humiliating enough, but afterwards there seemed to be a lot of ill-will on their side, with their players slating us in the press and calling us big-time Charlies and so on. I don't know where they had gotten that impression from because we didn't behave that way in front of them and we certainly didn't have any characters like that in the team – whether they thought that of the manager is a different thing. It was disappointing because they were fellow professionals and it did rankle with me because it didn't need to be done. They thoroughly deserved to beat us on the day and we were very, very poor, but sometimes amid the romance of the cup there are occasions such as this which aren't quite as pleasant as they're made out to be.'

The 2-0 victory did not flatter Bournemouth; it most certainly embarrassed and humiliated Ron Atkinson, especially after the Oxford defeat a few weeks earlier. 'That performance was an absolute disgrace to the name of Manchester United and we now owe it to the fans and to ourselves to win the championship,' he told the press afterwards. 'Good players didn't play well today. You don't have a divine right to play well, it can't be assumed automatically. It has to be fought for. You have to match fire with fire until you get the chance. Players who don't react to a result like this shouldn't be playing for Manchester United.'

In his 1984 book *United to Win*, Atkinson discussed how he addressed his team. 'Contrary to what the popular newspaper headlines sensationally declared, I did not at that time blast the players,' he insists. 'I kept the lads together in the dressing room with the door locked. My strong words were confined to stressing that we now owed it to the club, the supporters and ourselves to go hell for leather for the league championship and the European Cup Winners' Cup ... I ordered the players not to talk publicly about the defeat. I didn't want to see excuses trotted out across the back pages of the newspapers.'

He did not speak to the players on the journey home aside from when the team coach pulled into Old Trafford, and he told the players he expected to see them at The Cliff the following morning – Sunday (which was 'unheard of' according to Norman Whiteside) – at 10am.

There are contrasting memories of that training session, as you would imagine with almost 40 years' time passed. Whiteside recalls Atkinson ordering the players into the indoor gymnasium on the hard ground for running and staying there for an hour until finally blowing his whistle to allow them to stop.

According to Duxbury, though, Atkinson did not stick around: 'He sent us all running around in the gymnasium, which seemed to be nothing but a token message to let off some steam. Was that really punishing us? Why weren't we working on something that went wrong on the Saturday? He didn't even come into the gym – Mick Brown did. It's not the same kind of authority ... I suppose assistants need to be this way but he was very much a yes man to Ron, and having the assistant there rather than the manager wasn't really sending a big message to us. You could see the difference in later years with Sir Alex. He was always present, and you knew where you stood with him, for better or worse.'

One player who was given a let-off was Hogg. 'Bournemouth was a baptism of fire,' he says. 'I couldn't believe I was playing, I was delighted to be getting my debut. They turned us over but I did alright. Ron had us training inside at The Cliff on the shale. I was about ready to go in but Ron pulled me aside and said, "Do me a favour son and go and have a bath. I'm going to deal with the rest of these." That was enough from Ron for me to think I did alright.'

In training on Monday, Atkinson gave a stern talk to his players, reminding them that they owed it to the club and the supporters as well as themselves to make up for the cup humiliations with success in the league and in Europe.

The response was gradual. United drew three from their next four games and following the third of those results (a goalless draw at home to Norwich) were four points behind Liverpool. They might already look on draws at Loftus Road and St Andrews as four points dropped, and they would certainly look upon that Norwich result as two lost rather than one gained.

A response was needed and what better time than at Kenilworth Road, with the eyes of the world, and nation, watching? The game would be screened on television, while most interested observers were well aware that the big meeting with Edwards and Maxwell was due to take place that weekend. Edwards's position had been strengthened by reports of a consortium led by some Manchester-based businessmen and supporters who had expressed an interest.

On 9 February, Maxwell spoke to the press: 'If I am going to buy a First Division club, I might as well buy the best and the biggest,' he said, denying he would asset-strip the club. 'If anybody says that, they are idiots. Manchester United are a successful company that makes a profit now and I hope it will be more successful and more profitable. Some other people would invest in yachts or pictures but I prefer something that would give a lot of happiness to me and millions of people around the country. I don't have hobbies. You can't improve on Ron Atkinson as manager but anyway that is a premature question. I had said to Jim Smith (the Oxford manager) that I would take him with me if I moved into the First Division, but he fully understands that that would not be the case with United.'

Despite the numbers quoted, Maxwell never, in fact, made an offer. Edwards informed him the price was £15m, a price that was intentionally prohibitive as the United chairman had grown reluctant to sell. It was suggested that Maxwell thought he would be able to buy the club for half of that amount. With no deal in place, it was agreed that club solicitor Maurice Watkins would draft a statement for the press that would only confirm that initial talks had been held.

United defeated Luton 5-0. The game was effectively won at half-time as the visitors netted twice just before the break, but they rubbed salt in the wound with three goals to make a more emphatic statement. It could have been worse, with two efforts hitting the woodwork, but Atkinson was more than pleased. 'We had been threatening to do that to someone for a long time,' he said, quipping that each goal would add an extra million pounds on to the asking price of the club.

Edwards recalls travelling back to Manchester and hearing Maxwell on the radio saying negotiations had broken down, before a statement had even been released. And that, as far as Robert Maxwell and Manchester United was concerned, was that.

Atkinson's side drew at Wolves and won against Sunderland at Old Trafford. There was a renewed sense of optimism in the air. The United manager made a £300,000 offer for Spurs striker Steve Archibald, but it was rejected, despite the forward being on the transfer list. With the season drawing to its conclusion, and the transfer deadline nearing, the London club were not willing to sell unless they received a more attractive offer. That was something Atkinson could empathise with; in late February reports emerged that Sampdoria wanted to sign Bryan Robson. For the first time, the United boss had his head turned when he saw what was on offer. The Italians were willing to put up £2m, and also include Liam Brady and Trevor Francis – both players who had previously attracted Atkinson's attention – in the deal.

'As far as I am concerned the door to any Italian club remains shut, for the time being at any rate,' the United boss said, though he intimated that his position might change once his team were out of the title race. Robson put on a show for his admirers, starring in a comprehensive 3-0 victory over Aston Villa at the start of March 1984, which was effectively the start of one of the most crucial periods of the club's history under Ron Atkinson. Liverpool's draw with Everton had reduced the gap at the top of the table to just two points.

United had been drawn to face Barcelona in the Cup Winners' Cup, and travelled to Spain for the first leg. Barcelona had Diego Maradona and Bernd Schuster in their team, though the Argentina forward was most certainly the headline attraction. 'We won't be making any special plans for Maradona,' Atkinson insisted. 'We will play him just as we would play against any other world-class player … I'm happy with the way we are playing just now. We have a nice edge to our game and I don't think we'll be overawed.'

There was a slight difference between what was said publicly and what went on behind closed doors. That much was something which had certainly revealed itself over the past few months. The players had seen a different side to the manager once his pride had been wounded by the domestic cup defeats; they were already aware of the way he would often play one role for the press and another for them by the way he would prepare his side. For the players who had been trained by Dave Sexton and had experienced his meticulous approach, Atkinson may have seemed more relaxed by comparison, certainly in the eyes of a Bailey or a Duxbury; but, by and large, those who had only known Atkinson as the manager at the club were generally impressed by the attention to detail he wasn't often credited for.

'Ron was very polished when it came to preparation,' Graeme Hogg says. 'He would have had people watching our next opponents and he would go through the report with us. He went through every single individual in their team. He'd go through who he expected them to play and then he'd start explaining all the observations made about their players. "Their goalkeeper sometimes drops the ball, their full-back doesn't always track back." We had a routine on matchdays where we'd watch *Football Focus*, we'd sit there for maybe half an hour. The gaffer, Mick Brown and Jim McGregor would come in, order the television to be turned off and he'd go through our drills one last time. There'd never really be any team meetings, unless there was a crisis, on a Friday. It was always done on the day of the match. Ron would give us personal instructions, too, tailored to our own ability. If I was playing against Gary Thompson of Aston Villa, for example, Ron would tell me that I had to time my jumps earlier. Thompson had a way of jumping, a scissor-jump, that was awkward. We were the same height but I couldn't get near him if we jumped at the same time. Against Cyrille Regis, Ron would always tell me to make sure I would have a yard and a half. If he got closer than that he'd turn me. This advice would come before kick-off, while the banter was going around the dressing room. He would walk around to every single player to remind them of their personal responsibilities. He'd tell me to win my battles. That was the best part of my game so he'd have me on that, and if I was playing with Paul, for example, he'd tell Paul to get out the road and pick up the pieces. When the opposition had goal kicks, it was my job to push the defence up the pitch and contest the ball to try and get it down for Robson or someone in midfield to attack. Once I won the ball, if I had possession, I had to first look to give it to Arthur. If there was anything on in midfield, try and get the ball there as quickly as I could. The last thing he wanted us to do was to jab hopeful balls into midfield because there was a huge danger of the ball being intercepted in a bad area. If we had any trouble at all, wrap our foot around it and try and hook it as far as we could between the channel of their full-back and centre-half to give our players a chance to push up and challenge in their half.'

Aston Villa was one thing, and, even though they had enjoyed recent glory days, Villa Park was a world away from the Camp Nou. Whiteside had picked up a groin strain in that game, creating exactly the problem the manager had been concerned about when wanting to get a senior back-up. He was forced to select Mark Hughes, who would be making only his fifth appearance. There were further concerns. Kevin Moran had missed the win over Villa but would be fit for the Barcelona game. Atkinson had to choose between Hogg and McGrath to partner him. Hogg recalls: 'The Barcelona game was something that didn't really affect me at the time. It's only looking back and you appreciate how big it was. I remember that it was between me and Paul who would play, we were both breaking

Dave Sexton flanked by Frank Blunstone to his right and Tommy Cavanagh to his left, August 1977.

Gordon Hill celebrates scoring against Arsenal on 5 November 1977. But the Gunners won 2-1. The next time the two sides met was on Hill's birthday on 1 April 1978. That would be 'the last game 'Merlin' played for the club as Dave Sexton ruthlessly sold his top scorer.

Scousebuster! Jimmy Greenhoff celebrates ending Liverpool's double hopes in the 1979 FA Cup semi-final replay, two years after destroying the Anfield club's treble aspirations.

Manchester United squad picture for their centenary year.

Sammy McIlroy kneels dejected on the Wembley turf; his magical goal counts for nothing as Arsenal break United hearts with a last gasp winner in the 1979 FA Cup Final.

New Manchester United manager Ron Atkinson sits alongside Bryan Robson before the game against Wolverhampton Wanderers on 3 October 1981. Club secretary Les Olive watches on as Robson and club chairman Martin Edwards seal the signing with a handshake.

*'On me head!'
Atkinson was
infamous for
participating in
his team's training
sessions.*

Champagne Ron – but despite having cause for celebration after managing his team to victory in the 1983 FA Cup semi-final, Atkinson insists his glamorous reputation was largely staged.

Ron Atkinson gives his team-talk before extra time in the 1983 FA Cup Final.

Manchester United's players indulge in a lap of honour after overcoming Brighton in the 1983 FA Cup Final replay.

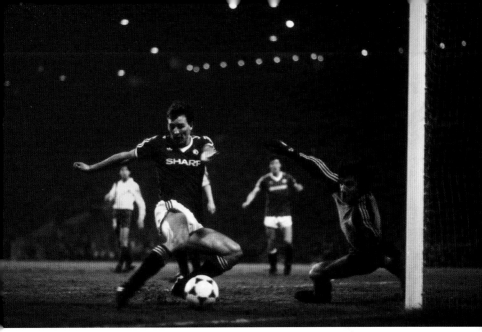

Bryan Robson scores his second goal in a famous win over Barcelona in 1984.

Australian national captain John Kosmina and national manager Frank Arok sit alongside Martin Edwards, Ron Atkinson and Gordon McQueen as Manchester United prepare to play three friendlies in Sydney and Melbourne in May and June 1984.

*Norman Whiteside uses Everton defender Pat Van Den Hauwe as a shield
to bend a seminal shot past Neville Southall, and win the 1985 FA Cup for
Manchester United.*

Celebrations after the 1985 FA Cup victory.

into the team at the same time. In the end I was given the job of marking Diego Maradona and Ron said, "Just do your best. Stay close to him. Let him know you're there. Kick him." It was simple as that. It doesn't matter how good you are, you always need space and time to do what you want to do. Okay, the very top players make their own space, but you have to be on their tail all the time in order to give them something extra to think about. Everyone talks about Old Trafford but he never did much in either tie ... There was 90,000 in the Nou Camp and I would say it was a nice atmosphere rather than hostile. It was strange.'

Hogg was unfortunate; making his European debut, he sliced a cross into his own net in the 35th minute. Other than that, he equipped himself well, as did his team-mates. An equaliser should have been forthcoming when Robson was put through one-on-one with the goalkeeper. However, the midfielder had the rarest moment of indecision, believing that he was offside, and flicked his shot without conviction. It still hit the crossbar, but came back to safety – and Robson was horrified to discover the linesman had deemed him onside. 'I was sick,' Robson admitted. Worse was to come. Having done a good job of keeping Maradona quiet, and seeing him get substituted, United felt they had done an adequate job until the last minute, when Francisco Rojo scored a fine goal to make it 2-0.

Back in the UK, United responded well from that disappointment to win 2-0 at Leicester; Hughes scored his first league goal for the club at Filbert Street. Liverpool won against Tottenham, with Kenny Dalglish scoring after he'd suffered a spell out with injury. The Anfield side were further bolstered by the signing of Ipswich midfielder John Wark. Wark had been a player United had been interested in, but Atkinson told reporters at Leicester, 'Wark is a player I have in mind, but so far no contact has been made and no fee has been mentioned.' He was beaten to the punch; Wark would have a fine impact for his new club.

United were set to face Arsenal and then Barcelona within days of each other at Old Trafford and were given a major boost when Liverpool lost against Southampton on Friday, 16 March. Even before that, Charlie Nicholas – lining up for the Gunners that weekend, having turned down both Liverpool and United – had tipped Ron Atkinson's side for the title. 'You can never discount Liverpool, especially with Dalglish back,' he said. 'But if you tied me down I would have to take United for the title. They impressed me more when we played against them.'

Arsenal had suffered against United in the cups in 1983 but did at least have a good track record of three consecutive goalless draws at Old Trafford in the league. Their resistance this time lasted just ten minutes as Atkinson went for a midfield diamond that had Robson, the jewel, appropriately atop it; Tommy Caton was the villain for the Gunners, conceding a penalty before later being sent off. Muhren – now the regular kick-taker – scored with ease and then had an effort deflected in just before half-time. Stapleton and Robson completed what became a rout with second-half strikes. Most impressive was the industry and intelligence of the midfield unit, with Wilkins controlling from deep as Robson penetrated time and again. Wilkins and Robson were 'invaluable', while Wilkins made Arsenal 'dizzy' with his passing, according to Paddy Barclay in *The Guardian*. The result was significant, as United were now top by one point with just ten games to go.

Due to its position sandwiched between the Barcelona games, people rarely look back at the Arsenal match and how it had positioned United so healthily for the closing weeks of the season. In years to come, people would talk more about the infamous season two years later and how close the team came to ending their First Division title wait, but it is fairer to say this period was the pinnacle of Atkinson's time at United in terms of the mood and general feeling of positivity – if not so much on the weekend, with the Barcelona game still to come, then most certainly in the days that followed the Catalan team's visit to Old Trafford.

'The fans must be patient,' Atkinson said about the second leg. 'We will have to open with caution because we don't want to give them an away goal.'

These were the right words to say from a manager who must nonetheless have felt hopes of progression were slim. Considering his recent attempts to strengthen his squad, he might well have wondered if only there were some secret ingredient, an intangible that could turn events in his favour. Whiteside was back. Moses would play alongside Muhren and Wilkins behind Robson.

Atkinson kept faith in Hogg to partner Moran. But it would still be asking an awful lot, even if not quite a footballing miracle, for a performance that would see United qualify. A conversation with the chairman early on matchday gave Atkinson some inspiration.

'I just remember telling him he would witness something he'd never seen before,' Martin Edwards said. 'And it was incredible, a fantastic atmosphere and a wonderful game. Robson was magnificent. One of the greatest nights in European football at Old Trafford. There was Benfica in '66 and Real Madrid in '68 and this was definitely up there.'

Atkinson remembers it well. 'The memory of the night of Wednesday, 21 March will, I am sure, live with me forever,' he said. 'Chairman Martin Edwards had repeatedly attempted to describe to me the very special atmosphere generated by a full house Old Trafford crowd on a big European occasion, and I certainly never experienced anything like it. The noise from the 58,000 supporters crammed into the ground was deafening. They cheered, they chanted, they sang their songs and roared their encouragement.'

Atkinson passed on that same information to his team. He reassured young Hogg, who would again come face to face with Maradona, who would surely be better than he was in the first game. 'It probably helped that I was a young kid who he would have known nothing about,' Hogg says. 'Before the second leg Ron reassured me I had nothing to be worried about. He said the crowd would help me, they would be our 12th man. The atmosphere at Old Trafford got to Barcelona and their big players. They folded after the second goal.'

An early chance fell to Whiteside as he looped the ball on to the crossbar after the Barcelona keeper came out of his goal. In the 22nd minute United got a corner; Hogg flicked it on and Robson was there at the far post to make it 1-0. The atmosphere was feverish anyway; the sort that would either be killed flat by an away goal or elevated to greater levels if hope was given. United supporters could now believe. The visitors navigated the rest of the first half safely but at the start of the second tried to play possession football near their own goal much too early. United pressed high and forced an error. A cross from Remi Moses was met at the near post by Ray Wilkins, whose shot was saved but spilled by Javier Urruticoechea

227

('Urruti') in goal. Robson snatched the rebound and fired it in from close range.

Barcelona responded with an effort of their own but they were rocking; from the resultant counter, Albiston found space on the left. His cross was headed back across goal by Whiteside; an effort, no doubt, but just off target. Thankfully, Stapleton was there at the far post to fire the ball over the line and give his team an aggregate advantage. With almost 40 minutes still to play, United had to settle any nerves and hope that Barcelona became too anxious. Hogg and Moses were absolutely outstanding in their marshalling of Maradona. Atkinson brought on Hughes for the tired Whiteside; it was a decision that almost backfired.

'The fans gave us a phenomenal lift,' Hogg says. 'Mark came on and near the end he made a challenge in the box which should have been a penalty. I've seen it two or three times since and I've definitely seen them given.'

United held on and claimed a famous victory. At the final whistle, hundreds of supporters raced on to the pitch and held Robson aloft their shoulders to carry him to the tunnel. Once there, he was greeted by Ron Atkinson, who hugged him; a television reporter then pushed a microphone in Robson's face and asked him what he made of it all.

'We were disappointed with the result in Barcelona as we felt we should have beaten them over there,' he admitted. 'But the lads have proved they've got a lot of character. The game really went just right for us, scoring in the first half to steady us down for the second.'

It was Atkinson's turn to take questions. 'That was one of the great Old Trafford nights, that's what European football is really about,' he beamed. 'The last quarter of an hour felt like three days. I felt we took the third goal too early!'

Later on, Atkinson described it as one of his greatest moments: 'When the final whistle went it was complete pandemonium ... The immense joy resulting from that famous victory surpassed anything I have experienced in the game. It was even better than winning the FA Cup at Wembley.'

The memory of the atmosphere at Old Trafford lived long in the memory of all who were there. 'I had never before heard such fervour and I haven't experienced it since,' remembered Norman Whiteside.

'At the end, explosions of joy just about took the roof off the place,' Bryan Robson said in his book *Robbo*. 'The players hardly had time to congratulate each other before they were mobbed by thousands of fans spilling on to the pitch. I was lifted off my feet and carried shoulder high. My name was being sung and my back slapped till it hurt, or at least it would have done if I hadn't been so elated. It was one of those nights you dream about and treasure for the rest of your life.'

Mick Duxbury agreed. 'I've never known anything like that at a ground,' he says. 'They always said about midweek European games, but that one was unbelievable, it really was. We were never going to get beat. The crowd sensed it and so did we. Maradona wasn't at his best. Schuster wasn't at his best. Everything they did, they just couldn't match us. Everything just felt right. And on the night, it just, it was unbelievable. Unbelievable. It will be right up there with the greatest nights in the club's history. Okay, the crowd is probably half the size of the crowd at Wembley. Maybe a bit more, whatever. It's a different occasion. It lives long in the memory and in the moment it gives you the same sort of boost as winning a trophy. But sadly you don't, and it doesn't matter how much you like it and how much you put it up there.'

You don't get a trophy, but still, nights and occasions like the game against Barcelona are worth just as much in terms of memories. Away from the finals, there are a handful of games – more than a handful when it comes to spoiled United fans – which stand up to be just as memorable, if not more, than those occasions when United won a trophy. The Santiago Bernabéu in 1968, Barcelona in 1984, Turin in 1999 one week after Villa Park, Paris in 2019; these words are synonymous with singular victories which were not rewarded with trophies (on the night, even if they were part of trophy-winning campaigns), but were singular victories and incredible atmospheres in unlikely turnaround comebacks. (Okay, well, technically Villa Park doesn't count as a comeback, but it was a victory in unlikely circumstances.)

Add that to the growing optimism from the win over Arsenal and this genuine sense of hope and expectancy that something magical was on the immediate horizon, and it's easy to see why this evening is crystallised as the ultimate moment, the grand pinnacle of Manchester United under Ron Atkinson. That's not to say it was all downhill from there. There were further peaks, big days, great moments and another trophy to say the very least. There were longer, sustained periods of great football. But ask any number of United fans to name their favourite moment under Atkinson and you can expect most of them to name the evening his team beat Barcelona at Old Trafford.

You would not get any mitigating circumstances when it comes to how those supporters present on the night remember the atmosphere. It is not comparable with anything else, and even that incredible night against the same opponents in 2008 did not quite reach the same feverish state as back in 1984.

Another debate many United fans of this era will not compromise on is the idea that Bryan Robson is the club's best-ever midfielder and the performance against Barcelona is the number-one display that comes to mind when recalling his individual brilliance and importance. That it came against Maradona, then one of the best players in the world, and Robson came out so emphatically on top, only served to cement that point of view. From those first few weeks since the player confessed to some initial anxiety due to the fee, Robson had blossomed into, comfortably, the best player in the league. That may sound like a bold statement considering Liverpool had what is generally considered their best-ever team, but this opinion had been shared and discussed by journalists for almost a year.

It was also held by most who played alongside him. 'Without a doubt Robson deserves to be mentioned alongside players like Maradona, and it's only the injuries he suffered that stop that being the case,' Hogg says. 'Robbo's problem was that he would already play when he was injured, he played with injuries when he shouldn't have. He was the driving force behind the whole side.'

Robson's midfield partner, Ray Wilkins, could not have held him in higher regard. 'He was the original action man, he used to throw himself into challenges, cover every inch of the pitch and then pop up in the box to score a goal,' Wilkins said. 'A truly wonderful player. From box to box, he was absolutely unbelievable. He had an engine that was second to none, and was aggressive in the middle of the pitch.'

Robson himself was feeling very confident indeed. He could trace the upturn in form to a specific time. 'I think being given the captaincy was probably another factor that helped me,' he said. 'Some players will tell you their own form suffered after becoming skipper because they found the added responsibility a burden and a distraction from their own game. Others shy away from it because they feel it's simply not for them. But I never found the job a burden or a handicap. In fact, I relished the responsibility and believed I thrived on it.'

Atkinson concurred with that consensus, though did believe his star man had only started getting the attention he deserved because of the increase in goals he was scoring at the head of the midfield diamond. A starring and definitive performance directly against Maradona only strengthened the opinion of Robson's brilliance. Maradona is thought by many to be the greatest, but Robbo had outshone him and made the difference for his team. The United skipper would be coming up against the man officially deemed the best player on the planet; United had drawn Michel Platini's Juventus in the next round.

One reporter took the opportunity to question Robson on his future, and the captain admitted he saw it at United. 'Things are going better at Old Trafford,' he said. 'It is making me want to stay.'

There was the opportunity that Robson's importance and brilliance would be forever marked in history by his contribution as the leader in United's glorious success in 1984. Instead, it would be a case of his reputation being enhanced by his absence, which ultimately contributed to the stronger, at times prevailing, narrative that he was merely the leader of a team of underachievers.

As United prepared to face Nottingham Forest, *The Guardian's* Robert Armstrong paid them the ultimate compliment: 'The startling transformation in the fortunes of Manchester United within the past eight days has brought back a whiff of the tingling atmosphere that was commonplace at Old Trafford during the 60s.'

Atkinson could not wait to get his team back on the pitch to try to benefit from this great momentum. He was stopped in his tracks when the game at Forest was postponed. Despite not playing – or maybe even because of not playing – the United boss would subsequently identify this moment as a pivotal one. 'Confidence at the club could not have been higher,' he said. 'We were in front with the last lap of the season to come, and there was not a man at Old Trafford who did not believe we were going to win the title at last. I confessed that, despite hours of soul-searching during the summer months, I still cannot put an accurate finger on why everything should suddenly go so horribly wrong ... We had pulled off the great European Cup Winners' Cup quarter-final victory over Barcelona and the team believed they were capable of playing any side in the world, anywhere at any time, and would be sure of victory. On the Saturday after this we faced a tough fixture against Nottingham Forest at the City Ground situated next to the River Trent. We were amazed when we were informed that the game would have to be postponed because of a waterlogged pitch ... On reflection, the postponed game at Forest might well represent the vital turning points in our fortunes. At the time I just couldn't see United losing another game. In fact, I believed we would win all of our last ten games to take the championship. Undoubtedly, the most crushing blow of all, though, was that Bryan Robson also got himself injured and was out of action in crucial matches. Even so, a club like United cannot put forward the loss of key players through injury as the main reason for our demise. But the loss of Robson and Muhren did affect us greatly because, just a few weeks previously, we had carefully devolved a new playing system in which we went into action without an orthodox winger. The idea was to put four men in midfield, allowing Robson the opportunity to exploit his talents in any area of the field. He had the freedom of the pitch and he had been expressing himself magnificently. Our game had been electric. We scored goals, played some superb football and Robson was in terrific form. With the injuries we lost our balance and shape; the playing system had to change because vital personnel were absent. Any manager will tell you that the most important aspect of a successful team is a settled side and a definite pattern. On this occasion our form spluttered and we managed to pick up precious few points ... We handed that championship to Liverpool on a silver platter. At the end of the day it had to be said that we at Manchester United squandered the greatest chance to date to establish ourselves as the top team in English soccer. But I am still convinced that the day when we will do so is not very far away.'

It was ten days before United were able to kick a ball in anger again, and when they did it was difficult to generate the same sort of bounce they had enjoyed against Barcelona. West Brom were stiff opponents and United slumped to a 2-0 defeat at The Hawthorns. Robson gave another demonstration of his importance when he scored the only goal in the next game against Birmingham at Old Trafford; the victory masked what Atkinson described as 'one of the worst home performances of the season'.

The boss knew he would be relying on Robson against Juventus anyway, but even more so after Wilkins had been booked against Barcelona, meaning he was suspended for the first leg at Old Trafford, and an injury to Muhren which had kept him out since the game against the Spanish side.

On the Monday before the game, Atkinson was sitting in his office talking to Italian journalists when he peered out on to the training pitch at The Cliff. The players were coming in, and Robson was kicking the footballs into the ball bag; in doing so, he tore his hamstring, and Atkinson squirmed as he instantly knew what that meant. He feared the journalists would know, too, but was thankful that Robson appeared to put a brave face on it and waited until he was back in the changing room to get treatment.

'In normal circumstances our task would have been formidable to say the least; without the injured Arnold Muhren and Bryan Robson, and the suspended Ray Wilkins, it was as if the heart of our team had been ripped away,' Atkinson admitted. 'With the very last kick of a training session before the game, Robson had injured his hamstring. There was no way he could make the match, even though he had walked away from the training ground without so much as a grimace so that the watching Italian journalists would not be aware of our terrible misfortune.'

Remi Moses was the only player who would normally get into the midfield who was available to play. He would be joined by John Gidman on the right, Arthur Graham on the left and Paul McGrath in the middle. After ten minutes, Gidman was withdrawn; he had been rushed back from his own injury too soon. It meant a first appearance of the season – in fact, since playing in the FA Cup Final in similarly strange circumstances – for Alan Davies, who had only made five reserve appearances all season due to his own injury struggles.

The terrible fortune continued. Three minutes after making the change, United fell behind; Paulo Rossi fashioned some space on the edge of the box and his effort deflected off the shin of the helpless Hogg to send Bailey off-balance. The ball went down the middle of the goal. With ten minutes left in the first half, a battling United side found a breakthrough; Albiston's clip into the box was met by Whiteside, who was struggling under the attention of the defenders, but did remarkably well to get a shot away. That was saved, but Davies had enough time to control the rebound before putting it into the net.

Despite a valiant effort, United were unable to add to their tally, but a 1-1 draw was a creditable result from a Juventus team many felt was the best in their history. 'Taking everything into account, our performance was better than against Barcelona,' Atkinson told the press. 'Better in terms of guts, in terms of sweat, in terms of people overcoming the odds. It wasn't classical to watch, but with the side we had out we had to keep up the pressure and keep throwing it at them. At half-time we talked about things I haven't talked about since I have been at this club – old-fashioned, rustic stuff ... if we play with the same positive attitude and commitment we have a good chance in Turin. They're hard men, I know that. But we're no pansies.'

There was little of that fighting spirit on show against Notts County in a 1-0 defeat or in a goalless draw at Vicarage Road. 'It is beginning to look as if injuries have literally knocked the heart out of Manchester United's attempt to win their first league championship for 17 years,' David Lacey said in *The Guardian*. It was made all the more frustrating by Liverpool's stuttering form; they had won against Watford and West Ham, but fell to a surprise defeat at Stoke and could only draw at Leicester. Still, the Anfield club now had a two-point lead again at the top despite what was shaping up to be the most lethargic 'title race' in years.

United were hoping that they could rush Bryan Robson back for the climax of the season. 'He is a big doubt for Saturday's game against Coventry,' said Atkinson, 'and we must work feverishly to get him fit for Juventus next week.'

Ahead of that game with the Sky Blues, the boss addressed the injury problems in his programme notes: 'Injuries have forced us to make changes and while the lads who have come in have played remarkably well there is no doubt that we have missed the touch of our senior men at times,' he said. 'It's the change in the pattern of player that has made the difference as much as the absence of experienced players. It always takes time to adjust and I think we had to accommodate too much too quickly to maintain our winning run. Not that I like dwelling on injuries because all teams are hit at some stage or another and the last thing we want is to start feeling sorry for ourselves. I suppose the biggest disappointment was losing at Notts County on the day Liverpool lost at Stoke. It was a missed opportunity to go into the lead at the top of the table. What made it so galling was because we dominated and County hardly posed a threat. Then we threw three points away by conceding the sloppiest goal we have let in all season. Having said that, though, we need to remind ourselves that at least we are still in with a great chance of the championship as we draw near the winning post.'

United got a much needed win over Coventry, with Hughes scoring twice, and McGrath and Wilkins netting in a 4-1 win. But even the confidence boost from that victory could not compensate for the continued absence of Robson who wouldn't make Turin. Wilkins was at least back, but Muhren was still out, and Atkinson decided to go with Hughes from the start in place of Whiteside.

Juventus started masterfully. Platini was pulling the strings against a depleted midfield, though Wilkins and Moses competed bravely. United had the first chance when Hughes pulled away to the left and shot across goal; his effort was parried by the goalkeeper, but McGrath's attempt to poke in the rebound was denied.

Boniek – recently linked to United – struck a hammer blow when he latched on to a through-ball, held off the attention of Albiston, and clipped the ball over Bailey. Having been outfoxed on that occasion, Bailey was outstanding for the rest of the game, making several fine saves. 'It was brilliant against Barcelona, but that was the standard we knew Manchester United should have been hitting more often,' Bailey admits. 'When we played Juventus, who were the best team in the world at the time, despite the injuries we weren't outplayed. It was a different story in the return, Rossi was brilliant, and I had probably my best game for the club.'

In the second half, Atkinson sent Whiteside on for Stapleton with the instruction 'put yourself about a bit and get stuck in.' Just seven minutes after coming on, he'd done quite a bit more than that. McGrath did well in the box to turn and find him, and Whiteside fired into the net with a strong first-time effort. The goal did wonders for United, who grew in confidence as the atmosphere within the home crowd became palpably anxious. With the game set to go into extra time, and the hosts' confidence draining, Juventus won a free kick high on the left. It was played into the box where defender Gaetano Scirea tried to fire an effort away; that was blocked by McGrath, but the ball fell kindly to Rossi who fired a winner past the brilliant Bailey to break the hearts of the United travelling party.

Robson and Muhren were still absent from the weekend game at home against West Ham. It was another goalless draw as United finally started to pay the significant consequence for their lack of width and lack of Robson through the middle. The result was made much more painful by the news Liverpool had drawn at home, meaning there was another missed opportunity. The same scenario happened the following weekend, as United at least got a goal in a 1-1 draw at Goodison Park (when Robson finally returned) and Liverpool drew at Birmingham.

'I thought we were going to win the league. That was our best chance,' Atkinson admitted in an interview for this book. 'Liverpool signed John Wark, a player I'd wanted, who did really well for them and gave them an instant boost. We lost Robbo. I don't want to say it's all down to that, but people say you can't be a one-man team, and my response to that is Argentina would never have won the World Cup in 1986 without Diego Maradona. One man doesn't make a team, but *can* make the difference. How good would Ajax have been without Cruyff? We had changed the system to play Robbo at the top of a diamond and he was getting quite a few goals. Losing him was a blow but not the only one. Our midfield against Barcelona was Remi, Ray, Bryan and Arnold. Against Juventus we ended with Alan Davies, Remi, Paul McGrath and Arthur Graham on the left. Decent enough players but, in comparison to what we had, it was difficult. Despite that, we were still only beaten in the last minute by a great Juventus side. But we took ten points from our last ten league games.'

Robson's absence had drawn admiring eyes to the performance of Ray Wilkins, who it seemed was more 'gettable' than his team-mate. AC Milan had scouts watching Wilkins at the Coventry game and it was intimated they may be interested in renewing their attempt to sign Whiteside, too. 'We are not selling anyone,' Atkinson said at the time. 'It's just the Italians in their hunting season. Wilkins, Whiteside and Robson will be here next season along with other good players who will be joining them.'

But there were developments. Milan offered United £1.5m for Wilkins after the defeat in Turin and it was enough to cause the manager to think again. More representatives from the Italian side were present at Goodison Park as it transpired that talks had been held. 'It's been a traumatic time,' Wilkins admitted. 'My wife and I have not slept for a week.' Perhaps this accelerated his decision to accept the move and draw a line under the matter; it was announced that Wilkins would indeed move to Italy that summer, but at the same time Atkinson warned there was now 'no chance' Robson would follow. For the last few games of the season, it seemed the manager was trying to discourage interest in Whiteside too, giving him a run of games from the bench as Mark Hughes started to become a first-team regular. If that was his intention, it had the opposite impact, as Whiteside confessed in his autobiography that he wondered whether he had made a 'serious error' in turning down the offer to sign for Milan.

The important moment in the title race came on May Day – Monday, 7 May. United entertained Ipswich Town at Old Trafford in the last home game of the season. With the title still a realistic possibility, Atkinson discussed the near future in his programme notes: 'Once again you have made Manchester United the best supported club in the country, and the vocal encouragement has undoubtedly been an important factor in our success this season,' he said. 'We have enjoyed a good following at away matches as well which we also appreciate. The only cloud on that horizon was being unable to organise any trips for the European matches, but as I have tried to explain before, this was simply not possible in the face of potential crowd trouble. This is most ironic because while Manchester United might have had a problem with hooligans a few years ago the behaviour of our fans these days is remarkably good ...

Our aim now is to try and deliver some reward in the championship for our fans. At the time of writing we are still in close contention with Liverpool with nine points still at stake ... whatever the outcome I think we can claim to have made progress with more points and more goals than last season. It's a pity we were unable to go into the last lap with our strongest team, but that's all part of the game, and on the positive side two or three of the younger players have impressed in their places. I believe the future is looking good for Manchester United ... so good in fact that it seems the Italian clubs want half our team! We cannot stop other people admiring our players, though I must say the endless speculation has been a bit trying. All I will say at this stage categorically is that nothing will be done which won't be in the best interests of Manchester United. I am not looking to sell our best players, but in the competitive world of football you have got to keep all your options open. Rest easy this summer, though, we will be back next August stronger than ever!'

It looked good at half-time; United led against Ipswich thanks to a Hughes goal, and although Liverpool had taken control of their own home game against Coventry just before the break, the teams were continuing to match stride for stride. That all changed over the following hour; Liverpool scored three second-half goals to triumphantly win 5-0, while United instantly conceded an equaliser and could not fashion a winner no matter how much pressure they put on the visitors. That kitchen sink philosophy backfired when Ipswich scored a breakaway winner in the 86th minute. Alan Sunderland – on loan from Arsenal, where he had destroyed United's trophy ambitions in the past – struck one of only three goals he would get for Ipswich which helped them avoid relegation. (This game was also the footnote for the famous statistic about the last time, at the time of writing, that United led at half-time at Old Trafford and lost the game.)

Liverpool now had a five-point lead at the top of the table with two games left. 'It will need a miracle now,' Atkinson admitted.

The following Saturday, the destiny of the title was confirmed when United could only draw at Spurs – a point earned through a goal from Norman Whiteside from the bench. Atkinson joked afterwards, 'If we can get 12 points from our last game against Forest, we've done it.'

'Big Ron' might have been in jovial spirits as it emerged that it was not only his players drawing envious glances from overseas. Barcelona, whom he had conquered a few weeks prior, were interested in hiring him as manager. 'All I can say is that Atkinson is in the middle of a contract with us,' Martin Edwards said. Barcelona eventually plumped for another Brit, Terry Venables.

United could not even get one point from their rearranged visit to the City Ground. Garry Birtles scored and Viv Anderson got the other in an effectively 2-0 dead rubber game which still carried a little bit of a sting. Liverpool had won their title but drew their last two league games; in fact, they won only two of their last eight league games, and those two wins represented the six point difference between them and United. More galling for United supporters was that they didn't even finish second; Southampton had leapfrogged them into that position, and it was even *more* embarrassing when Forest got third spot, not simply by virtue of that win against Atkinson's side, but the second goal, which made their own goal difference +31 and United's +30. The end-of-season collapse could not have been any worse.

Following the Barcelona win, United dropped 20 points in the league and needed only seven to win it outright (or maybe even six, as those points might have changed the goal difference enough in United's favour as Liverpool's goal difference was ten better). The home draw to West Ham and home defeat to Ipswich were easily five more points United should have picked up. Then it would have needed just one result on the road to have gone in their favour. Was it down to Robson's absence? Well, ten points were dropped without him, and ten were dropped after he came back, although you might look at the last two games when United knew the game was up and discount them.

It wasn't just Robson, it was Muhren's absence too. The Dutchman insists that he didn't feel as if that had so much of an impact that it 'cost' United anything. 'I don't think so. It's all part of the game,' he told *Red News*. 'These things happen all the time and besides, it's not a one-man band, it's a team performance. But the squad wasn't that big as it is now, so sometimes it was more difficult to find a replacement for certain players who got injured, but to say this concerned me … no.'

Muhren theorises that the growing pressure, particularly in the run-in, might have begun to creep into the minds of the players. 'Oh yes, the pressure was high but I felt different,' he said. 'I just did my utmost to play as good as possible (when fit) and that's all you can do. Maybe the ones who were playing at United for a longer period had some problems with it as they all wanted it so desperately for themselves and the supporters, but if you cannot cope with that pressure it goes at the cost of your performance.'

Martin Edwards concurs that he felt the squad was too thin to cope with the number of injuries it suffered at the worst possible time. 'We dropped off because Robson and Muhren got injured right with a few games to go,' he says. 'It all fell away at the end of the season. In those days the squads weren't as big; today you'd be able to handle that situation much better.'

That squad size is a particular bone of contention; Gary Bailey feels that a tighter squad would actually be beneficial, but it was the injuries which were costly. 'We should have won the league under Ron. There isn't just one reason why, there are loads,' he says. 'Aston Villa, for example, used a small squad when they won the league. They kept the same team as often as they could. If Ron had been able to do that, I'm sure we would have won it at least once. But we had injuries to Robbo and to other key players. We should have been more successful and it is very frustrating that we weren't.'

Another theory is that, after defeating Barcelona, the distraction of Juventus and the possibility of European glory shifted United's eyes from the domestic prize.

'They used to say that Bryan was a one-man team but I always thought that was a little bit disrespectful to the rest of the team,' Graeme Hogg says. 'I wouldn't use Bryan's absence as the only reason why we didn't win the league or lost against Juventus. There were other mistakes made as well. After beating Barcelona we took our eye off the ball a bit, concentrating too much on the Juventus game. We got carried away with how well we'd played against Barcelona and thought we only had to turn up to win.'

Mick Duxbury disagrees. 'I don't think we were distracted, no,' he says. 'We were obviously disappointed with the Juventus game. But then we were top of the league and you have all those games to look forward to, to hopefully be the first winners since 1967. If there was a distraction, it's only in that you're going for something else as well. Not in spite of, not instead of, but as well.'

It was likely, then, a combination of different things, hitting United at the most unfortunate period; though one might also suggest that a stronger squad, a better squad, might have been able to deal with the setbacks. That's what Liverpool did, after all. And that's another point; it has to be remembered that this is largely acknowledged as the best Liverpool side there has ever been. They won the League Cup, the league and then they went on to win the European Cup as Joe Fagan enjoyed an incredible first season as manager.

This was not the best Manchester United side of all time and yet in 1984, as they weren't even bridesmaids watching their rivals sweep up most of the major honours, they might well have felt they were Liverpool's equals, having defeated them in the Charity Shield and taken four points from them in the league. The strength of the opposition and the scale of their achievements in the context of their own history should go some way to redefining the perspective that Ron Atkinson's brilliant team are viewed with, and yet, it is that incredibly harsh label of underachievement that this Manchester United team are stuck with. They should have done better, even taking into account the mitigating circumstances around their late-season collapse, and it was for the players to raise their own standards for a renewed push at the championship in the 1984/85 campaign.

Money Spinner

THE SALE of Ray Wilkins raised £1.5m for Ron Atkinson to spend to bolster his Manchester United team, and in the summer of 1984 he duly obliged. There was also the matter of around half a million pounds of the compensation payout for Steve Coppell, but that had been earmarked for Jesper Olsen, the Ajax winger who had agreed to sign at Old Trafford in the winter of 1983. The petite Danish left-footer was courted by many top clubs in European football, but Atkinson had used the information that he was a United fan to his advantage and stole a march by negotiating a very early deal.

'Olsen, in particular, will be a revelation in the English First Division,' Atkinson boasted in his 1984 book *United to Win*. 'Olsen boosted our hopes [of signing him amidst strong competition] by declaring a marked reluctance to the idea of pursuing his career in Italian football, and I decided to fly out to Amsterdam for talks with him. The moment we came face to face proved to be a particular embarrassment for me. I had been sitting at a table waiting for him to arrive and when he walked in I sprang up from my chair to greet him. Unfortunately, the zip on my brand-new pair of trousers burst wide open. He looked at me in amazement and I mumbled hurriedly, "We don't pay a lot at Manchester United, Jesper, but we do have some fun" ... I am excited by the prospect of what Olsen can achieve in playing for United in the 1984/85 season because I truly believe he has the ability, character and ambition to become the most exciting player seen at Old Trafford since George Best. He is an old-fashioned dribbler who attacks defenders with tremendous skill and pace.'

As soon as the season had wrapped up, and the money for Wilkins was safely in the bank, Atkinson made clear his intentions with the reshuffling of his team. Bryan Robson would never have a goalscoring season as great as his 12 league goals and 18 strikes in all competitions in 1983/84, but the manager was not convinced about the benefits of the longevity of a midfield diamond when considering the sacrifice of natural width. One might conclude that Atkinson had dismissed a successful system somewhat prematurely, when it was the absence of players rather than the dysfunction of the formation which had proved costly.

In the final ten games of the previous campaign, United had failed to score on five occasions, and on four more had only scored once per game. Arthur Graham had done a good job but Atkinson wanted more pace down the sides and identified the relentlessly fit Gordon Strachan of Aberdeen to provide it. A £500,000 deal was agreed with Aberdeen in May, but the transfer would not be completed for another three months as German side Cologne claimed he had already signed for them.

While that saga was ongoing, Atkinson finally landed a long-term target when he brought in Alan Brazil to bolster the frontline and finally provide some senior competition for Norman Whiteside. The Spurs striker signed for £700,000 in late June and said: 'I would like to get a bit of my old form and consistency back. I don't regret joining Spurs initially. They were a big club and at the time what they had to offer was good.'

United coach Mick Brown said, 'It's no secret that we wanted another striker. We have now got four. It doesn't mean anyone will be leaving but it does mean we are in a better position with our strike force.'

Atkinson was delighted to have got his man at long last. 'I had always admired Brazil's talents,' the boss admitted. 'The lad was sharp and lively, and his priceless ability to turn defenders in their own penalty area was not shared by other strikers in Britain. In my opinion, he is to goalscoring what Bryan Robson is to midfield play. I was completely and utterly convinced that he was the player I must acquire for United. His skills look made to measure for our set-up ... Arnold Muhren, who had teamed up so successfully with Brazil in their days together at Ipswich, would often implore me to sign Brazil. He would insist that he could make his pal enough chances to win United everything that was going. Muhren believed quite strongly that Brazil was one of the best players in the world. Indeed, missing out on signing Brazil was in all probability the biggest mistake I made at United in those first two years as manager.'

Those words uttered in the summer of 1984 might feel foolish in retrospect, but one has to at least believe there is some substance to them. Atkinson *had* wanted Brazil, and United *had* struggled sometimes when Whiteside was particularly suffering with the heavy burden. The irony now was that he had brought in the player he wanted but the supply line he had planned for him was going to change; Muhren's playing opportunities would be restricted with the signing of Olsen.

Olsen's arrival was indicative of another change in British football. The deal had been negotiated by the agent Dennis Roach. This was nothing new in itself; Roach was first involved in a transfer at United when he arranged the deal of Nikola Jovanovic in 1979. He had also acted as representative in deals with United's own players over time, including Gary Bailey, Norman Whiteside, Paul McGrath and Mark Hughes. In the intervening years, Roach had ingratiated himself enough in the Old Trafford boardroom to act as an agent for the club, negotiating overseas friendlies and tours, and was involved in the arrangement of games in Spain against Roma and Bilbao in the summer of 1984. (Incidentally, Roach's relationship with United would prove important some years later as he was a part of the entourage around Frenchman Eric Cantona when he was moving to England.) He also had a hand in United's post-season schedule as they went on a trip to Hong Kong and Australia in May and June. Atkinson took a squad that was missing a number of star names; in fact, missing so many players that guest players had to be invited. These players included Frank Worthington – who, remember, had previously been linked to United but at the age of 35 would not be considered for a move now, despite reports in the Australian press that he was 'expected to sign' for Atkinson – and Peter Barnes, who would in fact one day make that move a permanent reality. Tommy Hutchison, the former Man City midfielder who had made his name at Blackpool and Coventry, made up the numbers with Bailey, Moran and McQueen the most senior players on the tour.

Atkinson had been greeted at Sydney Airport by a reporter who said, 'Mr Atkinson, I'd like to welcome you and Manchester United to the World Series of Soccer!' The United boss was bemused, even though there was a fairly big game on the tour as they resumed old hostilities with a far stronger Juventus team at Sydney Cricket Ground. The rookie and part-time United side achieved a goalless draw but lost on penalties. Atkinson took the opportunity to firmly rubbish the idea of Bryan Robson going to Turin.

By the time the pre-season campaign was underway, the deal for Strachan had also been concluded, thanks in part to the intervention of Aberdeen manager Alex Ferguson. Ferguson was keen for Strachan to sign for United because his club would receive a far bigger fee than if the winger went abroad. Cologne eventually agreed to drop the matter when United offered to play a friendly with them in which the German side could keep the gate receipts. As it transpired, the friendly never took place.

'In my judgement, Strachan is a player of similar calibre to Wilkins and in the same age bracket,' Atkinson said. 'We had also made a profit of £1m on the transactions. I have not necessarily finished buying new players; however, I would like to sign a top-class defender if possible, but for the moment my hope is that the new signings will provide a vibrant stimulus not only to the team but also for the fans ... The squad of players at my disposal is now bigger and stronger. The new acquisitions are good footballers who, I believe, will bring success to the club.'

While United had undoubtedly strengthened their squad, Liverpool had taken a big hit when one of their greatest-ever players, Graeme Souness, moved to Sampdoria. The Italians had failed in another bid for Robson (£2.25m, Liam Brady and Trevor Francis was the admittedly attractive package presented to United) but got Souness for a relative snip at £650,000. Atkinson stated that the summer's transfer activity encouraged him to 'believe passionately' that Manchester United were now on the very brink of becoming the major force in English football. We have more potential match-winners in the team than ever before. My major criticism of the United side last season was that we hardly ever managed to pick up a point we had not worked desperately hard to win. We always had to play exceptionally well to win matches because we did not possess the players to get us a goal out of the blue. Liverpool, on the other hand, often played below par but had Ian Rush standing by to produce for them a winning goal out of nothing. Now I believe we have players whom I can term potential match-winners ... My conviction that by the time I retire I will have won all the major prizes the game has to offer has never wavered. More than anything else, I want the league championship for Manchester United. The time is now right for United to win.'

Those words were written in the book he released that year and the level of expectation was not only matched by most at Old Trafford, it was becoming a demand. On 15 August, ten days before the season kicked off, fans sprayed graffiti on one of the walls at The Cliff which read: 'Do you hate Scouse enough?', 'League titles – Liverpool 15, United 7', and 'Edwards + Atkinson, do you cry at night?'

Mick Brown insisted that the manager was as frustrated as the supporters seemed to be. 'Look, when we faded out at the end of last season, I don't know about the boss being disappointed but he was bloody hell to live with,' he told reporters.

And Atkinson himself may have had a different tone than the bold statement in his book, but the message of ambition was the same: 'We're trying to play everything down,' he said. 'Graeme Souness said to me in the summer that we were going wrong by saying too much. You don't see stories about "Liverpool are going to win this or that" and, to be fair, I don't think I've ever predicted that my team is going to win anything. But that's the way it is written. All I want to say is that we feel we have made progress each year and that in signing three quality players, financed by the money we received for Ray Wilkins, we have a better squad.'

All three players would be in the first team for the opening game at home to Watford. The team sheet read: Bailey; Duxbury, Moran, Hogg, Albiston; Strachan, Moses, Robson, Olsen; Hughes, Brazil. Whiteside was on the bench as the manager decided to go with Hughes.

The 4-4-2 was clearly an emphasis on United's own style but the manager was not dismissive of the disruptive approach of the visitors to Old Trafford on opening day, as he complimented Watford's style and predicted they would trouble a lot of opponents in his programme notes for the game. 'Hopefully it won't be us too much this afternoon as we swing into action to make what I believe will be a stronger and sharper bid for the championship,' he said. 'We have got three new players in our squad who can make the difference between actually winning things and just missing out.'

It took just half of the first half for Gordon Strachan to make an impression. He had been United's most impressive player in pre-season and showed fine awareness to catch Watford's offside trap off guard. The referee followed Strachan's control as he chested the ball down and raced on to it; the Hornets backline had paused, expecting the linesman's flag to go up as Brazil and Olsen were in offside positions. The referee waved play on, and Strachan was brought down by the goalkeeper Sherwood. The new signing picked himself up and scored the spot kick. It was the right boost for Atkinson's side, who had endured a false start; as they lined up in the tunnel, the referee noticed their black socks clashed with Watford's, and sent the players back to change into white socks!

United were unimpressive after going in front. They could not get a second goal and did not seem to have great cohesion with their new system. Criticism of a lack of organisation could never be levelled at this Watford team, and as the anxiety of the crowd seeped into the home players, Graham Taylor's side struck a blow in injury time to snatch a draw. With quarter of an hour left, Atkinson had withdrawn the ineffectual Brazil for Whiteside. Journalist Paddy Barclay suggested that Brazil might be 'at this early stage, a question mark against the manager's judgement. United may need time, which money can't buy.'

Guardian reporter Ronald Atkin said: 'United will need to remedy the inconsistency in home games which cost them a crucial 18 points last season.'

Well, consistency certainly seemed to be the order of the day as far as Atkinson was concerned, as he prioritised continuity in the short term in an attempt to achieve long-term benefits. United drew their first four games but the manager kept the same team throughout, hoping that something would click. Despite the mounting pressure around the club, the boss projected the same image to his players, living up to the image of someone who genuinely loved being at Manchester United as opposed to a figure who could not bear the responsibility. He had not wavered in his belief that his approach was the right one.

'Training was still five-a-sides,' Graeme Hogg recalls. 'Ron would always join in and would often swap sides to join the winning team. We were training once on Littleton Road and it was pissing down. Ron was wearing a baseball cap because he didn't want to get his hair wet. I remember Robbo saying to Giddy he was going to knock it off, so he clipped a ball into Ron to force him to head it. Rather than risk his cap coming off, Ron ducked and fell in the mud. The price of vanity!'

But Atkinson was not so vain as to blindly stick to a pattern that wasn't working just because one of the players underperforming had been signed by him. Alan Brazil just did not seem to fit into the United style of playing; the change in approach with two speedy wingers and two industrious midfielders meant Brazil could not link up with the play as he had done with Muhren at Ipswich, and with Muhren not getting any game time, the chances of the new striker impressing had lessened.

Atkinson bit the bullet and dropped Brazil in order to play Whiteside and Hughes (with Frank Stapleton still convalescing after a knee operation in the summer) up front together against Newcastle. The result was emphatic, as it seemed a switch had been flicked and all of the issues about incompatibility in those opening games were immediately dismissed. Olsen in particular was fantastic, creating a golden chance for Robson before scoring a superb goal on the stroke of half-time, intercepting a defensive pass and rounding the goalkeeper to finish cutely. When Strachan scored a penalty in the third minute of the second half, United were in complete control and started to play with the sort of confidence one expected. Further goals followed. Hughes and Whiteside did not seem to feel the same sort of pressure as Brazil to stay up front and deliver the goals; the result was a more fluid style of play, though Hughes did help himself to a goal on the hour mark. It was a tough afternoon for the visitors who had Peter Beardsley in their ranks; the forward could not make an impression on his return to Old Trafford, with that decision to put the faith in Whiteside and Hughes fully justified.

Atkinson's side were flying and scored a magnificent fourth through Remi Moses; Albiston, Strachan and Hughes were also involved in a passage of super one-touch passes that ended with Moses drawing the goalkeeper out before sliding the ball in. It was a huge moment for Moses, wearing Wilkins's number four shirt, to show he was an able replacement.

The only damp spot on the second period was the inability of Whiteside to convert an Albiston cross to get his own name on the scoresheet. But a fifth goal followed soon after as Duxbury and Moses combined well to set Strachan away. The winger's dummy fooled a defender and he also became the third United player to embarrass visiting goalkeeper Kevin Carr by running around him with the ball before putting it into the net.

After the comprehensive 5-0 win which was, more importantly, delivered with style, Paddy Barclay wrote: 'Will Manchester United win the championship? I don't know; don't really care at the moment. I just wish there were another match at Old Trafford tonight. All the virtues the club had in mind when they replaced Dave Sexton with Ron Atkinson three years ago were in evidence as Atkinson's remodelled team overwhelmed Newcastle in the second half on Saturday.'

The same team achieved a handsome three-goal win at Coventry before Atkinson decided to give Strachan a rest for the UEFA Cup game against Raba Vasas at Old Trafford. Arnold Muhren was recalled and instrumental in a 3-0 win the manager described as a 'good, sound, all-round performance'.

Muhren scored the second and his performance meant the press were keen to talk to him after the game. He was realistic about the situation facing him. 'The side was more or less picked at the start of the season,' he said. 'I'm not happy that I wasn't in it but the manager spent £2m buying new players and he would not have done that if he had no intention of playing them. I'm certainly not sure of keeping my place. I will be very surprised if Strachan is not back soon and I will just have to accept it. It's the risk you have to take when you play for a club of this size.'

Quite whether Alan Brazil was so understanding about his own position is uncertain. Having not been given the chance to play against the Hungarians, Brazil might have hoped he was being kept back for the big game against Liverpool at the weekend, but instead suffered the ignominy of running out for the reserves at Sheffield United in between the games; a sign he would not be considered for the weekend.

The game against Liverpool, despite Brazil's absence, saw a lot of focus on United's expenditure. Jesper Olsen's star turn against Newcastle had caught the eye with those who wondered whether he might be too slight to adapt to the physical nature of the British game beginning to feel like they might be proved wrong. Olsen, though, admitted to some press that he was still coming to terms with it, which prompted a humorous response from his boss. 'Our lads were in stitches when they heard Jesper talking about the physical side of English football,' Atkinson said to reporters. 'I think he must have kicked everybody in training by now. He's a hard little player – make no mistake about that.'

United drew first blood in the important encounter; Strachan pushed Alan Kennedy into the box, forcing him to commit in an area where he didn't want to – penalty. It was converted with the usual unerring accuracy.

Robson and Moses were dictating the midfield battle and combined to set Olsen up for a fine chance which could have made it two; the captain then had a great effort saved in equally stunning fashion by Grobbelaar.

United had numerous chances to put the game to bed but Liverpool grabbed a barely deserved point with the kind of lucky goals scored by perennial champions; a Kennedy header was cleared off the line by Hogg, but the clearance hit the head of Liverpool's own new striker, Paul Walsh, who unwittingly got on the scoresheet. The wet and windy conditions made it difficult for either team to get into a genuine rhythm but United still felt they had done enough to win.

On BBC's *Grandstand* before the game, it had been suggested United were trying to buy their first league title since 1967. 'Seven players out there today cost us nothing,' Atkinson hit back. 'Anybody would think that we go out every summer and buy a team. This time we were in the fortunate situation of being able to sell one player and spend the money on three others.'

In a League Cup game against Burnley, youngster Billy Garton was given a chance while Muhren and Graham were asked to run the wings. Alan Brazil was also given a chance from the bench, but he came on for Whiteside only to be present alongside Hughes as the Welshman scored a hat-trick in a 4-0 win.

Robson scored the first in that game, and also again from a deflected free kick in the following game at his old club West Brom. For Brazil there had been a mini-reprieve as Whiteside's injury kept him out of the game at The Hawthorns, but the former Spurs striker was again unable to make an impression. It was a difficult game where the referee struggled; penalties were awarded to, and scored by, both teams as United won 2-1, though Atkinson confessed the decision for his team was generous. Robson claimed his former team had been over the top and that referees should offer United more protection.

'I had a word with the referee and told him that unless he took some names the game would get out of hand,' said Robson. 'I'm not asking for special favours, or saying that we are softies. But unless referees do give protection, especially to Olsen and Strachan, then it could become horrible.'

The Express's John Wragg said of the win: 'Evidence is mounting that unbeaten United are capable of winning the championship.'

Yet evidence also remained that they were reliant on their skipper; he was injured in the return game with Rabas (a 2-2 draw which earned a tie with PSV Eindhoven) and missed the trip to Villa Park where the hosts won 3-0. He was back for the next game – a 5-1 destruction of West Ham. Despite the return, the resilient, multidimensional qualities of this United team were instead praised.

'West Ham came to Old Trafford last season to defend, and sneaked away with a goalless draw, boring everyone but themselves,' Paddy Barclay wrote in his match report. 'On Saturday they tried it again and caught a thrashing from a team improved by the arrogant skills of Olsen and Strachan. Ron Atkinson's vision of a great new Manchester United is beginning to materialise.'

Other changes to the team included Brazil and McQueen making starts, and both got on the scoresheet, the former grabbing his first league goal for the club. The latter was in jovial spirits despite not featuring regularly. 'It was not a lot of fun,' McQueen joked about the lack of work the defenders had to do. 'Mind you, we did get a bit slack in the last ten minutes, when Remi stopped tackling my men as well as his own. I had to flick the ash off my cigar!'

Despite those draws, United were in third place and kept that position with a hard-fought win over Tottenham. 'Spurs have some ultra-competitive players and we had to stand toe to toe with and slog it out with them,' Atkinson said after a Hughes goal midway through the second half gave his team the victory. 'Last week we demonstrated how football should be played in terms of artistry but today we expected a totally different game and we got it. We earned the right to play. It was better when we got little Olsen moving down the left. He took some stick. He is a fiery little lad but I told him at half-time that the best thing to do was to hurt them with his ability.'

It had been quite a day for United, who had been boosted by the news of Bryan Robson agreeing a huge seven-year contract to remain at Old Trafford. Earlier in the month, it had been suggested that at the club's AGM, which would be held on 1 November, they would announce a record profit of £1,731,000.

From rude health to rude awakening; a difficult week shone a new perspective on the contemporary challenges facing United. First was a troublesome trip to Holland to take on PSV; after years of similarly controversial episodes for English clubs, things would come to a head in this campaign. Atkinson had been good to his word when restoring United as a European force. It had not been without its problems.

After the St Etienne incident in 1977, United's next foray into Continental competition was in the UEFA Cup in 1980. 'I went to Łódź in 1980 on a club trip organised by Dave Smith,' remembers supporter Bill Goodall. 'We stayed for two nights in Warsaw and travelled to and from Łódź by coach so we were in the town for only a short time. The only hint of trouble was after the game when their supporters entered the pitch and some Reds threw a bench at them from the terraces. The only issue we had was finding beer in Warsaw. It was around the time of the Solidarity movement and beer was only available when we had locals with us.'

That was a single tie – United were eliminated on away goals in the first round – and they were eliminated at the same stage two years later by Valencia in a game that was more problematic and something of a scene-setter; as mentioned earlier, the club were fined for the trouble in Spain. 'We travelled on a day trip organised by the club,' Goodall recalls of the Valencia trip. 'It started well and we were allowed into their trophy room to look around. We soon found some bars near the ground with Reds who had been in the nearby coastal towns. Word soon spread about trouble involving Reds at one of the resorts but it was calm around the ground until it neared kick-off. Two of us walked down the street to the ground to see the team arrive. As we walked back the local police were attacking Reds in the doorway of a bar. One of the policemen, a big bloke with a beard, reappeared in the ground hitting Reds indiscriminately with a baton. Trouble started in the upper section of the stand with what appeared to be Reds reacting to taunts from locals. After the match the police chased us on to our coaches for the airport and then let locals stone the coaches.'

United were reluctant to encourage their supporters to travel, going as far as refusing to sell tickets for European away games to their official supporters' club, but the 1984/85 European journey went by mostly without any newsworthy controversy. Most United supporters travelling to the games in Prague and Barcelona got tickets in the home section. 'For Prague we travelled independently by Inter Rail, finding a hotel in Frankfurt on the way,' says Goodall. 'It was a very relaxed atmosphere and we bought tickets for the home end on the day. We spent the first half on the terraces and then made our way into the one stand they had for the second. I would say the match was one of the best United games I have seen.'

Press reports – possibly scaremongering – suggested police in Barcelona had 'dungeons' waiting for supporters but no real trouble occurred. Turin was a different matter altogether. 'As soon as we entered the ground we were pelted with coins,' Goodall remembers. 'Our tickets were from Mike Ross and there were about 500 Reds in the lower section of the terracing. Juve fans pelted us again with missiles and attacked us with flagpoles from around the perimeter of the pitch. We regrouped under the stand, then ran out at the Juve fans, who scattered, and we settled down to watch the game. There were skirmishes ongoing throughout the game, mostly with the police. We were taken back to our hotel by coach with the National Guard outside to stop us getting out. That didn't stop us once the hotel bar was dry.'

Matters were made more complicated the following season. With two high-profile trips to Barcelona and Juventus in recent memory, United's next European adventure caught the public attention, and so it was newsworthy that the club were continuing to advise their supporters not to travel when they were drawn against PSV. United did not take up an allocation but they were not assisted in the matter by the local side or authorities. It was reported that the hosts had set aside a thousand tickets especially for people with British passports.

'This is very disturbing news,' chairman Martin Edwards said. 'We asked for no tickets for the match and have done everything we can to stop people travelling. But this is almost an invitation to them. It could undo all the good work we have been trying to do since the trouble in Valencia ... We have done everything in our power to prevent renegade fans from travelling.'

Club secretary Les Olive also spoke to the newspapers. 'After all our preparations this comes as a shock to us,' he said. 'We intend to let UEFA delegates know our feelings immediately. We have been working with PSV, who appeared to have done their best to prevent the sale of tickets to any unofficial outlet. And we had the Dutch police over to discuss the problem. Now it just seems like an open invitation to the troublemakers.'

Maybe it was; but there was a significant percentage of those fans just wanting to watch their team continue a tradition they had helped to pioneer for British football. For many, there was adventure to be found in the journey in the days before low-cost flights from budget airlines.

'Persil vouchers were used to buy 2-for-1 train and ferry travel and we set off for Eindhoven,' Bill Goodall says. 'When we arrived in Eindhoven the local police were handing out leaflets telling us how to get tickets. They had a sensible approach to our visit and they were really relaxed. I didn't see any trouble but we did see a bar that had been trashed by some Reds. The only person I know who didn't get in was a mate who was drunk outside the ground, and looking for a lad who had his ticket, who happened to be drunk and inside the ground.'

The letter handed out by police read thus:

To all Manchester United supporters
On behalf of the Municipal Police, welcome to Eindhoven.

Since Eindhoven is unfamiliar to you, we thought we should give you this pamphlet to let you know how things are done here.

A number of tickets will be available from the main ticket office at the PSV stadium from 10am. The stadium is within walking distance of the railway station. Policemen will show you the way. Tickets can only be bought on presentation of a British passport.

You can spend the whole day in the centre of Eindhoven. There will be a large police presence and the tolerance of the police is low. Just have a pleasant day so that you do not run the risk, after a long journey, of missing the match itself. If you have any questions or problems, please feel free to approach a policeman; he will be glad to help you.

The PSV Stadium has a number of house rules. The most important are:

- no objects which can be used as offensive weapons may be taken into the stadium (e.g. canned drinks, bottles, penknives, sticks, flagpoles, etc.)
- no supporter under the influence of drink will be allowed into the stadium
- everyone must agree, if requested, to be searched when entering the stadium.

A special section of the stadium has been reserved for you. If you do not have a ticket for that section (VAK X), do not simply go to the section for which you do have a ticket as you then run the risk of getting into a large number of PSV supporters with all the consequences that this may have. Contact a policeman. He will give you advice. You will be kept in your section for approximately 15 minutes after the end of the match. Then you will be accompanied by the police to your transport. For those travelling back via the Hook of Holland, there will be a special supporters' train waiting at the station. This train has a direct connection with the night boat to England. There are no trains after the match which make this connection. We hope you have an enjoyable stay in Eindhoven.

United drew 0-0 in a game that was as thankfully uneventful as the trip (there were actually a dozen arrests, but no major incidents). They would qualify for the third round with a narrow win in the second leg; more on that in a moment. All in all, the journey had been a fairly taxing distraction from the football, which had finally seemed as if it had been settling down. Maybe this had an impact on what was to follow.

The title challenge picture was not taking shape yet in the First Division, with Arsenal and Sheffield Wednesday leading the way and the usual suspects like Liverpool and United still trying to find their feet. Add to those names Everton, who themselves had stuttered in the first few weeks of the season, only to record a sensational win at Anfield through a brilliant Graeme Sharp goal. Now, one goal in October does not end a title race, but the impetus and confidence it gave to an Everton team which would go down as the greatest in the club's history cannot be understated. It was followed up by a seminal performance against United at Goodison Park, though it was also a game which proved to be a constant headache for Atkinson for various reasons.

Mick Duxbury was out injured and so too was his usual replacement, John Gidman. It meant that Kevin Moran had to deputise at right-back with McQueen and Hogg in the middle. Alan Brazil was in for Whiteside, with Stapleton the substitute. After just six minutes Everton took advantage of United's unfamiliar defence and then another head injury was suffered by Moran. By the time United could bring him off, they were 2-0 down. Stapleton came on and Strachan moved to right-back. A third goal was scored soon after and a heavy defeat became a huge embarrassment when the hosts scored two late goals to add some gloss to their victory. That is not to suggest United deserved any better; sportswriter

Peter Ball said they were defeated 'as thoroughly as the 5-0 scoreline suggests'.

Atkinson then saw his team beaten by Howard Kendall's side again three days later when Everton won a League Cup game at Old Trafford; Alan Brazil had scored an early goal, but the Toffees levelled it up and won when their former player Gidman converted a late cross into his own net.

The televised Friday night game against Arsenal came at the best possible time, then – an opportunity for Atkinson's side to get back on track in an encounter sure to be full of bite. 'There can be no doubt about our objective tonight,' the manager said in his programme notes. 'The memory of our last league game is burned unforgettably on my mind and I am sure our players won't forget it in a hurry either. Everton's five-goal win was the heaviest I have ever experienced as a manager. Manchester United have not had many like that and it beholds us all to wipe out a nightmare performance with a good show against the Gunners this evening … While I want our players to remember the experience and hate it, it would be foolish to let it destroy our confidence. We have to remember that we have scored a couple of 'fives' as well this season, one of the victories ironically being against another title-challenging side, West Ham, the team that has just topped Arsenal off the top of the table! That's the fascination of football, of course, and why it is difficult to give a sensible answer to the people who ask what went wrong at Goodison Park. The fact of the matter last Saturday was that Everton played very, very well and we played badly; put those two things together and you have the explanation for a five-goal difference. We still had enough good players out there to have done better.'

Arsenal were usually vulnerable victims for United to exorcise their demons; it seemed as if the London side might get a shock win at Old Trafford when they came back from Bryan Robson's early goal to lead at half-time, but Atkinson's side turned on the style in the second half, with three goals to secure a fine 4-2 victory.

Gordon Strachan scored two of those, and two late penalties in each of the next two games secured two more wins – first, an extra-time kick against PSV which was the only goal of the entire tie, and then a last-gasp winner in a topsy-turvy 3-2 win at Filbert Street.

Norman Whiteside, back from injury, then scored both goals in a 2-0 triumph over Luton. The win ensured United were in second place, above Arsenal on goal difference, and behind Everton by three points, that result at Goodison Park being the definitive separator.

The following five games suggested that United had some afflictions they needed to address. Moran had been out for a spell injured and he was joined on the sidelines by Hogg; Hogg was not the most talented defender on the books, but he had showed a reliability and a consistency which had led to him being the most commonly selected centre-half throughout 1984. McQueen was fit, but age (he was now 32) and injuries were now catching up with him. His time at United would soon come to an end and it was clear that at least one more senior defender would be needed. Atkinson was in the market for one; during that winter, he was linked with a move for Terry Butcher, the brilliant England and Ipswich defender, and Mark Wright, the Southampton centre-half.

United were 2-0 up at Sunderland after just 14 minutes through goals from Robson and Hughes but suffered a late capitulation as the hosts turned it around to win late on. A 2-2 draw followed in the first leg of the UEFA Cup tie with Dundee United; twice leads were thrown away. A routine 2-0 win over Norwich was followed by a trip to the City Ground, where Ron Atkinson brought in Arnold Muhren for Olsen, feeling his experience would be crucial in the return against Dundee, and so wanted to give him a run out against Forest. But for the second away game in succession, United had a two-goal lead only to lose in injury time. Forest won 3-2, and Atkinson was literally sick, having suffered food poisoning the night before the game. 'That was one of our finest performances this season and we have come away empty,' he said.

Next it was the trip to Scotland; a trip where United sensibly decided to relax their approach on supporters attending, such would have been the pointless nature of banning them.

'It was a day trip by train,' United follower Bill Goodall says. 'Some of us had been successful in the club ballot, and the rest bought forged tickets from Manchester tours. The tickets were printed on orange card and were so easy to forge. It was a bit of a shock for us when the pubs were open when we arrived at 10am and didn't close at 3pm, but we struggled through! The pubs in England still closed between 3pm and 5:30pm in 1984. Some locals told us to watch ourselves around the ground but the only trouble we saw was when a group of Reds burst into a pub we were in and then promptly apologised as they had attacked the wrong pub. And there was a rush at the home fans from our section during the game but it soon halted when a lad collapsed.'

The selection of Muhren was justified against Dundee as this time a 3-2 scoreline on the road went in United's favour. The Dutch winger scored the decisive third goal which was not only the winner but the security away goal, which meant Dundee would have needed to score twice. The former Ipswich man wasn't to know it at the time but this would be his final goal in United colours; he would, however, have known his time was surely coming to an end, due to Olsen's emergence.

'I was more off than on the pitch,' Muhren told *Red News*. 'They bought Jesper Olsen and he became first choice, and when you're 35 you feel written off. But when you hear fellow players and supporters saying that you still should be in the squad it gives you a boost to continue. I knew I was going to leave a beautiful club, although I had a contract for one more season, but as I was no longer first choice and having the feeling you still can play at the highest level, you have to make a decision. Johan Cruyff, manager with Ajax at that time, asked me to return to Ajax as he wanted an experienced player in his very young side. I played alongside Cruyff and knew him very well so was flattered he asked me to come back. Besides, the kids were at a certain age that you start thinking what is the best thing to do for them in reference to school, etc. and I could go and live in my home town again. So after seven years in England we decided to go back to Holland. I always had a very good relationship with Martin Edwards so we had a few talks about it and although he did regret my decision he also respected it and gave me his full support to finalise my transfer.'

That decision would be some months away; Muhren would still play a few more games for the club. Atkinson, though, continued to look for experience to back up Olsen on the wing, and considered bringing back Gordon Hill. Hill was now 30 and was back in the UK after playing in the NASL, which had recently folded; his English league career had been destroyed by that knee injury he had suffered at Derby shortly after leaving United. Atkinson invited Hill to participate in the five-a-side games he would have with coaches and other former professionals he knew on Fridays after the first team had trained and was impressed enough to consider offering him a contract. It never happened; United did still have Muhren on the books, as well as Arthur Graham; Graham had actually seemed certain to join Man City after the clubs agreed a £25,000 deal, but the player changed his mind. It is not certain, but this may well have been the final nail in the romantic idea of Hill returning for an Indian summer, although the prospect of his knee withstanding the rigours of the First Division doesn't seem very realistic. (It should be said that it is still more likely that Muhren and Graham's contracts, rather than Hill's injury, were the roadblocks.)

The more serious interest was in Butcher and Wright, but Atkinson could not convince either club to do business. After the win at Dundee, it was suggested the United boss was 'angry at reports on United's defensive failings rather than attacking attributes' and it certainly appeared that his post-match comments were engineered towards changing the narrative: 'We have been involved in some of the most exciting games in the country this season and that will continue to be our policy. I'm convinced what we are doing is right and will eventually bear fruit.'

Atkinson was given some vindication by the next two results, although identical scorelines prompted very different reactions. A 3-0 win over QPR was accomplished in some style and could have been more handsome if Gordon Strachan had not missed a penalty. That wasn't enough to encourage criticism from John Course for *The Guardian*, who instead paid the most incredible compliment to a number of United's stars, asking: 'Strachan, Stapleton, Hughes, Olsen – have United ever had a better quartet?'

Clearly, there had been enough evidence throughout Atkinson's three and a half years at Old Trafford to invite favourable comparisons with the greatest sides in the history of Manchester United. This wasn't the first time statements with such sentiment had been declared and it wasn't the first time that they would immediately be followed by words of caution; this time, though, those apprehensive words would come from one of United's own stars. John Gidman had been the star name over these performances, the right-back scoring in that victory over QPR and in a 3-0 win over Ipswich too. The latter victory was not quite as emphatic as the scoreline suggested, with plenty of criticism directed towards the defending, and Gidman, the adventurous right-back, admitted: 'All round we looked shaky. There were times when we should have been punished but we weren't. That's football and we got three.'

Gordon Strachan – scorer from the penalty spot for the ninth time already this season – insisted it was a team effort. 'The way we are built,' he said, 'we should be defending as a team as well as attacking as a team.'

At Christmas, Spurs led the table on 39 points, United were second on 38, Everton third on 37, with champions Liverpool languishing in eighth with 31 points. But the frailties which threatened to undermine Atkinson's team staging a challenge in the second half of the campaign were exposed again over Christmas as they lost at Stoke on Boxing Day before winning handsomely at Chelsea to close out 1984.

It had been a year which had seen United lose to Bournemouth and defeat Barcelona. They had matched Liverpool on a head-to-head basis on any occasion throughout the year and yet lacked the defensive discipline to see out games they were leading with 12 minutes to go, causing them to lose on both occasions in those recent weeks. With many journalists making forecasts in their end-of-year pieces, projecting Manchester United's fortunes remained as unpredictable as ever.

Alan Thompson of *The Express* said: 'The summer shows signs of being intolerable. If either Spurs or Arsenal win the First Division, Londoners will be telling the rest of us they discovered the game. But it is definitely on the cards, because Manchester United are too brittle in defence. They think they can play the game before they have scored the goals.'

Meanwhile, *The Guardian*'s David Lacey conceded that Bryan Robson's injury had a significant impact on United's chances of success in 1984, but was not willing to give the benefit of the doubt now. 'This time, however, with the title up for grabs, Atkinson's stock will surely fall if United fail again,' Lacey wrote.

Before the Chelsea game, former winger Mickey Thomas – now plying his trade at Stamford Bridge – had explained the difficulty facing players in the Old Trafford spotlight. 'You have to play for United to realise the constant pressure their players are under to succeed,' he said, 'and although on paper they have the best side in the country, they are not consistent enough.'

There was a great opportunity to remedy that with the first four games in 1985 at Old Trafford (it would actually turn out to be five), but injury problems worsened as the month went on. Hogg and Moran were still out, so too was Whiteside, and Jesper Olsen was also ruled out of the New Year's Day game with Sheffield Wednesday at Old Trafford. The Owls became the latest team to grab a late winner against Atkinson's side, with an Imre Varadi double; Strachan missed a penalty which would have still seen United only get an underwhelming draw. The Scot atoned by scoring the first in the FA Cup tie against Bournemouth; in a twist of fate, United were drawn against their conquerors from the previous season, but this time the Cherries were picked apart comfortably as the favourites won 3-0 to earn a tie against Coventry City.

That meant Coventry at Old Trafford would actually be United's next two games as they were scheduled to play in the league the following week. After remedying the inconsistent home form in the first half of the season, Ron Atkinson's team slumped to their second defeat on the spin in 1985; more costly than the three dropped points was the loss of Bryan Robson, who suffered a dislocated shoulder after the momentum from a forward run had carried him over an advertising board where he landed on the transformer box of the recently installed underground heating system. Robson was advised that surgery would keep him out for ten weeks, whereas rest and treatment should keep him out for no longer than six. The midfielder took the fateful decision not to have surgery; he would suffer further dislocations with even greater ramifications down the line. As it transpired, he would miss nine weeks anyway, which would have made surgery the most logical decision.

United also defied logical expectations – though maybe given their penchant for doing the unexpected, it should have been anticipated – by coping better without Robson than many would have ever counted on. That owed something to the beneficial impact of another disappointing injury, however, when Kevin Moran (who else, really?) was forced to come off after just 15 minutes of a game at Highbury.

Before that, however, United were continuing to prove themselves as reliably infuriating as ever. A hard-fought win over Coventry in the cup saw Atkinson defend his team's approach: 'Sometimes we try to be too tidy, but there are days when sheer drive is best.'

It was a bit tidier in a 2-0 home win against West Brom, but as soon as they promised to go on a nice run, they were stopped in their tracks when relegation-threatened Newcastle grabbed a late equaliser at St James' Park (Peter Beardsley rubbing salt in the wound by scoring the goal).

'An embarrassing pattern is beginning to emerge,' sportswriter Erlend Clouston said in *The Guardian*. 'How many times this season have Manchester United squandered leads, underestimated inferior opposition, studiously failed to seize opportunities to haul in the mathematical slack between themselves and the top of the table? When, on the stroke of half-time, Moran volleyed in Hogg's nod-on from Strachan's corner, that should have been that. It wasn't. Unless United sharpen up they are in danger of being considered challengers not in the league race but the caucus race – which, as the Dodo told Alice, merely involved starting when you want, and stopping when you want.'

Atkinson didn't know who or what he could depend upon. Seemingly not Bryan Robson's ability to stay fit. Not his defence to hold firm to secure a result on the road. Not Gordon Strachan's ability to score from the spot (he missed again against Blackburn in the cup, but scored to help his team win 2-0 nonetheless). And certainly not the fitness of Kevin Moran; when the Irish defender was forced to come off with a hamstring injury, the United boss might well have reconsidered his recent denial of reports that he was interested in the young Fulham defender Paul Parker. Parker would eventually find his way to Old Trafford in 1991.

Moran's replacement at Highbury was Norman Whiteside, from the substitute's bench. Paul McGrath moved from midfield, where he was deputising for Robson alongside Mick Duxbury who was also an emergency fill-in for Remi Moses. For Moses, a game at Highbury (though he didn't play this one) would signal another body blow to his career. Whiteside moved into the centre of midfield and became an accidental revelation. It was reminiscent of the occasion Tommy Docherty had been forced to play Brian Greenhoff in defence and suddenly found himself with a brilliant partnership of the Yorkshireman and Martin Buchan.

'The game was like a dream and I immediately felt comfortable in the role,' Whiteside said. 'For the first time I was facing forwards for long periods and instead of getting tangled up with defenders, fighting for the ball with back to goal, most of the field was constantly in my vision.'

Whiteside's class was in stark contrast to the more agricultural football played between these sides when things got petty. The Northern Irishman put on a masterclass fit for royalty, which was fitting as the King of Tonga, Tāufa'āhau Tupou IV, was present. On the half-hour, United broke from a corner; Stapleton played the ball to Olsen, who found Whiteside on the edge of the box. The new midfielder turned back on to his left side and curled a superb effort into the top corner.

The goal – the winner – marked a masterful display where Whiteside almost immediately reinvented himself from harrying forward to artistic midfielder and his manager joked that Robson might not be able to regain his place.

'It will be interesting to see if he gets back in the side when he's fit,' smiled Atkinson after the match. 'People thought when Robson was injured that it was Goodnight Vienna to Manchester United. Well, you've got to give full credit to what the team have done without him, although obviously he is missed. If they'd played the same way, with the same drive, last season when he was out, we would have been champions.'

Atkinson elaborates in 2019. 'In 1985 we were a little better equipped to deal with Bryan's absence,' he says. 'I always thought Norman was a great finisher, probably the best we had on the books. If we had a chance I would want it to fall to him. But I always felt he wouldn't be quite quick enough to be a great centre-forward. He reminded me of Ray Kennedy who Liverpool moved into midfield. Ray blossomed and I could see the same for Norman. It came about as a bit of an accident. In training before the Arsenal game in February 1985, Remi picked up a knock we thought was innocuous at the time, but it ultimately finished him. He was just about to get picked for England. Against Arsenal we got another injury early on, so I had to bring Norman on in midfield. He scored the winning goal from that position and that was it, he was moved.'

Moran would be out for a couple of months; Moses would miss the rest of the season in an attempt to return for the following campaign. Both he and Robson would still be absent for the next game; a crucial match with league leaders Everton at Old Trafford. Stapleton and Muhren were also on the injury list, but Atkinson decided to keep Whiteside in midfield and recall Alan Brazil. The Toffees had a seven-point lead and a game in hand; United were in third, and Spurs were in second place three points in front of Atkinson's team with a game in hand themselves.

A bumper crowd of over 50,000 were present to encourage their team and in just the third minute Olsen charged at Gary Stevens only to be felled in the box. It was the 15th penalty the club had been awarded that season.

Thankfully, this farce did not play out on the pitch, but it later transpired that after having missed four from the last five spot- kicks, Gordon Strachan was no longer first-choice taker. After the game, Atkinson claimed Olsen should have taken the penalty (though it is not clear whether the new routine had Olsen on penalties, or if it was to be the player who had been fouled who would take the kick). The manager claimed the player had been too shaken up by the foul; Olsen denied it. 'No, I just didn't fancy it,' he said. On commentary for *Match of the Day*, John Motson claimed he had spoken to Strachan earlier in the day, and had been told that the Scot did not expect to take the kick.

Strachan showed some guts to step up, but his kick was poor, barely even right of centre. The lack of conviction made it one of the easiest saves of Neville Southall's career. Strachan was not too hurt by the miss and continued to be at the heart of United's best moves. He and Olsen combined to set up Brazil, who rounded Southall but never had the ball under his control enough to get a shot away. And Brazil was unfortunate moments later; he controlled a long pass majestically, flicking the ball past two defenders. On the third bounce, the ball just got away from him so he couldn't get a shot away, but it fell perfectly for Olsen, who rattled in a drive from the edge of the box. The ball deflected past Southall and gave United a 37th minute lead.

One sign of champions, or great teams at least, is to come back from a setback quickly. Everton did just that before the break when Trevor Steven shrugged off being hit by an object thrown from the Stretford End to clip in a corner that was headed in by Derek Mountfield.

With the scores level at half-time, it was fairly evident that United viewed this as a last real chance to pull themselves back into the title race and threw everything at their visitors. Jesper Olsen played a fine ball to Brazil, whose inventive shot on his wrong side smashed against the crossbar and away.

With six minutes left, though, it seemed as if they would, in fact, lose; Albiston was unfortunate as his aggressive challenge on Steven was a little too forceful and was punished with a penalty. Kevin Sheedy stepped up, and his kick was delivered with much more power than Strachan's. It was, however, in a similar area, if slightly more to the goalkeeper's left, but Bailey was equal to it, pushing it wide.

The day after this game, the miners' strike ended, as Prime Minister Margaret Thatcher claimed a 'famous victory'. But neither United nor Everton could get their own from a game *Match of the Day* host Jimmy Hill described as 'as exciting as any' he had seen that season.

The circumstances of the game made it difficult to know whether to feel elated or deflated. 'The result hasn't helped us,' Atkinson mused, 'but Spurs have started to close in and you don't know how that might affect Everton.'

Stapleton was back, and back on the scoresheet, in a narrow 1-0 win over Hungarian side Videoton in the first leg of their UEFA Cup tie.

Whiteside continued to show impressive form, netting a hat-trick against West Ham in the FA Cup to set up a semi-final clash with Liverpool. And Whiteside was the hero again with a late winner in an impressive, and crucial, game at White Hart Lane. Three days later, United got a Friday night point at the Boleyn Ground when the returning Bryan Robson came off the bench for Whiteside and scored the leveller in a 2-2 draw.

Those dropped points did not dampen Atkinson's spirits, who said ahead of the return game against Videoton: 'We are showing signs of running into our best form. And our results over the last couple of years have proved that we pull out all the stops in Europe.'

What a time then to put in a flat performance. Videoton scored early on and United could not galvanise themselves to get a goal either in normal or extra time. It went to penalties, and Frank Stapleton blasted over the bar, giving the hosts the chance to win with the last kick of the regular five. That was fired wide, but Arthur Albiston gave them another chance when his awkward right-footed effort was saved. The hosts did not pass up their next opportunity to win the game, and United suffered an embarrassing exit from European competition, though Atkinson had attempted to temper expectations before the game, describing it as 'as hard a task as any British club has got in Europe'.

The trip was a lively one for the United fans who made it, but it passed largely without incident (the coach company that took a group of supporters made a complaint about their rowdy and drunken behaviour, but this was pretty insignificant taking all things into consideration). It was a setback and not quite a glorious way to end this year's Continental adventure in comparison with the games against Barcelona and Juventus a year earlier. Unbeknown to anyone at the time, it would be United's last foray into European competition for another five years. At the end of this 1984/85 season, English clubs would be banned from competing in Europe after the Heysel Stadium disaster that May, in the European Cup Final between Liverpool and Juventus. Liverpool supporters were accused of charging at Juventus fans, breaching a fence; as the Italians attempted to escape the violence, they were pressed against a concrete retaining wall. Many Juventus supporters were killed in the crush, but then the wall collapsed, killing more (39 in total died), but allowing some to escape to safety. Fourteen Liverpool supporters were found guilty of manslaughter and Heysel has been described as 'the darkest hour in the history of the UEFA competitions'. As a consequence, all English clubs were given a ban from UEFA which at the time was indefinite.

'We did try to appeal against the decision,' Martin Edwards said. 'Our argument was: how can you ban all clubs because of one incident that has happened abroad, that was out of all the other clubs' control, and that occurred in a stadium that was probably not fit to hold a final anyway? I appreciate some action had to be taken, but our feeling was that UEFA had tarred all English clubs with the same brush due to the actions of a minority of supporters. Our appeal fell on deaf ears.'

Heysel has often been referred to as an event which was inevitable. In 2005, Liverpool-following journalist John Keith described it in *The Independent* as 'the horror of a tragedy waiting to happen' (though it is important to note Keith is referring largely to the antiquated state of the stadium rather than the hooligan culture). In Chris Rowland's self-published *From Where I Was Standing: A Liverpool Supporter's View of the Heysel Stadium Tragedy*, the author takes a similar approach when he writes: '... in truth the ban was the bill English football had to pay not only for Heysel but for over a decade of violence by English football followers, in which Liverpool's supporters actually played very little part.'

United fans had been no angels on their jaunts away from England and indeed had been faced with more than one punishment from UEFA in recent years, and yet Bill Goodall insists that something as tragic as Heysel *had* to happen. 'I don't think I ever thought something as horrific as the loss of lives at Heysel would ever happen at a match,' he says. 'I remember watching the events on TV and thinking it was just another terrace fight. I know there was more to Heysel than the lack of organisation, but the positive approach the police took in Eindhoven really hit home with me. The only time I recall feeling uncomfortable in a ground while following United was in the Leppings Lane end at Hillsborough. I always went in the seats there after that. It stays with me that we could have been in that semi-final.'

It was a huge blow to the careers of the likes of Bryan Robson and other United club stalwarts like Mick Duxbury and Arthur Albiston. The peak of their careers – which Robson had now indefinitely committed himself to – would be spent without European football. Spare a thought too for the greatest Everton team in history who would have had a great chance of winning the European Cup. For Robson, at least, there was the consolation of winning the European Cup Winners' Cup in 1991 after United were allowed to compete again. But he was the only one from United's 1985 team (though Clayton Blackmore was in and around the squad) who would make it to Rotterdam.

Victory over Barcelona and the tightly contested game against Juventus suggested United were better than the underachieving tag they were given. In the aftermath of the Videoton game, there was a more immediate need for pride restoration, and it was an angry United team that took to the pitch for their league game against Aston Villa. Mark Hughes thumped in a hat-trick in the first 20 minutes as Atkinson's side won 4-0. It was a good way to compensate for the relatively below-par form Robson had showed since his return. A specialist had leaked to the press before the return game in Hungary that he didn't feel the midfielder was fit to play.

United then won against Leicester and Stoke to solidify their second-place position in the league; there was a gap of just four points to Everton, but the Toffees had two games in hand. The remote chances of winning the league were dealt a further blow after a 1-0 defeat at Hillsborough which came just a few days before the FA Cup semi-final. Lee Chapman had scored the winner for the Owls, giving some observers cause to question United's central defence which, in the absence of Moran, was McGrath and Hogg.

The player who had been tipped to come in and bolster that position gave a feature interview to *The Guardian*. 'Pressmen used to ring me up and suggest the best places to live outside Manchester,' admitted Ipswich's Terry Butcher. 'Eventually me and my wife thought, "bloody hell, this could really be on." But then I had a talk with my manager who said he was definitely not going to sell me, no matter what. So I went home and told the wife and after that it was just a question of buckling down and getting on with the job at Ipswich. It was all pie in the sky really.'

United and Liverpool contested a fantastic semi-final at Goodison Park. Atkinson had said the weekend would either be 'the best of the season, or the worst for many a long year' as he considered the prospect of playing out the final weeks with no prize to contest. He portrayed a calm persona on the touchline before the game but his nerves must have been wrought when Liverpool came back twice to equalise, first in the last few minutes of normal time, and then again in the last minute of extra time. The latter came in controversial circumstances, as the linesman flagged for offside, but Liverpool were allowed to play on by the referee and scored through Paul Walsh.

Atkinson, though, was not too cross. 'Unfortunately the referee was looking into the play and the linesman was behind him,' he said. 'We've no complaints about the referee, he had a great game. But it needed just one whistle at that point and we were at Wembley.'

The United boss preferred to praise the performance of Paul McGrath: 'Before the game I wondered how people like him would handle the situation. After all, it was his first domestic semi-final and he was against the European champions. But he played as if it were a testimonial match.'

Liverpool manager Joe Fagan also praised McGrath while conceding his side had been fortunate. 'To be quite honest they were the better side,' he said. 'I don't normally take much notice of the opposition but both of United's central-backs stood out for the strength and determination. I was very impressed.'

Less impressive was the behaviour from the terraces. Jesper Olsen was hit by an object thrown from the Liverpool end while taking a corner, while Liverpool fans fired flare guns at United fans. Two fans were stabbed, two policemen were injured and 46 people were arrested.

The replay at Maine Road was less troublesome and more memorable for the right reasons. Not for Paul McGrath, though, at first; having impressed so much in the first game, he made the first notable contribution for the wrong reasons, heading a cross into his own net just before half-time. There was time for Liverpool to almost get a second while their tails were up, but Nicol fired just wide. The scousers were made to pay for not killing off their rivals. Less than a minute into the second half, Robson played a one-two with Stapleton and then advanced, before firing a magnificent shot from 25 yards into the top corner. The perfect riposte to those who felt he wasn't at his best. United were buoyant and on the hour mark scored another fine goal; Strachan played Hughes through, and the Welsh forward fired in from the edge of the box, showing remarkable composure. The goal turned out to be the winner – Robson was once more carried off the pitch on the shoulders of supporters, though it was the match-winner who got most of the column inches after the match.

Paddy Barclay described Hughes as 'the most evocative player United have produced since George Best.' He was certainly a player the supporters absolutely loved. At 5ft 10in, he was not the most imposing of players, nor did he carry the sort of bulk which would go some way to justifying his remarkable physical strength. But he had tremendous upper body strength and possessed a bravery which helped him go if not eye to eye then certainly toe to toe with opponents who stood half a foot taller than him. There was no better shielder of the ball. The list of his unique qualities did not stop there. His thighs were extremely muscular, helping him generate superb power on his passes and shots. He was genuinely two-footed – enough to make you wonder what his stronger side was. He was a scorer of great goals but also timely ones; this winner in April 1985 merely the first of an illustrious list of crucial interventions by one of the most remarkable individual players in the history of the club.

Hughes explained his physical style. 'I get whacked about by defenders and just try to give as good as I get,' he said. 'It is not a question of going out to kick people. I just feel that, if I can get the physical side of my game going, put a few block tackles in or something like that, the rest will follow ... It will be difficult to maintain this year's level of success but that's what I'll be striving for because you are in the game to win things. Once you've had a taste of what I've experienced at Maine Road you want more. It's like a drug.'

Hughes was often cited as a scorer of great goals but not a great goalscorer. That would probably be a tad unfair, but it is true to say that this 1984/85 season would see his best-ever goal tally of 24. He also failed to score for the remainder of this campaign, but that feeling of an anticlimax was something which spread quickly over the club in their two games after Maine Road. Defeat at Luton was followed by a goalless draw at home to Southampton to end any realistic hopes of challenging Everton for the league title (though they would come up against them in the FA Cup Final). After that game against the Saints, United had played three games more than the Toffees (37 as opposed to 34) and had a nine-point deficit. United had a maximum of 15 points they could win; Everton had 24. It was as good as over.

A draw at home to Sunderland followed – Norman Whiteside missed a penalty, but the returning Kevin Moran rescued a point. Moran secured all three with the only goal at Norwich the following week, before the final home game of the season against Nottingham Forest.

'I believe we have given the game a lot of entertainment this season, both home and away, and I am looking for the FA Cup as the reward for our positive approach,' Atkinson said in his final programme notes of the campaign. 'We had a few problems in mid-season which spoiled our championship challenge, but they are behind us now ... I hope we can underline the fact that we are ready for Everton at Wembley by displaying some of our skills in a winning way against Forest this afternoon.'

United won 2-0, but if Atkinson was hoping for an uneventful build-up to Wembley to avoid a recurrence of Highbury in 1983, he was sadly mistaken. A trip to Loftus Road should have passed completely without event considering it was a dead rubber, with neither side having anything to play for. That didn't extend to the players, as some were keen to make a name for themselves for inclusion in the Wembley team. Alan Brazil, so often on the outskirts despite having been so coveted by Atkinson, scored in the first half. But the second half was far from a casual late-of-season affair. In the first minute, Graeme Hogg pulled up with the recurrence of a pelvic strain. The Scot was devastated; he knew it would keep him out of the final.

Eight minutes later and it all kicked off. Gordon Strachan scored a second for the visitors. QPR player Steve Wicks reacted angrily, calling the linesman a cheat as he believed Strachan was offside. Wicks was sent off and the home crowd were furious; a coin was thrown at John Gidman. With everything threatening to boil over, a message came over the public address system: 'Calm the proceedings down, cool things a bit.'

QPR pulled a goal back shortly after but Brazil made an emphatic point by scoring in injury time to make it three. He might not make the final team, but he was making a good case to be the substitute (teams could still only name one). If there was a place up for grabs in the team, nobody put in the best audition at Vicarage Road in the last game of the league campaign. Olsen and Robson were rested, providing chances for Duxbury and Brazil to try to prove themselves as best choice for 12th man. Moran and McGrath partnered each other in defence as they would have to be first choice for Wembley.

But a 5-1 battering by Watford put nobody in a good spotlight, including the manager, who was the first to admit fault: 'I knew Everton would employ Graeme Sharp and Andy Gray in attack and they would beat nobody for pace. Everton would pound it up to them and they would feed off the second ball. I did not want Gray and Sharp to spend all afternoon under our crossbar. I needed to keep them at bay. The best way to deal with them was to hold a high defensive line and I wanted to test the theory out at Vicarage Road. The flaw in that plan was the Watford attack was led by Luther Blissett and John Barnes, who had all the pace in the world. I went into the dressing room and announced, 'I have to tell you, lads, we won't be playing that way on Saturday.'

In the build-up for the FA Cup Final, *The Guardian*'s David Lacey at least evaluated performances over the season rather than the last seven days when commenting on the ability of Atkinson's team. Lacey said it was difficult to recall McGrath having a bad game, and that the Dubliner had ironed out his occasional tendency to lose concentration, 'if that's not tempting fate'. But Lacey *was* perhaps tempting fate when he reckoned Kevin Moran, 'one of the league's top-ten' defenders, and so an able replacement for Hogg, might even 'be a match-winner'. Hughes was described as 'footballing genius' while the praise for Olsen was even greater – 'to see him twist, turn and run with the ball is to appreciate a modified version of the incomparable George Best.'

Ron Atkinson meanwhile described Strachan as 'Steve Coppell with tricks'. The qualities of the likes of Robson, Bailey, Albiston and even now Whiteside, a veritable veteran with 148 first-team games under his belt, were on record and well documented. Despite the numerous missed penalties, Gordon Strachan had enjoyed an exceptional first year at Old Trafford. John Gidman had overcome injury and the challenge of Mick Duxbury to get the nod on this occasion.

'When it got down to the last training session before the final, I was more or less aware it was down to me or Alan Brazil who would get the nod as substitute,' Duxbury remembered. 'On Friday afternoon, Ron came over to me and told me that I'd be sub. I know that Alan was told some time later and I kept my news to myself – I think he was told on the coach going to the game that he wouldn't be included and he took it as a massive, massive disappointment.'

That disappointment would be short-term and long-term for Brazil. Despite that impressive brace at QPR, Atkinson had been informed by the physiotherapist Jim McGregor that the back problems Brazil had suffered from through the season were chronic. McGregor advised the manager that he would have to swiftly move the player on because in his opinion he would be 'finished' within 18 months. That move would come in January of the following season, but not before Atkinson had attempted to use him in a swap deal for Cyrille Regis, the Coventry City forward who he had worked with at West Brom in the 70s. Atkinson felt sorry for Brazil because the timing of the move when he eventually came to Old Trafford meant he was given chances ahead of Whiteside who was already a hero on the terrace. 'It was held against Brazil,' Atkinson said. 'Always.'

Brazil's plight made Duxbury appreciate his involvement a little more, instead of feeling too deflated about not being named in the starting team. 'It put it into some perspective for me that I was grateful to at least be in the squad, but it was still a huge disappointment compared to the fact I'd started in the last final,' the defender admitted. 'Everyone wants to be in the starting 11 in a final. You don't wish ill of your team-mates but you're hoping to get on as early as the first minute. I didn't, and neither manager appeared ready to make a change as the game remained very tense and close fought.'

As previously stated, this was the finest Everton team in history. They had stormed to First Division success with an 18-game unbeaten run from Boxing Day. Due to their phenomenal run in the FA Cup and European Cup Winners' Cup, they still had three league games to play *after* their trip to Wembley, but had guaranteed having won the league by at least ten points. They were arriving for the final on a high after their victory over Rapid Vienna in the European final – their only European success. Everton striker Andy Gray revealed how much he and his team-mates wanted to win at Wembley. 'We desperately wanted the double of the league and cup, and if we'd not played in Rotterdam I'm sure we'd have done it,' he said. 'Everyone was tired, aching and hoping that they would recover in time.'

In the league encounters, the two teams had played out that thrilling draw at Old Trafford, but there was that 5-0 humbling at Goodison Park, which would suggest that the game would be tight or won handsomely by Everton, though David Lacey refused to discount United. 'The popular feeling seems to be that United will win and thwart Everton's dreams of a treble just as they foiled Liverpool's threefold ambitions in 1977,' the journalist wrote. 'In more than one instance the wish may be father to the thought. United are the most entertaining team in the country – when they find the right blend and rhythm ... Their players catch the eye because so many of them are prepared to run with the ball and pit their wits against opponents on an individual basis ... but for every individual strength they can offer, Everton have the ability to match it. If United are going to win they will probably have to do the bulk of the work before half-time. Strong second-half performances have been a feature of Everton's success this season. Of course, Robson, Hughes, Whiteside, Olsen or Strachan can turn the 1985 final in one inspired moment.'

Inspired was not exactly how one would describe the dour first half. It seemed that Everton were keen to test Gary Bailey's nerve and, as they anticipated, the goalkeeper came out to punch a long throw after ten minutes; from the punch, Peter Reid hit an effort that was deflected on to the post by Gidman. United, for all their investment in width, found themselves with similar issues to the cup finals of 1976 and 1977. The Wembley pitch was simply too big for that strength on the wings to be exploited in any proper way, and the game instead became an attritional battle through the middle, as most tight finals seemed to be. To that end, United were hardly going to be found wanting, but Everton clearly felt as if they would live up to the pre-match predictions with a strong, confident start to the second half. Peter Reid did well to set up a chance for Andy Gray, but the striker lashed at it with little composure.

Robson was booked for a foul on Reid, and then Gray himself was booked as United began to come back into the game and exert their own pressure. Whiteside saw an effort saved by Southall. United had

Everton pushed back and the defenders appeared willing to take a chance to break them down; on one such occasion it almost proved cataclysmic. John Gidman stepped back from a rolling ball in the 78th minute to allow McGrath to take possession; but the centre-half was too far away to have it under his control, and Reid showed great anticipatory skills to intercept. Suddenly there were three Everton players against Kevin Moran, who committed and brought down Reid. It was some fifty yards from goal and in today's game a red card would be the only sensible outcome. Back then, sending a player off was so uncommon that referees would often just point to the sidelines instead of brandishing a red card (they had been introduced in 1976); it had certainly never happened in an FA Cup Final before. Peter Willis, a retired policeman by (former) trade, was the official who made history – in his last ever game as a referee. Moran was distraught and furious and initially refused to leave the field.

'It was a shock, a terrible shock,' Moran, who said his first instinct had been to 'smack the referee', recalled. 'I'd gone for the ball, not the man, you can see on the television replays that I kept my foot down. I almost got there, too, but as I followed through my body caught Peter and he was knocked into the air, which made it look far worse than it was. As I left the pitch I felt dreadful. I thought I'd cost United the cup, that ten men couldn't possibly hold out, particularly as the match went into extra time. I sat on the bench and could hardly bring myself to watch. I felt sorry for myself and even sorrier for my team-mates.'

Frank Stapleton was on hand to try to calm down his fellow countryman. 'I looked at Kevin and saw he'd gone,' he said. 'I grabbed hold of his shoulders and held on for all I was worth.'

Norman Whiteside felt the decision was harsh. '[It] was definitely unfair by refereeing standards of the mid-80s and may even have only earned a booking today, as Paul McGrath, who had given the ball away to Reidy, was haring back to cover,' Whiteside said. 'Peter would never have got to the ball and, to his credit, he immensely protested to the referee that Kevin didn't deserve it. Peter Willis, however, was not going to be swayed by character witnesses and made his mark in his last game, going out on the biggest note of all by sending off a player in the FA Cup Final for the first time in history.'

It was a battle for United to get through to extra time, and when Arthur Albiston was forced to come off for Mick Duxbury, further reshaping a defence that was completely unfamiliar, Ron Atkinson now had to hope his patchwork team of ten players could hold out for a replay. Or rather, Mick Brown did.

'We need to put Sparky on his own up front and hold out for Thursday and the replay,' the assistant told his boss.

But Atkinson, who later claimed that this game was the only big occasion at United he'd ever been sure of winning before the kick-off, smelled blood (though as we'll discover a little later, he did have one moment of doubt). 'I moved Frank Stapleton to centre-half but pushed Norman Whiteside up to join Mark Hughes in attack,' he said. 'I wanted Jesper Olsen and Gordon Strachan to play as far up the pitch as they could. I trusted Bryan Robson to protect the now-makeshift back four.'

Football is at its best and most primal in such circumstances. When backs are against the wall and a team feels a certain sense of injustice it can create a unique spirit in the moment. Being a man down did not hurt United in terms of fatigue as much as it might have done considering Everton's midweek final in Rotterdam in which the major exertion of energy had been in the second half. If that was a leveller, then maybe it was United's feeling of being hard done by which tipped the odds in their favour.

Strachan and Olsen, previously almost anonymous, worked relentlessly and showed energy that defied the fact they had spent 90 minutes on the draining Wembley turf. Stapleton applied himself admirably, and even if there was at times a frenetic and desperate approach to United's defending, that only heightened the tension and sense of occasion. Pat Van den Hauwe had a chance in the first half of extra time as Everton cleverly worked a free kick to him; Whiteside showed fantastic defensive nous to get across to him and block the effort. United accepted that their chances would come on the counter, but Everton's numbers meant it was difficult to make a real impression; on one break, Robson found Olsen, but the Danish winger could not get behind the line and his effort from 25 yards was weak and easily saved.

In the opening moments of the second period, Hughes laid on a great chance for Whiteside, but the ball got stuck under his feet and his shot was struck with no conviction. It was the very effort of a man exhausted from almost two hours of football.

Everton pushed United back but Atkinson's team were relentless on the counter. Olsen did well to find Hughes, who turned and surveyed his options before spreading a pass out to the right-hand side for Whiteside to chase and open the game up. The midfielder had three men stopping the route to goal as he changed gear and decided to cut infield. Strachan took note of the change of direction and galloped over to the right, providing an option. The Scot's run was absolutely crucial; Van den Hauwe was given cause to consider his options for the most slight of split-seconds. He didn't commit, and as he was pushed back Whiteside was able to use him as a shield. He performed a step-over and fired a left-foot effort around the defender and to the far side of goal.

'As soon as Pat obstructed my view of the far post, and, consequently, Neville's view of me, I hit it,' Whiteside remembered in his autobiography. 'And the distance the ball took to travel around Pat, the extent of Southall's blind spot if you will, was the same distance the keeper's hand was away from the ball as it crept in and hit his glove bag inside the far post.'

With a goal to protect and just ten minutes to see out, United were unapologetic about their tactics of playing it long for Olsen and Strachan to chase. Everton did not have the legs, pace or penetration to come back into the game, and United were able to see out the match and claim their sixth FA Cup – their third in eight years.

'As soon as Norman scored, I forgot about the sending off,' Moran said. 'It was a great weight coming off my shoulders. At the end, I was just like all the other players, on the pitch celebrating, applauding the fans … I didn't feel any stigma at being the first player to be sent off in the cup final. When people saw the incident on television, I think most people thought I was unfortunate rather than malicious. Certainly the support I got from the club, the supporters and people within football was overwhelming. Looking back on it now, I regard it as just a statistic for the record books.'

Atkinson was delighted, naturally, as he spoke to reporters after, choosing first to defend his player. 'After seeing the television replay I now know the referee made a mistake,' he said, before admitting that perhaps history in the shape of Moran's enforced withdrawal from the 1983 Milk Cup Final had influenced his reaction. 'We may have learnt from that. This time, instead of sitting back, we went at the game, although when the sending-off happened, I thought our best bet would be a replay.'

Atkinson also described it as 'arguably the greatest cup win any side will ever have at Wembley.'

Moran was not permitted to climb the 39 steps up to collect the medal and lift the trophy with his team-mates. In fact, it was not certain he would receive his medal at all. On the trophy parade back in Manchester, he was still the only player without one. There was a meeting with the committee on the Wednesday after the game where it was decided the humiliation Moran had faced for being sent off was 'sufficient punishment'. At the time of the meeting, Moran was with his team-mates flying over the Atlantic for a post-season mini-tour in Trinidad. The defender was called to the cockpit where he received a telephone call to inform him of the good news.

How this success would influence projections and expectations of United's fortunes for the following season could wait until the summer officially began, but this trip west was hardly the relaxing break it seemed. Just 24 hours after landing, they played Southampton at the National Stadium (in front of an impressive crowd of 19,000) and lost 1-0.

'A couple of days later we faced a local select 11 in a game we won in incredible heat,' Mick Duxbury remembered. 'Before one of the games, a gimmick had been arranged where a parachutist would come in and 'deliver' the match ball. I think he actually hit the stand on the way down and got injured – he certainly didn't do what he was supposed to. It was completely bizarre from start to finish. It would have been nice if the club had just taken us away for a few days to relax after another tough season, but I suppose, with the commercial pull that Manchester United have, it was never going to be that simple. Taking the rough with the smooth – it was just part and parcel of what we'd become accustomed to. I feel sorry for the players and supporters alike in these faraway destination tours. We're all human and we get tired. Of course we appreciate the opportunities but the players aren't in the best of conditions to put on their best performances, whether it's at the beginning or end of a season.'

This trip, to some, was perhaps the first time the line between having a good time and having strong disciplinarian leadership was blurred.

'We did have a good time when we could, after we settled,' Duxbury said in his autobiography. 'The first hotel we got to was so disappointing nobody even unpacked their bags. We were told we couldn't travel overnight because of bandits in the hills so we had to leave early in the morning in a minibus. Yeah, it wasn't the greatest of trips. The lack of discipline that Ron had instilled in the team meant that we all got a little carried away with indulging, and I include myself in that. Things are great when everything is going well – and after the FA Cup win, that's how it all seemed to be – but there comes a point when you have to maintain some control. Maybe the events of the next 16 months or so proved that the line between discipline and enjoyment had just become a little blurry for the manager. Yes, we'd be told to be at places at a certain time, so it was never unorganised as such, but what I mean is that normally there is a time and a place for letting your hair down. We'd all begun to do that but then there was nobody to rein us in but ourselves. At the end of a season, you don't see the damage in it because it's part of the fun and seems like the right time, but moving forward maybe it did play a part in what was to happen. The players had a choice and a responsibility too, and they took advantage of the freedom that was given. But maybe that's the point. I go back to the culture at the time and there must have been a fine line between instilling that discipline and maintaining consistency and what we were. Because I'm sure we had the ability.

'Do you blame the players for that, well partly yes, but the manager ought to take some of the responsibility. It may sound like I'm being overly critical of Ron and making him solely responsible for our failure to fulfil our potential, and I have to cut back a little and reinforce the fact that it was part of the culture in football. Perhaps Ron's reign is unfairly viewed because of what his successor did and it's easy to say anything with the benefit of hindsight. One thing I would never shirk away from saying is that the players were at least equally responsible for our supposed underperformance in the 80s. The plus point of our actions was that we were creating a bonding and a togetherness which we wouldn't have otherwise and perhaps that's what Ron was going for. The argument is whether that went too far, but certainly at the time our manager could say his management style was justified because it was bringing some success.'

One night in Trinidad, Whiteside remembered having too much to drink and walking head-first into a glass door thinking it was open. The door didn't break, but Mick Brown wasn't amused, and Whiteside overheard Brown telling Atkinson: 'Look at the state of him. He's an absolute disgrace.' Atkinson, however, defended the player, saying after scoring the winning goal in a cup final, he was entitled to enjoy himself.

Brown was frustrated by being the butt of jokes from some of the players. (Whiteside said: 'I often felt he let things go at home when he might have stepped in. But when he wanted to mouth off and be the disciplinarian, he had a knack of doing it at the wrong time.') On one occasion on this break, one of the players hid under Brown's bed, with the plan being that once Brown got in, they would whip the covers away and hopefully pull him off the bed. But the plan was frustrated when Brown went straight on to his balcony after an evening at the bar, sitting outside with a whisky and cigar. Numerous players – and Atkinson! – were hiding on the balcony of the next room, waiting to hear the fallout from the prank, and could only stifle a laugh as Brown took a large drag from his cigar, exhaled and proclaimed to himself, 'Aah, paradise!'

Atkinson had recently been introduced to Israeli journalist-turned-football agent Pini Zahavi, who appeared to have taken a leaf out of Dennis Roach's book and invited United to Israel for a friendly that would take place the following March (as United explored ways to financially benefit from their official ban from European competition). It is worth jumping ahead, whilst on the topic of Mick Brown, to that trip as it serves as a further example for the mayhem behind the scenes.

'We carried a dead turtle we had found on a beach up to Mick's room, put one of his beloved cigars in its mouth and left it in the shower,' Whiteside remembers. 'It took five of us to carry it up there and it stank so bad that they must have had to fumigate the hotel when we left. But Mick had lost his sense of smell and didn't notice it at all.'

Duxbury was one of the other four and remembers the story in more detail. 'One of the mornings we were out on the beach doing a bit of running and working on our fitness when we came across this giant turtle – well, it was a big turtle, probably not a giant but bigger than anything certainly I'd seen before,' he said. 'Gary Bailey, Lee Martin and myself decided we were going to take the turtle into the hotel. That night we were helped by a local to escape the hotel perimeters (which involved climbing over a barbed wire fence) and drove us to the beach. We were going to drive it back but for some reason that escapes me now, we couldn't put it in the car. Anyway, we carried it back and lifted it over the fence – we'd taken hotel bed sheets to wrap it in. There was a putrid smell coming from it, something seemed to be oozing. We hadn't actually decided what we were going to do with it but then we agreed – Mick Brown's bedroom. We went to reception and got his room key as he was still down having his evening meal. We take the turtle up into Mick's room and go into the bathroom, putting it in the bath, and ran a bit of water. We put the room flowers on the turtle's back, made a hasty exit and went into Gordon Strachan's room where a couple of the lads were playing cards. We were waiting for a reaction but what greeted us first was the smell – it absolutely reeked, and everyone on the floor must have been able to smell it. In the end it got so bad we had to go and take the turtle out before Mick came back. He might not even know about it to this day. We managed to smuggle it out of reception where the local who had helped us took it away. I think he said he was going to take the shell off but we never knew what became of it.'

Was it possible that Manchester United had enjoyed too much of a good thing? If you were to suggest that in May 1985, you would have been looked at as if you were mad.

Vision

THERE IS a popular adage in modern footballing vernacular that the game was invented in 1992. This is a reference to the creation of the Premier League and the television deal the Football League had with British Sky Broadcasting. Television cameras at games were nothing new, and neither was the live broadcasting of matches. But the introduction of it on a regular basis came in October 1983 when Tottenham Hotspur's 2-1 win over Nottingham Forest was shown on London Weekend Television, the ITV network franchise holder for Greater London at weekends. That was the first game of a contract between the Football League and television networks – the BBC and ITV worked together – that lasted two years, and was due for renewal and renegotiation in the summer of 1985.

In the meantime, the advent of sport on television had come at a detriment to the popularity of soccer. American football was now available for British viewers for the first time and other 'working-class' sports like darts and snooker were televised. The hooligan culture had done nothing to romanticise or glamorise the game and there were two horrific televised incidents in the May of 1985 which damaged the reputation of the sport furthermore. There was Heysel, and earlier in the month on the 11th there was a fire at Bradford City's Valley Parade. Cameras were present as City were expected to celebrate winning the Third Division, but those events were overshadowed by the fact that 56 spectators were killed and at least a further 265 were injured. This was not indicative of a

QUE SERA, SERA

violence problem, but the scenes were harrowing and gave further weight to the growing opinion of football stadiums being unsafe environments; it also made for unsuitable viewing for families.

While the FA Cup remained of significant national interest, and consequently of significant interest to the broadcasters, the television networks were less inclined to pay over the odds for regular league games; it was also felt by some senior officials that the football authorities had an inflated sense of worth. 'They have hooligans kicking each other on the terraces, lousy facilities and boring players and they say it's television's fault nobody goes to the game any more,' John Bromley, the head of ITV Sport, had blasted the day before the Heysel disaster. 'The crunch has come. I'm not talking idle threats, but the realities of life. Soccer has no god-given right to its slots on TV and if they don't want to talk sensibly there are plenty of other things to take their place.'

Despite all this, there was a truth accepted by most that in the future, live broadcasting would become increasingly popular. It appeared that the League, and many chairmen of football clubs, were concerned about the drop in attendances, though it had been agreed in the previous contract that, *should* there be a downturn, the television companies would provide compensation based on the average home gate. In his autobiography Martin Edwards says that he was one of a number of chairmen who felt the broadcasters were working together to keep the proposed value of the deal low. One suggested deal was worth £3.8m for 16 live matches as well as the semi-finals and final of the League Cup. Edwards recalls Robert Maxwell (remember him!), still chairman of Oxford United, reacting angrily to that suggestion, stating that £10m was a fairer figure. Maxwell's demands made the other chairmen realise they did not appreciate the value of the revenue made through television advertising and so they sought independent advice.

This was one battle but the chairmen of clubs in the top division were also fighting battles with clubs in the lower leagues; Edwards recalled one particular argument where the more financially strapped clubs vetoed plans to introduce names and squad numbers on shirts because of the cost involved, much to the frustration of owners of the 'top five' clubs in England, which were United, Liverpool, Everton, Arsenal and Tottenham. There was also frustration among the

284

top-level clubs that all clubs were paid the same amount when they were shown on television, despite the high-profile games naturally bringing in bigger audiences.

With no deal agreed with the season set to start, the result was a 'blackout', with no football shown on television at all. Despite this, average First Division attendances dropped dramatically (just about everywhere except for Old Trafford, which actually enjoyed an increase on average of around 4,000 per game from the last season!). Only four out of the first 44 First Division games were watched by crowds of over 30,000, and two of those were at Old Trafford; journalist David Lacey said that the trend 'remains a persistent comment on soccer's steepening decline as a spectator sport.'

The league sponsors, Canon, the camera and camcorder company, grew increasingly frustrated as their exposure dwindled; at one point, they threatened to cancel and withdraw their sponsorship, prompting the League to reach a compromise with the networks. That would not come for quite some time, and, as luck would have it, this period of time just so happened to coincide with the best football Manchester United ever played under Ron Atkinson. Or so we have been led to believe, anyway ...

Live television wasn't the only thing to be disassociated with English football at the start of the season; there was now prohibition of alcohol sold at football grounds, starting with the Charity Shield at Wembley where Manchester United were given a sobering experience against Everton in a replay of their May final. Sportswriter Hugh McIlvanney said of Everton's performance in a comfortable 2-0 win: 'They had been substantially the better team from the kick-off, more thoughtful, more fluently coordinated and far more confidently, persistently aggressive.'

It was quite a deflating way to begin the campaign, which had theoretically had a pre-season that should have been most conducive to a strong start; the ramifications of Heysel and the European ban meant no English clubs went abroad even for friendlies in the summer of 1985.

And manager Ron Atkinson also stayed on the British shores as he looked to strengthen his side; four years in the job and two FA Cups meant there was no shying away from the expectation of a First Division title challenge in the forthcoming season, and no

European journey to distract attention. His first port of call was to try to sign Leicester City striker Gary Lineker, who was reportedly available for around £900,000. Having signed Alan Brazil, and now being unable to offload him, Atkinson had to try to free up a squad place and accepted an offer of £500,000 from French side Bordeaux for Frank Stapleton. Having staved off advances from European clubs, United were now hopeful that the 29-year-old may be enticed to take what may be his last chance to play on the Continent. He turned it down, wishing to stay and fight for a league title.

'We put Bordeaux's offer to Frank, because it was a good one and from an overseas club,' Martin Edwards told the press. 'If it had come from an English First Division club I doubt we would have considered it. We are very pleased with this decision.'

United never pressed ahead with a serious move to sign Lineker; it could be argued that a more concerted case to bring the striker to Old Trafford was made in 1978 when he signed professional terms with boyhood club Leicester City. He had been spotted by Jimmy Murphy, who had identified him as a player to try to get, but his plea fell on deaf ears – one of a growing list of incidents causing the legendary coach to feel disillusioned with the club. Atkinson, a fellow former West Brom man, had made it a point to keep Jimmy around – 'He was always around, and rightly so, as well he should have been; there was always a place for Jimmy,' Atkinson said, but in the summer of 1985 the Welshman was 74 and scouting on a part-time basis (though in terms of hours, Murphy may as well have been a full-time servant to United until the day he died in November 1989).

United made just two signings that summer – Peter Barnes, the Coventry winger, and Chris Turner, the 26-year-old Sunderland goalkeeper, who was brought in to provide serious competition for Gary Bailey. It did not have the desired effect on helping Bailey take his game up a level; he was at fault for Everton's first in the Charity Shield, with McIlvanney saying he had a 'thoroughly wretched afternoon' which would 'intensify the rivalry between the miserable Bailey and Turner.' The manager, though, insisted afterwards that Bailey would start in goal against Aston Villa.

If you were to consider the following theory in purely the context of the three months which were to follow the Charity Shield, you may think it ludicrous; it does seem, however, that Atkinson was beginning to lose control of the balancing act that comes with being liked and being respected. Being liked is all well and good, but being respected is ultimately the crucial element which inspires players to give a little extra. It also helps if you have proof of the success of your choices and the conviction in which they are made. Bailey may well be an exception in that he has gone on record to say he welcomed Atkinson's tendency to try to get under his skin, but Stapleton for one might have had good reason to feel aggrieved after being one of the top performers and yet still touted for a sale that summer.

Likewise had Mike Duxbury, who started the Charity Shield as a right-sided midfielder but was brought off in the second half for the returning Remi Moses. Duxbury was miffed with being replaced at Wembley and was not best pleased with Atkinson's explanation of 'it's a chance to give your mate a game.'

'I was beginning to feel a little out of place and I wasn't very comfortable with it,' Duxbury recalled. 'Every professional wants to be playing, don't they? I accept that not everyone can. There's only 11 players after all. But I felt I was now being used as a makeshift player to fill in when someone else was unavailable – I'd suffered one dip in form and was instantly dropped and then asked to fill in elsewhere. I played as well as I could to try and force my way back into the reckoning, but it was admittedly a little difficult to do so when I always had at the back of my mind that I was never the manager's preference anyway. I did begin to wonder if it was personal, or if I was a bad player. I didn't rock the boat – admittedly, I wasn't exactly a superstar, but I felt I was applying myself well.'

The Charity Shield result was a disappointing conclusion to a thoroughly underwhelming pre-season campaign. 'For some reason I always remember our pre-season results as mostly being dreadful,' Atkinson says. 'It never unduly worried me as I always saw that time as preparation. That year we couldn't go abroad because of what had happened at Heysel. We were beaten by Everton in the Charity Shield. Everybody was doom and gloom in their forecasts. I felt the reaction was over the top even though I was disappointed by the result at Wembley.'

There were more wins than usual, but it was still hardly the stuff of dreams. A 3-2 win at Cambridge was followed by a 1-0 win at

Hereford and then another 1-0 win at Bristol City, before Bradford thumped United 3-1 at Huddersfield's Leeds Road stadium in a game to raise funds for the Yorkshire side. The most notable point from those pre-season games was the appearance of Moshe Sinai, the 24-year-old Israeli midfielder who was on a short-term trial from Hapoel Tel Aviv – possibly at the behest of Atkinson's new acquaintance Pini Zahavi. Sinai (who was capped 44 times for his national side and later was assistant coach for them) was substitute in the first two games and started at Ashton Gate before being brought off. That was the last that was seen of him, with not even a reserve game or two to see more of what he could do.

With Gordon Strachan out injured, Atkinson went for a 4-3-3 to start the league season against Aston Villa, with Olsen up front alongside Hughes and Stapleton. The manager appeared to be going for graft in the middle of the park, with Moses returning to the starting 11 alongside Whiteside, the man who had come in for him, and Robson. The first half was a physical battle; Moses was excelling before he was challenged rather crudely on the same ankle which had caused him to be out for so long. Steve McMahon was the guilty Villa player – soon after Moses was forced to come off injured, Robson aggressively went after McMahon, 'bowling him over' with 'the afternoon's most vigorous challenge' according to Paddy Barclay of *The Guardian*.

United earned the right to play. Within five minutes of the second half, Moses had been brought off for Duxbury, Robson had exacted his own sense of justice, and United had scored twice as their hosts were unable to cope with the movement down the right. First, Whiteside headed home, and then Hughes finished comfortably from a Gidman cross. That same combination linked up to make the game secure in the 75th minute, and Olsen got a fourth after a challenge high up the pitch from Hogg found the Dane in space.

The handsome win was a fine way to start the season, though Barclay suggested that the scoreline was a little flattering: 'As the players trotted off, there was a blood-curdling roar. United looked surprised, as if to say: "Hey, we were good, but not that good." And then they looked up at the electronic scoreboard which told of Everton's defeat at Leicester. The championship trail beckons once more.'

Strachan was back for the trip to Ipswich, but Gidman was injured with a badly cut shin just three minutes into the game and replaced by Duxbury. Atkinson's side had to wait a little longer for the breakthrough at Portman Road, but it was worth the wait; Duxbury, Hughes and Strachan were all involved in a fine passing move, with the latter putting the ball on a plate for Robson in the 63rd minute. 'He was playing much of the time from memory,' Atkinson said of the returning Strachan, 'but by God what a memory.'

That 1-0 success made United the only team to win their first two games, but they were certain to face a physical test at Highbury. Gunners boss Don Howe had identified United as 'the team to beat' this season, but his side were unable to do so. The visitors were comfortable from the first minute and took an early lead through Mark Hughes, dictating the play through a midfield dominated by Robson and Whiteside. Just after the break, Arsenal were awarded a penalty but Charlie Nicholas saw his effort saved; 15 minutes later, Paul McGrath netted the crucial second goal. Another penalty for Arsenal in the last minute was taken and scored by Ian Allinson, but the single-goal margin of the win was not reflective of the dominance of United.

Sportswriter Hugh McIlvanney described Robson and Strachan as 'splendid' with their 'influential mobility' and 'crisp, relevant interventions' which gave United an 'immediate superiority in midfield' alongside the 'thrilling excellence of Hughes'. The reporter noted there was a 'roughness that sometimes threatened to overflow' in United's approach. Atkinson conceded there had been a bit of luck with the missed penalty but insisted his team were only earning the right to win by winning the physical battle. 'They like to press us, we like to press them,' he said. 'When you get teams like this, it's a question of who gives way.'

A routine 2-0 win over West Ham at Old Trafford made it four wins from four, and 20 games unbeaten against London clubs. The Hammers had put on one of their stubborn defensive masterclasses in the first half but were undone straight after half-time as a quick double put them to the sword.

'The main reason United took so long to score seemed to be severe overcrowding in the environs of the visitors' penalty area,' reported Paddy Barclay. 'With McGrath and both full-backs repeatedly joining the attack, the home side often suffered from a surfeit of passing options. Strachan, watched by the Scotland manager Jock Stein, was in classic form, Stapleton back to his subtle best, Whiteside and Robson authoritative.'

Jesper Olsen suffered a cut lip but came back on to the pitch to be instrumental in both goals; however, he was injured late on when a tackle to his ankle would rule him out for a few weeks. In his place came Peter Barnes for the game at Forest. Brian Clough's team had been a bogey side for United in years gone by, but their resistance was broken in under two minutes – Mark Hughes scored a spectacular angled drive into the top corner. If not for the in-house closed circuit television footage clubs recorded, Hughes's remarkable effort would have been consigned to myth and legend. The United fans were still singing '1-0' when Barnes made it two shortly after. Strachan crossed for Stapleton to make it three goals, and three points, before the first half was over.

'United's leadership of the First Division is beginning to look serious,' said journalist Peter Ball. 'The manner of this victory ... was as compelling as the result. The feeling this year is that the unbeaten leaders are made of sterner stuff. Certainly the early moments here suggested that this time everything Atkinson touches is turning to his favourite commodity as his surprising gamble on the prodigal talent of Peter Barnes paid off with two goals in the first five minutes.'

The wins continued to come; Strachan to Stapleton was the combination again for two more early goals, this time against Newcastle, in a comprehensive 3-0 win at an Old Trafford, which had what one reporter described as a 'raucous fervour'.

'The way we are playing now, we could keep our 100 per cent record intact for a long time,' Ron Atkinson said, and that belief was vindicated by another home 3-0 win, this time over Oxford, giving United their best start to a season for over 80 years. Atkinson had been rewarded with the Bell's Manager of the Month award for August, but wasn't presented with the traditional bottle of whisky given to winners due to the continuing prohibition at football stadiums. Sportswriter Peter Ball had some sympathy for the visitors: 'For Oxford, coming to Old Trafford after losing 5-2 to

Coventry must have seemed like facing a real lion after being savaged by a toy poodle.'

One team who would have more incentive than most to put an end to the winning streak was Manchester City. 'It's the question on nearly everyone's lips: who'll be the first to stop Manchester United? Today it's our turn to try – and we've got a lot on our plates,' City boss Billy NcNeil wrote in his programme notes. 'It must be a long time since one team's performances have obtained such unanimous national acclaim and by all accounts United have deserved it ... I recognise that Ron Atkinson has assembled and blended the best team in the country at the moment. I was immensely impressed watching them win last midweek against Newcastle. They have power, skill and artistry. We can raise our game today. We must raise our game today. We must raise our game.'

City's average attendance for that season was 24,000 and it more than doubled to 48,773 for the visit of their neighbours (many of these day-trippers were in fact United fans who got tickets in the home end). McNeil's hopes of a stubborn resistance were also ended as this was another game effectively over by the half-hour mark. Hughes was brought down in the seventh minute and Robson tucked away the penalty, but Arthur Albiston hit a long-range, right-footed screamer in the 19th minute. In the second half, Albiston's fellow full-back Mick Duxbury got in on the act, scoring a tap-in, and celebrating with a forward roll.

United's run was technically ended by Everton in a game that did not go down on record as an official match; due to the European ban, the FA in their eternal wisdom created a tournament called the 'Football League Super Cup' so that all of the teams who qualified for Europe could play against each other. United played a strong team in this competition but did not take it as seriously as other games. In their group with Everton and Norwich, they lost both games against the Toffees and drew both against the Canaries. The inconvenience of the 'competition' was best summed up by Everton boss Howard Kendall's infamous team talk ahead of one of their games with Norwich: 'What a waste of time this is, but out you go!'

Thankfully, the result did little to derail United's winning momentum in official games but the additional match took a physical toll. Mark Hughes picked up an injury that kept him out of the game against West Brom, as did Peter Barnes. Graeme Hogg was struggling with a thigh strain but played through the injury. United raced into their customary early lead when Alan Brazil scored in the sixth minute. When Gordon Strachan made it two in the 22nd minute, he was also pushed into the goalpost by two defenders, injuring his shoulder. He came off, but United continued to plunder goals, winning by a big score of 5-1.

'I'd have preferred him not to have scored and stayed on,' Atkinson admitted, acknowledging the cost could be yet to come. 'We're really thin on the ground at the moment. It looks as if he could be out for about a month.'

The win at The Hawthorns gave United a nine-point lead at the top of the table, to match their nine consecutive league wins, and Peter Barnes then scored the only goal at Selhurst Park in the first leg of their second-round Milk Cup clash. Atkinson was hoping his team would record the 'perfect ten' league victories by defeating Southampton at home.

'How long can we keep it up? I suppose that is the question most people in football are asking about Manchester United,' the manager said in his programme notes. 'And the answer I have got to make as we welcome Southampton to Old Trafford this afternoon looking for our tenth successive league win is probably going to disappoint you. For, frankly, I just don't know ... We are certainly in the mood to do it. Success breeds confidence and provided it does not overflow into big-big-headedness it allows players to express themselves and stamp their authority on a game. I think you can assume that we are enjoying it out in front; it certainly beats being in West Bromwich Albion's place and it's better than chasing someone else as we did Everton last season and Liverpool for I don't know how many seasons before that! We are not nervous. It's not like a road race going too fast at the start and burning out, because no one can take away the points you have earned. We will carry on trying to add to them in threes; what makes the end of a winning run difficult to predict is the beauty of football.'

The tide did appear to be shifting, somewhat. The Saints were no pushovers and there were no early goals. In the 62nd minute United thought they'd got the breakthrough when they were awarded a penalty, but Peter Shilton saved Robson's kick. Then,

13 minutes later, the breakthrough finally came after Albiston made a fine run down the left and Hughes fired home.

'I was worried in the 89th minute; I thought they [Southampton] might mount a surge!' Atkinson joked after the game. 'I really did think it was just a question of time. We were not flagging. We were getting better. Any team would miss Strachan. But we are still capable of creating enough chances.'

At the end of September 1985 it couldn't have looked any better for United; ten wins from ten, the highest scorers in the league with the meanest defence, scoring an average of 2.7 goals a game and conceding an average of 0.3. At the back, United were the beneficiaries of all the rewards of patience. McGrath and Hogg had formed a fine partnership and understanding with Bailey. Albiston and Duxbury were playing as well as ever. Robson and Whiteside, in midfield, were dictating the tone and pace of every game, dominating opponents easily. Their physical prowess was matched by Hughes and Stapleton up front and complemented by the craft of Strachan and Olsen, and Olsen's stand-in Barnes, from the wings.

It is no surprise that many have gone on record to state just how brilliant it was to be associated with Manchester United at this time. 'Our football was devastating and the goals flowed,' Robson said. 'Just about everybody in the game agreed we looked unstoppable. It was the club's best-ever start to a season and many pundits were telling us we were already certainties for the championship. We weren't prepared to say that publicly at the time, but we believed we were at last on our way to claiming that title.'

For Whiteside, it was ultimate vindication of the way Atkinson wanted to play: '… our execution of his ultra-confident, flamboyant philosophy came close to perfection.'

'It was just so exciting,' Martin Edwards recalls. 'We had Gordon Strachan and Peter Barnes on the wing; everything seemed to be going for us. We were playing so well and taking teams apart.'

Sometimes the players were just as bewildered by the quality of the play as the supporters and most neutrals. 'There was a passage of play where Gary Bailey made a save, passed it to me, and I helped the ball on,' Duxbury remembers of the game at Forest. 'From then on we put together a move that I'm not even sure that we scored from but was incredible to watch. For a second, I lost myself, and felt like a supporter on the stand, marvelling at what I'd seen my colleagues do. Peter scored his first goal, a debut goal in a 3-1 win on that day. It was unbelievable. The confidence was really beginning to rub off on us all and we were all raising our own games as a consequence. For everything I've said that may appear negative about the manager, one thing I have to say is that under Ron Atkinson, Manchester United were always going to play good football. Whether that was a reflection of the manager and the freeness he encouraged, I don't know … It was without a shadow of a doubt the best football I've ever partaken in because it was so attacking and brought so many goals. My memories of great football start with Brazil in 1970 and then the latter days of Tommy Docherty's reign at United. That was what I considered the best football I'd seen but for that ten-game period at the start of 1985/86 I'd like to think we played as well as any United side could and it was a true privilege as a player to be a part of.'

Duxbury also remarked on the balance: 'It was the right sort of momentum rather than irresponsible – we were controlled and felt unbeatable.' It goes some way to underlining that idea of everything just being perfectly right for Atkinson in terms of squad composition, his decision making and the morale in the squad. At this time, every decision he made was easily justified by the results of the team, and the reality is that a dressing room that had strong characters like United should not have been brittle enough to be susceptible to an implosion the second things didn't go right.

'It was great,' Hogg says. 'Everybody knew their job and the most important thing was that we had a settled team. We took it game by game and it was unbelievable. We were beating everybody. It was attacking, flowing football. It was the Manchester United way. The Luton game really derailed our momentum. We drew but it ended that winning sequence.'

It is important to note that winning runs in football never go on forever and it is not a sign of bad management if they end. The counter argument to this is things went so wrong for United, so quickly, that the reasons *had* to be multiple, suggesting all was not as rosy as it appeared to be. The dropped points, when that time came, would feel as anticlimactic as they were inevitable, but it needn't be a disaster. And, when that time did come, it didn't *seem* to be a disaster.

All the talk before the game at Luton Town was about how United could equal the record of 11 league wins to start a season which had been set by Spurs in 1960. Two key players from that team, Ron Henry and the captain Danny Blanchflower, were talking to newspapers about the record and the game in the modern day.

'Football has become so negative,' Blanchflower said. 'You're offside as soon as you leave the dressing room. United may not be negative, but 80 per cent of the teams they play are. In our day there were no poor teams.'

Henry, meanwhile, bemoaned another change in the game: 'We wanted to play. We didn't get much money. In fact, I am absolutely certain that all the boys in the team would have loved to play. We loved doing what we did.'

Frank Stapleton was given right of reply and revealing something about his decision to reject a move away in the summer. 'We are more interested in achieving something,' the striker said. 'I am confident that most of the lads would promise to give up the whole season's bonuses if they could be sure of the championship. There's a lot of pride at stake.'

It seems that romanticising about the past always starts with two primary issues: the money and the rules. If a third player had been interviewed you might have expected to hear something about the conditions of the pitch, and perhaps it comes as no surprise that in this particular historical journey, that topic will come up again later in this book.

Luton Town had already invited some criticism by their decision to install an artificial pitch at Kenilworth Road (derided as a 'plastic pitch' just as the one at Loftus Road had been). Such pitches would eventually be banned, though it is worth mentioning that no United players blamed the surface for their first dropped points of the season. Atkinson had taken his team down a day early so they could train on the pitch the day before the game.

Kevin Moran was keen to put talk of the record in perspective. 'You can't get away from the cliché. You take every match as it comes,' he said. 'I'll tell you what's really thrilling supporters. I talked to an old man the other day and he'd come alive again. And it was the football that had done it. Not just the victories. No, he said, it was the football. That's what's happened this season. That's the exciting thing. Not the record.'

United seemed to apply themselves well, playing in a 4-3-3 without Strachan. Hughes scored with a looping, deflected effort on the hour, but ten minutes later Luton levelled; they were then incredibly resolute for the remainder of the game to become the first team to take a point from Atkinson's men that season. Any complaints about the surface were null and void as it turned out the plastic pitch at Loftus Road might have done United a favour; Liverpool lost at QPR, meaning the lead at the top was actually extended by a point. The only team celebrating on the day was actually Luton; their manager David Pleat was almost embarrassed by how happy the players seemed to be. 'You'd have thought we had won when the game ended, that's a measure of how much the players respect Manchester United at the moment,' Pleat said, 'but we did only get a point.'

The return game against Palace in the League Cup was navigated easily and United won 2-0 against QPR but paid a heavy price when Bryan Robson damaged his hamstring. It was clear that the captain would be missed against Liverpool in the crucial game on 19 October. Hogg came back in after being replaced by McGrath in defence since the game at West Brom. In that five-game spell, Atkinson had been sufficiently impressed by McGrath to now consider him first choice alongside Moran, but had to make a change with Robson's injury, so McGrath moved back into midfield as the manager opted for physicality and numbers with him, Whiteside and Moses. Olsen had played from the right against QPR but Atkinson's formation change meant the Dane was back in his number 11 shirt and Barnes was named substitute. One might reason that this was the first time the manager had named a cautious 11 when a more adventurous one was available to him, though it could easily be understood using the logic that Robson was missing and the most important thing to focus on was ensuring Liverpool did not close the gap.

Liverpool had recently appointed Kenny Dalglish as player-manager after the retirement of Joe Fagan, but they still had plenty of winning experience and used all of that experience to dominate.

They took the lead through Craig Johnston before McGrath made the sort of run to get on to a cross that he couldn't possibly have made from centre-half to fire in an equaliser. The game finished 1-1; not as bad as it could have been.

'I think that to play Liverpool without power and midfield is to hand the game over to them,' Atkinson insisted, defensively, after the game. 'McGrath is the best centre-half in the First Division; I didn't want to move him but as far as I was concerned it was a must.'

The intensity of the game, rather than the quality, would likely have made for good television, and there was news of renewed conversations with the Football League, BBC and ITV. The Football League suggested a package of 14 to 16 live league and cup games, comprised of two or three league games each and the rest in cup matches. The price for this would be £4m. The broadcasters were not happy with that so the talks rumbled on, until December, when the League finally acquiesced to a deal worth just £1.73m for nine league and League Cup games, with a separate deal struck for four FA Cup games. United would be shown three times – at West Ham on 2 February and Liverpool a week later, and at home to Sheffield Wednesday in April. A fourth would also be shown, when United and West Ham's FA Cup tie went to a replay in March.

There was more intensity at Stamford Bridge. Strachan and Robson were missing again whilst Moses had once more damaged his ankle against Liverpool; the combative midfielder would be out for almost another year after making just four league appearances so far that season. (In a desperate attempt to remedy the issue, Moses later flew to Holland to receive specialist treatment. This was not sanctioned by the club – in fact, it was deemed 'without club permission' and when the player promptly presented United with the medical bill, which was several thousand pounds, there was a dispute as to who should pay.) McGrath and Whiteside gave as good as they got in the middle of the park, but McGrath was forced to go back into defence when Graeme Hogg was sent off just before half-time, a headache for Atkinson just after Olsen had scored a fine goal after cutting in from the right-hand side. The United boss angrily reacted from the bench after seeing his player sent off and had his own name taken by the referee. Afterwards, Atkinson claimed he saw 'provocation and one or two tackles over the ball' by Chelsea players. But he would have been very pleased to see the reaction of his team when they conceded an equaliser in the 75th minute; within 60 seconds they had reclaimed the lead through a thunderbolt shot from Hughes.

Momentum continued with a win over West Ham in the League Cup but another injury – this time to Duxbury's hamstring – meant another reshuffle, with McGrath moving to right-back and Stapleton to midfield to see out the game. John Gidman was still not ready to play first-team football, so youngster Billy Garton was called up to play his first senior game in almost a year against Coventry City.

Atkinson was feeling positive in his programme notes: 'As far as our chances of winning the league championship are concerned, this has been a very satisfying period for us,' he said. 'Our last two matches were against the two teams pressing us the hardest. So when we took stock this week it was pleasing to note that we had held Liverpool at bay and knocked Chelsea behind. And all at a time when we have been without two or three of our classiest players.'

Two first-half goals from one of the classiest fit players, Olsen – making it four in recent weeks as he adapted admirably to his new position as a winger who would cut in from the right – sealed another comfortable win, prompting journalist Derek Hodgson to suggest that United being able to win without getting out of second gear was actually a bad thing. 'Even without four England players [Robson, Moses, Gidman and Duxbury] and the invaluable Strachan, United were so far ahead in this rather academic contest that it became a strong argument for the Super League,' he said. 'The gap between the top and bottom of the First Division is now such that four clubs must surely be pruned.'

Hodgson did, however, pay due credit to United's remarkable form, describing McGrath as 'an Irish Beckenbauer' and writing: 'Mr Atkinson has his critics but in two vital qualifications for soccer management, the judgement of players and tactical insight, he can rarely be faulted. He has overcome the absence of Robson, his crucial player 11 months ago when Coventry were the last team to win a league match at Old Trafford, by remodelling the formation, changing tactics and recruiting that spectacular but wayward Barnes.'

The win maintained United's ten-point advantage and unbeaten run which now stretched to 15 league games. The neutrals loved it; pundits were convinced. As is clear from the likes of Duxbury and Robson, and Martin Edwards, all at the club seemed delighted with a run of form that Norman Whiteside later described as a 'carnival of football'.

You might be surprised to learn, then, that the man in charge of it all did not view the late summer and early autumn of 1985 in the same way that others at the club seemed to. 'In a lot of those games, we didn't play well,' Atkinson insists candidly. 'We did in some, and when we turned up we played really well. A lot of the games were battles. But because they weren't being shown anywhere, our good solid wins earned us a reputation as if we were playing like the great Hungarian or the Brazilian sides! The reputation grew in the absence of the footage. There were some great performances amongst the wins.'

Try telling the supporters that what they were watching wasn't spectacular. They descended in hordes to the next game at Hillsborough, with newspapers describing it as a 'vast travelling support creating an atmosphere more akin to an FA Cup semi-final than a league fixture'.

United should have been boosted by the return of Bryan Robson from the start and Gordon Strachan from the bench, while John Gidman was able to provide more senior defensive cover for Olsen on the right. But it was just one of those games when everything seemed to go wrong. Robson fuelled speculation that he had been rushed back too quickly from his hamstring injury when he had to come off with just 14 minutes played. Stapleton moved into midfield as Strachan played behind Hughes. The unfamiliar system looked as if it might still possess enough craft to break down the Owls, but Wednesday grabbed the game's only goal in the 83rd minute. The home side, just as at Luton, celebrated as if they themselves had won a trophy.

United were held to a goalless draw at home to Spurs as they once more tried to cope without Robson. The reaction was not over the top, as one might suspect it would be in modern times. 'Even the 0-0 draws are classics at Old Trafford these days,' Paddy Barclay wrote in *The Guardian* after a game with plenty of craft, guile and physicality.

Peter Shreeve, the Spurs manager, posited a familiar phrase: 'You either stand up to United at Old Trafford or let them run over you.'

As United prepared to face Leicester City at Filbert Street, they were linked with John Sivebæk, the Danish international right-back who was playing part-time for Vejle. He was available for £250,000 and signed in the coming weeks to provide back-up for Gidman with Duxbury out. It would seem a fairly sensible move but one might argue that two international quality right-backs was enough, and the third choice *should* be a player like Garton. It is easy to understand why Duxbury might have felt as if it was insult added to hamstring injury.

There was certainly a very unpleasant mood in the air as United were thumped in the Midlands; the Foxes scored three times in the first 30 minutes and were already 2-0 up when Alan Brazil had to come on for Arthur Albiston in the 15th. Despite having Whiteside, Strachan, Hughes, Brazil, Stapleton and Olsen all on the pitch, United were unable to score a single goal in response, and Atkinson was so furious that he kept his team locked in the dressing room.

'Manchester United's players emerged single-file and long-faced after being kept in their dressing room for 55 minutes,' wrote John Wragg of the *Daily Express*. 'The door had been locked all that time. It had been one of those days.'

Wragg suggested United looked 'off-balance and clumsy' but Atkinson, despite his frustration, was sporting enough to praise Leicester's 'best day of the season'. Home boss Gordon Milne accepted his team were especially motivated: 'Wherever Manchester United go they attract big crowds, motivate opposition players, and make the game a special occasion.'

United saw out a November to forget by losing at Anfield (despite taking the lead) in the League Cup and then drawing with Watford at Old Trafford. Alan Brazil had come on for Moran in the 65th minute and scored just three minutes later, but the visitors equalised in injury time; an indication of where the luck was currently at.

The downturn in form did not bring vocal criticism for Atkinson at the club's AGM that week, as he insisted that he would continue with the same approach as he always had (though there was just the hint of defeatism in his words already): 'Before the start of this season, with football getting all sorts of knocks, we made a conscious decision to play entertaining football, even if it meant taking risks. We may be proved wrong, but ...'

On 7 December, Ipswich Town came to Old Trafford. Colin Gibson, a left-back, signed ten days prior to the game for a fee of £275,000, following the news that Albiston would be out until the turn of the year. The Scot was normally dependable but at 28 it was probably the right move to add some senior back-up. Atkinson also strengthened his defence by signing Mark Higgins, the former Everton defender who had retired in May 1984 after six operations. Due to insurance problems, United were not permitted to play him in league games but he was eligible to play in the Cup; should Atkinson wish to register him to play in the First Division, he would be forced to pay £60,000.

Gibson was straight in the team and Mark Dempsey, the young midfielder, was brought in to play alongside Whiteside. The biggest news was Atkinson's public confession that he was considering dropping Stapleton or Hughes. It had been seven games since Hughes had scored and twice as long for Stapleton. The manager said 'it was heads or tails' before deciding 'to give the strikers one more thrash together'; Stapleton scored the only goal in the first half before Hughes was replaced by Brazil in the 63rd minute.

Up until his recent dry spell, Hughes had been in fine form with ten goals before November. His spectacular efforts may have been missed by television cameras in his own country, but they had been noted with intent over 1,100 miles away in Barcelona, whose manager Terry Venables made it clear he wanted to bring the Welshman to the Camp Nou. United supporters felt the matter was over when it was announced that Hughes had signed a new five-year deal, but this did not derail the pursuit of the Catalan club, who learned of a clause in the contract which enabled Hughes to join them for a fee of £1.8m. Hughes was one of the first to try to fight for some sort of level playing field when it came to the difference in salaries and contracts United gave home-grown players as opposed to those who were signed. Norman Whiteside remembered feeling 'majorly hard done by' when he read that at least four players earned over £150,000 a year while his salary was £250 a week (£13,000 a year). When Hughes did agree his new deal, with Barcelona's interest obvious, many supporters were enraged that such a popular figure would have such a clause in his deal. So, despite the intention of the deal apparently being to dampen speculation, it only intensified it. Atkinson never made good on his idea to drop either Hughes or Stapleton for Brazil in the short term. Instead, he decided to once again explore the idea of using Brazil as collateral for a transfer, but that would take a few weeks to come together.

Hughes scored in a 3-1 win at Aston Villa, suggesting the blip was over, and giving one journalist the confidence to go ahead with a feature he must have had pencilled in for weeks. Christopher Hilton of *The Express* ran a number of articles through that week which spoke glowingly about Ron Atkinson; the first bore the headlines: 'A big lad born to be No. 1' and 'Making of the slick tactician'. Such features must have instilled the same fear in Manchester United managers as the dreaded 'vote of confidence'; those with long-enough memories might recall *The Mirror* running a similar feature on Frank O'Farrell's apparent revolution at Old Trafford in December 1971, right before things turned sour.

Just like clockwork, United lost their next game, against Arsenal at Old Trafford. Continuing the narrative of the season between these two sides, Norman Whiteside missed an early penalty – he later moaned to reporters 'it was more like a pass back' before Charlie Nicholas, who missed from the spot in that early season game, made amends by scoring a late winner. Despite the injuries and result, Atkinson felt it was important to stress he felt his team had played well. 'Our second-half performance was as good as we've given for a long time,' he insisted after the game. 'There was drive, verve and adrenaline – things I like.'

He later reflected on the frustrating afternoon, feeling it had been a blow to the confidence: 'It was quite a shaker, because, to put it bluntly, I thought we were very unlucky. I always try to avoid using bad luck as a reason or excuse for a disappointing result. You make your own luck in this game, and to blame a lack of it for losing is too easy an escape hole. But I have got to say that I was quite pleased with our performance. We were slow to start, perhaps, but after that, we played with plenty of drive and verve. I like these qualities. No one went under. There was purpose in our play, and while I was obviously disappointed with the 0-1 result, I was pleased with a lot that happened out on the pitch. You get nothing for losing, but if you have to lose, then we lost the right way still doing the right thing.'

Atkinson was still trying to put a brave face on it at Goodison Park on Boxing Day. But United had repeated their trick from the last time they went to Merseyside, scoring early and then capitulating and losing. Stapleton ended his goal drought but the champions were just too strong. 'We took the lead with a super goal from Frank Stapleton, a real classic,' the United boss said. 'That's when we asked our defenders to defend, but they didn't. Everton are a very good side but we should have done better with the start we had.'

It was a new year but the same old problems as Gary Bailey, Jesper Olsen and Graeme Hogg all dropped out injured for the visit of Birmingham. Colin Gibson scored his first goal for the club in a difficult win that saw McGrath brought off after just nine minutes with an ankle injury.

It forced Atkinson to call up Mark Higgins for the FA Cup game with Rochdale. Mike Duxbury was back, and alongside Albiston, Whiteside, Garton, Blackmore and Hughes, that made six youth-team players in the starting 11. 'We must never give up playing,' Atkinson said in a familiar battlecry beforehand. 'We are going to be positive and will play to win, but, if we do lose, we must die fighting.'

Stapleton and Hughes were the scorers in a 2-0 win and Hughes was once again netting in a 3-1 win at Oxford, amid renewed speculation about a move to Spain as the clause in his contract was revealed.

'If he wants to go, we can't really stop him,' said Atkinson. 'We just hope he doesn't want to go. But at least we've guaranteed ourselves a sizeable fee instead of the £350,000 or so we would have got if he had left at the end of his contract. We've had little chats with him about it but we won't mention it after today. We do not want anything to distract us from our main aim, which is to win the title.'

United were too anxious as Nottingham Forest visited Old Trafford; a Jesper Olsen double overturned an early deficit, but Clough's team went from 1-2 in the 80th minute to 3-2 winners at full time. 'We tried to go into overdrive and race the thing,' Atkinson explained. 'Sometimes it misfires, but that's the way we play.'

The much-needed composure of Bryan Robson was back for the following week's game at Sunderland in the FA Cup. The midfielder played a reserve game against Barnsley and said: 'Everything went fine and I'm quite pleased with the way I got through the game. I felt my legs a bit, but I really enjoyed the match. A few people said I'd finished my career but I knew all along that it was just muscle pulls and muscle tears and I was never really worried from the first instance.'

Robson once again failed to finish the game, but was sent off at Roker Park when he was accused of knocking over Barry Venison as the Sunderland player tried to get up. 'I didn't see the incident but Bryan told me that Venison was holding him down and his knee caught Venison on the side of the face as he got up,' Atkinson said. Robson was able to take part in the replay, which United won 3-0. Another 90 minutes took its toll once more as Strachan succumbed to injury again early on.

Atkinson returned to the transfer market to sign Terry Gibson, the Coventry City striker, for £350,000 plus Alan Brazil, thus ending one of the more disappointing and frustrating careers of an Old Trafford striker. Even on his better days, the supply line Atkinson now had from the sides did not suit the striker, whose confidence had been hit as Hughes emerged as a genuine star so early on into his career at the club. Gibson scored on his reserve-team debut against Sheffield United on 30 January (a game where Sivebæk was also introduced into the fold) and said: 'Now I've joined a big club I've got to think big.'

In their first televised game of the season, United started well at Upton Park. Robson scored in the 26th minute, a fine clip over the goalkeeper after a pass from Hughes. But West Ham equalised after half-time and it all started to fall apart. Robson suffered a recurrence of his shoulder injury and was forced to come off, and then the Hammers scored a late winner. It was a significant defeat – United were now second to Everton, their ten-point lead already completely obliterated.

Walk Through the Storm

IN THE first truly high-profile televised game of the season, English football was shrouded with more shame. Manchester United visited Anfield in a match broadcast live on the BBC, the cameras catching some of the most disgraceful scenes of the season. It seemed difficult to believe these two clubs had faced off in a relatively friendly FA Cup Final back in 1977, which concluded with United's players wishing Liverpool well for their forthcoming European Cup Final.

Tensions had undoubtedly risen since then, but the afternoon of Sunday, 9 February 1986 took them to previously unimaginable heights. Liverpool supporters pelted coaches packed with United fans, and when the team bus came in they redirected their attention. It seems unthinkable now, but there was little security for the United team as they left the bus; hordes of home fans packed into the space where they could to hurl abuse, chanting 'Munich' at their opponents. One threw a brick at the window where Mark Hughes was sitting; the window cracked, but Hughes fortunately escaped unharmed. Some Liverpool fans even held canisters of tear gas which they sprayed in the direction of the United players as they hurried into the stadium. Clayton Blackmore had made the conscious decision to try to avoid coming out behind Norman Whiteside as the fiery midfielder was as loathed by Liverpool fans as he was loved by United fans, but that didn't save Blackmore, who was the worst affected by the tear gas. At the same time, plenty of young Liverpool fans were also affected, and United's players took them into the away dressing room, where Bryan Robson was acting as an emergency nurse at the sink, pouring water into their eyes. Atkinson ushered the rest of the players out on to the Anfield pitch to clear their eyes and lungs.

'I didn't know what happened,' Blackmore said. 'We just stepped off the coach and someone sprayed something at us. My eyes poured with tears and I couldn't breathe. Whatever it was I caught most of it straight in the face. The boss got us out on the pitch immediately, but it was a bit frightening – we could have been sprayed with anything.'

The game itself (Whiteside later said it was 'amazing' that the game went ahead) was evenly contested. A Colin Gibson goal in front of an angry Kop was cancelled out by a John Wark equaliser; it ended 1-1, but nobody was talking about the football afterwards.

Atkinson told reporters Anfield had become a 'hell-hole' and expressed concern that a player could get killed, adding: 'A lot of fans were milling around, kicking and spitting at us, the usual thing. Then I realised that some of the lads were coughing and spluttering. I don't know what tear gas is, but obviously they had received some sort of aerosol spray as they left the coach. We just slipped the lads straight through on to the pitch to give them some fresh air. By the time the game started they were not showing any ill-effects. The pity is that you look forward so much to a game between two clubs like this. It's got to take a certain kind of lunatic to try and spoil it. We are trying to give the English game a better image but someone who does something like this cannot seriously call himself a supporter.'

Liverpool boss Kenny Dalglish was immediately defensive. 'This will appear in all the papers and the person responsible will feel proud of what he has done,' he said. 'It would be better if everybody kept quiet about it. I don't know what you can do about this sort of thing. After all, a team has got to get into the ground.'

Dalglish's hope that it would be shrugged under the carpet was as outrageous as it was unrealistic – Blackmore remembers it being one of the 'gongs' on *News at Ten* that evening – but he did find an ally in Ted Croker, the FA secretary who was in firefighting mood and chose instead to criticise Atkinson's comments. 'Ron Atkinson got himself involved in some very emotive statements,' Croker said. 'They made very impressive headlines but they were totally without foundation. There was one person with one can but unfortunately responsible people from within the clubs got involved. That disturbs me more than the incident itself. With the situations of violence in this country you could say that anyone could conceivably get killed in a riot. The vast majority deplore this sort of problem. I don't want people to think I have my head in the sand. We know there are problems but they exist in all aspects of life today.'

Liverpool secretary Peter Robinson criticised United players for talking to newspapers, saying they 'inflamed' the situation. Thankfully, after some reflection, Liverpool were more proactive as a club than Dalglish or Croker felt was necessary. They consequently announced they would erect new barriers to keep fans from the visitors' coach and install an extra CCTV camera behind the main stand. Future visits from United would get extra-special measures, with officials sat further back from supporters in the directors' box. *The Guardian* had reported how Liverpool fans 'continually spat at the United bench' whilst Blackmore – forced to watch the game from the directors' box – claimed he would rather be on the pitch where he was more shielded from the vitriol. United officials also worked with Liverpool representatives to draw up a 'peace plan' which would include rival mascots leading out the teams before the games, representatives of each club travelling on the opponents' coach, and even joint functions for supporters. Hopes of a rosy future were as equally pie in the sky as Dalglish's hopes it would all be forgotten.

A draw at Anfield in any circumstances is normally considered a decent result, especially without Robson. It was also achieved without Gary Bailey, who was replaced by Chris Turner. Bailey was dropped to the reserves. In fact, he would not play for Ron Atkinson again, with his final game being that recent loss to West Ham. Despite his England place being at risk, he was selected for the World Cup that year; a selection that was to have devastating consequences for his career.

United's central midfield for the game against West Brom was Blackmore and Stapleton, but they were still able to secure a comfortable win through a Jesper Olsen hat-trick – two first-half penalties and a fine effort in the second period.

In that second half, the Old Trafford pitch cut up terribly, with the hosts never able to get into any sort of rhythm. The club were having issues with their undersoil heating only heating some parts of the pitch, so £12,000 was spent on covers for the remainder of the playing surface to protect it.

Money was spent on the team, too; Peter Davenport came in from Nottingham Forest with Atkinson hoping for a similar contribution to that made by John Wark for Liverpool a couple of years previously. (Atkinson had enquired about Graeme Sharp of Everton, but the player had just signed a new contract at Goodison Park.)

Davenport, a United fan as a lad, was delighted. 'I used to stand at the Stretford End with my dad and my brother, and never missed a game for a long time,' he beamed. 'Considering we lived on the Wirral that wasn't a bad claim!'

Atkinson committed his own future to the club at the same time, amid rumours of Real Madrid being interested in appointing him. 'I consider I have got the best job in football already. I love it where I am,' he insisted.

There was to be no change in fortunes. A late defeat at The Dell was followed by an early blow in the FA Cup fifth-round tie at West Ham. In the third minute, Robson – who had returned for the game at Southampton – injured his shoulder again, the same which had caused him problems before. Atkinson's team battled but were eliminated in the replay at Old Trafford.

In between the games, United had been scheduled to send a team to play a fundraising game at Grantham Town in aid of leukaemia sufferer Chris Buckingham. The game, however, had been postponed because someone claiming to be Grantham manager Barry Shaw called United reserve-team manager Brian Whitehouse and said the floodlights were not working so the game had been cancelled. Five thousand fans had bought tickets and Grantham had to play a game with the first and second team instead. Atkinson said, 'We will be doing everything we can to make it up to him. The team is very upset. We thought it was a very cruel hoax.' (A game was rescheduled for the end of the campaign.)

Before the next league game, United flew out for that previously mentioned friendly in Israel, a trip which seemed to underline how out of control things were getting. At the very least, it was ill-timed, and a long journey that was as regrettable as forgettable.

It was yet another late goal on a tight pitch, this time at QPR, which brought yet another defeat. United left the field to their fans chanting 'what a load of rubbish!' Atkinson had opted to play Davenport instead of Hughes and defended his decision to take 'Sparky' out of the team: 'I believe the Barcelona business has affected Mark's game and I hope the rest will take the pressure off.'

It was another physical contest with plenty of fouls; Rangers boss Jim Smith spoke proudly of his team 'winning the battle'. And the 'b' word was once again in Atkinson's vocabulary as he insisted his own side 'keep battling on': 'I really expected us to beat Rangers and so did the players. We were not complacent and we might even have had penalties at both ends. Stapleton was fouled and Davenport was tripped. This result does our confidence no good at all.'

Without Robson, Whiteside and Moses, sportswriter Robert Armstrong said: 'United were rather like a Rolls-Royce without an engine, lacking the midfield drive to support the skills of their front runners.'

This was the first time you could consider the First Division championship being out of United's hands; they were now five points behind Everton on the same number of games, so even if they won the upcoming game between the two contenders, it wouldn't be enough to put, or keep, them top. There were three games before that – Luton Town, Manchester City and Birmingham City. It was clear nine points would be necessary if they were to feel confident of recapturing any sort of momentum.

Most, though, were beginning to accept that this was the fate of Manchester United, with the current season simply being their most spectacular failure yet. Having taken another gamble on Davenport, Atkinson was in danger of becoming characterised unfavourably. Journalist Ronald Atkin of *The Guardian* quipped, 'The big question now is, who else can Ron Atkinson buy?' Before the game at Loftus Road, copies of the new fanzine *When Saturday Comes* were sold and included the sort of satire for which publications of this nature would become loved: 'United are trying to sign Platini just in case they get a free kick on the edge of the box this season.'

Davenport had scored 54 times in 118 league games for Nottingham Forest and at the age of 24 (almost 25), he was seen as a pre-emptive replacement for Mark Hughes. It was almost the sort of signing Gary Lineker might have been if Atkinson had pulled the trigger and not been so concerned with Stapleton's position. It probably would not have needed hindsight to consider that, for roughly the same outlay, one Lineker might have been a better investment than Davenport and Terry Gibson, even if the logic on a deal-by-deal basis seems fairly rational.

It was that logic which was now being pooled together and questioned, though. The temporary boost of signing Peter Barnes, who hadn't played for the first team since November, now looked like another senior player with short-term prospects at the club stockpiled into the reserve team. Barnes would join a list of players that includes the likes of Davenport, Brazil, Terry Gibson, Garth Crooks; senior players who all had good careers but were never likely to establish themselves at Old Trafford in the long term.

When this was put to Atkinson in an interview for this book, he defended his record. 'I did get stick about the short-term signings that people thought were gambles but I brought in Arnold Muhren for free and he was great; I also intervened to sign Arthur Graham when I heard he was going to Coventry for £40,000,' he says. 'I thought for that money he could do a job for us, and he did. He was a good little player. Peter Barnes only cost us £30,000 and if he hadn't been so stupid he would have got back in the England team. I always thought it was worth sometimes taking a little punt on somebody, giving them a little chance to see what they could do. One of the biggest chances I took was on Paul McGrath; I was sure he had something but I was never quite sure what, but he developed into a great centre-half, for me still the finest there's been in the Premier League ... I always think your centre-halves should be your most durable players, but at United we always seemed to have an injury problem. Eric Harrison suggested Higgins because he'd had him at Everton. He insisted Mark could still play, so we looked at him in training and I agreed with Eric. At £60,000, paying his insurance money back, it was less than you would pay for a Third Division defender. He was a good lad and did alright.'

It is true to say there were plenty of success stories to counterbalance the ones that didn't work out, but by now the balance of disrupting the squad morale was becoming too far in the negative direction for Atkinson to resolve. The manager had done a wonderful job at creating a unique atmosphere at the club and in the dressing room, but the transfer gambles made this season were running the risk of putting one too many noses out of joint.

It was playing surfaces, and not transfer punts, which Atkinson concentrated on ahead of the visit of Luton Town in March. 'I am not going to make excuses about the difficult playing conditions,' he wrote in his column for the match programme. 'Over the course of an English winter you have to expect to play two or three times on snow or a frozen pitch. It's all part of the long haul of a league championship and it's the same for everyone. At the same time I have got to say that I will welcome the return of a decent surface. When it comes to banging the ball down the field and chasing after it, our lads might not be as good as some of the other people. We don't really train them for that and so we shouldn't be too surprised if they don't excel at that kind of game. But hopefully now the weather has turned and we can look forward to playing on the kind of pitches that saw us at our best early in the season.'

The manager selected Hughes and Davenport from the start but was forced to bring on Stapleton when Kevin Moran broke his arm again in the 13th minute. The forward, who had moonlighted in midfield, now went to centre-half, and looked awkward; it came without cost as Luton were unadventurous and lost 2-0. Journalist Stephen Bierley said the lowest league gate of the season of 33,668 was 'surely the quietest at OT for many weeks'.

Hughes had scored the first goal but had given Atkinson a huge headache before the game by giving an exclusive interview to a newspaper where he said he wanted to leave. The following Monday, United released a statement alongside an announcement that Hughes had in fact already signed for Barcelona and would join them at the end of the season. The statement read: 'Mark has apologised to the club for his recent newspaper article and wishes to put on record his appreciation of the treatment he has always received at Manchester United.'

The injury to Moran caused United to pay the £60,000 insurance money to register Mark Higgins so that he was eligible for league football. Atkinson had delayed that decision for as long as he could and was doing the same with Bryan Robson's shoulder dislocation; there was pressure from tabloid newspapers insisting that the captain of club and country should be immediately sent for an operation in order to ensure he would be ready for the World Cup in Mexico. The United boss risked the wrath of a nation by insisting the club's interests would come first. Robson played with a special shoulder harness in a reserve game against Leicester on 26 March to prepare him to come straight back into the team against Birmingham at the weekend.

Before that, Higgins made his league debut against Manchester City. United went 2-0 up but conspired to throw it away and end up with only a point. Against Birmingham, somewhat unbelievably – though not, considering the way it had all happened – Mark Higgins broke his arm. He continued through to the end, and United shared his battling spirit, with Robson netting a late equaliser. 'We are out of hamstrings into broken arms,' lamented Atkinson.

Birmingham boss John Bond remarked: 'I don't want to be critical of anyone, but if it were me I would have to ask myself if I would allow Robson to play. I found it sad to see Bryan playing like this. He seemed to be operating in a role where he would get protection for his injury. You have to wonder what the mileage is in playing someone who is only 80 per cent fit. Robson wasn't so powerful, dangerous or committed as usual. Ron Atkinson values him so highly he would play him even if he had a wooden leg.'

The player himself insisted he was fine: 'Everything was okay. I got more pain from an ankle I twisted in the first half than from the shoulder.'

United welcomed Everton to Old Trafford on the last day of March (Easter Monday), two days after their trip to St Andrews. Atkinson was reluctant to play Higgins and claimed he asked Stapleton to play centre-half, but he refused. He eventually came on in the 62nd minute for Davenport, who had yet to score for his new club. But the game finished 0-0, a result that did nobody any good as Liverpool seized the opportunity to go to the top of the table.

'Manchester United were ambitious but unimaginative, Everton efficient but uninspired,' David Lacey reported.

Atkinson was relieved to see his team claim an important victory at Coventry to close the gap at the top to two points. 'Ron Atkinson is now talking of the last few matches as a mini-season,' reported sportswriter Stephen Bierley. 'More like a mini-skirt, really. If

United have the legs, everything might still be lovely. If not it would be best not to look.'

Big Ron's side had the opportunity to get a potentially mentally important result when they took on Chelsea at Old Trafford before either of the Merseyside clubs played again. They would have games in hand, but United could go top with a game in hand. As was par for the course, though, disaster struck; Gordon Strachan had come off with an injury and, even though his team-mates rallied back from a Kerry Dixon goal to equalise, the Chelsea forward netted an injury-time winner as United threw everything forward and saw themselves hit on the counter.

Liverpool and Everton won their next game, and United played their televised fixture with Sheffield Wednesday. Stapleton and Whiteside joined Strachan in the physio room and Atkinson was forced to select two right-backs, Duxbury and Sivebæk, in his midfield. There was commitment but little creativity as the Owls stifled Olsen. Two goals early in the second half for the visitors, to which United had no response, appeared to be the final death knell in the title challenge. A five-point gap with just four games left (leaders Liverpool had five, and Everton had six) was not yet a mathematical impossibility to overcome, but it was now a huge improbability.

'Ron was usually never a manager where you would see the pressure getting to him,' Graeme Hogg recalls. 'Possibly the only time I ever saw him affected was when we played Sheffield Wednesday at home at the end of the season. He was exasperated on that day. There was an air of "I can't do any more."'

The preceding five months now had an important relevance in how Ron Atkinson's almost-five years at the club were perceived and the general consensus had gone from 'steady building' to 'habitual underachievers'. They were stuck in a cycle they were forever doomed to repeat, and, as far as Atkinson was concerned, there was little patience or sympathy. The first rumours of a dismissal for Manchester United began to emerge following the defeat to Wednesday as there was now significant doubt that Big Ron was the man who would end the wait for a league title.

Yet he remained hugely popular; especially so with the majority of the dressing room who he hadn't upset, and with many journalists,

who enjoyed his personable nature. He certainly had a supporter in
Express reporter David Emery, who wrote on 16 April that it was
'No Time To Sack Atkinson'.

'Those daunting figures and the strength of their achievements
have shed too large a shadow for a succession of fine men,' Emery
said of the likes of Busby, Charlton and Best. 'Wilf McGuinness,
Frank O'Farrell and Dave Sexton all failed to meet the exceptional
requirements. Only Tommy Docherty seemed to have the force of
character and the depth of feeling to communicate with the Old
Trafford worshippers – until he was consumed by an even greater
love and forced to quit. Now Atkinson, big flamboyant Ron whose
public image shields a sensitive soul, is on trial. His crime? Winning
the FA Cup only twice in five years, reaching the Milk Cup Final
and never being worse than fourth in the league championship. Only
two clubs can match that consistency of the same period, and they
both come from Liverpool.'

Emery considered the possible replacements – Venables was
happy in Spain, Graham Taylor was a possibility if he had outgrown
Watford, Howard Kendall was 'hardly' likely to come and Brian
Clough was 'unthinkable'. 'Away from such candidates, who has
achieved enough to have the right to depose Atkinson? No one
as far as I'm concerned. For the good of United, Edwards and
his board must close their ears to the siren cries of the fickle. To
change again now would surely condemn Old Trafford to another
prolonged period of confusion. And consign another ex-manager to
the tombstone inscription: "They expect to win everything."

United won at Newcastle, but, as per the script, with every
positive came a negative; Robson, who scored at St James' Park,
would miss the final three games of the campaign and faced a race
against time to be ready for the World Cup.

Atkinson made Norman Whiteside, about to turn 21, his
skipper, as he had done earlier in the season; back in October,
the manager had even instructed Whiteside to take charge of an
indoor training session. *The Guardian* reporter Robert Armstrong
described Whiteside as 'the anchorman in an injury-hit season'.
Armstrong said the season had been the 'kind of setback' ... 'that
would almost certainly have cost' Atkinson his job a couple of
years ago.

United lined up for their last league game at Old Trafford with a team that looked utterly unfamiliar – Turner; Gidman, McGrath, Garton, Albiston; Duxbury, Whiteside, Blackmore; Hughes, Stapleton, Davenport.

'It's been a season of tremendous highs and lows,' Atkinson admitted in his programme notes. 'Personally I shall never forget those opening weeks when the lads not only made goalscoring look easy but provided some of the most exhilarating football I have seen for many a year. Many supporters wrote to me to say that they considered it vintage stuff, the most exciting they had ever seen at Old Trafford, and I gathered that some of them had been coming for quite a long time. I am still getting letters from fans, though most of them expressed in slightly more critical terms. Not to put too fine a point on it ... some of them would like to see me fired! All I can say is that I am equally bitter about the way the season has ended. I felt so despondent in the second half of our last home game that I felt like joining in with the fans shouting for my head. But that was one game. When I look at the season overall I am still thrilled by the potential at this club and I truly believe we are very, very close to having something really exceptional at Old Trafford. Critics say we tossed our ten-point lead away, somehow implying we were either careless or didn't even care. That's rubbish; what really happened was that our form and rhythm was broken by injuries. I'm not moaning about that because it's something that happens in soccer and presents problems that have to be beaten. We failed at the end of the day, but my word how close it was! If we had beaten Chelsea at Old Trafford a fortnight ago we would have gone top of the table and I believe we would have been inspired to go on and take the title. The maddening thing is that we deserved to beat Chelsea that night, and so, as I take an overall look at our season, I am no longer despondent. I am just all the keener to have another crack at that elusive championship.'

Stapleton scored early on and United netted three times in the last seven minutes to record an emphatic win. A penalty in the 87th minute even presented the opportunity for Davenport to step up and score his first goal for the club after an incredibly difficult start.

The season concluded at Vicarage Road. Hughes scored an exceptional goodbye goal in a 1-1 draw. United went from certain champions to underwhelming runners-up, but it had got even worse; West Ham had usurped Atkinson's side, who had to settle for fourth, leading to the stinging barb that United were experts at finishing fourth in a two-horse race.

At Watford, Atkinson appeared to accept his time was up. He was sitting alongside Martin Edwards and informed him that he felt his time may have come to an end: 'After the game at Watford, Ron turned and said to me, "Maybe my time's up, chairman." I persuaded him. I said don't go, give it more time. I felt that perhaps because of the injury crisis we might do better. I certainly put it down to injuries rather than poor management. I felt he could turn it around.'

Atkinson, however, insists he wasn't serious. 'It might have been in a fit of pique,' he says. 'Something exasperated like, "I don't know with this lot!" but I didn't want to resign.'

Many at Manchester United may have felt that 1984 was the best chance Atkinson had to win the league, but the circumstances behind the 1985/86 season make that the most infamous of all the near-misses. There was something of everything in there, too, for the sceptics. The short-term signings, the injuries, the dreadful pitches, the tendency to switch off and lose results in the dying minutes of matches against lesser teams. All factors came into play in an eventful campaign.

This was one occasion where describing the injuries sounds more like a reason than an excuse. Ironically (given the reputation he would earn in his later years), just about the only player in the defence and midfield to have an injury-free season was Paul McGrath, who played 40 league games, his best tally for the club. The same could be said for Whiteside, who was dependable in his 37 First Division appearances. But Bailey, Duxbury, Gidman, Moran, Hogg, Albiston, Strachan, Robson, Moses, Olsen and Barnes all had spells out of the team that were long enough to be deemed significant. Up front, Hughes and Stapleton played almost every game, but they often had to change their approach on a game-by-game basis. Furthermore, Stapleton later confessed it was not always easy to play alongside Hughes, due to the Welshman's individual style. Stapleton said his strike partner would often suffer a drop in confidence if he went a few games without scoring.

Another way of looking at it is to list the number of league appearances made by those players who had injury absences. Bailey made 25, Duxbury 23, Gidman 24, Albiston 37 (deemed significant because his five matches absent were in a row and forced Atkinson to sign a player), Hogg 17, Moran 19, Robson 21, Strachan 28, Barnes 13, Olsen 28, and Moses four. Apart from Albiston, all of the list missed at least a third of the campaign.

And so the curtain hadn't even closed on the season before thoughts turned to how United, and Atkinson, could recover; hopefully more successfully than Bryan Robson would that summer.

Borrowed Time

DESPITE MARTIN Edwards's insistence that Ron Atkinson should continue as Manchester United manager, the chairman was beginning to have misgivings about the future before May 1986 was over.

Predictably, there was plenty of speculation about how United might strengthen their team. The primary name was Terry Butcher, and now Ipswich seemed willing to do business. Ipswich chairman Patrick Cobbold said, 'I won't deny that his future with us is very much in the balance.'

Atkinson was keen on Butcher but made a fateful decision to accept ITV's offer of a commentary position for the World Cup in Mexico, deciding he would deal with such matters on his return. He went there from Hong Kong, where United had played the last of three post-season friendlies.

'Ron went off to the World Cup, and I felt he would have been better served staying in Manchester and sorting out the squad,' Edwards remembers. 'But he went and came back and suddenly wanted to buy a couple of players; one of them was Terry Butcher. It was right at the beginning of the season. If we were going to try and buy a player of that calibre you needed to be working on it right at the start of pre-season, so I did wonder if there was an element of panic in Ron's transfer strategy. It didn't happen and the season started poorly.'

Atkinson, meanwhile, was unhappy in return with Edwards when he came back from Mexico. United had just opened a new

318

museum at Old Trafford and, following on from the increase in popularity of American sports due to the exposure of them on British television, Edwards was discussing the idea of establishing a basketball team under the United name. Atkinson believed these were unnecessary distractions.

'I felt I had done the job Martin had brought me in to do,' he said in his 2016 book *The Manager*. 'He asked me to re-establish Manchester United as a force in the English game. From 1968 to 1981 they had finished in the top four twice – which was scandalous for a club of its stature. The top four had no real meaning then, and anyway English clubs were banned from Europe. But Manchester United had finished no lower than fourth in my time at Old Trafford and won the FA Cup twice ... Board meetings at Manchester United consisted of endless discussions about the basketball team the club was then running and about ten minutes on football.'

Atkinson told Edwards that he wanted Butcher, and that he had been informed the player would cost £750,000. He says Edwards admitted he was a good player but said the money was allocated for the museum. 'Well that will be handy when we're three down – I'll bring the museum on for a corner,' Atkinson told him.

He wasn't the only one returning from Mexico with woes. England had selected Bryan Robson and Gary Bailey for their World Cup squad. Bailey, however, picked up a knee injury in training and had to return to Manchester for an operation. The gamble on Robson, meanwhile, had backfired. Clearly in discomfort, he was finally forced to come off after 40 minutes of the second group game against Morocco. He too would finally be sent for an operation when he returned.

In his absence, Diego Maradona led the England midfield on a merry dance as the Argentine superstar scored two famous goals – one brilliant, one controversial. The brilliant goal is rated by many as one of the greatest ever scored. One can't help but wonder how easily Maradona would have raced through a midfield that had Robson in it. Their previous head to head in 1984 suggests the United legend might have come out on top. On such moments, legacies are built and reputations earned.

While Maradona led Argentina to World Cup glory, England – and Manchester United supporters – were left only to wonder what they might have accomplished if their captain had not suffered with his shoulder. The injury would put him out of the start of the season.

With the European ban now relaxed enough to allow English teams to play in friendly games, United went to Holland to play against Dynamo Kiev and Ajax. There were some reports of supporter unrest, but it was the players' drinking which hit the headlines. A number of the squad were dubbed 'The Magnificent Seven' after being spotted in a bar. Three of the seven, Terry Gibson, Mick Duxbury and Clayton Blackmore, left the group early to go back to the team hotel. It was only 7.30pm but they were already the worse for wear.

'Ron called the police,' Blackmore remembers. 'Terry, Micky and I arrived back at the hotel to be confronted by Mick Brown, who was going out of his mind. He goes, "Where've you been, where've you been, he's called the police!" "Where is the fat bastard?!" answered a drunken Micky.'

Blackmore admitted the mood around the club 'wasn't great'. The guilty players were fined. If it felt like things were unravelling out of control, Atkinson was doing his level best to maintain a brave face, although it was seemingly impossible for him to put on that larger-than-life act in the season's opener at Highbury. Charlie Nicholas scored the only goal of the game in the 80th minute; *Guardian* reporter David Lacey said Atkinson looked 'a little world-weary, his permanent suntan a trifle sallow'.

'We put a lot of effort into the game,' Atkinson said. 'A bit more steadiness in possession would have helped us.'

Lacey, however, felt he had seen this sort of performance from United before, saying they 'gave the sort of energetic but mundane display that led to Atkinson succeeding Dave Sexton as manager'.

United got their Old Trafford campaign underway two days later on the August Bank Holiday Monday but were shambolic and low in confidence. They went a goal down within 60 seconds and two down in the 39th minute. It provoked something of a reaction as Stapleton and Davenport scored either side of half-time (Davenport's equaliser was credited to McGrath in some of the morning papers) to level it up, but the Hammers scored again eight minutes from time to record a famous victory. Whiteside and

Blackmore's commitment to winning the ball back, and playing adventurous football, could not be questioned, but it was clear that the natural defensive qualities of Moses and Robson were desperately missed. For all of the talent in McGrath and Moran, the organisation that one of them would have enjoyed the benefit of from Butcher was also pretty evident.

Atkinson had enjoyed a record-breaking start to the previous campaign and was doing so again now for all the opposite reasons. His team fell to a third consecutive defeat, this time against Charlton at Old Trafford. Whereas in the past they had been caught by late sucker punches as they tried to win the game, here the Addicks scored in the 49th minute, and the hosts had no response. The United team left the pitch to boos.

When Martin Edwards was questioned by reporters after the game, his reassurance was not exactly watertight. 'We gave him another chance last season, but we're not fickle enough to think about changing after only three games,' the chairman said. 'I am as disappointed as much as the crowd at our poor start. I can fully understand their feelings.'

Atkinson suffered a slip of the tongue afterwards, saying, 'Bad players ... sorry, good players, don't become bad players overnight,' but otherwise came out with stock phrases which are always associated with a manager reaching the end such as 'keeping belief'.

United drew at Filbert Street in their next game to at least halt the run of defeats, and Atkinson was pleased to see Bryan Robson come through an 'A' team game unscathed, fit to play against Southampton. 'I am not prepared to take it easy,' Robson said. 'If I ever thought that was necessary it would be time to pack it in ... I know I've had a problem, but it's not going to worry me.'

The boss insisted that better was to come from his team. 'I guess this is the testing time for Manchester United,' he wrote in his programme notes. 'To open a season with three defeats is a nightmare start for any club, big or small. Inevitably, as manager, the finger points at me, and I have no complaints about that, because success or otherwise is my responsibility ... Our present position hurts, but don't worry, we'll soon change it.'

United hammered Southampton on a day that was shaping up to be crucial as far as Atkinson was concerned. One newspaper that week had speculated that Robson may be offered the position of player-manager; *The Guardian*'s Stephen Bierley scoffed at that suggestion, but said of Atkinson: 'He was not and is not trusted. All very unfair, for in Atkinson ambition to take United back to the top has burned fierce ... the truth is that in the last year or so Atkinson has lost his way, and Edwards has allowed matters to drift.'

The two crucial incidents cited were the deliberating over Hughes's move and the refusal to send Robson for surgery. Robson was superb against Southampton, and those concerns about a lack of goals were answered with Davenport and Whiteside both on the scoresheet in a 5-1 win over the Saints.

It was a false dawn. United lost at Vicarage Road.

'We paid for a moment of casualness at the back, but for that we would have run out comfortable winners,' Atkinson insisted. 'But the drive and the pace of the side tonight was tremendous.'

After the game, Robson insisted that the players remained behind the manager, while Atkinson himself kept tight-lipped about his future. It was heavily suggested that Aston Villa wanted to hire the United manager to take over; as grand a club as Villa were, it was a far cry from the links to Madrid at the start of the year. Villa were the only team below United in the First Division.

Renewed speculation came around of Atkinson getting the sack if United lost at Goodison Park. But they did, and he didn't, even if his insistence that 'the daft thing is that apart from the Charlton game we have played well' seemed rather hollow, and even if the 3-1 defeat at Everton was a *little* harsh. It was United's first game on television. They were scheduled to play Chelsea and Manchester City on TV in the coming weeks, with broadcasters presumably hoping they might be witness to a live execution.

The Chelsea game was particularly excruciating. Kerry Dixon scored in the second minute, exploiting a big gap left by Sivebæk before smashing past Turner. United's attempts to get back into the game were agonising for a paltry crowd of just over 33,000 at Old Trafford. Remi Moses was back in the team to try to add some bite, but clearly looked unfit. There was nothing of the fast, industrious play of 12 months before. Anxiety replaced composure in the second half, with another poor result on the horizon. Davenport thought he had levelled things up on the hour, but the goal was disallowed;

it turned out there had been a push on Stapleton, and the referee had awarded a penalty. United would have rather taken the goal. The kick was taken by Olsen, who had literally just come on for Moses (Robson had missed from the spot in a League Cup game against Port Vale in midweek). The Dane's kick was weak and easily saved by the Chelsea goalkeeper. 'Nothing goes right for United!' said the ITV commentator Brian Moore, and he didn't realise how right he was.

Just a couple of minutes afterwards, Olsen was then brought down in the box and the referee awarded another penalty. This time Gordon Strachan stepped up. The Scot shot to Tony Godden's right, but Godden guessed right again – this time his save was a little better, though the kick was still poor.

'If this was reality, it was a waking nightmare,' reporter Bierley wrote in his report for *The Guardian*. 'A mass of incident could not compensate for football that was very much bottom-of-the-table standard.'

Godden – who had put Atkinson on the brink – suggested he should have been brought to Old Trafford. 'He should have signed me in the summer when I was on a free, then it might have been different today,' goaded the Chelsea stopper.

The Times reported United as 'flying on the wings of outrageous misfortune'.

'This is the worst position I have been in as a football manager,' Atkinson admitted. 'We have got to buckle down and start winning matches.'

The next game was Nottingham Forest's City Ground; not for the last time, that venue was tipped to be the scene of the final game for a Manchester United manager. Brian Clough, enjoying a brief resurgence with his team in fine form after a few years of post-European Cup mediocrity, insisted he would not be taking it easy.

'It's the law of the jungle,' said Clough. 'I can't be concerned if United lose and Ron is in the dole queue on Monday. It could be me on the dole next. It's the survival of the fittest.'

However, Clough had publicly supported Atkinson when United dropped to the foot of the table and Atkinson phoned to say thanks. 'I said then there was no manager in Europe under more pressure than Atkinson and nothing has changed. I would like us to have 30,000 people in the ground against United, three points and Ron Atkinson to keep his job. He has talent as a manager and his players have talent. He has support and the biggest club in Europe. He ought to be able to get out of trouble.'

Not for the last time, those reports of the Manchester United manager's exit were premature, though in this case not so much. Forest were league leaders but United looked anything but short on confidence as they equipped themselves well. They needed a Robson goal to secure a draw, but as reporter Bob Houston put it, 'United's luck, deservedly, held. Mr Atkinson's cards can reside safely in the Old Trafford office safe, and there should be no need to get the bike out of the shed. For the moment …'

Robson – comfortably the man of the match, and most vocal in his support for the manager – felt the return to a 4-4-2 shape, as had been the case at the City Ground, would be the sign of better things. 'When we were playing with three in midfield, Remi Moses was doing the defensive job with Norman Whiteside on the left side,' Robson said. 'That made it more important for me to get forward so I was doing a lot of running instead of getting the ball. But today we changed to a style which I prefer. I like letting Gordon Strachan, Norman and Jesper Olsen go forward while I sit in there and get plenty of the ball. That's what happened today. It is a style which suits me more than anything and I think it suits the other lads. I see a lot more of the ball and I still get involved in the build-up.'

Nobody could ever accuse Robson of not having a realistic sense of perspective, but his comments seemed to be founded more in hope than expectation. The stay of execution earned by the result was just that, and not a turning point.

The following week, one of the most infamous incidents of indiscipline took place at The Cliff, when Jesper Olsen and Remi Moses were involved in an altercation.

'Oh, it was good!' laughs Atkinson. 'I was the only one who saw it. I was playing sweeper. Jesper was a little bugger in training, he could be nasty … I can remember Arthur Albiston once saying he felt Jesper might injure somebody. In matches he wasn't like that, I wish he had been. In this one training session, he went over the top on Remi, and Remi got up like Lloyd Honeyhan as quick as a flash. Boom. I couldn't believe it. I knew no one else had seen anything, so quick as I could I said, "How did you two bang heads like that?!" and I looked down at Jesper and warned him not to say a word. It was a collision. Until Jesper started talking to Danish journalists. The last thing I wanted was Remi out of the team. That kind of situation can happen in training. It stopped Jesper going over the top again! Remi is the quietest footballer I ever met, off the field, but on it he wouldn't shut up. He trained like a lunatic. He would work out in the gym even when he was injured, he didn't need supervision.'

That was Atkinson's candid admission in 2019; back in 1986, the incident was treated like a state secret. Bryan Robson was the first to go on record with an eyewitness account in his own autobiography. 'Remi wasn't a big lad, but he absolutely battered Jesper,' he wrote. 'The fight took place on the training pitch. Jesper went over the top on Remi, who wasn't happy about the tackle and gave Jesper a menacing stare. Jesper came back at him with a defiant, "Yeah, what are you going to do about it?" kind of response. Remi showed him. He went bang, bang, bang, and that was the end of it. There was blood all over the place.'

Jesper Olsen's bruises – and the 11 stitches in the cut above his eye – seemed to allude that something had gone on that was more than just, as the manager told reporters, 'a clash of heads'. United defeated Port Vale and Sheffield Wednesday before the visit of Luton. Journalists were adamant all was not well at Old Trafford, as seemed further apparent when Atkinson abruptly left his pre-match press conference as he was questioned about Frank Stapleton's contract. He was probably anticipating further questions about Olsen as it emerged the winger apparently wanted to move to Germany.

'Victory, rather than the manner of it, matters most to United at present,' wrote reporter Paul Fitzpatrick of United's 1-0 win, which came courtesy of a ninth-minute Stapleton strike. That sentence in itself spoke volumes, considering just how strongly Atkinson had adhered to the philosophy of entertaining first and foremost as a matter of principle.

United drew at Maine Road, and then at home against Southampton in the first leg of their League Cup tie. Ahead of the game against Coventry at home, Atkinson banged the drum of a slowly shifting momentum. 'It was maddening to find victory slipping through our fingers at Maine Road on Sunday,' he wrote in his column for the programme. 'But we also created chances, and while a draw was probably a fair reflection of the play, I felt we had our moments. So I was not at all disheartened, and I feel sure that if we can maintain our recent momentum through November, we will soon begin to climb.'

United were held again; a 31st-minute goal from Davenport was cancelled out after the break by David Phillips. Atkinson's heart must have sunk as Robson came off injured in the 11th minute.

At The Dell in the second leg against Southampton, it was a familiar tale as the manager was forced to make both his substitutions (two were now allowed, and thankfully so, as they were needed!) in the first half. Youngster Nicky Wood came on in the 38th minute with the scores level, and Atkinson wanted to get his team in level at half-time to reorganise. It didn't happen. A goal for the Saints just before the break changed the complexity of the match. With 20 minutes to go, Atkinson instructed his side to go for an away goal, with disastrous consequences. Southampton scored three times in the last 19 minutes, and although Davenport netted in the 88th minute it wasn't even a consolation.

'This has to be the lowest point of my time in Manchester and it's up to me to turn it around,' Atkinson said after the game. 'I'll be taking stock of our injuries tomorrow. But I've no plans to recruit at the moment. We'll be going with the staff we've got. It's a challenge but I believe they will pull us through. In the meantime I certainly don't want anyone going around feeling sorry for themselves. There must be no moping. We went for a result at Southampton and thought we'd get it. But that's history. What we must get now is some First Division respectability.'

Atkinson may well have breathed a sigh of relief when the following day came and went and he was still Manchester United manager. That would account for the apparent shock he felt on the morning of Thursday, 6 November 1986, when he was informed he was dismissed.

On Good Terms

ONE THING nobody could ever accuse Ron Atkinson of was shying away even when things were tough. Just a few hours after United released a statement which began with the fateful words 'In the light of the team's poor performances over the last 12 months ...' Atkinson was facing television cameras talking in a straightforward manner about the decision.

'My pride's hurt,' he said. 'It's the first time I've been out of work since I left school. I've been out of work for a morning and I'm bored. I'm itching to get back again.' Asked if he felt Martin Edwards had been under pressure to dismiss him, Atkinson seemed appreciative of the choice the chairman had to make. 'The fans were frustrated,' Ron admitted. 'I could understand that. There was a suggestion, which may be the case, that the gates were going to fall because the results haven't been very good. I would say this now, Martin Edwards never put me under any pressure, he left me to get on with it. I didn't feel that whatever pressure was supposed to be heaped on him was reflected in his attitude towards me.'

He was even more complimentary, surprisingly, about the chairman to the newspapers than he had been to the cameras: 'If you're positive you don't look on the black side so I wasn't prepared for it. But I feel no bitterness, I have no axe to grind. I've worked with a chairman believed to be as good as any in the game. You couldn't get a more supportive man. My successor has got to get the players fit and then I'm sure the good times will return. I've no idea what the turning point was here. But I'll always remember the five great years I had in my five-and-a-half-year stint here. They were magic.'

And so to the events of earlier in the day. 'Our boots had not been laid out for training and there was a message for Mick Brown and me to report to Martin Edwards's office,' Atkinson remembered. 'I turned to him and said, "I wouldn't be asking for a rise today, Mick." I didn't, however, think we'd be sacked.'

He remembered Edwards telling him that he needed to make a change, and that the secretary would sort out the details of his contract. It was, apparently, as straightforward as that.

'After the Southampton game I took stock of the various factors,' Edwards says. 'Ron had said to me he wasn't sure about carrying on, then there was the fact that we had started badly, and he hadn't devoted the summer to team building, it made me realise we probably weren't going to win the league with Ron. It was sad at the end, though, because we'd had five good years. But we weren't knocking on the door enough.'

The decision had more or less been taken on the night of the Southampton game. Edwards talked it over with director Mike Edelson on the plane journey back to Manchester, and then had a meeting on the Wednesday with Bobby Charlton and Maurice Watkins, where the decision was made. Edwards had already decided on Atkinson's successor – Alex Ferguson, the Aberdeen manager who had broken the Old Firm stranglehold on trophies in Scotland – but, feeling hesitant after the public embarrassments of trying to replace Sexton, wanted to ensure he had an agreement with Ferguson before dismissing his current manager.

'I think by Ron's reaction when we told him of our decision to let him go he wasn't totally surprised,' Edwards said in his autobiography. 'It must have been on his mind and he had considered the possibility. He accepted it with a single shrug and a placatory handshake. It wasn't an easy decision because after five years we had built up a good relationship. But the club had to come first.'

Atkinson went to The Cliff. In the car park, he bumped into Whiteside, took him to his office and said, 'Tell you what, I've just been up to Old Trafford and they've sacked me. You're the first to know.' Atkinson asked Whiteside to inform Brian

Whitehouse and gather the players in the gymnasium where he could inform them.

Some reserve-team players who had made the leap to first team still hadn't 'graduated' into the first-team dressing room at The Cliff. That room only had so many seats so only when a senior player left could a junior one come in. Alan Brazil's departure meant Hughes could leapfrog Hogg into a seat, and Hogg and Blackmore were still in the reserve dressing room as the rumour filtered through.

'It was always in the back of your mind that a change might come because of how poor things had become,' Hogg said. 'Results were bad, the newspapers were speculating but at the time, when Mark Hughes was still there, there was a group of us younger players who hadn't made the move up to the senior dressing room at The Cliff. Sparky, Clayton Blackmore and me would get changed in the reserves dressing room and so we wouldn't hear the same sort of stories and conversations, we'd hear bits that came through, but we weren't part of that circle of lads yet. Mark Hughes got a peg in the first-team room over time but even when I was a regular I was still in the other room. There was a feeling, though, I knew some of the senior lads were of the mind that they had to try and get their fingers out and try and turn it around because they were worried they were only two or three games away from losing their manager. It's a different world – you hear today about players trying to get their manager sacked. For us it was the opposite. We felt guilty. No one I knew wanted Ron to go. He was very popular, top class. He was always upfront with us, with me. He never bottled anything with regards to that. Most of the squad had nothing but respect for him. That only lasts for so long, it only counts for so much, if you're not getting results, though.'

In typical fashion, Atkinson marked his exit by holding a party at his house in Rochdale, and invited the players. Some felt it in bad taste; others didn't want to hurt the outgoing manager's feelings by not going. Whiteside recalls that just him, Robson, Strachan and Bailey attended, partly because they knew they weren't fit enough to play at the weekend and, in Whiteside's words, could get 'stuck into the drink'. Gordon Strachan acted as DJ and played tracks in good humour like 'Big Spender' and 'Goldfinger'; the Scot was not a big drinker but got himself into a spot of bother. 'When he tried to drive home to the other side of Manchester, his car passed a football ground and he wondered how he had managed to get to Maine Road,' remembered Atkinson. 'He hadn't. He had driven to Leeds. He was outside Elland Road.'

Atkinson had taken two phones call earlier that evening; the first from a journalist friend who informed him that Alex Ferguson would be taking his job, and the second from Jesus Gil, the chairman of Atlético de Madrid, asking if he wanted to take over at the end of the season. The outgoing manager said his attitude to things was 'Que Sera, Sera.' How incredibly apt.

It was a relatively small group of players wishing farewell to a manager who was apparently so popular. 'Norman and I went together. There weren't many more there and I remember thinking that no matter what your issue was with the manager, you should turn up and wish him well,' Bailey remembers. 'It made me think that maybe there was a deeper resentment I hadn't really been aware of, or maybe some of the players just did not appreciate the work that he had done.'

One of the senior players most affected by what people might say was short-term thinking from the manager in terms of team selection and signings was Mick Duxbury. Duxbury hadn't always seen eye to eye with Atkinson but resentment would seem a little too strong a term for how he appeared to feel. 'We were gathered in the gym and Ron came bouncing down the steps, trying to be as lively as he ever had been,' Duxbury says. 'There was a bit of nervousness as he announced he'd been let go, and then he went around the group shaking our hands. In typical fashion, Ron threw a party that night and invited the players to go. I can't speak for who went or didn't, I just know that I didn't turn up. Why do it? It didn't make any sense. I wasn't particularly disappointed that he'd gone and wouldn't have gone to one of Ron's parties anyway.'

This attitude seems representative of many of the squad, and although there could be no accusation of unprofessionalism or lack of desire to win games, it would be entirely understandable to consider that the events of the last 12 months had given some players cause to wonder whether the approach of the manager was working. If they felt they might be taken out of the team without a proper explanation, or if they felt the formation and game plan had changed without due diligence, they might not feel as if they could apply themselves as best they could.

It is important to note Bryan Robson's words of the time and since about this period – he felt almost personally insulted, and took Atkinson's dismissal personally, as he felt it was indicative of the players and their performance. 'Our bid nose-dived and I still say the main reason was the catalogue of injuries with which we had to contend,' he said. 'The league was already out of the question. We hadn't been able to pull it off with stronger teams than the one we had that season, so what chance was there? The truth is that we had one or two players who were not good enough for Manchester United. There was no question of Ron "losing the dressing room". The players liked him as a bloke and respected him as a manager.'

Robson could have no reason to question the manager given his own significance in the Old Trafford dressing room. If it seems like Atkinson indulged his star man, then let us at least consider the alternate side of the coin – that he was showing good management. Atkinson and Edwards had both come under immense criticism for postponing surgery on Robson's shoulder, but it later transpired that Robson himself made that decision. Like his successor, Atkinson was strong enough to bear the brunt of the accusatory columns and opinions to deflect the pressure from his player. Either way, Robson is the last place you would start if you felt some players were disillusioned with the direction the club was heading under the management.

Even in the players who might have felt disgruntled, Atkinson had actually instilled a strong enough team spirit and a strong enough sense of pride in the club again that their desire to win a league championship at Manchester United superseded any concerns they may have. Stapleton and Duxbury are prime examples, the former turning down that move to Bordeaux, and the latter refusing to join Everton in early 1986, even if that decision was partly motivated by the belief that Atkinson may actually soon be gone.

'Change might have been on the cards for me too as I received the crushing blow that Ron had accepted an offer from Everton for me,' Duxbury said in his autobiography. 'Gary Stevens, their right-back, had got injured, and so Howard Kendall made a £250,000 offer for me. I can remember the lads saying to me that they were shocked that the club had accepted an offer so low. It never got so far as me having to turn Everton down, though, because I said in no uncertain terms that I would not leave United. I don't know if that was stubbornness on my part or if a part of me believed that the Atkinson era would soon be over, so all I had to do was wait … I had no regrets over turning down Everton even though I could've won a league medal with them because it wouldn't have meant the same to me as winning it with United. They were my club, the only place I'd played and the only place I wanted to play.'

What went wrong, then? There is an obvious red flag and that is the high-profile nature of the way United collapsed after such a strong start to the season a year before. Prior to that there had been a running joke among the press that going to watch United was like going to view a new house (two up, two down) such was their prolific tendency to throw away leads; so this grandest capitulation created a scenario that, once continued into the next season, made the manager's position untenable.

'The players were good enough. I'm convinced of that,' Gary Bailey says. 'Maybe it was the turf. On the good pitches in August, September and November, we destroyed teams with Strachan and Olsen. But then the turf tore up and got muddy. Little Jesper would kick the ball, it would stop in the mud, and some brute would kick him into a stand. We had a skilful team who liked to pass the ball so the winter did affect us. It wasn't just Jesper and Gordon, even our defenders like Micky Duxbury, Giddy and McGrath, they all liked to play on the ball. It was a top-class team. Everyone was on the top of their game. I can remember going on England duty that November and Gary Lineker said to me, "No one's going to catch you now. You've gone." It gave me confidence. But six weeks later Lineker and Everton were just a couple of points behind us and as early as that I remember thinking, "Here we go again."'

Bailey feels that injuries played a huge part, not only in the way the lead was frittered away, but also the dreadful start to the following season. Whiteside had an operation after the World Cup and managed to play a part in pre-season but said he had to 'learn how to run again' and admitted he definitely rushed back before he was ready. By the goalkeeper's recollection, there was nothing that suggested morale was at rock bottom.

'That summer, Bryan, Norman and I spent a lot of time in the physio's room together,' he says. 'We were three of the big organisers in the team, in terms of position we were crucial and of course the extra qualities Norman and Bryan brought need no explanation. The days in the physio room would be long and boring so we came up with games to amuse ourselves. I remember Robbo bringing in a box of eggs. The game was to support a whole egg in our mouths for as long as we could before it cracked. If it lasted a minute you passed it to the next person. So Robbo went first and lasted the minute. He passed it to Norman who won. When it was my turn I crunched it within a few seconds. I lost and had to do press-ups! Today there are international replacements for every single player. We had a smaller squad and a tighter budget and if we lost a star name, while we would still have a good replacement, that might well represent the one or two per cent I said earlier that we lacked.'

It is worth pointing out that the fairly positive team spirit that remained among some of the team was in stark contrast to the difficult final days under Sexton, where the tension did feel more present to Bailey. 'It did turn sour then,' he says. 'I started to feel that when I was injured and I came back and wasn't in the best of form. The atmosphere was tense on the terrace and in the dressing room. I can remember making a mistake in one game and one of the lads, who shall remain nameless, grabbed me by the neck against the dressing room wall and told me I had cost him his clean-sheet bonus. It wasn't a happy time.'

Graeme Hogg feels that injuries affected the momentum of the team, and consequently it had an inevitable impact on the form: 'It's difficult to say exactly what went wrong but a major reason was that our confidence drained away so quickly and so badly when we started losing and we just couldn't get it back. We picked up injuries which disrupted the side, myself included, and we couldn't get that rhythm back.'

Duxbury, as you may think, feels the manager does need to take some of the flack for interrupting the rhythm. 'I don't think the injuries helped,' he concedes, 'but then Ron changed the side. Having been that successful at the start, and then you had the players available and fit again, you would have thought they'd be given a chance again to play as a team, but it never seemed to happen

... if you're not playing well, then you look at yourself. And you can understand that's why the manager is bringing other people in. But I didn't think that at any time through his managership that I wasn't playing well.'

Injuries may have been the major factor for the way the 1985/86 season had disintegrated, but it is never a valid reason for explaining why a manager was sacked. So if there was no player revolt to speak of, and injuries aren't applicable, is there a more brutal truth? Perhaps United just weren't good enough?

'We had a good team but we missed two or three world-class players,' Arnold Muhren told *Red News*. 'The squad those days wasn't as big as it is nowadays and injuries to key players can be very decisive then. Liverpool was the team with more better, stronger players than we had and they just dominated the 80s like United did in the 90s.'

The other way of looking at it is appreciating the quality of the opponents. As many as four clubs had arguably the best sides in their history during Atkinson's tenure – Nottingham Forest, Aston Villa and the clubs on Merseyside.

'They were obviously very good,' Duxbury admits. 'Everton won the league, Liverpool were always there, but those type of teams we always used to seem to get good results against. It was a failing that against the so-called lesser teams, we struggled or got beat. There must have been something mentally there.'

Complacency?

'Maybe ... but it probably happened too often for it to just be one of those things,' he says. 'Maybe for those players who weren't brought up through the United system and understand that every team wants to beat you, it can be difficult. I'd never level it at anybody, but there must be something there and it doesn't have to be the ones that always like shouting and bawling, you don't always need that. But, there certainly must be something there. But again, if I looked around our dressing room, I wouldn't say, you know, "You're not going to turn up today", or anything like that. You know, "You only put a half a shift in"... no, I'd never say that.'

Maybe there is a strong truth within that idea which relates to the players Atkinson had brought in over the last 18 months of his reign. None of them lasted in the long term and it could be said

– with some justification considering they never won the medals to prove otherwise – that the intensity that came with playing for Manchester United was too much of a culture shock. The desire to defeat United was strong. Paul Parker tells a story about Trevor Francis's time as manager of QPR about a game that took place a couple of years after Atkinson was sacked. Francis celebrated a dead-rubber end of season win at Loftus Road by bringing champagne into the dressing room. The sting of rejection lingered long, it seems.

'On our travel to an away game once, we went to see Liverpool play at Luton Town,' Duxbury remembers. 'They were playing on a Saturday and we were on the Sunday. The ground wasn't full. They nicked it late on, a result they probably didn't deserve, just as we'd probably done before and United would certainly do for years afterwards. My lasting memory of that, though, was thinking how horrible it must be to be Liverpool and not play in front of packed houses. The subsequent effect was that it was a reminder just how fortunate I and the rest of my team-mates were to be playing for Manchester United. How lucky we were. And that magnified how importantly other teams saw their games with United.'

The very idea of the allure of Britain's biggest club was under the spotlight again in the wake of the news of another managerial change. Certainly much of this was influenced by the reporting by the press and, according to some, it was no coincidence that Atkinson had gone from being heralded as one of the great under-rated tacticians of the time to having his appearance constantly juxtaposed against the idea of his perma-tanned, perma-smiling reputation.

Journalist Frank Keating, writing for *The Guardian*, suggested that Atkinson's decision to contribute an exclusive column to *The Sun* newspaper had come at a cost to his relationship with the press at large: 'If only one paper is getting the quotes, then all the rest can do is pillory their rival's star next day. Until it all turns nasty and suddenly a full-scale witch-hunt is under way. Would Atkinson still be in a job today had he told all to everyone and not just one? The rest of Fleet Street has been gunning for him since he started his 'exclusive' each week in one paper. Traditionally, of all clubs, you always hoped United were above this sort of thing. But not anymore.'

(It is worth pointing out, whether this contradicts or even exemplifies Keating's point, O'Farrell had an exclusive column with *The Mirror* throughout 1972, and decided to stop writing it when his team's form dipped drastically. Keating also suggested Clough as the ideal replacement for Atkinson. The idea of the Forest manager taking charge at Old Trafford had already been dismissed as far back as when O'Farrell was sacked and Tommy Docherty was hired.)

'Poor bargains, erratic team selection and an increasing tendency towards safe options have combined to unseat the Sun King from his throne,' theorised David Lacey, also in *The Guardian*. 'Atkinson has also paid the price of loyalty to Mick Brown, his assistant at West Bromwich Albion, who continued to hold the post at Old Trafford when it was obvious that something other than the basic disciplines was needed to inspire the players ... Atkinson, who liked wearing gold, led from the front, was always able to give the press a tasty headline and, in short, seemed just the man the club needed. However, the Manchester supporters never took to him as they had taken to Docherty, discerning the difference between a likeable rogue and a pleasant but at times distant showman. The strange thing is that some time ago Atkinson, no fool and realising that the gold bracelets, cufflinks and whatever were in danger of bringing him derision, made a conscious effort to tone himself down. He has not glittered for a long time now, and with the dulling of his image the light seemed to go out of his management ... the most important player in his managerial career has been Bryan Robson, both at West Bromwich and Manchester United. Had Robson stayed fit so much might have been different. In the end it all comes down to players. Ask Bobby Robson.'

This brings us on to another significant topic often associated with United's relative failure (if discussed in terms of winning a league championship) under Atkinson: the hitherto undiscussed (in this book) 'drinking culture'.

The best place to start with this is the captain, Bryan Robson, who said in his autobiography that he didn't 'want anyone running away with the idea that Ron was happy for us to go out boozing every night, far from it.' He admitted the manager felt it could be good for morale and that he put his trust in players, treating them with respect. Robson had his own rule that he wouldn't drink for two days before a match, which most of his team-mates respected and adhered to. 'We didn't abuse that trust and I don't think our drinking cost us in terms of performances or results,' Robson insisted. 'We went out for a drink only at the start of a week when we didn't have a match until the Saturday or Sunday. So because we had so many midweek cup matches, we'd maybe go out no more than once a month or even two months. Then we'd go out for lunch as a group of players after training on Monday and take it from there. The likes of Moran, McGrath, Whiteside, McQueen, Hughes and me would sometimes be out till two in the morning ... It didn't take the edge off my game because if I'd had a session on the Monday, I wouldn't have another drop for the rest of the week. The morning after, I'd train hard and sweat it out. When you are comparatively young and fit, you can cope with it. I always made sure the drink didn't affect my job.'

Norman Whiteside remembers that after the European ban the Monday sessions might also cross over on to Tuesdays, but even if they did play in midweek they would still find time to have a drink. 'We would go to one of our Mat's pubs on Wednesday night after games,' he said. 'Even if we'd played away, we could knock him up in the early hours and he would let us sit in the bar, unwinding over several pints, and would allow us to carry on. If he called it a night and trooped off to bed. Then we would sleep it off on Thursday and go back to training pretty fresh on Friday. Whenever I was fit enough to be picked, I never once had a drink from Wednesday night until Saturday night.'

This isn't laid out bare to cast aspersions or point fingers at players. It was not as if Manchester United Football Club was the only club who had players who indulged in alcohol during the week; it would have been newsworthy indeed, as it eventually was, when clubs actually actively worked to identify it as a real problem. Whiteside isn't the only one to remark that all the big achievers at the time were doing exactly the same. 'I know that by today's abstemious standards our drinking sounds horrendous, but I must stress that we weren't the only ones who had a carefree attitude to nights out,' he says. 'Liverpool did it, Everton certainly did it ... I'm not saying it was right, but on the other hand I cannot see that it was all that wrong either.'

Many of the players recall that Atkinson had said so long as the players turned up fit and ready to train and be picked for the team, that was all that mattered; Whiteside insisted that even if Atkinson had imposed a ban on drinking, the players would have probably 'found a way around it ... because when you're 20 years old and as fit as you'll ever be, you're never going to be persuaded that a night out is going to do you any harm.'

Bailey was not one of the drinkers; coming from South Africa, and having trained on the Continent, he could not understand the culture of drinking – he did, however, appreciate that it could help others.

'I felt alone in every sense; I trained as a goalkeeper away from the rest of the team, I wasn't a drinker and I was academic,' he says. 'I was culturally alone in almost every sense. When we weren't doing well it really was a lonely existence, though when we were winning games, playing really well and doing well, and I was a bit more mature too, I was able to enjoy it ... Psychologically it helped some of the players to have that culture. It helped them deal with the pressure. Could we have been better without the drinking? Perhaps, of course. But the margins weren't great. We only needed that rub of luck sometimes, there was only one or two per cent between us winning a league title and not. Bryan and Kevin were our biggest drinkers and they were not only reliable on a Saturday, but they'd be at the front of running in every training session, every single morning. Paul was one of the greatest defenders I've ever seen so it didn't seem to bother him that much. It was part of the culture. Maybe if there wasn't the drinking, some of the players might have been susceptible to the pressure. When I was training with Hamburg before I signed for United, they would train in the morning and then again in the afternoon, where they would work more on the tactical side. In England we trained for two hours in the morning and the players went to the pub in the afternoon! I went back for extra training. That was my preference but I couldn't argue that the German approach was genuinely more effective considering how successful English teams were in European competition.'

Atkinson recalled going on a trip with Liverpool abroad while he was United manager – presumably in his role as commentator for

ITV – and said he witnessed them drinking to excess in a manner that made him feel his own team were lightweights.

Mick Duxbury was one who did occasionally join in but was not of the main crowd. He too believes that it is important to view it in the perspective of the contemporaneous footballing landscape, and the fact that United's better players were the biggest indulgers.

'In fairness, if it was a problem, then it was a problem in football, not just United,' he said in his autobiography. 'It's important to acknowledge that just because there was a drinking habit and a culture, it didn't mean there was a drinking problem per se. But I suppose it's natural to wonder what might have been if Ron had had more discipline and cut it out in the way that Sir Alex tried to do later. Bryan Robson and Norman Whiteside were absolutely fantastic players. Bryan was captain of his club and country, he carried the team so many times and scored so many important goals. Norman was a colossal player for us too. They both got us out of so many holes ... if you were to look at it logically and ask that, without the drink, could we and they have achieved more and done better, you would have to say yes, but then it's hard to fathom just how good they might have been because they were, for me at least, world-class players who were vital to our team as they were. Easy as it is to point out the drinking culture as a problem, the fact that it existed at all the top clubs meant that nobody had an advantage over the others. Of course, without the drink, we'd have all played better, but at the end of any given game if you were to start pointing the finger at someone and wondering if they'd done their jobs, then Norman and Bryan would always be safe. I don't think you could ever do that at any United player but those two especially could never be questioned. If I could choose any team-mates from my career to have beside me in the trenches those would be the top ones I'd select. There were some unbelievable stories I've heard about what happened at Liverpool – none I can print! – but their best trait was consistency. Perhaps it would have been a sign of good management to see the stop of it as a potential advantage but at the time we didn't feel like it put us at a disadvantage.'

Looking back and knowing what we do now, we can surely conclude that United would have been better off if they had attempted to eradicate the drinking culture at the club earlier. There is no telling what the impact of this may have been, or how successful it could have been, but it is largely accepted that it was a massive positive step in the right direction when Alex Ferguson took those measures. Paul McGrath appeared to be the most deeply affected (and his autobiography is most definitely high on the list of this author's recommended reads), demonstrating that indulgence can lead to addiction. McGrath also bluntly describes the drinking culture as the biggest reason why Atkinson was sacked. Robson and Whiteside can be absolved of never letting it affect their performance, at least in the way they could control it, but what about the physical effects that they could not?

Considering the number of muscle injuries and strains suffered over the years, and the frequency with which some players suffered them, it is difficult to reasonably conclude anything other than a more prohibitive attitude to drinking would have had beneficial impacts on the injury problems often suffered at the club. Bailey reckoned only a one or two per cent improvement might have brought a league title and surely that one or two percent improvement could have come from not drinking. Clayton Blackmore agrees, whilst still naturally remaining protective of his colleagues.

'I know a lot of people blame what's come to be known as the 'drinking culture' at the club and I can see what they mean,' he admitted. 'Bryan was a big drinker but the difference with him was that it didn't affect his performance, or at least it didn't seem to. The others often associated with him were big Gordon McQueen, Norman Whiteside, Paul McGrath. I don't know if it's fair to say these were all favourites of Ron so they got away with it – he liked to have big lads in his side and they all fit into that category too. They weren't the only ones drinking. I could be just as bad and so could Arthur Albiston; we certainly kept up with them as well as we could. Since retiring, Arthur doesn't drink – there are obviously cases in football where the habit becomes an addiction, but I think Arthur's case proves that it was simply a routine that we were in. Robbo's rule was no drinking 48 hours before a game and at the time we thought it was sensible, but look, there's just no other way of saying it, that kind of lifestyle is obviously going to affect your body and it is going to have a negative impact on you if you're a professional sportsman. Sure, we tried our best, and for players like Bryan the effects weren't obvious, but you just can't be at full tilt.'

Ferguson's implemented change was easier said than done and it took a long time. The public face of the change was the sale of Norman Whiteside to Everton in August 1989, and Paul McGrath to Aston Villa that same month. Whiteside was 24, McGrath was 29; those sales coincided with Ferguson's big summer spend and so it has to be said that the departure of two hugely popular players contributed to some of the pressure from the terraces that following autumn and winter.

With the benefit of hindsight, those decisions are often cited as examples of Ferguson's genius; but is genius a little generous? There was foresight and bravery, without a shadow of a doubt, yet it was only logical that a diet which was more in tune with that of a professional sportsman would yield better results physically and consequently in performance too.

Did Atkinson lack the bravery to make such a call? That would be a little unfair; however, it could well be that he didn't even perceive it as a problem at the time. Bryan Robson was the captain of his team and the leader of that smaller group of players who would grace any United side in history; he was the strength of the team, and it stands to reason that Atkinson would not associate any weakness with that area of the dressing room.

The very idea of a 'drinking' culture in the United team was something more or less invented in the 1980s. That doesn't mean it doesn't extend further back; Paddy McGrath's Cromford Club was often attended by United players in the 60s and 70s, after all. Despite this, only George Best was ever singled out as one who drunk to excess, and, even then, many remain defensive of Best and say he only drunk in his later years. Alcoholic excess wasn't noted as a trait of a Busby team, nor was it ever used as a reason for failure by any of his successors. Tommy Docherty appeared to take a hard line with it, for the times – though the version of George Best's final exit from United differs depending on who tells it. One thing that is consistent in all recollections is that the Northern Irishman had grown unreliable because of his illness and that was a big factor in determining his exit. Dave Sexton, as has been noted, was a hard taskmaster on the training pitch, so much so that even the goalkeepers became physically sick.

Maybe it became more associated with Atkinson and his team because the idea of 'Champagne Ron' was a personality and image he cultivated and indulged. Many have gone on record as saying Ron would pour the bottle and let others drink. The characterisation was one the United hierarchy were happy with following the dichotomous Sexton.

Still, that is a matter of image and perception and not a matter of assessing the impact of the action. At the time, attitudes towards alcohol in sport were more relaxed. This much is proven by accounts of players from other teams. And it is fairly important to note that the chronic injury issues suffered by McGrath and Whiteside were mostly post-Atkinson issues, and so the discussion of the involvement of alcohol and its effects on, and impairing of, recovery are not strictly associated with the issue at hand of how those problems contributed to United's perceived underperformance in the earlier period of the decade.

There is still a cumulative effect, though. The point is that it wasn't in the bigger number of games or lengthier spells out, such as the ones suffered by Robson, but the minor spells out of the team and the opportunity taken by players with a week off to indulge in drinking more than they should have. If we are to believe that the difference between Manchester United and a league title was caused by fine margins, maybe this is one of those. It is far too simplistic to categorise attitudes towards drinking in sport as a fine margin.

United didn't only do enough to get over the line under Ferguson, but their entire outlook was changed; the increased physical fitness levels that were a consequence of changes to diet helped when it came to smarter conservation of energy and game management. United became famed for the way they would win games late on, not only in injury time or Fergie time, but after having the patience to wear down teams for more than an hour or so. And let us not forget how one of the major disappointments of the Atkinson era was the number of late goals conceded. United conceded 36 goals in the 1985/86 season, which is pretty impressive; 17 of those – a staggering 47 per cent – were conceded later than the 70th minute.

It speaks volumes. These kind of results are not achieved overnight or by addressing small margins.

So we return to the suggestion that Atkinson was not bold enough to start with his strongest aides in Robson, Whiteside and McGrath and propose a change in attitude. Again, though, it barely feels like a matter of bravery or boldness; these players were among his strongest performers. A message from those players to the rest of the squad could have had a profoundly strong impact – imagine even Robson saying there was room for improvement?

It is more reasonable, though, for a manager to concentrate first on addressing the weaknesses in his squad rather than his strengths. It was also not quite the same as Ferguson's situation; for the former Aberdeen boss, these players had not won a trophy and were beginning to miss matches. Under Atkinson it was very much a case that Robson in particular was capable of sinking five pints on a Friday night (according to team-mates, despite the Monday Club insistence) and being the best player on the pitch on Saturday; there wasn't really a cause to think, 'Just how good could he be without the five pints?'

Clayton Blackmore suggests: 'Under Ron, United had all the tools to win the league – he just didn't have them all at the same time and in a league as competitive as the First Division, and at a team as big as Manchester United, you need everything to fall into place.'

That summary is surely pretty close to the truth. Those fine margins never quite fell into place – the number of injuries, the timing of the injuries, the pitches, the unfortunate timing of the strength of British football in general – at crucial points, when Atkinson needed the rub of the green, he never got it. If you are to cite the drinking and the underwhelming signings as self-inflicted issues, and the will of the opposition who still saw United as the biggest scalp in the country as a club-specific historical affliction, there is still much more evidence to suggest Ron Atkinson was a good manager for Manchester United than one who ought to have his reign tainted by the tag of underachievement.

If the strongest criticism of Atkinson's reign has its foundations in the idea that he simply wasn't the man who introduced a revolution in the British game (as it was, because this was not just an issue at United), then it seems a little unfair. *Express* journalist

Mike Dempsey took a month or so before penning a feature which suggests the thought at the time was that the demoralisation of the previous year had unsettled United as a club.

'It has been 19 years since that elusive [First Division championship] flag fluttered above Old Trafford – 19 years that will haunt Ferguson,' Dempsey wrote. 'Ferguson has to chase a dream that has eluded his four predecessors. But where does he start? United's lurch towards the lower reaches has been accompanied by charges laid mostly at the feet of the players. THEY lacked discipline. THEY were unfit. THEY were injury prone. THEY had lost contact with their fans. AND, worst of all, people were saying some were not giving their best. The fans were restless. The board was embarrassed. Even United's £500,000 sponsors, Sharp Electronics, were said to be inscrutably concerned. Ferguson has injected the one thing the fans had yearned for: discipline. It would be silly to suggest this is merely a question of short hair cuts, club blazers and three bags full, Mr Ferguson. His way is the common-sense way. He insists that a Manchester United player behaves like one. He must look the part, play the part. He must have pride, dedication, respect and a bearing. Ferguson has inherited, on paper, a high-quality squad. He has also inherited some of soccer's most highly paid players. Like every true Scotsman, he will want his money's worth.'

Dempsey listed the seven reasons for Big Ron's 'Downfall':

1 No more cash for buying, without first selling
2 The Hughes transfer to Barcelona devastated fans
3 Robson, Bailey and Whiteside went to the World Cup despite not being fit and all faced surgery on return
4 Injuries to Strachan, Moses, Colin Gibson and Sivebaek
5 Moses was sent to Amsterdam for specialist treatment without the club's approval and there was a row about who should pay the treatment bill
6 Moses/Olsen punch-up, Atkinson covered up then admitted he'd lied
7 Buys Atkinson didn't make

… with the latter point having the elaboration that 'Terry Butcher was the biggest miss of all.' Butcher would go down as Atkinson's big miss, just as Tommy Docherty regretted not signing Peter Shilton, and Alex Ferguson twice failed to sign Alan Shearer.

The most salient of those, aside from the injuries, was surely related to point six, with the prevailing issue being the increasing lack of discipline. That was something Atkinson could not control without taking drastic action – maybe some of it had been beyond his control to begin with. He couldn't help the injury situation, which impacted virtually every single game of the previous season, and it was practically impossible for him to swim against the tide and keep morale high when those injuries inevitably influenced results. Yes, he could have thought more carefully about the short-term signings and the potential damage on morale, but the pressure was on him to win the league and this was his big chance to control it. It didn't work. What might he have done in the summer of 1986 to turn it around? If the first step was to have the prescience to eradicate the drinking, he would have risked alienating those players who had his back the most by suggesting their 'improper' preparation was what had cost the club previously. If he had hired new staff he might have been implicitly confessing that he had got it wrong before. Hindsight is a fantastic thing. We all, as general consumers of football, have a tendency to dramatise things, so that every new beginning must involve a complete change in direction or every ending has to be catastrophic. Sometimes things just run their natural course. That seems to have been the case here, though it has to be said, but for terrible luck, Ron Atkinson was certainly a good enough manager, and his team were a good enough team, to have ended that long wait for a league title. As Edwards says, 'I felt he did a good job ... we were close but just not quite there ... So I don't look on Ron's tenure as a failure at all. It was a stepping stone to great things in the 1990s.'

Unfortunately, the hard fact that it was followed by the most successful reign in English football history projects a pretty harsh perspective on the period, much harsher than it should. In a funny sort of a way, Atkinson became the victim of his own success, as United's focus of winning the league title gradually became the Holy Grail. It was probably during the period of 1981–86 when the idea of United having to be serious contenders and more than just a good football team was born. The scale of Ferguson's achievements and the time it took to build suggest the club was in desperate need of a rebuild. Maybe the reality is that everyone's confidence was knocked hugely by the injury crisis, and the momentum had shifted so far the other way that a change in management was the only solution.

Is history, then, unfair on this Manchester United side? 'Very much so,' Bailey insists. 'It is an annoyance. We just needed one bit of luck in one year and we would have been remembered as the team that won the league either in 1984 or in '86 after we won the first ten games. Instead, here we are more than 30 years later talking about what could have been done or what should have been done. But we have to live with that. The reality is, being at Manchester United, coming second doesn't count for much.'

Hypothesising

THERE WERE one or two remarks about Ron Atkinson made by journalists while he was Manchester United manager, referring to his likability and popularity amongst supporters. After his sacking, he was compared to Tommy Docherty, but Docherty's dismissal was unique in that he went out on a high in terms of the football. There was a perfect storm with the Scot because he was such a polarising figure and inspired such extreme evocation. His reign is almost crystallised to deity level because he was taken from adoring United supporters before the potential of his team was realised. Even Sir Matt Busby and Sir Alex Ferguson do not have this sort of benefit – most perceive the timing of their retirements as just, and some even feel they were overdue. Docherty's critical assessment of the managers who followed him did little to damage the love felt for him by the supporters who had grown up with his team. The way United appeared to officially distance themselves from the controversial figure in the years which had passed since only serves to strengthen the conviction of those who still believe he should not have been sacked, or that he was the victim of a conspiracy from a group out to use any excuse to sack him.

If Docherty had been sacked after the club's relegation in 1974, he would not have complained and neither would most supporters. Conversely, if Atkinson had been dismissed after winning the FA Cup in 1983 or 1985, the reverence which the newspapers suggested was held for Docherty instead might at least be shared. There are many variables, but even within the affection held by football supporters who sometimes have a leaning for the cult and perhaps unpopular, there is always a line. Dave Sexton was a likeable man by all accounts. His reign is not remembered with fondness.

There is little point hypothesising over an imaginary popularity contest; it is probably fairest to say there is a generation of supporters who feel the same way about Atkinson and his side as the generation before who grew up idolising the Docherty side. At their best, both teams shared the same characteristics and personality, which is no coincidence considering the footballing education of each manager. They played with adventurous full-backs, defenders comfortable on the ball, tricky wingers and unpredictable forwards who were more about thrills than they necessarily were about 25 goals a season. If there was a significant difference it came in central midfield, where the craft and pocket-pinching of Macari and McIlroy was replaced by the drive and power of Robson and Moses or Whiteside. You can have a preference; you can love both. United supporters old enough are fortunate to have the choice to pick their favourite.

What helps cultivate that affection for the Atkinson side is the relationship supporters had with the team. Sir Alex Ferguson's reign was so long and reached so far that it is now most commonly associated with the 90s, the turn of the century, and the incredible impact live broadcasting on television would have. Atkinson's reign is the exclusive property of the 80s, a time of The Cliff, of standing at the Stretford End, of being able to approach players on matchday (with intentions more genuine than spraying them in the face with CS gas).

Then there is the money. It is this factor Gary Bailey feels rules more than any other when it comes to the difference in relationships between supporter and football team. 'Maybe it is the money; the money the players earn which makes them inaccessible, or the money in the game which has changed it just as much for the players,' he says. 'I remember after a game against Manchester City, and we had beaten them comfortably, players from both teams went to a nearby pub and I remember a lot of journalists being there. The players were hurling abuse at each other in a jokey way, but nobody got upset and nothing was written about it in the papers. A couple of years ago I went to do a talk at the supporters' club. There's no limo to pick me up, just one of the fans. The games were more physical, more aggressive, players would pick up bumps and bruises and continue to fight for the team. Supporters would respond and feel a part of it. Today a player can be nudged and fall over and stop the game. Spectators want to be entertained. It's nobody's fault, it's just the way it moved on, like life in general. Back then, there might be one or two times a year that you would be on television. That's why the cup final was such a big deal. Now you can stream any game wherever you are in the world and those viewers are consumers who want to be entertained rather than supporters who have that strong emotional connection.'

Atkinson believes that aggression and commitment – the quality which, funnily enough, probably distinguishes his side from Docherty's – is the main reason for the connection supporters had with the team from this era. 'There was a way of playing,' he says. 'The game has changed, of course, but fans love aggression. They love flair, they love quality, but they love aggression. They love people who can tackle. Players like Robson, who had it all.'

It probably spoke volumes as to why so many of that team were so highly regarded by fans. Whiteside and Hughes stand out, as do Kevin Moran and Remi Moses, two players who get less attention only because of just how dominant others were as characters (Moses in particular was notorious for being media-shy). But there was no little flair; Robson and Hughes were known for the spectacular, and even Stapleton fell into the category of a forward who would generally score 15 to 20 goals of quality rather than 20 to 30 in quantity. In Coppell and Muhren, Atkinson had graft and guile, trading it for speed and trickery in 1984 with Strachan and Olsen.

Mick Duxbury and Arthur Albiston were as reliable and consistent as most of the best full-backs in United's history, and in Paul McGrath, who had finally found his best position as a centre-half towards the latter end of Atkinson's tenure, the club had a player whose talent was the equal of any player to ever grace that position. It was a genuine sporting tragedy that his time as the cornerstone of the centre defence wasn't longer. In goal, Gary Bailey won out against everything – early nerves, and early doubters, among the press and even his new manager in 1981. He showed remarkable character to overcome some high-profile errors and become one of the most dependable stoppers to play at Old Trafford. He played 375 times for the club. (Until David De Gea surpassed him in 2019, he was the longest-serving player in the club's history to have not scored a goal, due to Peter Schmeichel and Alex Stepney's relatively prolific exploits!)

United became a delight to watch again, earning – and deserving – comparisons with some of their greatest sides. Remember, at one point Atkinson had fielded a quartet which was rated 'the best' the club had ever put out. Comparisons with the likes of Best, Law and Charlton may *seem* like ridiculous hyperbole, but it is worth bearing in mind that at the time the eras of those players was closer and fresher in the memory.

There were statement successes and landmark performances. Defeating Arsenal in two semi-final appearances in 1983, defeating Barcelona in 1984, and overcoming Liverpool in the FA Cup semi-final in 1985 – and much more than that, the manner in which those wins were achieved – meant arguably as much as the two FA Cup wins of the 80s. Ron Atkinson had a commitment to playing football the right way, and it was the Manchester United way.

Whilst taking the time to summarise the events of this book, Dave Sexton's efforts as United manager should not go unmentioned or unappreciated, nor should the achievements be necessarily swept under the carpet – finishing second in 1980 was a fine accomplishment. In April 1984, sportswriter Simon Inglis wrote of Sexton's time at OT: 'It was not that he failed, but the manner in which he succeeded.' Frustratingly for this book, Sexton remained mostly silent about his time at the club. There were little telling clips, such as this remark from January 1983, when he was at Coventry: 'I have not got the sort of mind that can put a newspaper story uppermost, although I had to do it at United. I won't have a go at anyone because I don't want to see headlines like "Sexton bollocks Thomas", even if I have done. Anyway, I find if I have to bollock someone it is usually my fault in the first place because I am the manager.'

In the same month, Sexton confessed he had been 'shattered' when he left United, but insisted he was still 'a soccer romantic'.

His tenure was a valuable lesson, with positive and not-so-positive outcomes. His ideas and theories for how football should be played were not completely different to that of his predecessor or his successor. But he wanted consideration where Docherty and Atkinson preferred instinct. It was that latter quality the Old Trafford crowd, and players, were more receptive to. It could be argued that United have repeated those mistakes in their managerial appointments of recent years. Sexton was also a sacrificial lamb when it came to persona; as the opposite type of character to Docherty, it was discovered that the manager needed a certain personality in order to survive the week-to-week pressure, understanding that it needed a certain character, even if that character was a performance.

But Sexton deserves immense credit for being wise beyond his years; anticipating the value of a ball-retaining midfielder, and appreciating that every member of the team should work as hard as his colleague. His patient attitude and experience of working with young players helped the club immensely; a benefit they reaped the rewards from long after Sexton was dismissed. Without many of the young players he brought to the club, Atkinson's reign may not have been as successful or memorable. Whiteside, after all, did score in all three cup finals under Big Ron. Mark Hughes was still scoring in finals (spoiler, he returned to the club) in 1994.

There was, in the end, an incompatibility, but Dave Sexton's era remains an important one in the history of the club for all that was learned throughout. As does Atkinson's; as discussed at length earlier in this book, although it was not an intentional decision to hire him based on this factor, Big Ron's footballing ideals were as close to the philosophy of the Busby Babes as any manager before (Docherty) or since. You can even include Sir Alex Ferguson in that – Ferguson came with his own ideas, and United were very much in his own mould even if he did stay faithful to the tradition created by Sir Matt Busby. This is to say he combined his ideals with the heritage of the club.

Atkinson probably felt he was doing the same sort of thing, but the key is that he believed in the same principles which were taught to the Busby Babes on the training pitch because it was the same education he had received. He and Docherty were unique in that they were taught directly by Jimmy Hogan, a rite of passage that no other Manchester United manager had, or will ever be able to claim to have. No matter if someone comes along who believes in the same ideas, it will never be as pure and natural as it was in this period. In this writer's opinion, this is the single biggest reason why those teams – despite their failure to win the league title – remain as loved as any in the club's history by those who were fortunate enough to experience them. If those years taught Manchester United supporters anything, it was that memories can be created from regular games just as much as they can from a match which ended with a trophy celebration, so long as the conditions are right; a hugely important part of that is a dedication to playing the right brand of football. And if the ability to create positive memories is the most important quality of any football team, then Ron Atkinson's Manchester United were as successful as any.